I Hated,
Hated, Hated
This Movie

Other Books by Roger Ebert

An Illini Century

A Kiss Is Still a Kiss

Two Weeks in the Midday Sun:
A Cannes Notebook

Behind the Phantom's Mask

Roger Ebert's Little Movie Glossary

Roger Ebert's Movie Home Companion
(annually 1986–1993)

Roger Ebert's Video Companion
(annually 1994–1998)

Questions for the Movie Answer Man

Roger Ebert's Book of Film: An Anthology

Roger Ebert's Movie Yearbook
(annually 1999 and 2000)

Ebert's Bigger Little Movie Glossary

With Daniel Curley

The Perfect London Walk

With John Kratz

The Computer Insectiary

With Gene Siskel

The Future of the Movies:
Interviews with Martin Scorsese,
Steven Spielberg, and George Lucas

I Hated, Hated, Hated This Movie

Roger Ebert

**Andrews McMeel
Publishing**

Kansas City

00 01 02 03 04 RDH 10 9 8 7 6 5 4 3 2 1

Library of Congress Cataloging-in-Publication Data

Ebert, Roger.
    I hated, hated, hated this movie / by Roger Ebert.
       p. cm.
    ISBN 0-7407-0672-1
    1. Motion pictures—Reviews. I. Title.
    PN1995.E317   2000
    791.43'75—dc21

                             00-036167

Design by Holly Camerlinck
Composition by Kelly & Company, Lee's Summit, Missouri

This book is dedicated to
Gene Siskel
1946–1999
. . . who liked to ask, "Is this movie better than a
documentary of the same actors having lunch?"

Introduction

The purpose of a movie critic is to encourage good films and discourage bad ones. Of course, there is much disagreement about which is which. The films in this book, however, have few defenders. The degree of their badness ranges from those that are deplorable to others that are merely hilariously misguided. Some of them are even fun, although not so much fun you would want to see them twice.

For years I had a law that I would give the zero star rating only to films I believed were immoral in one way or another. Any other movie, however wretched, would get at least a half-star. In making this selection I find that I have not always adhered to that rule. While everyone would agree that *Jaws the Revenge* or *Little Indian, Big City* are very bad movies, for example, few would find them evil—unless it is evil to waste two hours in the lives of unsuspecting ticket buyers, which it may well be. Other films are in the zero-star category as a sort of default; any star rating at all seems irrelevant to John Waters' *Pink Flamingos,* which exists outside critical terms, like the weather.

Some of the worst films in the book are so jaw-droppingly bad they achieve a kind of grandeur. With all of the "making of" documentaries available these days, why did no one record the making of *An Alan Smithee Film,* or *Frozen Assets*? What values were expressed at the story conferences on *North,* the movie that inspired my title? What was the thinking on the set the day they first saw Rosie O'Donnell as an undercover cop in S&M gear in *Exit to Eden*? Or when they did screen tests for the karate-chopping infants in *Baby Geniuses*? Or when they added a P.C. disclaimer to *Mr. Magoo* for fear of offending the nearsighted?

The easiest movies to write about are always the ones at the extremes. Good and bad movies dictate their own reviews; those in the middle are more of a challenge. In writing strongly negative reviews, I am tempted to take cheap shots, and although I have fought that temptation on occasion, there are other times when I have simply caved in to it. I am not proud of all the smartass remarks in this book, but remember that the reviews were written soon after undergoing the experience of seeing the movies, and reflect that when a film insults your intelligence, your taste, and your patience all at once, it brings out the worst in you. The movies made me do it.

ROGER EBERT

Ace Ventura: Pet Detective

(Directed by Tom Shadyac; starring Jim Carrey, Sean Young, Courteney Cox; 1994)

You know that the French consider Jerry Lewis the greatest screen comedian of all time. You've looked at some Lewis comedies, but you don't get the joke. You know that a lot of critics praised Steve Martin in *The Jerk,* but you liked him better after he started acting more normal. You are not a promising candidate to see *Ace Ventura: Pet Detective.*

The movie stars Jim Carrey, best known as the all-purpose white guy on *In Living Color,* as a Miami detective who specializes in animals. He'll find your missing bird or your kidnapped pedigree dog. And as the movie opens he's hired by the Miami Dolphins football team to find their mascot, a dolphin named Snowflake which is mysteriously missing from its home in a large tank at the stadium. The plot deepens, if that is the word, when Dolphin quarterback Dan Marino also goes missing.

Carrey plays Ace as if he's being clocked on an Energy-O-Meter, and paid by the calorie expended. He's a hyper goon who likes to screw his mouth into strange shapes while playing variations on the language. He shares his house with so many animals, he's like those zookeepers on late-night talk shows who always have pets crawling out of their collars. And he is simultaneously a spectacularly good and bad detective.

The story eventually involves Sean Young, who is much too talented for roles like Lieutenant Einhorn of the Miami police department; Udo Kier, once a distinguished German actor-director, now Ronald Camp, sinister millionaire; Courteney Cox as the Dolphin's chief publicist; and Noble Willingham as the team's owner. Most of the people look as if they would rather be in other movies. Sean Young is a trouper, however, and does her best with dialogue like, "Listen, pet dick. How would you like me to make your life a living hell?"

The movie basically has one joke, which is Ace Ventura's weird nerdy strangeness. If you laugh at this joke, chances are you laugh at Jerry Lewis, too, and I can sympathize with you even if I can't understand you. I found the movie a long, unfunny slog through an impenetrable plot. Kids might like it. Real little kids.

Ace Ventura: When Nature Calls
(Directed by Steve Oedekerk; starring Jim Carrey, Ian McNeice, Simon Callow; 1997)

I knew a guy once who had an amazing party trick. He could tilt his head way back, and stick a straw all the way up his nose. I hesitate to recount this memory, because if my review falls into the hands of Jim Carrey, we'll see that trick in the next Ace Ventura movie and, believe me, it's not the kind of trick you want to see again.

Carrey is an actor who gives new meaning to the term "physical comedian." In the course of *Ace Ventura: When Nature Calls,* he regurgitates in order to feed a starving eaglet; shows how he can push his eyeballs around with his fingertips; sticks his arm down a man's throat to the elbow (in order to save him from choking on an apple core); and spits so copiously that he covers himself and two other characters with dripping mucus.

Of course it wouldn't be an Ace Ventura movie if he *only* expectorated. First he has to snort long and loudly, in order to gather his mucus supply, which he seems to be drawing not only from the sinus area but from every inner bodily crevice. The fundamental principle of this series is that less is not more, and more is not enough.

Consider, for example, the scene where Ace wants to conceal himself while spying on some suspected African bat thieves. He hides inside a giant mechanical rhinoceros. But it's hot in there, under the African sun, and so he strips. Then the rhino develops operational difficulties, and it's time for Ace to escape. No points for guessing which of the rhino's orifices the naked detective chooses for his exit.

With my hand over my heart I have to confess that I did not find this movie very funny. Not funny enough to recommend. Not as good as the original *Ace Ventura,* which I also did not recommend (but which, on reflection,

I probably should have awarded two stars instead of one). Not as filled with incident and invention. And yet I confess I'm inspired by the *spirit* of the enterprise. Jim Carrey makes no little plans, takes no hostages, cuts no corners, and allows no compromise. I like his attitude.

The movie begins with a wicked satire on the opening scenes of Sylvester Stallone's *Cliffhanger,* as Ace desperately tries and fails to save a frightened raccoon, which slips from his grasp and falls off a mountain. Depressed by his failure, Ace goes to live in a Tibetan monastery (inspired by *Rambo III*). Then he is brought out of retirement by the mysterious disappearance of the sacred bat, which is the symbol of an African tribe.

The tribal scenes are not very funny, and one would say they are not tasteful, except that there is no connection between taste and any scene in an Ace Ventura movie. They reminded me of similar scenes in old B-movies where cannibals stirred pots full of missionaries. With just a little more effort, the sequences could have satirized Political Correctness rather than offending it. (There is an admirable scene where Ace is offended by a woman's fur neck-piece, and in retaliation knocks out her escort and wears *him* around his neck.)

The supporting cast includes the invaluable Simon Callow, who, after wonderfully playing the friend who dies of a heart attack in *Four Weddings and a Funeral,* should have held out for something better than being sodomized by King Kong.

Carrey himself is so manic he makes Jerry Lewis look like a narcolepsy victim. There are laughs in the movie, and an anarchic tone that I admire. But there aren't enough laughs, and the African tribal stuff doesn't work, and by the end of the movie I was thinking, if this goes on any longer, he's going to start sticking straws up his nose.

An Alan Smithee Film Burn Hollywood Burn

(Directed by Alan Smithee; starring Eric Idle, Ryan O'Neal; 1998)
An Alan Smithee Film Burn Hollywood Burn is a spectacularly bad film—incompetent, unfunny, ill conceived, badly executed, lamely written, and acted by people who look trapped in the headlights.

The title provides clues to the film's misfortune. It was originally titled *An Alan Smithee Film.* Then *Burn, Hollywood, Burn!* Now its official title is

An Alan Smithee Film Burn Hollywood Burn—just like that, with no punctuation. There's a rich irony connected with the title. "Alan Smithee," of course, is the pseudonym that Hollywood slaps on a film if the original director insists on having his name removed. The plot of *AASFBHB* involves a film so bad that the director wants his name removed, but since his *real* name is Alan Smithee, what can he do? Ho, ho.

Wait, it gets better. The movie was directed by Arthur Hiller, who hated the way the film was edited so much that, yes, he insisted his name be removed from the credits. So now it really *is* an Alan Smithee film. That leaves one mystery: Why didn't Joe Eszterhas, the film's writer, take off his name, too?

I fear it is because this version of the film does indeed reflect his vision. Eszterhas is sometimes a good writer, but this time he has had a complete lapse of judgment. Even when he kids himself, he's wrong. "It's completely terrible!" a character says of the film within the film. "It's worse than *Showgirls!*" Of course Eszterhas wrote *Showgirls,* which got some bad reviews, but it wasn't completely terrible. I was looking forward to explaining that to him this week, but he canceled his visit to Chicago, reportedly because his voice gave out. Judging by this film, it was the last thing to go.

Have you ever been to one of those office parties where the p.r. department has put together a tribute to a retiring boss? That's how this film plays. It has no proper story line. No dramatic scenes. It's all done in documentary form, with people looking at the camera and relating the history of a doomed movie named *Trio,* which cost more than $200 million and stars Sylvester Stallone, Whoopi Goldberg, and Jackie Chan, who play themselves as if they are celebrity impersonators.

The film stars Eric Idle as Smithee, who eventually burns the print, and checks into the Keith Moon Psychiatric Institute in England (ho, ho). Ryan O'Neal plays the film's producer. I love the way he's introduced. We see the back of a guy's head, and hear him saying, "Anything!" Then the chair swivels around and he says "anything!" again, and we see, *gasp!*—why, it's *Ryan O'Neal!* I was reminded of the moment in Mike Todd's *Around the World in 80 Days* when the piano player swivels around, and, gasp! it's—*Frank Sinatra!*

These actors and others recount the history of the doomed film in unconvincing sound bites, which are edited together without wit or rhythm. One is accustomed to seeing bad movies, but not incompetent ones. Sophomores in a film class could make a better film than this. Hell, I have a movie here by Les Brown, a kid who looks about sixteen and filmed a thriller in his mother's basement, faking a fight scene by wrestling with a dummy. If I locked you in a room with both movies, you'd end up looking at the kid's.

In taking his name off the film, Arthur Hiller has wisely distanced himself from the disaster, but on the basis of what's on the screen I cannot, frankly, imagine any version of this film that I would want to see. The only way to save this film would be to trim eighty-six minutes.

Here's an interesting thing. The film is filled with celebrities playing themselves, and most of them manifestly have no idea who they are. The only celebrity who emerges relatively intact is Harvey Weinstein, head of Miramax, who plays a private eye—but never mind the role, just listen to him. He could find success in voice-over work.

Now consider Stallone. He reappears in the outtakes over the closing credits. Such cookies are a treat for audiences after the film is over. Here they're as bad as the film, but notice a moment when Stallone thinks he's off camera, and asks someone about a Planet Hollywood shirt. *Then* he sounds like himself. A second later, playing himself, he sounds all wrong. Jackie Chan copes by acting like he's in a Jackie Chan movie, but Whoopi Goldberg mangles her scenes in a cigar bar, awkwardly trying to smoke a stogie. It's God's way of paying her back for telling Ted Danson it would be funny to wear blackface at the Friars' Club.

Alien Resurrection
(Directed by Jean-Pierre Jeunet; starring Sigourney Weaver, Winona Ryder, Ron Perlman; 1997)

Between *Alien* and *Aliens,* fifty-seven years passed, with Ellen Ripley in suspended animation. Between *Aliens* and *Alien3,* she drifted through space in a lifeboat, before landing on a prison planet. In all three films she did battle with vile alien creatures constructed out of teeth, green sinew, and goo. In *Alien3* she told this life form: "I've known you so long I can't remember a time when you weren't in my life."

I'm telling the aliens the same thing. This is a series whose inspiration has come, gone, and been forgotten. I'm aliened out. The fourth movie depends on a frayed shoestring of a plot, barely enough to give them something to talk about between the action scenes. A "Boo Movie," Pauline Kael called the second one, because it all came down to aliens popping up and going "boo!" and being destroyed.

I found that second film dark and depressing, but skillfully directed by James Cameron *(Terminator II)*. I lost interest with the third, when I realized that the aliens could at all times outrun and outleap the humans, so all the chase scenes were contrivances.

Now here is *Alien Resurrection*. Ripley (Sigourney Weaver) is still the heroine, even though 200 years have passed since *Alien3*. She has been cloned out of a drop of her own blood, and is being used as a broodmare: The movie opens with surgeons removing a baby alien from her womb. How the baby got in there is not fully explained, for which we should be grateful.

The birth takes place on a vast spaceship. The interstellar human government hopes to breed more aliens, and use them for—oh, developing vaccines, medicines, a gene pool, stuff like that. The aliens have a remarkable body chemistry. Ripley's genes are all right, too: They allow her reconstituted form to retain all of her old memories, as if cookie dough could remember what a gingerbread man looked like.

Ripley is first on a giant government science ship, then on a tramp freighter run by a vagabond crew. The monsters are at first held inside glass cells, but of course they escape (their blood is a powerful solvent that can eat through the decks of the ship). The movie's a little vague about Ripley: Is she all human, or does she have a little alien mixed in? For a while we wonder which side she's on. She laughs at mankind's hopes of exploiting the creatures: "She's a queen," she says of the new monster. "She'll breed. You'll die."

When the tramp freighter comes into play, we get a fresh crew, including Call (Winona Ryder), who has been flown all the way from Earth to provide appeal for the younger members of the audience. Ryder is a wonderful actress, one of the most gifted of her generation, but wrong for this movie. She lacks the heft and presence to stand alongside Ripley and the grizzled old space dogs played by Ron Perlman, Dominique Pinon, Dan Hedeya, and Brad Dourif. She seems uncertain of her purpose in the movie, her speeches lack conviction, and when her secret is revealed, it raises more questions than it answers. Ryder pales in comparison with Jenette Goldstein, the muscular Marine who was the female sidekick in *Aliens*.

Weaver, on the other hand, is splendid: Strong, weary, resourceful, grim. I would gladly see a fifth *Alien* movie if they created something for her to do, and dialogue beyond the terse sound bites that play well in commercials. Ripley has some good scenes. She plays basketball with a crewman (Perlman) and slams him around. When she bleeds, her blood fizzes interestingly on the floor—as if it's not quite human. She can smell an alien presence. And be smelled: An alien recognizes Ripley as its grandmother and sticks out a tongue to lick her.

These aliens have a lot of stuff in their mouths; not only the tongue and their famous teeth, but another little head on a stalk, with smaller teeth. Still to be determined is whether the littler head has a still tinier head inside of it, and so on. Like the bugs in *Starship Troopers,* these aliens are an example of specialization. They have evolved over the eons into creatures adapted for one purpose only: To star in horror movies.

Mankind wants them for their genes? I can think of a more valuable attribute: They're apparently able to generate biomass out of thin air. The baby born at the beginning of the film weighs maybe five pounds. In a few weeks the ship's cargo includes generous tons of aliens. What do they feed on? How do they fuel their growth and reproduction? It's no good saying they eat the ship's stores, because they thrive even on the second ship—and in previous movies have grown like crazy on desolate prison planets and in abandoned space stations. They're like perpetual motion machines; they don't need input.

The *Alien* movies always have expert production design. *Alien Resurrection* was directed by the French visionary Jean-Pierre Jeunet *(City of Lost Children),* who with his designers has placed it in what looks like a large, empty hangar filled with prefabricated steel warehouse parts. There is not a single shot in the movie to fill one with wonder—nothing like the abandoned planetary station in *Aliens.* Even the standard shots of vast spaceships, moving against a backdrop of stars, are murky here, and perfunctory.

I got a telephone message that *Inside Edition* wanted to ask me about *Alien Resurrection,* and what impact the movie would have on the careers of Weaver and Ryder. Financially, it will help: Weaver remains the only woman who can open an action picture. Artistically, the film will have no impact at all. It's a nine days' wonder, a geek show designed to win a weekend or two at the box office and then fade from memory. Try this test: How often do you think about *Jurassic Park: The Lost World*?

Alligator

(Directed by Lewis Teague; starring Robert Forster; 1980)
This movie was probably inevitable. What's amazing is that they took so long to make it. *Alligator* is inspired by one of the most persistent fantasies of recent years: That countless pet alligators, given as gifts when they were babies, were flushed down toilets when they grew too large . . . and that down there in the sewers of our major cities, they're growing to unimaginable size.

My own fantasies about sewers go all the way back to the old *Honeymooners* TV skits, with Ed Norton breathlessly telling Ralph Cramden about the beasts he encountered on his daily patrols beneath the city streets. But Norton never met anything like the alligator in this movie. In the tradition of *Jaws,* this creature is gigantic, voracious, and insatiable. It will eat anything (as you might imagine, considering where it lives).

The story opens as it's gobbling down dead dogs from a laboratory that's experimenting with new growth hormones. You got it: The alligator reacts to the hormones and grows to a length of thirty or forty feet. People start disappearing down in the sewers. A New York cop (Robert Forster) goes down with his buddy to see what's happening. The alligator eats the buddy. But Forster can't get anyone to believe his story.

These early scenes in the movie are probably the best, because they work on the dumb fundamental level where we're all afraid of being eaten by an alligator in a sewer. (Show me a man who is not afraid of being eaten by an alligator in a sewer, and I'll show you a fool.) Forster splashes along with his flashlight and the alligator slinks around just out of view.

Come to think of it, the alligator does a lot of slinking in this movie—maybe because it was too difficult to show the whole alligator. There are a couple of fairly phony special effects shots, as when the alligator bursts up through the sidewalk, but for the most part we just see parts of the alligator: His mean little eyes, his big tail, and his teeth. Especially his teeth.

The plot is absolutely standard; this story has been filmed dozens of times. You have, of course, the small-minded mayor who is concerned only with re-election. The police chief, a folksy character who fires Forster for not catching the alligator, but later rehires him. The girl scientist, who falls in love with the hero and helps hunt for the alligator. The villain, an out-of-town big-game hunter brought in to replace Forster.

All of these people do incredibly stupid things, like walking into dark alleys after the alligator, or putting a dynamite charge on a time-delay fuse while they're still trapped in a sewer with the alligator and the dynamite.

The alligator, on the other hand, is smart enough to travel all over the city without being seen: In one shot, he's in a suburban swimming pool, and seconds later, he's midtown. You would not think it would be that easy for a forty-foot alligator to sneak around incognito, but then, New Yorkers are awfully blasé. Meanwhile, I suggest a plan: Why not try flushing this movie down the toilet to see if it grows into something big and fearsome?

American Anthem
(Directed by Albert Magnoli; starring Mitch Gaylord, Janet Jones; 1986)
American Anthem is like a very bad Identikit sketch of *Purple Rain,* the previous movie by the same director. You can almost hear the police artist as he tries to make his drawing, based on half-witted descriptions of the big hit from the summer of 1984:

Q. Who is the star?
A. A major superstar in another field who has never acted before.
Q. What is his personal crisis?
A. He has an unhappy home life and a father who mistreats him.
Q. What is the suspense?
A. Will he conquer his inner demons and perform once again at the peak of his ability?
Q. Who is his girlfriend?
A. A future star in his field whose excellence inspires him to start trying again.
Q. What's the movie's visual style?
A. Kind of a cross between a concert film and an MTV video. Be sure to overedit. And put in lots of shots where the camera peers into the light source, so the heroic youth can be seen in silhouette as he tosses back his head and sweat flies through the air.

With this incomplete description, a filmmaker from Planet X might have made *American Anthem* from the basic ingredients of *Purple Rain.* The hero this time is not a rock star like Prince, but a gymnast played by the Olympic champion Mitch Gaylord. But since the movie treats him like a rock star, photographing him not as a sweating, breathing, striving athlete but as a pinup for the girls' locker room, the difference isn't as big as you might imagine.

In the movie, Gaylord plays a guy who has dropped off the gym team and refused a college scholarship because his father doesn't love him. His father, we learn, does indeed love him but is frustrated because he doesn't have a job. Gaylord sneaks into the gym to spy on his former teammates as they train, and one day he spots a beautiful newcomer (Janet Jones). She has arrived to train under the famous coach who is preparing everyone to try out for the U.S. Olympic gymnastics team.

It's love, and so Gaylord decides to get in shape again, which he does by working out on a bar that he has suspended between two trees in the forest. He especially enjoys practicing during fierce rainstorms when the thunder and lightning make for a better MTV video.

The plot is dumb and predictable, but so what? Everything depends on dialogue and character. And *American Anthem* is a curious case: The screenplay seems to have been written by people who, on the one hand, were intimately familiar with every commercial and salable ingredient in every hit movie of the last five years, and yet who, on the other hand, had never heard a cliché before. My favorite moment comes after a family fight when the kid brother whines, "Why can't we be like other families?"

A large portion of the movie is given over to gymnastics competitions, which are not explained or photographed well enough to be very interesting. Seeing a champion gymnast zip through his routine isn't half as interesting as a beginner being taught a thing or two about dealing with the parallel bars would have been. Skilled moviemakers know that, in sports movies, you don't create suspense by making something look easy, but by making it look difficult. Yet Gaylord's competitive routines in *American Anthem* are the equivalent of a Rocky movie where *Rocky* knocks his opponent unconscious with the first swing.

One thing is especially annoying about the movie. During the final match, there are dozens of strobe lights flashing incessantly and distractingly behind the contestants. I guess these are supposed to represent camera flashbulbs. Two thoughts are inspired: (1) If the gymnastics were really interesting, they wouldn't have to be tarted up with flashing lights, and (2) have you ever thought what it says about our national IQ that a lot of people believe you can take a flash picture from the twentieth row?

An American Werewolf in Paris

(Directed by Anthony Wallers; starring Tom Everett Scott, Vince Vieluf, Phil Buckman; 1997)

Now that *Scream* and *Scream 2* have given us horror film characters who know all the horror clichés, the time has come for a werewolf movie about characters who know they're in a werewolf movie. Not that such an insight would benefit the heroes of *An American Werewolf in Paris,* who are singularly dim. Here are people we don't care about, doing things they don't understand, in a movie without any rules. Triple play.

I was not one of the big fans of John Landis's original 1981 film, *An American Werewolf in London,* but, glancing over my old review, I find such phrases as "spectacular set pieces," "genuinely funny moments," and "sequences that are spellbinding." My review of the Paris werewolves will not require any of those phrases.

The new movie involves three callow Americans on a "daredevil tour" of Europe. Played by Tom Everett Scott (of *That Thing You Do*), Vince Vieluf, and Phil Buckman, they climb the Eiffel Tower by moonlight, only to find a young woman (Julie Delpy) about to leap to her death. They talk, she leaps, and Scott leaps after her, luckily while tethered to a bungee cord. (Hint: always be sure the other end of a bungee line is tied to something else before tying this end to yourself.)

The girl survives, the lads track her to her home, she has blood on her hands, her friend invites them to a rave club, she's not there, Chris finds her locked in a cell in her basement, the ravers are werewolves, so is she, etc., etc. Please don't accuse me of revealing plot points: In a movie with this title, are you expecting that the girl who leaps from the tower is not a werewolf, her friends are exchange students, and the club is frequented by friendly tourists?

One of the pleasures of a film like this is the ritual explanation of the rules, in which we determine how werewolves are made, how they are killed, and how they spread their wolfiness. Here it doesn't much matter, because the plot has a way of adding new twists (like a serum that makes moonlight unnecessary for a werewolf transformation). By the end of the film, any plot discipline (necessary so that we care about some characters and not the others) has been lost in an orgy of special effects and general mayhem.

But let me single out one line of dialogue. After the three American college students are trying to figure out what happened at the tower, one says, "The kind of girl who jumps off the Eiffel Tower has issues, man."

Starting with that line, a complete rewrite could be attempted, in which the characters are self-aware, know the werewolf rules, and know not to make the same mistakes as the characters in *An American Werewolf in London* (not to mention *The Howling, The Howling II: Your Sister is a Werewolf, Howling III, Howling IV: The Original Nightmare, Howling V: The Rebirth,* and *Howling VI: The Freaks*). I even have a great title: *Howler.*

And God Created Woman
(Directed by Roger Vadim; starring Rebecca De Mornay, Vincent Spano, James Tiernan, Frank Langella; 1987)

Is this the first time a title has been remade, instead of a movie? *And God Created Woman* shares little with the 1956 Brigitte Bardot movie except for its name and, to be sure, its director, Roger Vadim. It's a great title, and although I can only barely, dimly remember moments from the original movie, I am prepared to bet that this is a better one. The movie stars Rebecca De Mornay, who in her uncanny first shot looks for a moment like Bardot. Then the Bardot imagery is abandoned and the movie gets on with its business.

De Mornay plays a woman prison inmate (wrongly sentenced, of course), who is determined to be free. She escapes, but makes the mistake of hitching a ride in the limousine of a politician (Frank Langella). Instead of turning her over to the authorities, he helps her break back into the prison. Then he supplies some helpful advice: If she can find a responsible person on the outside who will vouch for her, she can probably be paroled.

This suggestion leads to the movie's best sequence, when De Mornay discovers a local handyman (Vincent Spano) who is making some repairs on prison property, and seduces him. Then she makes him an offer. She will give him her inheritance, $5,000, if he will marry her and help her be paroled. He agrees, and that leads to another good series of scenes, as these two incompatible people form an unlikely and apparently unworkable couple.

The whole middle stretch of *And God Created Woman* is good, in part because De Mornay and Spano work so effectively together, and partly because

Vadim tells the story efficiently and has a good story to tell. De Mornay plays a young woman who knows her own mind, firmly and without question. Although she had sex with Spano in prison, she won't sleep with him now: "This is business," she explains. He's astonished. She is, too, when she discovers Spano already has a family; he lives with a son and a kid brother. Then she makes adjustments, although Spano remains angry that she'd rather rehearse for a rock band than get a day job or keep house.

Meanwhile, she meets Langella again, and gets publicity as the deserving kid he has helped to rehabilitate. The two of them flirt, have a brief affair, and then separate after Langella's wife (Judith Chapman) suspects something. And then—the movie has gotten pretty dumb by this point—there's the threat that De Mornay will have to go back to jail, and then a dramatic moment at a political rally, and then, of course, the heartwarming ending.

Movies like this frustrate me because they do not have enough ambition to match their imagination. De Mornay and Spano have created two very interesting characters, in the reform-school girl and the carpenter who's trying to be a single father. Why did this plot, and these people, need the mechanical manipulation of the plot about the politician, his wife, and the melodramatic events of the last reel? Wasn't there a story here already?

I think so. De Mornay brings so much to this performance that it lifts off the screen and threatens to redeem the bankrupt plot. She makes the character live, and Spano is just as good, creating a whole world of hard work and pick-up trucks, mortgage payments and romantic confusion. In a movie like this, people are enough. The experience of De Mornay and Spano simply learning to talk to one another is more dramatic than the whole showdown at the political rally. In fact, the characters they create are so convincing that I resented seeing them manipulated by the rigid requirements of the plot: The young woman has broken out of one prison, only to find herself in another.

Is this a movie worth seeing? Sort of. You have to put the plot on hold, and overlook the contrivances of the last half hour, and find a way to admire how De Mornay plays the big scene, even while despising the scene itself. If you can do that, you'll find good work here—even by Vadim, who may have been as trapped by the plot as everyone else. Now that they've remade the title, I have an even better idea. They should remake the movie. Not the first one; this one.

Anna and the King

(Directed by Andy Tennant; starring Jodie Foster and Chow Yun-Fat; 1999)
King Mongkut of Siam is one of the slimiest characters in fiction, and Anna
Leonowens, the English schoolmarm who tries to civilize him, one of the
smarmiest. Here is a man with twenty-three wives and forty-two concubines
who allows one of his women and her lover to be put to death for exchanging
a letter. And here is Anna, who spends her days in flirtation with the king, but
won't sleep with him because—well, because he isn't white, I guess. Certainly
not because he has countless other wives and is a murderer.

Why is she so attracted to the king in the first place? Henry Kissinger has
helpfully explained that power is the ultimate aphrodisiac, and Mongkut has
it—in Siam, anyway. Why is he attracted to her? Because she stands up to him
and even tells him off. Inside every sadist is a masochist, cringing to taste his
own medicine.

The unwholesome undercurrents of the story of Anna and the King of
Siam have nagged at me for years, through many ordeals of sitting through
the stage and screen versions of *The King and I,* which is surely the most
cheerless of Rodgers and Hammerstein's musicals. The story is not intended
to be thought about. It is an exotic escapist entertainment for matinee ladies,
who can fantasize about sex with that intriguing bald monster, and indulge
their harem fantasies. There is no reason for any man to ever see the play.

Now here is a straight dramatic version of the material, named *Anna and
the King,* and starring Jodie Foster opposite the Hong Kong action star Chow
Yun-Fat. It is long and mostly told in the same flat monotone, but has one
enormous advantage over the musical: It does not contain "I Whistle a Happy
Tune." The screenplay has other wise improvements on the source material.
The king, for example, says "and so on and on" only once, and "et cetera" not
at all. And there is only one occasion when he tells Anna her head cannot be
higher than his. Productions of the stage musical belabor this last point so
painfully they should be staged in front of one of those police lineups with
feet and inches marked on it.

Jodie Foster's performance projects a strange aura. Here is an actress
meant to play a woman who is in love, and she seems subtly uncomfortable
with that fate. I think I know why. Foster is not only a wonderful actor but an
intelligent one—one of our smartest. There are few things harder for an actor
to do than play beneath their intelligence. Oh, they can play dumb people who

are supposed to be dumb. But it is almost impossible to play a dumb person who is supposed to be smart, and that's what she has to do as Anna.

She arrives in Siam, a widow with a young boy, and finds herself in the realm of this egotistical sexual monster with a palace full of women. Yes, he is charming; Hitler is said to have been charming, and so, of course, was Hannibal Lecter. She must try to educate the king's children (sixty-eight, I think I heard) and at the same time civilize him by the British standards of the time, which were racist, imperialist, and jingoistic, but frowned on chaining women in the rain until they surrendered.

By the end of the movie, she has danced with the king a couple of times, come tantalizingly close to kissing him, and civilized him a little, although he has not sold off his concubines. She now has memories she can write in her journal for Rodgers and Hammerstein to plunder on Broadway, which never tires of romance novels set to music.

Foster, I believe, sees right through this material and out the other side, and doesn't believe in a bit of it. At times we aren't looking at a nineteenth-century schoolmarm, but a modern woman biting her tongue. Chow Yun-Fat is good enough as the king, and certainly less self-satisfied than Yul Brynner. There is a touching role for Bai Ling, as Tuptim, the beautiful girl who is given to the king as a bribe by her venal father, a tea merchant. She loves another, and that is fatal for them both. There is also the usual nonsense about the plot against the throne, which here causes Anna, the king, and the court to make an elaborate journey by elephant so that the king can pull off a military trick I doubt would be convincing even in a Looney Tune.

Credits at the end tell us Mongkut and his son, educated by Anna, led their country into the twentieth century, established democracy (up to a point), and so on. No mention is made of Bangkok's role as a world center of sex tourism, which also of course carries on traditions established by the good king.

Armageddon

(Directed by Michael Bay; starring Bruce Willis, Liv Tyler, Ben Affleck; 1998)
Here it is at last, the first 150-minute trailer. *Armageddon* is cut together like
its own highlights. Take almost any thirty seconds at random, and you'd have
a TV ad. The movie is an assault on the eyes, the ears, the brain, common
sense, and the human desire to be entertained. No matter what they're charging
to get in, it's worth more to get out.

The plot covers many of the same bases as *Deep Impact,* which, compared to *Armageddon,* belongs on the AFI list. The movie tells a similar story
at fast-forward speed, with Bruce Willis as an oil driller who is recruited to
lead two teams on an emergency shuttle mission to an asteroid "the size of
Texas," which is about to crash into Earth and obliterate all life—"even
viruses!" Their job: Drill an 800-foot hole and stuff a bomb into it, to blow up
the asteroid before it kills us.

Okay, say you do succeed in blowing up an asteroid the size of Texas.
What if a piece the size of Dallas is left? Wouldn't that be big enough to
destroy life on Earth? What about a piece the size of Austin? Let's face it:
Even an object the size of that big Wal-Mart outside Abilene would pretty
much clean us out, if you count the parking lot.

Texas is a big state, but as a celestial object it wouldn't be able to generate
much gravity. Yet when the astronauts get to the asteroid, they walk around
on it as if the gravity is the same as on Earth. There's no sensation of weight-
lessness—until it's needed, that is, and then a lunar buggy flies across a
jagged canyon, Evil Knievel–style.*

The movie begins with a Charlton Hestonian voice telling us about the
asteroid that wiped out the dinosaurs. Then we get the masterful title card,
"65 Million Years Later." The next scenes show an amateur astronomer spot-
ting the object. We see top-level meetings at the Pentagon and in the White
House. We meet Billy Bob Thornton, head of Mission Control in Houston,
which apparently functions like a sports bar with a big screen for the fans, but
no booze. Then we see ordinary people whose lives will be Changed Forever

---

*Okay, there's some nonsense about air jets to push them down—but what happens
when they bend over?

by the events to come. This stuff is all off the shelf—there's hardly an original idea in the movie.

Armageddon reportedly used the services of nine writers. Why did it need any? The dialogue is either shouted one-liners or romantic drivel. "It's gonna blow!" is used so many times, I wonder if every single writer used it once, and then sat back from his word processor with a contented smile on his face, another day's work done.

Disaster movies always have little vignettes of everyday life. The dumbest in *Armageddon* involves two Japanese tourists in a New York taxi. After meteors turn an entire street into a flaming wasteland, the woman complains, "I want to go shopping!" I hope in Japan that line is redubbed as "Nothing can save us but Gamera!"

Meanwhile, we wade through a romantic subplot involving Liv Tyler and Ben Affleck. Liv is Bruce Willis's daughter. Ben is Willis's best driller (now, now). Bruce finds Liv in Ben's bunk on an oil platform, and chases Ben all over the rig, trying to shoot him. (You would think the crew would be preoccupied by the semidestruction of Manhattan, but it's never mentioned after it happens.) Helicopters arrive to take Willis to the mainland so he can head up the mission to save mankind, etc., and he insists on using only crews from his own rig—especially Affleck, who is "like a son."

That means Liv and Ben have a heartrending parting scene. What is it about cinematographers and Liv Tyler? She is a beautiful young women, but she's always being photographed flat on her back, with her brassiere riding up around her chin and lots of wrinkles in her neck from trying to see what some guy is doing. (In this case, Affleck is tickling her navel with animal crackers.) Tyler is obviously a beneficiary of Take Our Daughters to Work Day. She's not only on the oil rig, but she attends training sessions with her dad and her boyfriend, hangs out in Mission Control, and walks onto landing strips right next to guys wearing foil suits.

Characters in this movie actually say: "I wanted to say—that I'm sorry," "We're not leaving them behind!" "Guys—the clock is ticking!" and "This has turned into a surrealistic nightmare!" Steve Buscemi, a crew member who is diagnosed with "space dementia," looks at the asteroid's surface and adds, "This place is like Dr. Seuss's worst nightmare." Quick—which Seuss book is he thinking of?

There are several Red Digital Readout scenes, in which bombs tick down to zero. Do bomb designers do that for the convenience of interested on-lookers who happen to be standing next to a bomb? There's even a retread of the classic scene where they're trying to disconnect the timer, and they have to decide whether to cut the red wire or the blue wire. The movie has forgotten that *this is not a terrorist bomb,* but a standard-issue U.S. military bomb, being defused by a military guy who is on board specifically because he knows about this bomb. A guy like that, the *first* thing he should know is, red or blue?

Armageddon is loud, ugly, and fragmented. Action sequences are cut together at bewildering speed out of hundreds of short edits, so that we can't see for sure what's happening, or how, or why. Important special effects shots (like the asteroid) have a murkiness of detail, and the movie cuts away before we get a good look. The few "dramatic" scenes consist of the sonorous recitation of ancient clichés ("You're already heroes!"). Only near the end, when every second counts, does the movie slow down: Life on earth is about to end, but the hero delays saving the planet in order to recite cornball farewell platitudes.

Staggering into the silence of the theater lobby after the ordeal was over, I found a big poster that was fresh off the presses with the quotes of junket blurbsters. "It will obliterate your senses!" reports David Gillin, who obviously writes autobiographically. "It will suck the air right out of your lungs!" vows Diane Kaminsky. If it does, consider it a mercy killing.

Ash Wednesday

(Directed by Larry Peerce; starring Elizabeth Taylor, Henry Fonda, Helmut Berger, Keith Baxter; 1973)

Ash Wednesday is a soapy melodrama that isn't much good as a movie but may be interesting to some audiences all the same. It's about how a fiftyish wife (Elizabeth Taylor), her marriage threatened by a younger woman, has a face-lift in order to keep her husband. It doesn't work, but she gets a nice winter in a ski resort out of it and an affair with Helmut Berger.

The movie opens with clinical precision; a famous plastic surgeon explains his techniques to Miss Taylor as we see them being carried out. He outlines the areas of skin to be removed, and her face looks almost like one of those butcher's charts with all the cuts marked. Then he begins, with scalpel and needle, and when he has finished and she finally gets the bandages off, voilà! She looks as good as Elizabeth Taylor.

It's quite an improvement, because when the movie opens, she looks pretty bad. It must have taken some measure of courage for Taylor to allow herself to be made up and photographed so unattractively; maybe she got a double-reverse kick, though, out of knowing that she's so beautiful she has to be made up to look dowdy. And she is beautiful, which is what the movie's about, in a way. There are lots of close-ups in which she's frankly vain as she examines her face with delight; that face is a national treasure by now, and we support any measures to preserve it.

Most of the movie takes place at an expensive resort, where she goes to await the arrival of her husband (Henry Fonda). She hasn't told him about the face-lift: "At first," she says, "I didn't say anything because I was afraid it would seem like a silly thing to have done." A pause, and then: "Now my only regret is that I didn't do it years ago." Her husband is delayed in Washington on "business," which is part business and partly an affair he's having with a girl younger than their daughter. Taylor carries on a flirtation with Helmut Berger, mostly to test her new attractiveness, and eventually they make love. The fact that this affair takes about half an hour to develop, and requires yards of schmaltzy Maurice Jarre music to consummate, adds little to its interest.

The whole movie, indeed, feels longer than it is. It's fifteen minutes short of two hours, and still it takes forever to be over. The problem is that not enough happens; she waits at the resort, she drinks, she eats, she meets her daughter for a tearful lunch, she talks with a friendly fashion photographer, she waits, she has the affair, she waits, sighs, telephones, looks at herself, and models the Edith Head wardrobe. It's all so slight.

And yet, as I suggested, the movie may interest some audiences. Stars of Elizabeth Taylor's magnitude lead lives so public and famous that the details of their beauty become important to millions of people. Has she really had a face-lift? Does she need one? It's that kind of off-screen gossip that gives *Ash Wednesday* a sort of separate reality. The movie's story is not really very interesting, but we're intrigued because the star is Taylor. Weak as the role is, she was nevertheless just about the inevitable choice to play it. The unofficial crown for most beautiful woman in the world gets passed around a lot; one year it's Ursula Andress, then it's Candice Bergen, then Catherine Deneuve. But Taylor has won it so many times she ought to get possession. She's forty or forty-one now, and she looks great. There's a kind of voyeuristic sensuality in watching her look at herself in the mirror (which she spends no end of time doing). If you're Elizabeth Taylor, it's not vain to appraise your beauty, just as if someone's really after you, you're not paranoid. Maybe the fundamental problem with the movie is that we can't quite believe any man would leave Elizabeth Taylor. It's a good thing we never see Henry Fonda's bimbo, because if we did, we wouldn't be convinced. It's the same problem that sunk *Ryan's Daughter:* What woman would leave Robert Mitchum for . . . Christopher Jones? And the final confrontation between Taylor and Fonda is stiff and unconvincing; the movie has really been about the woman, not about the marriage, and Fonda doesn't so much interact with her as recite an announcement of termination. We can't buy it.

The movie's title was inspired, I guess, by the Catholic practice of wearing a smudge of ash on your face on Ash Wednesday as a reminder of man's inescapable mortality. In Taylor's case, however, mortality has at least temporarily been held at bay. For that, we can all be thankful—and she, I imagine, most of all.

Assassins

(Directed by Richard Donner; starring Sylvester Stallone, Antonio Banderas, Julianne Moore; 1995)

I know how to believe stuff when it happens in the movies. I believe bicycles can fly. I believe sharks can eat boats. I even believe pigs can talk. But I do not believe *Assassins,* because this movie is filled with such preposterous impossibilities that Forrest Gump could have improved it with a quick rewrite.

The movie stars Sylvester Stallone and Antonio Banderas as professional hit men. They haven't met when the movie opens, but they receive their orders on matching laptops (the kind where you just put one hand on the keyboard and rattle it in one place, and words get perfectly typed). Stallone is sent to kill a guy at a funeral, and is startled when somebody else does the job.

It is Banderas, hiding behind a nearby tombstone, and he's soon captured by the police—only to escape and get into a taxi that Stallone has stolen, in order to pick him up and find out who he is. (Stallone's own brilliant plan for the hit was to conceal a weapon in a cast on his arm and mingle with the mourners. His getaway plan was not explained.) The men are soon shooting at one another, for reasons that are explained without the explanations explaining anything, if you get my drift.

Soon the two men find themselves once again working on the same case and competing for the same prize—a $2 million reward for a stolen computer disk. The disk is in the possession of a woman named Electra (Julianne Moore), a cat fancier and computer whiz who has set up an elaborate scheme for exchanging the disk with some Dutch bad guys. (She has a radio-controlled toy truck in a hotel air shaft . . . but never mind.) Once again, Stallone and Banderas leave bodies littered all over the hotel, and then, as the reward is raised to $20 million, they find themselves in Mexico for a final showdown.

What follows is a *Spoiler,* so please stop reading if through some insane impulse you are compelled to see this movie. The endless last sequence of the film (which is very long and very slow) involves a situation where Stallone plans to enter a bank, collect $20 million in cash, and leave, and Banderas plans to shoot him from the window of the ancient abandoned hotel across the street. But Stallone knows that Banderas will do that, and enlists Electra in a plan to sit in a café and radio him updates.

He knows (for reasons buried in the past) that Banderas will eventually grow impatient while waiting, and after six or seven hours will be compelled to go into the bank to see if Stallone is still there. And Banderas will of course have to leave his guns outside. Sure enough, that's exactly what happens; the two men nod and chat a little, Banderas goes back outside and returns to his sniping post in the crumbling hotel, and Stallone collects the money and goes outside to be shot.

Say what? Well, there's some kind of a cockeyed plan in which Electra is supposed to sneak into the hotel while Banderas is in the bank, and snatch his rifle. But this hotel is *really* crumbling, and she falls through the floor. It is the first of many times in which several characters fall through so many floors it is a wonder the hotel is standing at all. And so when Stallone emerges from the bank, Banderas is in the window with the rifle aimed at him, and what does Stallone do? Duck for cover? No, he turns to accept his fate, or whatever, but then is saved through a unique application of the Fallacy of the Talking Killer. That is of course the old movie ploy where the killer talks instead of shooting. This is the first time I can remember where the killer is talking to himself.

There were many, many moments in this movie that left me puzzled. One of them involves the movie's key shooting. When you see it, you will know which one I mean, and you may find yourself, as I did, puzzled about how it happened. The mechanics of it seem to violate the laws of logic, not to mention physics.

Other problems in the movie: (1) How, when a guy is hanging outside the window of a cab and you crash it against the side of a bus, can he avoid being hurt? (2) If you hold a table up in front of you, will it really save you after a gas explosion blows you out of a third-floor window? (3) If you were holding a briefcase containing a bomb, would you throw it out of the car window, or hold it until you could drive down an alley and place it in a convenient Dumpster? (4) If you knew a sniper was waiting for you to emerge from the front door of a bank, would it occur to you to leave through the back, sneak up on the guy, and kill him—rather than depending on a ditzy computer nerd who says she's unable to shoot anyone? (5) Would you question the political and history credentials of a man who tells you he had to fake his death in 1980 because "the cold war was ending?"

Examining the movie's cast list for the answers to these and many other questions, I see that the characters played by Stallone and Banderas are named Rath and Bain. Rath becomes Wrath. Bain is French for "bath." Wrath and Bath. Has a nice ring. I was looking up Electra when the telephone rang, bringing me back to my senses.

Assault of the Killer Bimbos

(Directed by Anita Rosenberg; starring Christina Whitaker,
Elizabeth Kaitan; 1988)

Assault of the Killer Bimbos is one of those movies where the lights are on but nobody's at home. It is the most simpleminded movie in many a moon, a vacant and brainless exercise in dreck, and I almost enjoyed myself sometimes, sort of. The movie is so cheerfully dim-witted and the characters are so enthusiastically sleazoid that the film takes on a kind of awful charm.

The title is, of course, the best thing about it. I saw this film advertised at last year's Cannes Film Festival, where it was a finalist, along with *Space Sluts in the Slammer* and *Surf Nazis Must Die!* in my annual search for the most unforgettable bad-movie title since *Blood-Sucking Monkeys of Forest Lawn*. The amazing thing about the title is that it does, indeed, accurately describe the movie.

Assault of the Killer Bimbos begins at a go-go club located somewhere in the twilight zone. On a tiny stage in front of leering creeps, go-go dancers in weirdly decorated bikinis bounce around to bad music. They never take off any clothes, and when a waitress gets her "big break" and is allowed to dance, she's fired after the bananas on her brassiere fly off and strike several customers in their drinks. "You can't strip!" bellows the club owner. "This is a go-go joint, not a strip club!"

After plot complications too simple to describe, veteran dancer Peaches (Christina Whitaker) and newcomer Lulu (Elizabeth Kaitan) are unfairly framed for the murder of the club owner. They escape to Mexico in an old Dodge convertible, pausing along the way to kidnap a truck-stop waitress (Tammara Souza), who decides to join them. In the middle of their escape, they meet three pothead surfers who accompany them, and they are chased by various sheriff's deputies.

Students of grade-Z exploitation films may want to take notes about the employment of nudity in this film. Although the bimbos do not remove their clothes in the go-go joint, there is a later scene where they change clothes on the roadside, and we see their bare breasts. However, we never see the faces and breasts of the same women at the same time; the film is carefully edited to show nudity only from the neck down. That leads to the suspicion that body doubles were used to supply the nudity, and that the actresses actually starring in the film never took off anything.

Was this because (a) they refused to, or (b) they were assured there would be no nudity in the film, and then matching nude shots were spliced in later? Good questions, both of them, and I expect we can look forward to the answers in the sequel to this film, which is advertised during the closing titles and will be called *Bimbo Barbeque*.

At the Earth's Core

(Directed by Kevin Connor; starring Peter Cushing, Doug McClure; 1976)
Peter Cushing has never said the name "David!" so often before in his life.
You remember Peter Cushing. He's the one in all those British horror films,
standing between Vincent Price and Christopher Lee. His dialogue usually
runs along the lines of, "But good heavens, man! The person you saw has
been dead for more than two centuries!" This time all he says is "David!"

David is played by Doug McClure. You remember Doug McClure. Good.
I don't. McClure plays a rich young American inventor who has financed the
Iron Mole, which is a gigantic steam-powered screw, designed to penetrate to
Earth's core. The Mole has been designed by Cushing, an eccentric British
inventor, as who would not be after such an invention?

McClure and Cushing settle into their seats and push the appropriate levers
and the Mole goes berserk. It forgets all about the hill and screws itself right
into the very mantle of the planet itself, emerging in Pellucidar, that mysterious
land within Earth. Pellucidar is inhabited by the kinds of characters whose
names make me chuckle aloud even as I type them down. There's Dia, the
beautiful slave girl with the heaving bodice, and Ra, her boyfriend, and the
evil Ghak, not to mention the impenetrable Hooja. All of these people speak
English, you understand, except when it comes to the matter of proper names.

Well, anyway, Doug and the professor step out into this sinister underworld, which is filled with telepathic giant parrots, and the next thing you
know they're on the chain gang. The chain gang spends all day breaking up
rocks. You wouldn't think there would be a rock shortage at Earth's core, but
there you are.

About here, we begin to notice the Captain Video effect. You remember
Captain Video. He was a science-fiction hero on the old DuPont TV network.
He and his trusty sidekick (Bucky? Rocky?) were forever landing on strange
planets and sneaking around rocks. After three weeks, you realized that the
rocks were always the same.

Same here. Doug and the Professor sneak around one strange man-eating
vegetable, and there's another one—which is the original vegetable, photographed from a new angle. Meanwhile, the telepathic parrots wander by,
opening and closing their beaks by spring action. It's along about here we
begin to really zero in on Dia's bodice. Let somebody else break up the rocks
and clean up after the parrots.

The Awakening

(Directed by Robert Solo; starring Charlton Heston, Susannah York; 1980)

The Awakening is bad in so many ways that I'll just have space to name a few. It is, for example, completely implausible in its approach to the science of archaeology—so hilariously inaccurate, indeed, that I can recommend this movie to archaeologists without any reservations whatsoever. They'll bust a gut.

Example. Charlton Heston, a British archaeologist, is searching for the long-lost tomb of the Egyptian queen Kara. He finds it. Well, no wonder: It's "hidden" behind a gigantic stone door in a mountainside, with big, bold hieroglyphic written all over it. It's about as hard to find as Men's Clothing at Marshall Field's. Anyway, having found this priceless and undisturbed tomb, Heston immediately begins pounding away at the door with a sledgehammer.

Now, even if your knowledge of archaeology is limited to leafing through back issues of *National Geographic* at the dentist's, you know that when they make a major find, they're supposed to spend years dusting off everything with little brushes and making a fetish of not disturbing anything. Not Heston. He even has a team of laborers with pickaxes standing by as backup.

Well, wouldn't you know, every time Heston hammers at the tomb, his pregnant wife back at the camp doubles up in pain. That's because, as the movie makes abundantly clear, the spirit of Kara is being reborn in Heston's baby daughter. There's also some nonsense about how Heston ignores his wife-to-be with his comely young assistant (Susannah York), and then the movie flashes forward eighteen years, and we veteran *Omen* watchers prepare for the scenes in which the child becomes aware that she is possessed by a spirit, and that Her Time Has Come.

Great! And none too soon, we're all thinking. But the movie's climax is so filled with impossibilities that we're too busy with the mental rewrite to get scared. For example: Do you believe a priceless tomb would be left open, eighteen years later, so that people could walk right into it? That the operation of a secret door could elude generations of grave robbers, but be solved twice in a matter of minutes? That Heston could walk into a modern museum, move a sarcophagus around on a freight elevator, light candles, lift a two-ton lid with his bare hands, and conduct arcane rituals without attracting the inquiry of a security guard?

If you can believe all those things, then, at the end, when the reborn priestess Kara turns and snarls at the audience, you'll believe that *The Awakening* is set for a sequel. Call me an optimist, but I believe this movie is so bad it'll never be reborn.

BBBBBBBBB

The Babe

(Directed by Arthur Hiller; starring John Goodman, Trini Alvarado; 1992)
Say it ain't so, Babe.

Say you weren't a sad, tortured person who just happened to be able to slam homers out of the park better than anyone else.

Say this movie is all a lie, and that you were indeed a glorious American hero, the grandest of all the boys of summer, and that it was great fun, at least sometimes, to be the most famous baseball hero of all time.

Let us believe. We need our heroes.

But *The Babe* doesn't give us one. Apart from being a bad film in the first place, aside from being superficially written, aside from being shot with little sense of time or place, the movie portrays Babe Ruth as a man almost completely lacking in the ability to have, or to provide, happiness.

Spending these 115 minutes with the Babe is a little like being jammed into the window seat on a long-distance bus, next to a big guy with beer and cigars on his breath and nothing to talk about but his next meal and his last broad. Babe Ruth comes across as a pathetic orphan lacking in all social graces, who grew up into a self-destructive bore and hit a lot of home runs in the process. And then, in the end, when time caught up with him, he never got the message, and almost destroyed the myth that had grown up around him.

No matter how many homers he hit, Ruth would have never become a Great American Hero in the television age. On the radio and in the newspapers, maybe he came across as quite a guy. But to see and hear him—at least as he is portrayed in this movie—is to cringe. After the magical innocence of baseball as painted in *Field of Dreams,* after the life-affirming *Bull Durham,* here is a baseball trading card that looks like it was found in the gutter.

The fault is not John Goodman's. He plays the Babe as written. You can see, watching this movie, that he could have played a lot of other sides of

Babe Ruth and made them work. But John Fusco's screenplay doesn't seem to like Babe very much. It shows him as an overgrown, recalcitrant kid who had one skill. He could hit the ball. And then it shows him growing up into a human pig who wenched and cheated on those who loved him, who was drunk during many of his games, who was small-minded and jealous, who wasn't much of a team player, who lost his temper and screamed at the fans, and whose little trot around the bases looked like the outing of a constipated alderman.

Much has been made of the movie's use of Wrigley Field and a ball park in Danville, Illinois. They're supposed to re-create the look of the diamonds of Ruth's day. But the movie seems to keep showing us the same two parks, while giving us subtitles trying to convince us we're in Baltimore, or Boston. There don't seem to be many fans in the stands. There is no sense here of baseball. No smell of peanuts and roar of the crowd.

Babe's first wife, played by Trini Alvarado, is a nice girl who finally can't stand the reports of Babe's raids on the brothels and his demands for three girls at a time. The second wife, a Ziegfeld Follies girl played by Kelly McGillis, has been around the block a few times and is less easily shocked. She stays with the Babe, but more out of loyalty and stubbornness, we sense, than because of love.

Her loyalty is more than organized baseball can muster. Ruth is paid well and tolerated by the Yankees as long as he's hitting, but when his legs and eye start to go, there's no love lost between them, and no sense of loyalty. He ends up in Boston, where his final days are portrayed as a mixture of shame, anti-climax, and betrayal.

The famous moments are here. The dying kid in the hospital, who Ruth promises he'll hit two home runs in the next game. The "called shot" in the World Series. The home run record that has never been beaten, except by an asterisk. But at the end of the movie, when we're thoroughly depressed any-way, do we really need that maudlin scene where a young man follows Ruth off the field after his final game, introduces himself as the kid whose life was saved by those two homers, and gives back the ball that Babe autographed beside the hospital bed? Talk about shameless.

Baby Geniuses

(Directed by Bob Clark; starring Kathleen Turner, Christopher Lloyd; 1999)
Bad films are easy to make, but a film as unpleasant as *Baby Geniuses* achieves a kind of grandeur. And it proves something I've long suspected: Babies are cute only when they're being babies. When they're presented as miniature adults (on greeting cards, in TV commercials, or especially in this movie) there is something so fundamentally *wrong* that our human instincts cry out in protest.

Oh, you can have fun with a baby as a movie character. *Look Who's Talking* (1989) was an entertaining movie in which we heard what the baby was thinking. *Baby's Day Out* (1994), with its fearless baby setting Joe Mantegna's pants on fire, had its defenders. But those at least were allegedly real babies. *Baby Geniuses* is about toddlers who speak, plot, scheme, disco dance, and beat up adults with karate kicks. This is not right.

The plot: Kathleen Turner plays a woman with a theory that babies can talk to each other. She funds a secret underground lab run by Christopher Lloyd to crack the code. Her theory is based on the Tibetan belief that children have Universal Knowledge until they begin to speak—when their memories fade away.

This is an old idea, beautifully expressed by Wordsworth, who said that "heaven lies about us in our infancy." If I could quote the whole poem instead of completing this review, believe me, we'd all we happier. But I press on. The movie involves a genius baby named Sly, who escapes from the lab and tries to organize fellow babies in revolt. The nauseous sight of little Sly on a disco floor, dressed in the white suit from *Saturday Night Fever* and dancing to "Stayin' Alive," had me pawing under my seat for the bag my Subway Gardenburger came in, in case I felt the sudden need to recycle it.

Every time the babies talk to one another, something weird happens to make it look like their lips are in synch (think of talking frogs in TV commercials). And when the babies do things that babies don't do (hurl adults into the air, for example), we lose all track of the story while trying to spot the visual trick.

There's only one way the movie might have worked: If the babies had been really, really smart. After all, according to the theory, they come into this world "trailing clouds of glory" (Wordsworth again: The man can write). They possess Universal Knowledge. Wouldn't you expect them to sound a little like Jesus, or Aristotle? Or at least Wayne Dwyer? But no. They arrive on this mortal coil (Shakespeare) from that level "higher than the sphery chime" (Milton), and we expect their speech to flow in "heavenly eloquence" (Dryden). But when they open their little mouths, what do they say? "Diaper gravy"—a term used four times in the movie, according to a friend who counted (Cleland).

Yes, they talk like little wise guys, using insipid potty-mouth dialogue based on insult humor. This is still more evidence for my theory that the greatest single influence on modern American culture has been Don Rickles.

B.A.P.S.

(Directed by Robert Townsend; starring Halle Berry, Martin Landau; 1997)
B.A.P.S. is jaw-droppingly bad, a movie so misconceived I wonder why anyone involved wanted to make it. As a vehicle for the talents of director Robert Townsend and actors Halle Berry and Martin Landau, it represents a grave miscalculation; I hope they quickly put it behind them.

The title stands for "Black American Princesses." Its two heroines are more like tacky Cinderellas. Berry and Natalie Desselle play vulgar and garish homegirls from Decatur, Georgia, whose artificial nails are eight inches long, whose gold teeth sparkle, and whose hairpieces are piled so high on their heads that the concept passes beyond satire and into cruelty.

There is a thin line between satire and offensiveness, and this crosses it. Its portraits of these two working-class black women have been painted with snobbery and scorn. The actresses don't inhabit the caricatures with conviction. The result is a hurtful stereotype, because the comedy doesn't work to redeem it. We should sense some affection for them from the filmmakers, but we don't—not until they receive a magic Hollywood makeover in the later scenes of the movie, and miraculously lose their gold teeth. The movie invites us to laugh at them, not with them, but that's a moot point since the audience I joined did not laugh at all, except incredulously.

The plot: Berry plays Nisi, a waitress, who hears on MTV about a contest to choose a dancer for a music video and national tour by Heavy D. She shares this news with her friend Mickey (Desselle), a hairdresser, and it fits right into their plans for marrying a rich guy and living on easy street. So they say good-bye to their shiftless boyfriends and fly to L.A. wearing hairstyles so extreme no one behind them on the airplane can see the movie. Funny? No. It could have been funny, but not when the reaction shots are of annoyed white businessmen asking to change their seats.

In L.A. they're spotted at the audition by a mysterious figure who makes them an attractive offer: Room and board in a Bel Air mansion, and $10,000. What's the deal? He represents Mr. Blakemore (Landau), a dying millionaire, who has only experienced true love once in his life, many years ago—with Lily, his family's black maid. Nisi will pose as Lily's granddaughter and cheer the old guy in his final days on Earth.

There's more to it than that, of course; it's all a scam. But Mr. Blakemore inexplicably takes to the women from the moment he sees them. (Nisi, dressed in pink latex and high heels, looks like a hooker, and Mickey looks like her coach.) The plot later reveals details that make it highly unlikely Mr. Blakemore would even for a second have been deceived by the story, but never mind; the movie's attention span isn't long enough for it to remember its own setup.

Even though the movie fails as a comedy, someone should have told Landau it was intended to be one. He plays Mr. Blakemore with gracious charm and great dignity, which is all wrong; his deathbed scene is done with such clunky sincerity that one fears Landau actually expected audiences to be moved by it. Not in this movie. The cause of his ill health is left a little obscure, and no wonder, because shortly before his dreadful deathbed scene he's well enough to join the women in a wild night of disco dancing. You have not lived until you've seen Martin Landau discoing. Well, perhaps you have. He is both miscast and misdirected, and seems to labor under the misapprehension that his role should be taken seriously.

Another key character is Manley (Ian Richardson), Blakemore's butler, who turns up his nose at the first sight of the women, but inevitably comes to like them. The message of the movie, I guess, is that two homegirls can find wealth and happiness if only they wear blonde wigs, get rid of those gold teeth and country vocabularies, and are nice to rich old white men. It gets even better: At one point, the boyfriends from Georgia are flown out to L.A. to share the good luck, and they vow to get their acts together and Plan for Their Futures in a scene that comes way too late in the film for us to believe or care.

The movie was written by the actress Troy Beyer, who has a small role as a lawyer. What was she thinking of? I don't have a clue. The movie doesn't work, but was there any way this material could ever have worked? My guess is that African Americans will be offended by the movie, and whites will be embarrassed. The movie will bring us all together, I imagine, in paralyzing boredom.

Battle of the Amazons

(Directed by Al Bradley; starring Lincoln Tate, Lucretia Love; 1973)
Dear Mr. Ebert: I would like to object to consumer fraud in the ads for *Battle of the Amazons*. They taught us in Greek mythology class that the real Amazons had only one breast so they might better shoot their bows and arrows. So I went running down to the Michael Todd with the intent of seeing an eighty-inch boob and instead I got conned with a pair of forties.
Signed, Dennis Boy

Dear Mr. Boy: Ah, but those Amazons were Greek; these Amazons live someplace in Asia Minor. That is all the more puzzling because none of them is Asian and only three are minors. The drinking age was well below nineteen at that time in history, however, you will be glad to learn.

The Amazons and their captives are also interesting because, if I read lips right, they spoke Italian dubbed into English. Many historians are of the opinion that neither language existed then, but American-International, the distributor, may be onto something. One thing is for sure: No movie in the last twenty years has been dubbed more ineptly. No, not even *Godzilla vs. the Smog Monster.* In one scene, a man has his head split open with a ferocious blow from a sword. On the screen we see his lips opening in an anguished scream. On the sound track we hear him say, in English: "Oh, no!" It is possible to respect his opinion while questioning his sincerity.

Another problem in the movie is that the actors who were hired to dub it into English have a hard time not laughing. There was one speech that went something like: "Zeno, surely you agree that no matter what Ilio, Antiope, Medio, Eraglia, and Sinade say, Valeria is right!"

An additional difficulty is that most of the pretty girls in the movie are Amazons. No wonder the men of the village will not fight to resist capture.

It's hard to be sure exactly when the movie takes place; there are spears and bows and arrows and swords, which suggests early times, but then again all of the women on both sides are fresh from the hair dryer. They also employ impressive advances in the art of brassiere design.

One of the most intriguing aspects of *Battle of the Amazons* is that it was released only four weeks before the scheduled opening of *The Amazons,* a big-budget epic directed by Terence Young, who made some James Bond pictures.

Sometimes a schlock picture will be rushed in to exploit the publicity of an expensive movie, but here's the funny thing: *both* movies are from American-International, which by ripping itself off solidifies its reputation as the best exploitation outfit in the business. I am waiting confidently for the first Kung-Fu Amazon movie. No, wait: One's due before long. It's called *Red Hot China Doll,* which used to be the name of an interesting Szechwan-style chicken dish served in a nice little place on Clark Street.

Beautician and the Beast

(Directed by Ken Kwapis; starring Fran Drescher, Timothy Dalton; 1997)
Fran Drescher is a taste I have not acquired, but I concede that one could acquire it. It would help if she made a silent film. Her speaking voice is like having earwax removed with a small dental drill. And yet, doggone it, there's something lovable about her. I picture her making the coffee at Stuart Smalley's AA meetings, or doing the ringside announcements for pro wrestling.

You have seen her on *The Nanny* and on countless talk shows. Most talk-show guests say something and then laugh, so you know it's supposed to be funny. She laughs, and then says something, so you know it was supposed to be a laugh and not a respiratory emergency. Not every role would be suitable for her. I cannot visualize her, for example, in *The English Patient,* saying "Promise you'll come back for me." Or as Sheriff Marge Gunderson in *Fargo,* saying, "And I guess that was your accomplice in the woodchipper."

Beautician and the Beast contains a role that seems to have been whipped up out of two parts of Drescher's public persona and one part of nothing else. She plays Joy Miller, who teaches beauty secrets in a Queens night school. After a smoking mishap leads to a wig fire and the school burns down, she is hailed on the front pages as a heroine (for saving the lab rats), and approached by a representative of the obscure central European nation of Slovetzia.

That nation has recently emerged from communism into a dictatorship controlled by Boris Pochenko (Timothy Dalton), a despot who wants to soften his image and thinks maybe importing an American tutor for his children might help. (Pochenko is also the name of the European exile who is killed at the beginning of *Shadow Conspiracy,* but I cannot think of anything to say about this coincidence, other than that they are both named after a popular Japanese pinball game.) Dalton plays the role as if he had somehow found himself the villain in a James Bond film instead of the hero.

Slovetzia is not an advanced nation. There are sheep on the runway of the national airport. Pochenko lives in a castle possibly mortgaged from Young Frankenstein. Joy makes a bad first impression, when she is late for her official welcoming ceremony because she hasn't finished her hair and nails.

The dictator (known to his subjects as the "Beast for Life") has three children, who have grown restive under his iron fist while nevertheless managing to speak in American accents after their first few scenes. The daughter is unhappy about her approaching arranged marriage. The son bites his nails. "Don't do that!" Joy tells him. "Do you want to grow a hand in your stomach?"

Joy's wardrobe runs toward day-glo stretch pants and pullover blouses. She is sublimely indifferent to the veiled threats of Pochenko, so he tries un-veiled ones, which she tut-tuts away. Meanwhile, she has the castle running like a catering kitchen, and is able to save precious currency reserves by planning a diplomatic reception around frozen Chung King egg rolls.

The trajectory of this story is clear from its title. The beautician will get the beast, and in the subplot Juliet will get her Romeo. The direction is by Ken Kwapis, whose *He She, She Said* (1992) is invaluable for getting you from John Tesh to the Addams Family in the Kevin Bacon game. Kwapis tries to build suspense where none can possibly exist, which is always an annoyance; is it a crime for a movie to know as much about its story as the audience does?

But there are some genuine laughs here and there, and a certain charm emanates from Fran Drescher, who I suspect is easier to stand in real life than she lets on in her acting. And we are not disappointed in our wait for the Obligatory Transformational Entrance Scene, which all movies like this lead up to. After being an ugly duckling for three-quarters of the movie, the heroine turns up at the top of a staircase looking regal and beautiful, and descends while trying to keep one of those "are they looking at poor little me?" looks on her face. *Beautician and the Beast* made me laugh, but each laugh was an island, entire onto itself. They didn't tie together into anything very interesting. Drescher never really seems to be interacting with the other characters. Like Mae West or Groucho Marx, she eyeballs the stiffs while they're talking, and then delivers her zingers. We don't care about her character because we never feel she's really uncertain, insecure, or vulnerable. Here's a woman who will never grow hands in her stomach.

Beethoven's 2nd

(Directed by Rod Daniel; starring Charles Grodin, Bonnie Hunt, Debi Mazar; 1993)

There is a scene in *Beethoven's 2nd* in which Beethoven, who is a large St. Bernard dog, takes his girlfriend Missy, also a large St. Bernard, to a drive-in theater for the movies. They sit on a hill above the parking lot, where they have a good view of the screen. This much I was prepared to believe. Some dogs are very clever. But when Beethoven came back with a box of popcorn for Missy, I realized these were not ordinary dogs but two of amazing intelligence, and when it was revealed that Missy got pregnant later that night, I found myself asking if they'd never heard of taking precautions.

In due time Missy's four puppies are born into a world filled with human problems. The central tragedy is that Beethoven and his lady love have been separated. Beethoven of course lives with a large and loving family, the Newtons. But Missy has been dognapped from her loving owner by his bitter estranged wife, a woman who in appearance and behavior resembles the witch in *Snow White*.

The three Newton kids manage to rescue and cherish the puppies, after winning over their dad (the priceless Charles Grodin, who must have charged a high one for appearing in this). Mom (merry-faced Bonnie Hunt) of course loves the pups at first sight. And then the screenplay provides a vacation trip to a lake, where Missy's evil dognapper (Debi Mazar) and her goon boyfriend (Chris Penn) are also visiting.

That sets up the entirely predictable ending, in which the evil villains attempt a puppynapping. It also sets up a scene so unsavory that it has no place in a movie rated PG. The oldest Newton girl, Ryce (Nicholle Tom) is trapped in a locked bedroom by a slick boy she knows from the city. "Ummm," he says, dangling the keys and advancing on her, "this is gonna be great!" Luckily Beethoven saves the day before a sexual assault takes place, but were the filmmakers so desperate they could think of no scene more appropriate for a family movie?

The dogs are of course cute. All St. Bernards are cute. But their best features are not their eyes, which tend to be small, red, and runny—something director Rod Daniel should have considered before shooting so many soulful close-ups of Beethoven, who looks like he needs doggy Visine.

One of the film's genuine blessings is that we do not hear the dog's thoughts, although we do get several songs on the sound track that reflect their thinking. Missy and Beethoven are first smitten with each other while Dolly Parton and James Ingram sing "The Day I Fall in Love," and I'm telling you, there wasn't a dry face on the screen, mostly because the dogs were licking each other.

This movie has one clear reason for being: The success of the original *Beethoven*, which grossed something like $70 million. That film was no masterpiece, but it made good use of the adorable Beethoven, and in Charles Grodin it had a splendid comic actor who made the most of his role as a grumpy dad who didn't want a dog causing havoc around the house. This time, with Grodin elevated to an innocuous role and Debi Mazur acting as if she were being paid by the snarl, it's up to the dogs. You know you're in trouble when the heroes of a comedy spend more time swapping spit than one-liners.

The Believers

(Directed by John Schlesinger; starring Martin Sheen, Helen Shaver, Robert Loggia; 1987)

Here's another one of those movies where a Caribbean voodoo cult wants to practice a blood sacrifice using the child of a Manhattan psychiatrist. Can't they think of anything new to make a movie about? I'm getting tired of the dingy tenements in Spanish Harlem with the blood-soaked chicken feathers on the floor, and the scenes where the shrink realizes he needs a witch doctor to save his child.

Most religious movies are about peace and love and friendship, and how one day all of humanity is going to hold hands and be brother and sister. Movies about Caribbean religions are always about guys with blank eyes who stare at you for ten seconds and you're volunteering to wring the chickens' necks yourself.

I am as ignorant as most people on the facts about such religions, including the ancient Cuban cult in *The Believers,* which keeps its diabolical gods a secret by disguising them as Catholic saints. I would like to imagine that most Caribbean religions, like most religions everywhere, are a comfort to their believers, and hold up a prospect of a saner, more joyous life.

I would like to believe that, but the movies give me little reason to. Every voodoo movie ever made has depicted bloodthirsty cults of savagely sadistic murderers, vengefully thirsting for innocent blood. There has been a lot in the papers recently about "Arab-bashing," the practice of creating strongly negative stereotypes of Arabs on TV and in the movies. I'm in agreement. But what about voodoo-bashing? Isn't it just as prejudicial?

In *The Believers,* which is an awesomely half-witted movie, Martin Sheen plays a psychiatrist whose wife is electrocuted by touching the coffeemaker while standing barefoot in a pool of spilled milk. This event has absolutely nothing to do with the rest of the story. It's simply a pretitle sequence. So much for the wife.

After Sheen and his young son start anew in Manhattan, they attract the attention of a Cuban cult that sacrifices children in order to gain all sorts of fringe benefits, such as success, a better mental attitude, and so on. Sheen has these benefits explained to him by an old friend who secretly is a convert, but demurs at the opportunity of sacrificing his own child.

Meanwhile, he has a tempestuous pre–AIDS-era affair with his gorgeous landlady (Helen Shaver), while a police lieutenant (Robert Loggia) investigates a series of child killings. (One of Loggia's big scenes involves missing his coffee cup with the little plastic container of cream, so that Sheen can stare at the puddle on the desk and have a flashback to his wife's death.)

This is one of those movies that use the paraphernalia of expertise instead of the expertise itself. "Are you a Catholic?" people keep asking Sheen, who is, and there's the implication that his church affiliation somehow will protect him or endanger him—it's not clear which. There are lots of shots of ashes and blood and weird little voodoo charms, but no real explanations of what's going on—possibly because it doesn't matter. *The Believers* should be ashamed of itself.

Ben

(Directed by Phil Karlson; starring Joseph Campanella,
Meredith Baxter; 1972)

I wonder how Ben learned English. I seem to recall from *Willard,* last summer's big rat movie, that Willard trained Ben to heel, beg, roll over, play dead, and sic Ernest Borgnine. Not bad for a rat. But when did Ben learn English? It takes Berlitz six weeks of intensive training to get a French businessman to the point where he can proposition an American girl, and here's Ben learning instinctively.

Ben also talks in his new movie. It's hard to understand what he says, however, because all he does is squeak in various octaves. He sounds like Rubber Ducky being goosed. The movie's hero is Danny, an eight-year-old with a heart condition. Danny loves Ben. Danny apparently understands Rubber Ducky talk, too, maybe because he's a graduate of Sesame Street. Do you ever get the feeling that when Earth is finally conquered, it won't be by rats but by tiny, beady-eyed, preschool superintelligences who attack us with nuclear alphabets?

Ben and his friends head for the sewers and plan their assault on mankind. This involves being thrown through the air by invisible animal trainers, so that they land onscreen and scare hell out of sewer workers. Everyone knows this is nonsense. If Art Carney could go down in the sewers day after day and fearlessly face alligators, what's a few rats?

Doesn't matter, though. This isn't a thriller but a geek movie. In a thriller, we're supposed to be scared by some awesome menace to mankind—the Green Blob maybe, or Bigfoot, or the Invincible Squid and his implacable enemy, red wine sauce. But in a geek movie, the whole idea is to be disgusted because the actors have rats all over them.

You know what a geek is, or at least you do if you grew up near a county fairgrounds like I did. He's the guy who bites the head off a living chicken.

I used to hate the geek show, but I sat through it manfully because that was a test of your courage. If you passed it, you got to pay the extra quarter and see the lady who was tattooed all over. Also the Half-Man, Half-Woman, who, to my intense disappointment, turned out to be the wrong half of each.

Besieged

(Directed by Bernardo Bertolucci; starring Thandie Newton, David Thewlis; 1999)

Bernardo Bertolucci's *Besieged* is a movie about whether two people with nothing in common, who have no meaningful conversations, will have sex—even if that means dismissing everything we have learned about the woman. It is also about whether we will see her breasts. How can a director of such sophistication, in a film of such stylistic grace, tell such a shallow and evasive story?

But wait. The film also involves race, politics, and culture, and reduces them all to convenient plot points. The social values in this movie would not have been surprising in a film made forty years ago, but to see them seriously proposed today is astonishing. In a hasty moment I described the film as "racist," but it is not that so much as thoughtless, and lacking in all empathy for its African characters, whose real feelings are at the mercy of the plot's sexual desires.

The film opens in Africa, with an old singer chanting a dirge under a tree. We see crippled children. A teacher in a schoolroom tries to lead his students, but troops burst in and drag him away. The young African woman Shandurai (Thandie Newton) sees this. The teacher is her husband. She wets herself. So much for the setup. The husband will never be given any weight or dimension.

Cut to Rome, where Shandurai is a medical student, employed as a maid in the house of Mr. Kinsky (David Thewlis). He will always remain "Mr. Kinsky" to her, even in a love note. He is a sardonic genius who plays beautifully upon the piano, and occupies a vast apartment given him by his aunt and hung with rich tapestries and works of art. Given the size and location of the apartment she was a very rich aunt indeed. The maid's quarters are spacious enough for a boutique, and Mr. Kinsky's rooms are reached by a spiral staircase to three or four levels.

Thandie Newton is a beautiful woman. She is photographed by Berto-lucci in ways that make her beauty the subject of the shots. There's a soft-core undertone here: She does housework, the upper curves of her breasts swelling above her blouse. Little wisps of sweaty hair fall down in front of those wonderful eyes. There is a montage where she vacuums and Mr. Kinsky plays—a duet for piano and Hoover.

It is a big house for two people, very silent, and they move around it like stalkers. One day she drops a cleaning rag down the spiral staircase and it lands on Mr. Kinsky's head. He looks up. She looks down. Mr. Kinsky decides he loves her. There is a struggle. "Marry me! I'll do anything to make you love me!" She throws him a curve: "You get my husband out of jail!"

He didn't know she was married. Other things divide them, including their different tastes in music. He performs the classics, but one day plays rhythmic African rhythms for her. She smiles gratefully, in a reaction shot of such startling falseness that the editor should never have permitted it. Later Shandurai has a speech where she says how brave, how courageous, her husband is. Eventually we gather that Mr. Kinsky is selling his possessions to finance the legal defense of the husband. Even the piano goes.

All of this time the film has been performing a subtle striptease involving Shandurai, who has been seen in various stages of partial or suggested nudity. Now, at the end, we see her breasts as she lies alone in bed. I mention this because it is so transparently a payoff; Godard said the history of cinema is the history of boys photographing girls, and Bertolucci's recent films (like *Stealing Beauty*) underline that insight.

I am human. I am pleased to see Thandie Newton nude. In a film of no pretension, nudity would not even require any justification; beauty is beauty, as Keats did not quite say. But in *Besieged* we have troublesome buried issues. This woman is married to a brave freedom fighter. She says she loves and admires him. Now, because Mr. Kinsky has sold his piano to free her husband, she gets drunk and writes several drafts of a note before settling on one ("Mr. Kinsky, I love you"). She caresses herself and then steals upstairs and slips into his bed. In the morning, her freed husband stands outside the door of the flat, ringing the bell again and again—ignored.

If a moral scale is at work here, who has done the better thing: A man who went to prison to protest an evil government, or a man who freed him by selling his piano? How can a woman betray the husband she loves and admires, and choose a man with whom she has had no meaningful communication?

To be fair, some feel the ending is open. I felt the husband's ring has gone unanswered. Some believe the ending leaves him in uncertain limbo. If this story had been by a writer with greater irony or insight, I can imagine a more shattering ending, in which Mr. Kinsky makes all of his sacrifices, and Shandurai leaves exactly the same note on his pillow—but is not there in the morning.

The film's need to have Shandurai choose Mr. Kinsky over her husband, which is what I think she does, is rotten at its heart. It turns the African man into a plot pawn, it robs him of his weight in the mind of his wife, and then leaves him standing in the street. *Besieged* is about an attractive young black woman choosing a white oddball over the brave husband she says she loves. What can her motive possibly be? I suggest the character is motivated primarily by the fact that the filmmakers are white.

The Beyond

(Directed by Lucio Fulci; starring Catriona MacColl, Giovanni De Nava; 1981)
The Beyond not only used to have another title, but its director used to have another name. First released in 1981 as *Seven Doors of Death*, directed by Louis Fuller, it now returns in an "uncut original version" as *The Beyond*, directed by Lucio Fulci.

Fulci, who died in 1996, was sort of an Italian Hershell Gordon Lewis. Neither name may mean much to you, but both are pronounced reverently wherever fans of zero-budget schlock horror films gather. Lewis was the Chicago-based director of such titles as *Two Thousand Maniacs, She-Devils on Wheels,* and *The Gore-Gore Girls.* Fulci made *Zombie* and *Don't Torture the Duckling.* Maybe that was a temporary title, too.

The Beyond opens in "Louisiana 1927," and has certain shots obviously filmed in New Orleans, but other locations are possibly Italian, as was (probably) the sign painter who created the big DO NOT ENTRY sign for a hospital scene. It's the kind of movie that alternates stupefyingly lame dialogue with special-effects scenes in which quicklime dissolves corpses and tarantulas eat lips and eyeballs.

The plot involves . . . excuse me for a moment, while I laugh uncon-trollably at having written the words "the plot involves." I'm back. The plot involves a mysterious painter in an upstairs room of a gloomy, Gothic Louisiana hotel. One night carloads and boatloads of torch-bearing vigilantes converge on the hotel and kill the painter while shouting, "You ungodly war-lock!" Then they pour lots of quicklime on him, and we see a badly made model of his body dissolving.

Time passes. A woman named Liza (played by Catriona MacColl, who was named "Catherine" when the director was named "Louis"), inherits the hotel, which needs a lot of work. Little does she suspect it is built over one of the Seven Doors of Evil that lead to hell. She hires a painter, who falls from a high scaffold and shouts "The eyes! The eyes!" Liza's friend screams, "This man needs to get to a hospital!" Then there are ominous questions, like "How can you fall from a four-foot-wide scaffold?" Of course, one might reply, one can fall from anywhere, but why did he *have* a four-foot-wide scaffold?

Next Liza calls up Joe the Plumber (Giovanni de Nava), who plunges into the flooded basement, wades into the gloom, pounds away at a wall, and is grabbed by a horrible thing in the wall, which I believe is the quicklimed painter, although after fifty years it is hard to make a firm ID.

Let's see. Then there is a blind woman in the middle of a highway with a seeing-eye dog, which later attacks her (I believe this is the same woman who was in the hotel in 1927), and a scene in a morgue, where the wife of one of the victims (the house painter, I think, or maybe Joe) sobbingly dresses the corpse (in evening dress) before being attacked by acid from a self-spilling jar on a shelf.

But my favorite scene involves the quicklimed decomposed corpse, which is now seen in a hospital next to an oscilloscope that flatlines, indicating death. Yes, the rotting cadaver is indeed dead—but why attach it, at this late date, to an oscilloscope? Could it be because we'll get a shot in which the scope screen suddenly indicates signs of life? I cannot lie to you. I live for moments like that.

Fulci was known for his gory special effects (the Boston critic Gerald Peary, who has seen several of his films, cites one in which a woman vomits up her intestines), and *The Beyond* does not disappoint. I have already men-tioned the scene where the tarantulas eat eyeballs and lips. As the tarantulas tear away each morsel, we can clearly see the strands of latex and glue holding it to the model of a corpse's head. Strictly speaking, it is a scene of tarantulas eating makeup.

In a film filled with bad dialogue, it is hard to choose the most quotable line, but I think it may occur in Liza's conversations with Martin, the architect hired to renovate the hotel. "You have carte blanche," she tells him, "but not a blank check!"

The movie is being revived around the country for midnight cult shows. Midnight is not late enough.

Beyond and Back
(Directed by James L. Conway; starring Brad Crandall; 1978)

The makers of *Beyond and Back* were also responsible, if memory serves, for another film called *In Search of Noah's Ark*. It figures. At the end of that one they were still searching for Noah's Ark—they never found it. At the end of *Beyond and Back* we're back, all right—but were we beyond?

The movie's another one of those pseudo-scientific laundry lists of half-baked psychic theories. There may be something to the theories, all right, but there's never anything to the movies. They're booked into half the theaters in town and promoted with a hard-sell TV campaign, on the theory that enough suckers will be parted from their money before the word gets out that it's a turkey.

Beyond and Back gives turkeys a bad name. It exists on about the same cinematic level as an army training film or one of those junior high chemistry movies in which the experiments never quite worked. To be sure, the narrator is presented as a genuine authentic intellectual; we can tell because he's got a beard and glasses and stands in front of bookshelves and learnedly caresses bound volumes of the *Journal of the American Psychical Society*. But what does he tell us, really?

Well, he tells us for one thing that there is strong scientific evidence that human beings have souls, but that dogs do not. We see a nineteenth-century scientist making this discovery. He measures people and dogs at the time of their deaths to see if their bodies lose weight at the moment their souls depart. The people lose weight but the dogs do not. (The scientist had "delicate scales" attached to the deathbeds—scales so delicate, the narrator intones, they could measure to within two-tenths of an ounce! That is not a very small weight, as anyone who has observed the gradual shrinkage over the years of Hershey bars will have noticed.)

But never mind: The scientist discovered that his patients did lose weight when they died, and deduced that the human soul weighs "between half and three-quarters of an ounce." Given the factor for error in the experiment, which was a fifth of an ounce, you will see that this was not exactly the most precise experiment since Franklin flew his kite. (I cannot resist recalling that in Catholic school, we were told about a similar experiment; the only difference was that the experiment revealed *no* difference in weight—because the soul, of course, is not physical, and so scientists were stupid to even try to weigh it.)

There are other tiny flaws in the picture, as in the episode depicting the death of an army private during World War II. He was dead, all right: The doctor and the nurse agreed. But he still had consciousness, and his astral body, he tells us, rose from his physical body and walked around the room, saw strange bright glows coming from the sky, witnessed a display of lights, walked down a strange street in a strange city, talked to God, and was back in bed. All in nine minutes.

The flaw here is that although the man's spiritual body could not touch anything (his hands passed right through telephone poles with a whoosh), he is clearly seen opening the closet door in his hospital room. Fair's fair: They can't have it both ways.

But perhaps I'm being too hard to please. This is a film, after all, which permits certain inconsistencies, as when we share with Louisa May Alcott the experience of seeing her sister's soul rise from the body, looking like a small puff of steam from a teakettle and obviously weighing nothing like half an ounce—give or take a fifth of an ounce, of course.

Beyond the Door

(Directed by Oliver Hellman; starring Juliet Mills, Richard Johnson; 1975)
"Where's Jessica?" asks her worried husband, when she disappears during a birthday party for the children. He finds her in the bathroom, regurgitating pints, maybe gallons, of blood. "Honey, are you all right?" he asks, in the

understatement, or underquestion, of the year. She allows that she feels a little weak. They agree she ought to get more rest. The whole movie is this way: maddeningly inappropriate in the face of its horrors.

And yet *Beyond the Door* is one of the top-grossing movies in the country right now. Why? Maybe because at some dumb, fundamental level, it really does live it up to, or down to, its promise. It's not well acted, its "Possessound" audio sounds routed through the ventilation system, and the print looks like it was left too long in demonic possession.

But it's got one hell of an ad campaign. The TV spots and the trailer on the viewer in front of the theater show all sorts of delightful horrors, a menacing voice dares you to see it and, inside the theater, there's a party atmosphere. Parts of the movie play almost as comedy. I'm usually disturbed when people laugh at violence, but in a movie like *Beyond the Door,* the laughs seem almost appropriate.

That's during the earlier parts of the movie, when mysterious hands reach out to touch shoulders in darkened rooms, and it turns out it's just the husband patting his wife. In the later stages, though, when Jessica (Juliet Mills—yes, Juliet Mills) begins to turn green and talk like the Big Bopper, the movie's just conventionally disgusting. We get green vomit, brown vomit, blood, levitations, and other manifestations of the devil.

He is, by the way, in Jessica's womb. She has this short-order pregnancy that proceeds so rapidly she's three months' pregnant within a week (if that's the way to describe it). The mysterious stranger seems to have the answer, and after saving her husband from being run over by a truck, he offers several enigmatic epigrams such as, "Some people attract . . . misfortune."

Beyond the Poseidon Adventure
(Directed by Irwin Allen; starring Michael Caine, Sally Field,
Karl Malden, Shirley Jones; 1979)
The original *Poseidon Adventure* began, of course, with the giant ocean liner *Poseidon* being flip-flopped by a massive tidal wave. What happened then has become legend. In the midst of a New Year's Eve celebration, the movie's cast was trapped in the upside-down ballroom, which is what New Year's Eve feels like anyway, and, in one of the greatest coincidences in the

history of casting, all of the stars were saved and all of the extras were drowned.

The stars then had to struggle up the down staircase to the bottom of the boat, which, if you are following me closely, was by then above the water. And, to save their lives, they had to attempt to cut through the thick steel bottom and thus to daylight and so on. So far so good. But what do you do for a sequel?

I posed this question to Irwin Allen, creator of the Poseidon movies and *The Swarm* and *The Towering Inferno,* during one sunny afternoon in southern California when disasters were the last thing on his mind. He said he had an idea. It was, in all candor, he said, a great idea. The survivors of the *Poseidon* would be rescued and taken to land in Italy and be placed on a train which would go through a tunnel in the Alps, and the tunnel would collapse and everyone would be trapped under the mountain.

Irwin Allen cleared his throat modestly. What, he asked, did I think about his idea? It was, I said, a great idea, terrific if not actually stupendous. But I had a better idea. Allen didn't seem too enthralled, but I told it to him anyway. (There is, by the way, nothing quite so glazed as the eyes of a movie producer who has just seen his interviewer put his Pentel Rolling Marker away and start to speak, but I persisted.)

Here's what happens, I said. After everybody fights his or her way to the top and/or bottom of the boat, surviving fires and floods and explosions, another big tidal wave comes along *and turns the great ship over again!* And so the hapless survivors have to retrace their steps!

It makes no sense, said Allen, because (a) he probably wouldn't be able to reassemble the original cast, and (b) lots of the original cast members, like Shelley Winters and Gene Hackman, were killed in the original movie—so who you gonna top-line?

Hackman's gone for sure, I conceded. He lost his grip and fell into the flaming oil. But in the case of Winters—well, she says in the movie that she won the underwater swimming competition at the Young Womens' Hebrew Association, and so maybe at the beginning of the sequel she comes up gasping, and you go on from there. Irwin Allen mulled over that for a fraction of a second, and then, almost inevitably, our interview was over.

Therefore it was with a great deal of curiosity that I went to see *Beyond the Poseidon Adventure* in order to see how he'd finally worked out the sequel, without my help. And I know you think at this point that I'm going to give away the ending, but don't stop reading now. I wouldn't dream of giving away the ending. What I will give away is the beginning.

On the morning after the *Poseidon*'s disastrous night, tugboat captain Michael Caine and sidekick Sally Field get back on board the *Poseidon* and find leftover survivors who were not drowned during the original movie, and then bad guy Telly Savalas puts them all in jeopardy, and then . . .

But what did we really, sincerely, expect anyway, from a movie in which Slim Pickens plays a character named "Tex"? If you can think of a single line of dialogue that Slim Pickens, as "Tex," wouldn't say in *Beyond the Poseidon Adventure,* please do not miss this movie, which will be filled with amazements and startling revelations.

Bigfoot

(Directed by Robert F. Slatzer; starring John Carradine, Joi Lansing, Lindsay Crosby; 1971)

Why, you are asking, did I decide to see *Bigfoot*? Why am I taking your time—time you could spend trimming your toenails and talking to your plants, telling them what nice plants they are—to review *Bigfoot*? What strange light in the sky, what weird whistling in my ear, what blood-soaked note tied to a rock and thrown through my window, sent me to see *Bigfoot*?

These are good questions. The cast alone convinced me. Let me put it as simply as I can. If you have ever wanted to see a movie starring John Carradine, Joi Lansing, Lindsay Crosby, Chris Mitchum, and Ken Maynard, then *Bigfoot* is almost certainly going to be your only chance. Not since Joan Crawford starred in *Trog* has there been such an opportunity.

Joi Lansing began her career as a model for men's magazines. She is still startling, especially with a jumpsuit. She parachutes wearing the garment, which conceals a minidress slit to the waist, and a top that is slashed to the belt, and she runs away from Bigfoot for about five minutes in this costume, bouncing through the woods but not (for some reason) from her blouse.

No matter. There is always John Carradine. He plays a backwoods trader with a line of goods packed into the rear of his 1958 Ford station wagon. He stops at a general store run by Ken Maynard (yes, Ken Maynard) and Ken makes a phone call while standing in front of a poster from one of his old movies (*Texas Gunfighter*, if I remember correctly) wearing the same ten-gallon hat that's on the poster.

"There have been a lot of strange things going on up in those hills," he informs the sheriff, after Chris Mitchum's girlfriend has been carried away by a half-human, half-animal creature with big feet. But the sheriff refuses to go up on the mountain after dark, and so Chris enlists his buddies in a motorcycle gang led by Lindsay Crosby (yes, Lindsay Crosby).

This is no ordinary motorcycle gang. All of its members ride identical brand-new medium-size Yamahas, which are credited in the titles to a Hollywood Yamaha agency. The gang members also wear bright-colored nylon windbreakers with pull-strings at the bottom, and they wear new knit shirts and dress loafers. The girls wear bikinis. The gang's hairstyle is set by Lindsay Crosby's receding ducktail.

Meanwhile, Lansing and another girl are tied to trees (saplings would be a better word) by the creatures, and then Lansing is carried off and given to Bigfoot. Bigfoot is usually shot from a camera angle between his toes, making him loom over the camera like King Kong, but when we see him straight-on he looks about five feet ten inches or eleven inches tall. He wears a shaggy costume stitched together out of old, dirty brown shag rugs.

There is an exciting chase through the woods, which is only slowed down a little by the fact that the movie has nine unidentified extras who have to file past the camera. Then Bigfoot runs into a cave. This has us hoping that Joan Crawford will appear and explain that the creature has been misunderstood (in *Trog*, she went into the cave with a twenty-nine-cent bunch of carrots, calling "Here, Trog?").

But, no, a motorcyclist pulls a bundle of dynamite from his belt and throws it into the cave. No fuse, just the dynamite. Then we cut to footage apparently taken from another film, showing towers of flame. The mountain shakes. Yards below, an old Indian woman cocks her head and nods wisely at the sky. Mountain speak with big voice. Then we cut to a sound stage set decorated with trees, bushes, and a steaming pile of rocks in one corner—the remains of the cave and the mountain, too, for that matter. "Do you—think it's dead?" Joi Lansing asks. "Nothing could live through that," Lindsay Crosby assures her. I hope he's right.

The Big Hit

(Directed by Che-Kirk Wong; starring Mark Wahlberg, Lou Diamond Phillips; 1998)

Hollywood used to import movie stars from overseas. Then directors. Then they remade foreign films. Now the studios import entire genres. It's cheaper buying wholesale. *The Big Hit* is a Hong Kong action comedy, directed by Che-Kirk Wong *(Crime Story, Hard to Die),* starring an American cast, and written by Ben Ramsey, an American who has apparently done as much time in the video stores as Quentin Tarantino.

The movie has the Hong Kong spirit right down to the deadpan dialogue. Sample:

Hit Man: "If you stay with me you have to understand I'm a contract killer. I murder people for a living. Mostly bad people, but . . ."

Girl He Has Kidnapped: "I'm cool with that."

The characters in these movies exist in a Twilight Zone where thousands of rounds of ammunition are fired, but no one ever gets shot unless the plot requires him to. The bullets have read the screenplay.

As the film opens, we meet four buddies working out in a health club. They're played by Mark Wahlberg (of *Boogie Nights*), Lou Diamond Phillips, Bokeem Woodbine, and Antonio Sabato, Jr. The guys are hunks with big muscles, which we can study during a locker-room scene where they stand around bare-bottomed while discussing Woodbine's recent discovery of masturbation, which he recommends as superior to intercourse, perhaps because it requires only one consenting adult.

Then they dress for work. They're all garbed as utilities workers, with hard hats, toolboxes, and wide leather belts holding wrenches and flashlights. As they saunter down the street to Graeme Revell's pumping sound track, they look like a downsized road company version of the Village People.

The plot: They attack the heavily defended high-rise stronghold of a rich pimp who has just purchased three new girls for $50,000 a head. They break in with guns blazing, and there's an extended action sequence ending with one of the heroes diving out of an upper floor on a bungee cord, just ahead of a shattering explosion. And so on.

They kidnap Keiko (China Chow), the daughter of a rich Japanese executive. Complications ensue, and she ends up in the hands, and later the car trunk, of the leader of the hit men, named Melvin Smiley (Wahlberg). This is most likely the first movie in which the hero hit man is named Melvin Smiley. But he does smile a lot, because his weakness is, "I can't stand the idea of people who don't like me." You would think a hit man would have a lot of people walking around not liking him, but not if he is a good enough shot.

Keiko falls in love with Melvin with astonishing rapidity. Sure, she tries to escape, but by the end she realizes her future lies with his. Will this complicate Melvin's life? Not any more than it already is.

He has a black mistress (Lela Rochon), who looks at a dismembered body in their bathtub and says, "He's kinda cute." And he has a Jewish fiancée (Christina Applegate), who is Jewish for the sole purpose of having two Jewish parents (Elliott Gould and Lainie Kazan), so they can appear in the middle of the movie like refugees from a Woody Allen picture and provide crudely stereotyped caricatures. Gould makes crass remarks about his wife's plastic surgery, gets drunk, and throws up on Lou Diamond Phillips, in a scene where both actors appear to be using the powers of visualization to imagine themselves in another movie.

Many more action scenes. Cars explode. Cars are shot at. Cars land in trees. They fall out of trees. Remember those old serials where someone got killed at the end of an installment, but at the beginning of the next installment you see them leap quickly to safety? That trick is played three times in this movie. Whenever anyone gets blowed up real good, you wait serenely for the instant replay.

I guess you could laugh at this. You would have to be seriously alienated from normal human values and be nursing a deep-seated anger against movies that make you think even a little, but you could laugh.

Birds in Peru
(Directed by Romain Gary; starring Jean Seberg; 1969)
Oh yes, she has a lovely face. When the camera moves close and Jean Seberg arches that magnificent neck and looks into the middle distance and her lips part slightly . . . yes, Preminger knew what he was doing when he cast her as Joan of Arc.

So, yes, she has a lovely face. We see it for minutes on end in *Birds in Peru.* Looking up at us, down at us, away, in profile, turning toward, blank, fearful, seductive, nihilistic. It would almost seem that the face was Romain Gary's reason for making the movie. So that with a camera he could worship the face of his wife. Alas, Gary and Miss Seberg did not get on well while the movie was being made, and shortly afterward there was a divorce. Ah.

The story goes that Gary wanted to direct this movie because he was so displeased by the two previous movies made from his books: *Lady L* and *Roots of Heaven*. Those were stinkers, yes. So Gary took his short story *Birds in Peru* and directed it himself this time. Now there are three stinkers made from his work.

His story involves a frigid beauty (Miss Seberg) who arrives in Peru in the midst of a round-the-world trip in search of fulfillment. She is accompanied by her husband and his chauffeur, who complete a masochistic ménage à trois. The morning after the carnival, we find her on a beach with the bodies (some dead, some alive) of the lovers who tried and failed last night. She wanders away in shock. Arrives at a bordello on the seashore. Makes love with the madam and one of her customers. Wanders away again. Meets a sensitive young artist. Waits with him for her husband and the chauffeur to arrive. When they do, they will kill her. Then the chauffeur has instructions to kill the husband. There is a houseboy involved, too, whose function is to look startled and run about.

This material could have been made into an interesting movie. What was needed was a sense of pace, less impersonal dialogue, and an end to artistic game-playing. In short, it would have worked as a movie but it doesn't work as a photographed literary idea.

Gary holds his close-ups much too long, especially in the case of Miss Seberg; instead of providing dramatic impact and pacing, they drag the movie to a halt. Gary doesn't like to move his camera much, either; his ideas of composing a scene are painfully elementary. Shots on the beach are invariably photographed by arranging his actors in a geometric pattern and having them march dreamily ahead.

The beach photography, by the way, was apparently meant to be surrealistic. We get long vistas of barren beach, with figures here and there in the landscape, old Peruvian masks and feathers and dying birds stuck in the sand, and strange rocks on the horizon, as if this were a Salvador Dali retrospective. But none of it works. The movie doesn't grow. The characters drift through their vacuum. Rarely has so much pretension created so much waste.

But there is one, and only one, good cinematic moment. The woman and the artist are alone in the cabin. They embrace each other. Then they hear a strange sound: tap-tap . . . tap-tap . . . two quick taps, silence, two quick taps again. They look up. It is the chauffeur, come to murder them, impatiently tapping his foot.

The Blue Iguana
(Directed by John Lafia; starring Dylan McDermott, Jessica Harper, Dean Stockwell; 1988)

The Blue Iguana is as close to a no-brainer as you can get, and still have anything left on the screen at all. It's a smart-aleck parody of private-eye movies, but it knows as little about private eyes as it does about parodies and movies. It's the kind of experience where you sit in stunned silence, looking at the screen, knowing that even the actors can hardly be blamed, since if they had been allowed to improvise almost anything that came into their heads, it would have been better than the dialogue they've been given.

Horrible movies like this sometimes have a chance of working, in a perverse way, if they bring energy and style to the screen. We will never know, alas, whether energy and style could have saved this one. It's an expensive professional version of the kind of inane spoofs that college students sometimes try to shoot on video—movies where the big thrill is seeing your pals in costume. The movie's so bad, there isn't even anyone in it who knows how to smoke. The hero, a private eye named Vince (Dylan McDermott), plays every scene with an unfiltered cigarette stuck in his mouth, and yet he doesn't come across as a chain-smoker, he comes across as a nonsmoker who detests having this smelly thing under his nose.

Vince is broke, and so he accepts an assignment from the IRS, which wants him to travel to Diablo, a mythical Central American republic where a dragon lady (Jessica Harper) launders crooked money in her bank. The other players in this banana republic (none of them apparently Latinos) include James Russo as Reno, the local hoodlum, and Pamela Gidley as Dakota, who runs the saloon. The IRS agents, who follow Vince south, are played by Dean Stockwell, wearing thick glasses and a neck brace, and Tovah Feldshuh, who has evidently been spending a lot of time pumping iron lately and wants us to know it.

What happens in Diablo will be familiar to any regular viewer of the late movie on the cable station from hell. You know the one. That mystery station on your cable service that seems to show up in the unassigned gaps between the regular channels. The one with no name, no IDs, no number, and no call letters, that always seems to be showing movies that apparently do not exist. In those movies, as in this one, people drive around in old cars, shoot at each other, and say things like "I've got fifteen men out there!" The plots always involve coffins full of foreign currency, guys with mustaches, women with garter belts, and a voice-over narration in which the hero does a cynical whine.

I have no idea why this movie was made. I have no notions of what the actors in it thought they were doing. I have no clues as to whether the writer-director, John Lafia, thought it was funny. I do not know why Paramount released it. I do know that they say if an iguana loses its tail, it can grow another one. I do not know, however, if that is true. Wouldn't you think that in a movie named *The Blue Iguana,* in which nothing of interest happens for ninety minutes, they'd at least answer a few fundamental questions about iguanas? But the only iguana in this movie is a cigarette lighter.

Blue Velvet
(Directed by David Lynch; starring Isabella Rossellini, Kyle MacLachlan, Dennis Hopper; 1986)
Blue Velvet contains scenes of such raw emotional energy that it's easy to understand why some critics have hailed it as a masterpiece. A film this painful and wounding has to be given special consideration. And yet those very scenes of stark sexual despair are the tipoff to what's wrong with the movie. They're so strong that they deserve to be in a movie that is sincere, honest, and true. But *Blue Velvet* surrounds them with a story that's marred by sophomoric satire and cheap shots. The director is either denying the strength of his material or trying to defuse it by pretending it's all part of a campy in-joke.

The movie has two levels of reality. On one level, we're in Lumberton, a simpleminded small town where people talk in television clichés and seem to be clones of 1950s sitcom characters. On another level, we're told a story of sexual bondage, of how Isabella Rossellini's husband and son have been kidnapped by Dennis Hopper, who makes her his sexual slave. The twist is that the kidnapping taps into the woman's deepest feelings: She finds that she is a masochist who responds with great sexual passion to this situation.

Everyday town life is depicted with a deadpan irony; characters use lines with corny double meanings and solemnly recite platitudes. Meanwhile, the darker story of sexual bondage is told absolutely on the level in cold-blooded realism.

The movie begins with a much praised sequence in which picket fences and flower beds establish a small-town idyll. Then a man collapses while watering the lawn, and a dog comes to drink from the hose that is still held in his unconscious grip. The great imagery continues as the camera burrows into the green lawn and finds hungry insects beneath—a metaphor for the surface and buried lives of the town.

The man's son, a college student (Kyle MacLachlan), comes home to visit his dad's bedside and resumes a romance with the daughter (Laura Dern) of the local police detective. MacLachlan finds a severed human ear in a field, and he and Dern get involved in trying to solve the mystery of the ear. The trail leads to a nightclub singer (Rossellini) who lives alone in a starkly furnished flat.

In a sequence that Hitchcock would have been proud of, MacLachlan hides himself in Rossellini's closet and watches, shocked, as she has a sado-mashochistic sexual encounter with Hopper, a drug-sniffing pervert. Hopper leaves. Rossellini discovers MacLachlan in the closet and, to his astonishment, pulls a knife on him and forces him to submit to her seduction. He is appalled but fascinated; she wants him to be a "bad boy" and hit her.

These sequences have great power. They make *9½ Weeks* look rather timid by comparison, because they do seem genuinely born from the darkest and most despairing side of human nature. If *Blue Velvet* had continued to develop its story in a straight line, if it had followed more deeply into the implications of the first shocking encounter between Rossellini and MacLachlan, it might have made some real emotional discoveries.

Instead, director David Lynch chose to interrupt the almost hypnotic pull of that relationship in order to pull back to his jokey, small-town satire. Is he afraid that movie audiences might not be ready for stark S&M unless they're assured it's all really a joke?

I was absorbed and convinced by the relationship between Rossellini and MacLachlan, and annoyed because the director kept placing himself between me and the material. After five or ten minutes in which the screen reality was overwhelming, I didn't need the director prancing on with a top hat and cane, whistling that it was all in fun.

Indeed, the movie is pulled so violently in opposite directions that it pulls itself apart. If the sexual scenes are real, then why do we need the send-up of the *Donna Reed Show*? What are we being told? That beneath the surface of Small Town, U.S.A., passions run dark and dangerous? Don't stop the presses.

The sexual material in *Blue Velvet* is so disturbing, and the performance by Rossellini is so convincing and courageous, that it demands a movie that deserves it. American movies have been using satire for years to take the edge off sex and violence. Occasionally, perhaps sex and violence should be treated with the seriousness they deserve. Given the power of the darker scenes in this movie, we're all the more frustrated that the director is unwilling to follow through to the consequences of his insights. *Blue Velvet* is like the guy who drives you nuts by hinting at horrifying news and then saying, "Never mind."

There's another thing. Rossellini is asked to do things in this film that require real nerve. In one scene, she's publicly embarrassed by being dumped naked on the lawn of the police detective. In others, she is asked to portray emotions that I imagine most actresses would rather not touch. She is degraded, slapped around, humiliated, and undressed in front of the camera. And when you ask an actress to endure those experiences, you should keep your side of the bargain by putting her in an important film.

That's what Bernardo Bertolucci delivered when he put Marlon Brando and Maria Schneider through the ordeal of *Last Tango in Paris*. In *Blue Velvet*, Rossellini goes the whole distance, but Lynch distances himself from her ordeal with his clever asides and witty little in-jokes. In a way, his behavior is more sadistic than the Hopper character.

What's worse? Slapping somebody around, or standing back and finding the whole thing funny?

Body of Evidence

*(Directed by Uli Edel; starring Madonna, Anne Archer, Joe Mantegna,
Willem Dafoe; 1993)*

I've seen comedies with fewer laughs than *Body of Evidence,* and this is a
movie that isn't even trying to be funny. It's an excruciatingly incompetent
entry in the *Basic Instinct* genre, filled with lines that only a screenwriter
could love, and burdened with a plot that confuses mystery with confusion.

The movie stars Madonna, who after *Bloodhounds of Broadway, Shanghai
Surprise,* and *Who's That Girl?* now nails down her title as the queen of
movies that were bad ideas right from the beginning. She plays a kinky
dominatrix involved in ingenious and hazardous sex with an aging millionaire
who has a bad heart. He dies after an evening's entertainment, and Madonna
is charged with his murder.

But she's innocent, she protests—and indeed there is another obvious
suspect, the millionaire's private secretary (Anne Archer), who is also his
spurned former lover. Willem Dafoe plays the defense attorney who firmly
believes Madonna is innocent, or in any event very sexy, and Joe Mantegna
has the Hamilton Burger role.

The movie takes place in Portland, Oregon—a city small enough,
Madonna volunteers from the witness stand, that she once dated a guy who
dated a girl who dated Mantegna. That's a typical exchange in the courtroom
scenes, which involve Dafoe being reprimanded by the judge for just about
every breath he draws.

I don't know whether to blame the director, the cinematographer, or the
editor for some of the inept choices in this movie. One example. Dafoe is
addressing his opening remarks to the jury, and the camera pulls focus so that
we see an attractive young female juror sitting in the front row. She gives
Dafoe an unmistakable look. We in the audience are alerted that the movie is
establishing her for a later payoff. We're wrong. She's just an extra trying to
grab some extra business.

But enough on the technical side. What about the story here? It has to be
seen to be believed—something I do not advise. There's all kinds of murky
plot debris involving nasal spray with cocaine in it, ghosts from the past,
bizarre sex, and lots of nudity. We are asked to believe that Madonna lives on
a luxury houseboat, where she parades in front of the windows naked at all
hours, yet somehow doesn't attract a crowd, not even of appreciative lobster-

men. What does she dedicate her life to? She answers that question in one of the movie's funniest lines, which unfortunately cannot be printed here.

When it comes to eroticism, *Body of Evidence* is like Madonna's new book. It knows the words but not the music. All of the paraphernalia and lore of S&M sexuality are here, but none of the passion or even enjoyment. We are told by one witness that sex with the Madonna character is intense. It turns out later he's not a very reliable witness.

Bolero
(Directed by John Derek; starring Bo Derek, George Kennedy, 1984)
Bolero is a film starring Bo Derek as a woman who believes that the cure for a man's impotence is for his woman to train as a bullfighter. *Bolero* is also the name of the composition by Ravel that Dudley Moore played in *10* while making love with Derek. So much we already know. Also, let's see here, paging through the old dictionary . . . a bolero is a Spanish dance, characterized by sharp turns and revolutions of the body and stamping of the feet, and it also is a jacket of waist-length or shorter, usually worn open. So that explains the jacket of waist-length or shorter, usually worn open, which is Bo Derek's only item of clothing during one scene in the movie. It also explains the sharp turns and revolutions of her body during the same scene, although there is no stamping of the feet, except by the viewer.

But I am still a little confused by the relationship between Derek and the bullfighter who is her lover. If you have not seen the movie, let me explain. Derek has graduated from a fancy women's boarding school, and after mooning her professors she departs in search of a tall, dark, and handsome man.

First she meets a sheik, but he turns out to be a dud, maybe because he spends too much time inhaling the magic fumes of his hookah. So Bo goes to Spain, where she meets this all-around guy who herds cattle on a mountaintop, owns a winery, and is a bullfighter. If he also was an investment banker whose last book read was *The Prophet,* he could be a Dewar's Profile. Bo and the guy make love at sunrise. Unfortunately, the sun rises directly into the camera at crucial moments. Then her lover goes into the ring to fight with the bull, and is gored in that portion of his anatomy he can least afford to spare in any continuing relationship with Derek. He is brave. While doctors fight to save his life, his only thought is for his dog. He asks Bo to be sure that the dog gets home safely.

Before long, Bo is observing that her lover is acting depressed and distant. Could this possibly be because of his horrible injuries? You would think so, and I would think so, but Bo tells him it doesn't matter, and then she vows that he will live to fight again another day, so to speak. Then she starts taking bullfighting lessons. Oh, but I almost forgot. The Arab sheik tears himself away from his hookah long enough to fly to Spain and kidnap her. She is tied up in his open biplane, but manages to untie herself and jump off the plane. Then Bo is immediately back in her lover's hacienda again. How did she get to the ground? For anyone with Bo's faith, all is possible, and I think this is a real good omen for the lover. If she can get down in one piece, think what he might be able to do.

Let's face it. Nobody is going to *Bolero* for the plot anyway. They're going for the Good Parts. There are two Good Parts, not counting her naked ride on horseback, which was the only scene in the movie that had me wondering how she did it.

Breaking the Rules
(Directed by Neil Israel; starring Jason Bateman, Annie Potts, C. Thomas Howell; 1992)
Breaking the Rules is a movie about a guy who finds out he has a month to live, and decides to spend it in the worst buddy movie ever made.

The movie has to be seen to be believed. It is a long, painful lapse of taste, tone, and ordinary human feeling. Perhaps it was made by beings from another planet, who were able to watch our television in order to absorb key concepts such as cars, sex, leukemia, and casinos, but formed an imperfect view of how to fit them together.

This is the kind of movie where a scene is intended to make you cry, but you're not crying, you're wondering just how bad the dialogue can possibly be, and whether the filmmakers are indeed lacking in all instincts about what is believable or acceptable behavior, and what is not.

The movie opens with three childhood chums whose idea of a good time is to ride inside the dryers at the laundromat. One of the buddies throws up inside a dryer, and they get in trouble. One wonders, watching this scene, if the filmmakers know it is dangerous for kids to play inside laundry dryers? If they think it's funny to show such a practice? If they couldn't think of any other kind of prank?

The payoff comes when the kids are confronted by angry adults, and all three of them simultaneously point at the other two guys while chiming in unison, "He did it." This establishes the ground rules: These characters know they are in a movie, and are reading dialogue, not performing ordinary human speech.

Flash-forward ten years. One of the kids stages a reunion between the other two, who are no longer on speaking terms. Reason: He has leukemia, and a month to live. All three young men immediately decide to get a van and set off cross-country to California, where it is the dying lad's final wish to appear on *Jeopardy.*

Along the way, they stop off for some Nevada casino action, and meet a waitress who instantly marries the dying kid and asks him to sleep with her because she wants his baby. Nope, says the doomed one; it's my buddy who wants to sleep with you. Ever the good sport, the waitress sleeps with the buddy on her wedding night—on a couch in the same room where the other two friends are sleeping. How do they react? They pull the sheets over their heads, and giggle.

One appalling scene follows another. The illness, the death, the funeral, the videotape. Was there no one to cry out, "Stop this madness?" No one to read the script and see that it was without sense or sensibility? No one to listen to the dialogue and observe that nobody in the whole world has ever talked like this? No one to say that you cannot inspire sympathy for characters who act in a manner contrary to all common human decency? A good documentary about the making of *Breaking the Rules* might perhaps provide a useful record of the decay of intelligence and sanity in our time.

Brother Sun, Sister Moon

(Directed by Franco Zeffirelli; starring Graham Faulkner, Alec Guinness; 1973)
Franco Zeffirelli's *Brother Sun, Sister Moon* is a big, limp Valentine of a movie, filled with an excess of sweetness and light. What a shame. His subject

is Francis of Assisi, one of the most interesting and natural of saints, but Zeffirelli has portrayed him as sort of the first flower child.

Well, maybe he was. It may be true that Francis went out into the fields and spoke to the birds. But is it true, as Zeffirelli seems to believe, that the birds had more to say than Francis did? He hardly gives us six lines of intelligent or perceptive dialogue in the movie; the rest is empty, pretty phrasing. After a while we long for a cynic to wander into the movie and ask Francis a few pointed questions.

The movie shows every sign of having been taken apart and put back together again. The opening—a rambling, confused editing job—looks as if it's meant to cover up for an original beginning that ran too long. While Francis tosses and turns on his bed, we get flashbacks to a field of battle and memories of how he went off to be a soldier. The task of a movie's first ten minutes, at the very least, is to orient us and give us a general idea of what to expect. *Brother Sun, Sister Moon* opens on confusion and complexity, which is bad enough; what's worse is that once the opening is out of the way, the movie levels off into one note, indefinitely held.

Francis is portrayed as a wispy-bearded youth with a glow in his eye; if we didn't know he was a saint we might think he was a little tetched in the head. That's especially true when he leaves his sickbed and walks out onto a rooftop to catch a bird. It's not the bird that matters; it's the way he walks, waving his arms and teetering back and forth, always about to fall off. Surely even a saint can keep his balance.

After a suitable period of standing on the rooftop, Francis goes out into the fields and finds there a ruined church. He takes unto himself a band of followers, not omitting the obligatory local aristocrat who comes to scoff and stays to plaster, and they rebuild the church. The local church authorities, who are gowned and bejeweled as if they had first dibs on Marco Polo's plunder, are scandalized. Who ever heard of a Christian who embraced poverty and humility?

But Francis perseveres, and eventually the local bad guys set his church on fire. I guess it's set on fire, anyway; clouds of smoke pour from behind the church, but we see no flames. Did Zeffirelli decide to go with a smudge pot and save the rebuilt church? I dunno, but this is the kind of movie where you think of things like that. Anything to stay awake.

Now comes the big scene, where Francis and his followers go to see Pope Innocent, who is played by Alec Guinness. Zeffirelli has constructed a set for the papal chambers that makes Anthony Quinn's digs in *Shoes of the Fisherman* look like the ballroom of the Honolulu Hilton.

Dozens—perhaps hundreds—of altar boys swing incense burners. Squadrons of Swiss Guards swing open massive bronze doors. The College of Cardinals sits almost immobile, their robes so heavy they can hardly move. Scheming papal advisers are arrayed behind the throne. And Guinness is costumed in such a manner as to remind us of the ecclesiastical fashion show in *Fellini Roma*. Did Zeffirelli mean his scene to be satire, or merely wretched excess? Also, does the pope always have 200 divines on hand just to hold an audience for a few barefoot monks?

Well, believe it or not (there are gasps of dismay from the cardinals), the pope comes out in favor of poverty and self-denial, and gives Francis his blessing. Whereupon Francis presumably goes out and incorporates the Franciscan Order, although that's not in this movie; maybe we'll get a sequel. Zeffirelli himself says you can't think too much about his movie; you have to accept it as a simple experience. "You have to hang your brains outside by the door before you go into this film," he said, and it looks as if he started with himself.

CCCCC**C**CCCCC

. . . .

Caligula
(Starring Malcolm McDowell, John Gielgud, Peter O'Toole; 1980)
Caligula is sickening, utterly worthless, shameful trash. If it is not the worst film I have ever seen, that makes it all the more shameful: People with talent allowed themselves to participate in this travesty. Disgusted and unspeakably depressed, I walked out of the film after two hours of its 170-minute length. That was on Saturday night, as a line of hundreds of people stretched down Lincoln Avenue, waiting to pay $7.50 apiece to become eyewitnesses to shame.

I wanted to tell them . . . what did I want to tell them? What I'm telling you now. That this film is not only garbage on an artistic level, but that it is also garbage on the crude and base level where it no doubt hopes to find its audience. *Caligula* is not good art, it is not good cinema, and it is not good porn.

I've never had anything against eroticism in movies. There are X-rated films I've enjoyed, from the sensuous fantasies of *Emmanuelle* to the pop absurdities of Russ Meyer. I assume that the crowds lining up for admission to the Davis Theater were hoping for some sort of erotic experience; I doubt that they were spending $15 a couple for a lesson on the ancient history of Rome.

All I can say is that the makers of *Caligula* have long since lost touch with any possible common erotic denominator, and that they suggest by the contents of this film that they are jaded, perverse, and cruel human beings. In the two hours of this film that I saw, there were no scenes of joy, natural pleasure, or good sensual cheer. There was, instead, a nauseating excursion into base and sad fantasies.

You have heard that this is a violent film. But who could have suspected how violent, and to what vile purpose, it really is? In this film, there are scenes depicting a man whose urinary tract is closed, and who has gallons of wine poured down his throat. His bursting stomach is punctured with a sword. There is a scene in which a man is emasculated, and his genitals thrown to dogs, who eagerly eat them on the screen. There are scenes of decapitation, evisceration, rape, bestiality, sadomasochism, necrophilia.

These scenes—indeed, the movie itself—reflect a curiously distanced sensibility. Nobody in this film really seems to be there. Not the famous actors like Malcolm McDowell and (very briefly) Peter O'Toole and John Gielgud, whose scenes have been augmented by additional porn shot later with other people and inserted to spice things up. Not the director (who removed his credit from the film). Not the writer (what in the world can it mean that this movie is "Adapted from an Original Screenplay by Gore Vidal"?) Not even the sound track. The actors never quite seem to be speaking their own words, which are so badly dubbed that they sometimes seem at right angles to the drama itself.

Caligula has been photographed and directed with such clumsiness and inelegance that pieces of action do not seem to flow together, the plot is incomprehensible, the events are framed as if the camera is not sure where it is, and everything is shot in muddy, ugly, underlit dungeon tones. The music is also execrable.

So what are we left with? A movie that may be invulnerable to a review like this one. There are no doubt people who believe that if this movie is as bad as I say it is, it must be worth seeing. People who simply cannot believe any film could be this vile. Some of those people were walking out of the Davis before I did Saturday night; others were sitting, depressed, in the lobby. That should not, I suppose, be surprising.

The human being is a most curious animal, often ready to indulge himself in his base inclinations, but frequently reluctant to trust his better instincts. Surely people know, going in, that *Caligula* is worthless. Surely they know there are other movies in town that are infinitely better. Yet here they are at *Caligula*. It is very sad.

My friendly recommendation is that they see *The Great Santini*, to freshen their minds and learn to laugh and care again in a movie. People learn fast. "This movie," said the lady in front of me at the drinking fountain, "is the worst piece of shit I have ever seen."

Camille 2000

*(Directed by Radley Metzger; starring Daniéle Gaubert,
Nino Castelnuovo; 1969)*

It is said that Orson Welles saw John Ford's *Stagecoach* 200 times before directing *Citizen Kane*. According to a press release here on my desk, Radley Metzger has seen John Huston's *The Treasure of the Sierra Madre* 103 times. That was not enough.

I think Metzger was better—or worse, that is—back when he had only seen it maybe twenty times. Blinking his eyes as he emerged into the sunlight, he directed *I, a Woman*, which was the worst movie of all time (up until then).

Then he went back to see *Sierra Madre* another, say, two dozen times, and after that he directed *Carmen, Baby,* which was almost as bad as *I, a Woman* but made less money. Then, a glutton for culture, he saw *Sierra Madre* forty-one more times, and made *Therese and Isabel,* which was even worse than *I, a Woman.*

So that made eighty-five times he had seen *The Treasure of the Sierra Madre.* Eighteen times to go. I wonder if he was the guy who sat behind me the last time I saw it at the Clark. He was reciting the dialogue under his breath and when the usher protested, he flashed a card with the name Fred C. Dobbs on it. (This is not made up.)

Anyway, after seeing *Sierra Madre* 103 times, Metzger was ready for the big time. *Camille 2000* is shot in color. It is dubbed into English instead of subtitled. It is wide screen. It has a pretty girl in it. Her name is Daniéle Gaubert. Whoever painted that big sign in front of the theater has an accurate critical sense. The sign says: "See Daniéle Gaubert presented in the nude . . . and with great frequency." That captures the essence of Metzger's art.

Well, Daniéle Gaubert is presented in the nude all right, amd she has a lot of love scenes with Nino Castelnuovo. The way they make love is interesting. Their key technique is to assume the conventional configuration and then . . . not move! Mostly, they're looking at themselves in the mirrors. There are mirrors all over her bedroom. No matter where they look, they see themselves in the mirror. Daniéle and Nino aren't too bright, I guess. They're just about to start making love when their eyes wander, and they get interested in that beautiful couple up on the ceiling.

Anyway, after twenty minutes of this, Metzger speeds up his pace. There's a fascinating close-up of a flower, and as it goes in and out of focus we hear a lot of heavy breathing and see Danié1e's face on the left side of the screen. Apparently something is happening to her. Maybe a manicure.

I'm not sure, but I think the heavy breathing was dubbed in from Metzger's *Therese and Isabel.* That one starred Essy Persson, the all-time heavy-breathing champ. It was a movie about a woman who looked at the ceiling and breathed heavily. She didn't need a lover, she needed a Vicks Inhaler.

Candyman: Farewell to the Flesh
(Directed by Bill Condon; Kelly Rowan, Tony Todd; 1995)
In the original *Candyman* (1992), a couple of Ph.Ds from the University of Illinois theorized that the Candyman was an urban legend, brought to life by the faith of all the people who believed in him. But it turned out there was a much more Gothic and supernatural explanation, and we learn more about his origins in the new *Candyman: Farewell to the Flesh.*

The Candyman stories, based on books by Clive Barker, are an attempt to make an intelligent fable out of a bogeyman, and Bernard Rose's 1992 film did a good job of it, with Virginia Madsen and Kasi Lemmons as the researchers who track down tales of a slasher with a hook for a hand. He was terrorizing Chicago's Cabrini-Green housing project, but in the second film he has moved back home to New Orleans, and started preying on his own descendants instead of innocent bystanders.

In the new film, directed by Bill Condon, there's once again an attempt to establish a real world in which Candymen aren't possible. Kelly Rowan stars as a New Orleans schoolteacher whose father was killed years earlier, Candyman style. Now her brother has been accused of killing a Candyman expert, and a student in her class has started drawing the Candyman. How does the kid know about him?

The movie doesn't develop, alas, with the patience and restraint of the earlier film. It's got one of those sound tracks where everyday sounds are amplified into gut-churning shockaramas, and where we are constantly being startled by false alarms. There's a scene, for example, where a character walks up behind the teacher, and the sound track explodes. My notes read: *Scream! Shock! Rumble! Crack!*—followed, of course, by the guy saying, "Sorry, I thought you heard me."

The movie also pulls the old "It's only a cat routine," where a shrieking, snarling presence from out of frame turns out, yes, to only be a cat. There is even an "it's only a raven" sequence, no doubt in honor of Clive Barker's predecessor in the macabre, Edgar Allan Poe.

The story proceeds. Characters near and dear to Kelly are slashed Candyman style. Eventually, led by the little student from her class, who seems tuned in to the Candyman, she is led to an old plantation, where all is explained. Read no further if you would rather not know that the Candyman turns out to have been a slave who fell in love with his master's daughter, and she with him. When she became pregnant, the enraged plantation owner set a mob on the slave, which cut off his hand and smeared him with honey, so that he was stung by thousands of bees, which is how he got the name Candyman.

Is there an entomologist among us? Are bees attracted by honey? I would have guessed they'd be rather blasé about it, and would be more quickly attracted if the victim had been smeared with one of those perfumes they advertise on cable TV. Never mind. The slave, whose name is Daniel Robitaille, sees his bee-stung face in his lover's mirror, and somehow his spirit goes into the mirror, so that if you look in a mirror and say "Candyman" five times, that's going to be more or less the last thing you do. (I have tried this, and it doesn't work.)

The story goes to some lengths to develop sympathy for the terrible tortures he was subjected to, as a victim of racism who dared to love a white woman. (Because the Candyman is played by Tony Todd, who has more than a passing resemblance to O.J. Simpson, there are several scenes that have a curious double resonance.)

I suppose that Clive Barker would be happy to explain for us how *Candyman: Farewell to the Flesh* is a statement against racism, and maybe it is, although it sure does go the long way around. The message may be that because slaves were mistreated, we pay the price today, perhaps every time we look in the mirror and see our racism reflected back at us. (Hey, I didn't take those EngLit symbology classes for nothing.)

Like many movies with morals at the end, however, it has its slasher and eats him, too. If the last fifteen minutes of the movie are devoted to creating understanding for Daniel Robitaille, the first eighty-five are devoted to exploiting fears of slasher attacks by tall black men, with or without a hook for a hand. And the flashback is rather overelaborate: Did the mob vote against lynching Robitaille, deciding, "Naw, let's just cut off his hand and smear him with honey, so he can become an urban legend?" If not, it seems they went to a lot more trouble than most mobs in those sad days.

I am left with questions. Why did the Candyman visit Chicago? Why did he prey on innocent young black victims who had done him no harm? Which is he? A mythical force brought to reality by psychic mind power, or an immortal being fueled by the life force of the bees, who lives in mirrors? I spend my days pondering questions such as these, so you won't have to.

Cannonball Run II
(Directed by Hal Needham; starring Frank Sinatra, Burt Reynolds; 1984)
The clue to *Cannonball Run II* is in Frank Sinatra's first scene, but you have to look carefully. The scene starts in Sinatra's office, and we're looking over Sinatra's head at Burt and some other people. At least, it looks like Sinatra's head, except there's something a little funny about the ears. Then we see Sinatra. He talks. We see Reynolds. He talks. And so on, until, if we know something about movie editing techniques, we realize there isn't a single shot showing Sinatra and Reynolds at the same time. Also, there's something funny about Sinatra's voice: He doesn't seem to be quite matching the tone of the things said to him. That's the final tip-off: Sinatra did his entire scene by sitting down at a desk and reading his lines into the camera, and then, on another day, Reynolds and the others looked into the camera and pretended to be looking at him. The over-the-shoulder shots are of a double.

This is the movie equivalent to phoning it in. You can't blame Sinatra. Everybody else is walking through this movie, so why shouldn't he? Refusing to appear in a scene with your fellow actors is no worse than agreeing to appear in a scene that nobody has bothered to write. *Cannonball Run II* is one of the laziest insults to the intelligence of moviegoers that I can remember. Sheer arrogance made this picture.

The movie stars Burt as J. J. McClure, cross-country racer. Dom DeLuise is back as his sidekick. Some of the other familiar faces from the first awful Cannonball movie include Dean Martin and Sammy Davis, Jr., and they are joined here by Shirley MacLaine, Jamie Farr, Susan Anton, Marilu Henner, Telly Savalas, Catherine Bach, Foster Brooks, Sid Caesar, Jackie Chan, Tim

Conway, Richard "Jaws" Kiel, Don Knotts, Ricardo Montalban, Jim Nabors, Louis Nye, Molly Picon, and the pathetic Charles Nelson Reilly. It's a roll call of shame. Some of these actors are, of course, talented. Shirley MacLaine won an Academy Award the same year she made this. Burt can be good, but you can't tell that from this movie. *Cannonball Run II* is a day off for most of these performers, who are not given characters to play, readable dialogue to recite, or anything to do other than to make fools of themselves.

The name of the director is Hal Needham. He is a crony of Reynolds's, a former stunt driver who has brilliantly demonstrated the Peter Principle by becoming a director, thus rising far above his level of competence. This is the sixth time Needham has directed Reynolds. Greater love hath no actor, than that he sacrifice his career on the altar of friendship. When Reynolds appeared in Needham's awful *Stroker Ace* in 1983, he excused himself by saying the role had been intended for Steve McQueen; he stepped in after McQueen's death as a favor to his friend Needham. What's his excuse this time?

Cannonball Run II was made for one reason: The original picture made money. There may be a sucker born every minute, but so many of them fell for *Cannonball Run* that there may not be many left who are willing to fall twice for the same scam.

Caveman
(Directed by Carl Gottlieb; starring Ringo Starr, Barbara Bach, Shelley Long, Dennis Quaid; 1981)
Selections from Caveman Basic, a word guide that was handed to patrons as they entered the theater to see *Caveman:*

AIEE: Help! Save me!
ALOONDA: Affection, desire.
BO-BO: Man, friend, human.
CA-CA: Excrement.
FECH: Bad, no good, ugly
GWEE: To go.
HARAKA: Fire, burning thing.
KUDA: Come here, where are we now this way right here.
MA: Me, myself

MACHA: Wild animal, beast, nonhuman.

NYA: No, none, not happening, negative.

OOL: Food.

POOKA: Hurt, injured, messed up no good.

WHOP: Stop whoa, hold it!

ZUG-ZUG: Sexual intercourse.

Selections from my thoughts after having seen the film:

Aieee! This movie is fech! We can hardly wait for the end so we can gwee. We kill time in between by eating popcorn and other ool. The movie is ca-ca. There are a few good moments, mostly involving the giant prehistoric dinosaurs and other machas, especially during zug-zug. But the movie is mostly fech, nya, and pooka, if you ask ma.

And yet *Caveman* is fairly successful, maybe because there's a real hunger for an *Airplane!*-type satirical spoof. It gets good laughs with scenes like the one where John Matuszak throws himself over a cliff along with a rock. But it has a basic problem, which is that there is no popular original material for it to satirize. There has never been a really successful movie set in prehistoric times, although God knows they've tried, with movies like *When Dinosaurs Ruled the Earth* and *One Million Years B.C.* Those movies were self-satirizing; by the end, they were making fun of the way they started out.

Caveman seems more in the tradition of *Alley Oop,* crossed with Mel Brooks's *Two Thousand Year Old Man.* But the only artistic cross-reference it can manage is from the opening scene of Stanley Kubrick's *2001: A Space Odyssey.* In *Caveman,* the cavemen are shown in the process of discovering modern fire, cooking, and music. During their epochal discoveries, the sound track teases us by quoting from Strauss's "Thus Spake Zarathustra," but never quite getting it right. Why bother to rewrite Strauss? He's out of copyright.

The movie has an interesting cast—or would have an interesting cast, if the actors were given interesting things to do. Ringo Starr plays the leader of a wandering tribe, and onetime Oakland Raider Matuszak is the leader of the stronger tribe and the boyfriend of Barbara Bach, who wears push-up skunk skins. Starr feels great aloonda for Bach, and whenever he sees her, zug-zug is not far from his mind. But Matuszak is the kind of guy who can break a dinosaur's drumstick in two, and so Starr has to outsmart the big guy. Thus, intelligence is born.

It's a little depressing to realize how much time and money went into *Caveman,* an expensive production shot on location in Mexico. This very same material could have been filmed quickly and cheaply on a sound stage, since the production values are obviously not going to make us laugh any louder. And with the added flexibility and the lower stakes, maybe a little spontaneity could have crept into the film. As it stands, the filmmakers seem to learn comedy as slowly as the cavemen learn to whop before they step in the haraka.

Christopher Columbus: The Discovery
(Directed by John Glen; starring George Corraface, Marlon Brando; 1992)
Christopher Columbus: The Discovery makes a voyage of its own, back through time to the 1930s and 1940s, when costume dramas like this were made with great energy and style. Something seems to have been lost in the years between. The movie takes one of history's great stories and treats it in such a lackluster, unfocused manner that Columbus's voyage seems as endless to us as it did to his crew members.

The movie stars the French actor George Corraface in the title role, which he occupies as if it were a Ralph Lauren ad. He looks great, has a terrific smile, and sure fills out a breastplate, but where is the anguish and greatness that Columbus must have possessed? Corraface is not helped by a peculiar supporting cast, headed by Marlon Brando's worst screen performance in memory.

As Torquemada, the inquisitor, Brando sulks about the set looking moody and delivering his lines with the absolute minimum of energy necessary to be audible to the camera. Brando has phoned in roles before, but this was the first time I wanted to hang up. Self-conscious about his weight, Brando is swathed in vast black cloaks that are always tucked up right under his chin (they don't even move when he walks around). Orson Welles, also a big man, had the grace to accept his body instead of trying to hide it from the camera.

After Columbus survives a weird grilling from Torquemada, which sounds like the oral exam for his doctorate in theology, he convinces King Ferdinand and Queen Isabella (Tom Selleck and Rachel Ward) to allow him to sail in search of the New World. Here as elsewhere in the movie, dialogue and motivation seem to be missing; there is a hint that Isabella is smitten with Columbus, and that Ferdinand is jealous, but the scenes have been edited so severely that only hints remain, in the form of lots of furrowed and/or lifted brows.

Once Columbus and crew sail for the New World, the movie breaks down into routine travelogue shots and equally unsurprising vignettes of shipboard life, some centering around the decision of Columbus to give a young Jewish cabin boy a free ticket out of intolerant and anti-Semitic Spain. As the crew threatens mutiny, Columbus offers to be beheaded if land is not sighted in three days, and indeed the ax is descending on his bare neck when the wind picks up and land arrives, just in time.

Curious that I do not remember this near-beheading incident from my school days; you'd think it would rank right up there with George Washington and the cherry tree. One of the many odd things about this film is the way Corraface, as Columbus, is so philosophical and cheerful about the prospect of losing his head. He seems to consider it just one of those things.

Columbus and his discovery of America are of course not Politically Correct subjects just at the moment (Native Americans point out, not unreasonably, that from their point of view he discovered nothing). And of course Columbus and other early European visitors brought disease and genocide as their cargos. Nothing if not Politically Correct, the producers, Alexander and Ilya Salkind, supply a zoom shot to the *Santa Maria* at anchor at San Salvador, and we see a rat scurry down the anchor rope and swim ashore.

This shot symbolizes all the evil that Europeans brought to the New World, I guess. The Salkinds and their director, John Glen, are more generous in showing us what the visitors found here. True to the traditions of all historical romances set among native peoples, Columbus and his men encounter a large group of friendly Indians, of which one—the beautiful daughter of the chief—is positioned, at length, bare-breasted, in the center of every composition. (My survey of the other friendly Indians leads me to the conclusion that the chief's daughter is chosen by cup size.)

Columbus sails back to Europe, there are various silly fights and killings among the men he left behind, and Brando utters another portentous word or two, after which the movie is over. Another Columbus movie is promised us this fall, starring Gérald Depardieu. It cannot be worse than this one. I am especially looking forward to the chief's daughter.

The Clan of the Cave Bear

(Directed by Michael Chapman; starring Darryl Hannah; 1986)

What was it like, back there at the dawn of time? What was it like to be a human being, and yet have none of the things we take for granted, such as houses, feminism, and shoes? How did we take that first great leap out of the caves and into the Iron Age? Or, if you really want to roll back the clock, that leap out of the rain and into the caves?

The Clan of the Cave Bear attempts to answer those questions by making a great leap backward in the imagination, to that precise moment when the first Cro-Magnons were moving in and the last Neanderthals were becoming obsolete. Unfortunately, the movie never really does reconcile itself to the prehistoric past.

It approaches those times with a modern sensibility. It shows us a woman winning respect from a patriarchal tribe, when, in reality, the men would have just banged her over the head real good. It isn't grim enough about what things were probably like back then. It tells a nice little modern parable about a distant past that is hardly less idealistic than the Garden of Eden. Instead of people who are scarred, sunburned, scrawny, and toothless, it gives us graduates of the Los Angeles health club scene, and a heroine who looks as if she just walked over from makeup.

It also packs a lot of things into a short span of that long-ago time. Although whole eons were available to it, the movie covers just a few short seasons, as a wandering tribe of primitive Neanderthals encounters an amazing sight: a Cro-Magnon woman (Daryl Hannah), tall and blond and smarter than they are. The girl is adopted into the tribe, and right away she causes trouble.

She can't understand why the men get to have all the fun, and use all the weapons, and make all the decisions. One day she sneaks out and practices on the slingshot. On another day, she challenges the tribe's attitudes about sex, seniority, and even about self-defense. In her spare time, she invents arithmetic and becomes chief adviser to the medicine man. This isn't the first Cro-Magnon, it's the first Rhodes Scholar.

The movie dresses its actors in furs and skins, and has them walk about barefoot and talk in monosyllables. But it never quite makes them seem frightened, ignorant, vulnerable, and bewildered. To capture the sense of wonder of those days when the human race reached its turning point, *The Clan of the Cave Bear* needs great images, not tidy little dramatic scenes with predictable conclusions. It needs sights such as the opening of *2001,* when the bone went flying into the air. Or it needs the muddy, exhausted desperation of the characters in *Quest for Fire,* a movie that did feel like it took place in pre-history. *The Clan of the Cave Bear* is about the first generation of designer cavemen.

The performances are doomed from the start, because the actors are asked to play characters who are modern in everything but dress and language. Every one of these people has motives that are instantly recognizable and predictable. There is no sense of the alien and the unknown, no sense that these people have ideas and feelings that would be strange to us.

Even their quasi-religion is familiar: They believe each person has an animal spirit, which is its partner or symbol, and that if a person's spirit is strong, it gives them strength. This is pseudo-anthropology crossed with Indian folklore and the Boy Scouts.

The ending of *The Clan of the Cave Bear* emphasizes its bankruptcy, because there isn't really an ending, just a conclusion—a romantic shot of the woman continuing on her lonely quest. The great failure of the movie is a failure of imagination.

The filmmakers made no effort to empathize with their prehistoric characters, to imagine what it might have really been like back then. They are content to assemble the usual narrative clichés and standard story lines and apply them to some actors in costume. If modern men came from beginnings like this, why did they even bother to develop civilization, since they already possessed its most wretched excesses?

Clifford
(Directed by Paul Faherty; starring Martin Short, Charles Grodin, Mary Steenburgen; 1994)

I felt a little glow as the opening titles rolled up for *Clifford:* Martin Short . . . Charles Grodin . . . Mary Steenburgen . . . Dabney Coleman. Funny people. Even the technical credits were promising. John A. Alonzo, great cameraman; Pembroke Herring, skilled editor. I settled in for some laughs. And waited. And waited. In a screening of some 150 people, two people laughed, once apiece. The other some 148 did not laugh at all. One of the laughers was me;

I liked a moment in a showdown scene between Short and Grodin. The other person laughed right after I did, maybe because he agreed, or maybe because my laugh is darn infectious.

A movie like this is a deep mystery. It asks the question: What went wrong? *Clifford* is not bad on the acting, directing, or even writing levels. It fails on a deeper level still, the level of the underlying conception. Something about the material itself is profoundly not funny. Irredeemably not funny, so that it doesn't matter what the actors do, because they are in a movie that should never have been made.

The story opens in the year 2050, when a kindly old priest is trying to reason with a rebellious kid in a home for troubled kids. The priest (Short) tells the kid that he was once a troubled kid, himself. That sets up three flashbacks that make up most of the movie. To deal with the 2050 scenes right up front: They are completely unnecessary. Their only apparent function is to show Martin Short made up as an old man.

Now. Back to the main story, which takes place in the present. Martin Short stars as little Clifford, a brat, about ten years old, I guess. Short plays him with no makeup other than a wig and little boy's suits, and the camera angles are selected to make him look a foot shorter than the other actors. Clifford is a little boy from hell, a sneaky practical joker, spoiled, obnoxious. We meet him with his parents on a flight to Hawaii. He wants the plane to land in Los Angeles so he can visit the Dinosaur Park amusement park. So he talks his way into the cockpit and shuts off the plane's engines.

This sets up the body of the movie, in which Clifford's uncle Martin (Charles Grodin) agrees to take the lad for a week, partly to convince his girl-friend (Mary Steenburgen) that he does, indeed, like children. But no one could like this child, who grows enraged when his uncle won't take him to Dinosaur Park, and plays a series of practical jokes, beginning with filling his uncle's drink with Tabasco sauce and ending with the destruction of his uncle's plans for the Los Angeles transportation system.

Many of the jokes are of a cruel physical nature, involving a hairpiece worn by the uncle's boss (Dabney Coleman), or face-lifts, or phony bomb threats. What they boil down to is, little Clifford is mean, vindictive, spiteful, and cruel. So hateful that if a *real* little boy had played him, the movie would be like *The Omen* filtered through *The Good Son* and a particularly bad evening of *Saturday Night Live*.

But Martin Short is clearly not a little boy. He is a curious adult pretending to be a little boy, with odd verbal mannerisms, like always addressing his uncle with lines like "Oh, yes, My Uncle!" and fawning to strangers like a horny spaniel. If Clifford is not a real little boy, then what is he? The movie doesn't know and neither does the audience, and for much of the running time we sit there staring stupefied at the screen, trying to figure out what the hell we're supposed to be thinking.

Grodin emerges relatively unscathed, because as a smooth underactor he is able to distance himself from the melee. Steenburgen is given a scene where Coleman assaults her in the back of a limousine, for no reason that the movie really explains. Short has a couple of dance routines that have more to do with his *SNL* history than with this movie.

And then there is the "climax," in which Uncle Martin finally does take little Clifford to the Dinosaur Park. The movie treats the sequence as a bravura set piece, but actually it's an embarrassing assembly of shabby special effects, resulting in absolutely no comic output. At one point the movie sets up an out-of-control thrill ride, and we in the audience think we know how the laughs will build, but we're wrong. They don't.

To return to the underlying causes for the movie's failure: What we have here is a suitable case for deep cinematic analysis. I'd love to hear a symposium of veteran producers, marketing guys, and exhibitors discuss this film. It's not bad in any usual way. It's bad in a new way all its own. There is something extraterrestrial about it, as if it's based on the sense of humor of an alien race with a completely different relationship to the physical universe. The movie is so odd, it's almost worth seeing just because we'll never see anything like it again, I hope.

Color of Night

(Directed by Richard Rush; starring Bruce Willis, Leslie Ann Warren; 1994)
Color of Night approaches badness from so many directions that one really must admire its imagination. Combining all the worst ingredients of an Agatha Christie whodunit and a sex-crazed slasher film, it ends in a frenzy of recycled thriller elements, with a chase scene, a showdown in an echoing warehouse, and not one but two clichés from *Ebert's Little Movie Glossary:*

the Talking Killer and the Climbing Villain. I am compelled to admit that the use of the high-powered industrial staple gun is original.

The film stars Bruce Willis as an East Coast psychologist who loses his faith in analysis after he talks tough to a patient and she hurls herself through the window of his skyscraper office, falling to the ground far below in the best suicide effect since *The Hudsucker Proxy*. (The pool of bright red blood under her body turns black, as Willis develops psychosomatic color blindness right there on the spot.)

Desperate for a change, Willis heads for Los Angeles, where his best friend (Scott Bakula) has a psychiatric practice that finances a luxurious lifestyle. He is a guest one night at a group therapy session run by the friend. The group is an updated, kinky version of one of those collections of eccentrics so beloved by Dame Agatha, who in plot exercises like *The Mousetrap* introduced a roomful of weirdos so that all of them could have their turn at being the Obvious Suspect.

In no time at all a suspect is required: Willis's friend is found murdered in his high-security mansion, and of course there is a reason why each member of the group seems guilty. The group includes Sondra (Lesley Ann Warren), a nymphomaniac with a nervous giggle and a careless neckline; Clark (Brad Dourif), who lost his job at a law firm after he started compulsively counting everything; Buck (Lance Henrickson), an ex-cop who foams at the mouth with anger at the least provocation; Casey (Kevin J. O'Connor), a neurotic artist; and Ricky, a young man with a gender identity problem, of whom the less said the better.

Willis, who wants to retire from psychology, takes over the group at the urging of Martinez, the detective in charge of the murder investigation, who is played by Rubén Blades as an anthology of Latino cop shtick (during a chat with Willis on a sidewalk, he slams a passerby against a car and frisks him while continuing the conversation). The therapy group is of course a seething hotbed of neurosis and suspicion, and the screenplay (by Matthew Chapman and Billy Ray) sends Willis to visit each of the group members in turn, so they can spread paranoia about the other members while establishing themselves as possible suspects.

Meanwhile, a beautiful young woman materializes in Willis's life. She is Rose (Jane March, from *The Lover*), who seems to come from nowhere, who is lovely, who adores him, and who quickly joins him in a swimming pool sex scene that contained frontal nudity by Willis before the film was trimmed to satisfy the MPAA's censors. (The best possible argument for including Willis's genitals would have been that the movie, after all, contains everything else.)

Readers of *Ebert's Little Movie Glossary* will guess that Rose is explained by the Law of Economy of Characters, which teaches that there are no unnecessary characters in a movie. Either she is there simply to supply him with a partner in the sex scenes, or she is somehow involved with the mystery surrounding the murder. How and why and if this is true, I will not reveal.

There is, indeed, not much I can say about the rest of the movie without revealing plot points so subtle and cleverly concealed that they would come as astonishing surprises to Forrest Gump. So let's move on to the chase scene, in which a bright red car with blacked-out windows tries to force Willis off the road. It fails, but comes back for more, and there is a scene where Willis's car is driving on a street next to a parking garage, and a high-angle shot shows the red car on the roof of the garage, stalking him.

It is clear that from this angle the driver of the car cannot possibly see over the edge of the garage, and thus could not have any idea of where Willis's car is, but wait, there's more: A little later, the red car pushes another car off the top of the parking garage, so that the falling car barely misses Willis. How could the person in the red car know where a pedestrian six floors below would be by the time he pushes a car over the edge? Answer: This movie will do anything for a cheap action scene, and so we should not be surprised, a little later, when people who should be perfectly happy to remain at ground level go to a lot of trouble to climb a tower so that one can almost fall off, and the other can grab him, during and after heated dialogue in which the plot is explained.

Miss Christie would have loved the explanations. Her plots always ended with puzzled questions and serene answers ("The dog did not bark because the poisoned dagger . . ."), and so does this one. By the end of *Color of Night* I was, frankly, stupefied. To call the movie absurd would be missing the point, since any shred of credibility was obviously the first thing to be thrown overboard. The movie has ambitions to belong to the genre of *Jagged Edge, Fatal Attraction, Basic Instinct, Single White Female,* and other twisto-thrillers, but why did it aim so low? The movie is so lurid in its melodrama and so goofy in its plotting that with just a little more trouble it could have been a comedy.

The Concorde—Airport '79

(Directed by David Lowell Rich; starring Robert Wagner, John Davidson, Mercedes McCambridge; 1979)

Q. Gee, Mr. Science, what's a Concorde?

A. A Concorde is an airplane like the one you see in this movie, Penrod. It flies faster than the speed of sound. It can go from Washington, D.C., to Paris, France, in less than four hours.

What does it do then?

It lands, Penrod. Then it flies on to Moscow in the morning.

But . . . golly whillikers, Mr. Science! Why doesn't it just fly to Moscow in the first place!?!

Because then, Penrod, there wouldn't be the scenes in Paris where Robert Wagner takes Susan Blakely out to dinner, and George Kennedy takes Bibi Andersson out to dinner.

But . . . gosh all get out, Mr. Science! Why does Robert Wagner take Susan Blakely out to dinner in Paris!?! After all, she has the secrets that could destroy his industrial empire, and so, when the plane was flying to Paris, he tried to shoot it down with one of his guided missiles?

When you are a little older, Penrod, you will learn that there are great restaurants in Paris.

But . . . when he has her alone, why doesn't he just shoot her or stab her or something? Instead of trying to shoot down the plane when she's on board? And then the next day, he tries to bomb the plane. Wouldn't it be simpler if . . .

Nothing is simple, Penrod. you do not buy a woman dinner in Paris only to shoot or stab her.

But . . . why did the people get back on the plane in Paris after it had been attacked by guided missiles and fighter jets, and had done a loop-the-loop in the air and almost crashed in the ocean? Weren't they scared?

Not scared enough to turn in their Concorde tickets for tourist class on Aeroflot, I guess, Penrod.

Golly, Mr. Science, that plane sure was going fast!

As I said, Penrod, two thousand miles an hour.

Remember that scene where the pilot opens the cockpit window and sticks out his hand with the flare gun, Mr. Science???

Who could forget it, Penrod? It was a high point of the movie.

But . . . at two thousand miles an hour, wouldn't the air tear the side off the plane, and pull the pilot out of the cockpit through the open window?

The plane had slowed to one thousand miles an hour by then, Penrod. Pay better attention.

But . . . the pilot wanted to fire a flare gun because the heat from the flare would distract the heat-sensitive guided missile chasing the plane, but wouldn't the plane's engines be hotter than a little old flare?!?

Only seemingly, Penrod.

Thanks, Mr. Science!!!

Critters II

(Directed by Mick Garrett; starring Scott Grimes, Liane Curtis; 1988)
Critters II is a movie about furry little hand puppets with lots of teeth, who are held up to salad bars by invisible puppeteers while large numbers of actors scream and pronounce unlikely dialogue. It lacks all of the style and sense of fun of the original *Critters* (1986), and has no reason for existence—aside, of course, from the fact that *Critters* is a brand name, and this is the current model.

I mention the hand puppets because they are so obvious. Unlike the original film, which was a genuinely entertaining rip-off of *E.T.,* this movie is not even a competent rip-off of *Critters.* It is quite obvious, in many shots, that the critters—who are about the size of a bowling ball and have lots of teeth— are lined up along the edges of tables and other flat surfaces so that unseen puppeteers can operate them. It is rare to see a critter moving anywhere on his own, except as a ball being pulled along by an invisible string. The critters in the first movie had personality. In this movie, they're only props.

The plot is as before. The Cripes, a toothy, voracious race of interstellar garbage disposal units, have landed on Earth. They are followed here by bounty hunters, who blast them down with weapons that look as if they were made out of old tailpipes. The bounty hunters can assume the appearance of actual human beings, which means that the producers didn't have to spend any extra money on special makeup; all they had to do is hire an actor and say that he was an alien.

Anyway, the Cripes attack the same town they attacked the first time around. And the movie attacks the same plot it attacked the first time around—

right down to the cantankerous local sheriff and the townspeople who band together to fight the invasion. But while the first movie had considerable wit, this one is a demoralized enterprise from beginning to end. And it particularly misses the presence of M. Emmet Walsh, who played the sheriff in the first film with his usual oily charm.

Which leads me to a helpful suggestion. In the case of a movie like *Critters II*, the story is by definition utterly inconsequential. The only element from the original movie that interests the financial backers is the title. Since *Critters II* can be used as a title by anyone who holds the copyright to *Critters,* and the title alone will lure people into the theater, why bother with a mere retread? Why not have some fun?

My suggestion for *Critters III:* Make it a satire on sleazoid critter movies, starring the hapless and unseen employees who operate the hand puppets. Take us backstage. Show us the crummy special effects, but make fun of them. Pillory the crass financial guys who cynically demand a no-brainer remake. Make the hero a bright young film-school grad who dreams that his version of *Critters* will win an Oscar.

Opportunities for satire are everywhere. In *Critters II* there is an amazingly bad sequence in which all of the critters roll themselves up into one gigantic ball, and roll out to flatten the town. Anyone reading this review could write a funny scene about the difficulties of manufacturing and operating a critter ball. What is it made out of? Does it smell? Do the local dogs have a tendency to pay it rude visits? What happens if you're an extra who has to be crushed by the hairy ball, and you suffer from allergies? And what about the pecking order between puppeteers who operate the starring critters, and others who are relegated to the obscure critters?

I make these notes only to illustrate the bankruptcy of imagination behind *Critters II*. The makers of this film could not generate a single idea that was not provided for them by the makers of the original film. They went into the project with a rip-off on their mind. Since there is inevitably going to be a *Critters III,* I offer my story ideas free of charge to whoever is condemned to make it. If you want to dedicate the film to me, that would be nice.

Cyborg

(Directed by Albert Pyun; starring Dayle Haddon, Vincent Klyn, Jean-Claude Van Damme; 1989)

I am not sure I remember the opening words of *Cyborg* exactly, but I believe they were, "After the plague, things really got bad." I do remember laughing heartily at that point, about thirty seconds into the movie. Few genres amuse me more than postapocalyptic fantasies about supermen fighting for survival. *Cyborg* is one of the funniest examples of this category, which crosses *Escape from New York* with *The Road Warrior* but cheats on the budget.

The movie takes place in a future world in which all civilization has been reduced to a few phony movie sets. Leather-clad neo-Nazis stalk through the ruins, beating each other senseless and talking in Pulpspeak, which is like English, but without the grace and modulation. It's cold in the future, and it's wet, but never so cold or wet that the costumes do not bare the arm muscles of the men and the heaving bosoms of the women.

The plot of *Cyborg* is simplicity itself. The movie's heroine (Dayle Haddon) is half-woman, half-robot, and wears a computer under her wig. Her knowledge may include the solution to the plague that threatens to destroy mankind, but first she must somehow return to headquarters in Atlanta. Her enemy, Fender Tremolo (Vincent Klyn) wants to destroy her because he believes that if anarchy is unleashed upon the world, he can rule it. The hero, Gibson Rickenbacker (Jean-Claude Van Damme) is on a mission to escort her safely to Atlanta.

(If you look at the names "Fender Tremolo" and "Gibson Rickenbacker" and wonder why they set off strange stirrings in your subconscious, it is because both characters, according to the movie's press book, "are named after equipment and techniques associated with electric guitars." This rule presumably also applies to the characters Furman Vox, Nady Simmons, and Roland Pick.)

Once we know the central players, the movie turns into a sadomasochistic passion play, in which the village tries out varieties of unspeakable tortures on the hero, including crucifixion, before the formula is (of course) delivered safely after all. The movie reduces itself to a series of smoking, smoldering cityscapes (which look a lot like urban neighborhoods slated for renewal), and the Pulpspeak is the usual combination of vaguely biblical formalisms, spiced with four-letter words and high-tech gibberish.

Movies like this work if they're able to maintain a high level of energy and invention, as the Mad Max movies do. They do not work when they lower their guard and let us see the reality, which is that several strangely garbed actors feel vaguely embarrassed while wearing bizarre costumes and reciting unspeakable lines.

DDDDD**D**DDDDD

· ·

Dancers

(Directed by Herbert Ross; starring Mikhail Baryshnikov; 1987)

The idea is not exactly new: The story of a ballet is echoed by the real lives of the people who are dancing in it. But Herbert Ross's *Dancers* easily is the most dim-witted recent example of the genre, using *Giselle* to so little effect that perhaps the only way to save this movie would have been to substitute *Peter and the Wolf.*

See if any of this sounds familiar. Mikhail Baryshnikov plays Tony, the greatest male dancer of his age. While rehearsing for a film version of *Giselle* in Italy, he finds himself overtaken by a vague discontent. Things are just not right. Then, one day across a crowded restaurant, he spies the newest member of his company, a seventeen-year-old American teenager with big eyes and long hair. In a grand gesture, he sends her an entire ice-cream cake, and their romance is under way.

So far, the story's not implausible. I know a lot of people who would go to bed for an ice-cream cake. What is unacceptable about the movie is its refusal to supply the teenager (Julie Kent) with any human qualities other than hero worship and to assume that she would fall in love with Baryshnikov just because he is a famous man and he wants her to. Doesn't decency require them to at least pretend to have something in common?

The movie is so ineptly structured that maybe it doesn't even matter. The Baryshnikov character lays his usual line on her, something about a tall white tree he saw in his childhood, and meanwhile rehearsals for *Giselle* continue. But this is not even an interesting movie about show business.

Everything I have ever heard about the filming of ballet movies leads me to believe that the set usually resembles Fassbinder's *Beware of a Holy Whore,* in which venomous and embittered malcontents hang around the hotel bar telling lies about each other, but not here. On the set of *Giselle,* much depends on Long Looks. Baryshnikov's current and former lovers lurk in the wings, looking significantly at him and each other. We read volumes into their gazes, because we have to, and because the movie gives us little else to think about.

One of the best gazers in the movie is Kent, who learns after the magical white-tree story that Baryshnikov has told it to other women—that, indeed, she may not be the only woman in his life. This causes her such distress that she stands in the wings during a dance sequence and provides not one but two Long Looks. We see in her eyes that she is shaken and in despair. If we look closely enough, we see something else. It appears that the editor, William Reynolds, has had to use the same close-up twice.

The girl runs out of the theater. The dance continues. Then there is a search for her. "Call the police!" Baryshnikov cries, and then her jacket is found in the sea, soaking wet. This turns out to be a real mystery after she turns up on land, dry. The movie eventually ends after more dancing.

Dancers does not provide (a) interesting ballet sequences, (b) a coherent plot, (c) a romance of any description beyond the unsatisfactory requirements of Unrequited Love, or (d) pretty pictures. It has one distinction, though. It is one of the worst movies of the year.

The Dark

(Directed by John "Bud" Cardos; starring William Devane, Cathy Lee Crosby; 1979)

Movie critics aren't supposed to give away the plots of thrillers. That's part of the unwritten agreement with their makers. The other part of the unwritten agreement, though, is that thrillers should have plots. Since *The Dark* breaks its side of the bargain, I feel blameless in forging ahead.

This is without a doubt the dumbest, most inept, most maddeningly un-satisfactory thriller of the last five years. It's really bad: so bad, indeed, that it provides some sort of measuring tool against which to measure other bad thrillers. Years from now, I'll be thinking to myself: Well, at least it's not as bad as *The Dark*.

The movie involves a Jack the Ripper from outer space, who has super-human strength, can tear down brick walls with his bare hands, and has eyes that emit lightning flashes. He kills someone every night. The police are trying to catch him.

That's about it. The killings are not only unmotivated, but uninvolving, since only strangers get killed. They appear in the movie, walk into dark parking garages, and are murdered. The creature's favorite means of attack is to pull off his victim's heads. Wonderful. The press nicknames him "The Mangler," a title that could more accurately be bestowed on the director.

The Dark alternates the nighttime attacks with endless scenes of cops lecturing each other on how important it is to catch the Mangler. But the case is finally broken open when the father of one of the victims (William Devane) and a local TV newscaster (Cathy Lee Crosby) team up to solve it. A psychic has predicted that a young actor will be the next to go, so they pub-crawl through actors' haunts to find him. They do, he speeds drunkenly away in his car, they follow, the police tail them, and everyone ends up in a deserted monastery where the Mangler is cornered.

He's a tough creature to destroy. He's about six feet six inches, looks like the Wolf Man, snarls and growls a lot, and zaps everybody with his lightning bolts. The special effects are so bad, by the way, that at times the lightning bolts do not seem to come from his eyes, or to hit their targets—but never mind, the victims topple over anyway. Gunshots don't affect the creature, but after he's set on fire, he disappears in a puff of smoke.

What is this creature? Where does it come from? How to explain its chemistry, its appetites, its violence? Great questions, I guess, for the sequel. The movie ends with a panorama of Los Angeles and a narration assuring us that mankind must always be afraid of the Dark, because in the vastness of the universe, etc., we are like blind men tapping our way into infinity, etc.

One of the amazing things about *The Dark* is that it's only about 85 minutes long—short for a feature film, if more than long enough for this one. If they'd gone all the way and shot for 120 minutes, they might have qualified for the most stupefyingly boring movie ever made. Maybe they win that one anyway.

Day of the Dead

(Directed by George Romero; starring Joseph Pilato, Lori Cardille; 1985)
The zombies in *Day of the Dead* are marvels of special effects, with festoons of rotting flesh hanging from their purple limbs as they slouch toward the

camera, moaning their sad songs. Truth to tell, they look a lot better than the zombies in *Night of the Living Dead,* which was director George Romero's original zombie film. His technology is improving; perhaps the current emphasis on well-developed bodies (in *Perfect, Rambo,* etc.) has inspired a parallel improvement in dead bodies.

But the zombies have another problem in *Day of the Dead:* They're upstaged by the characters who are supposed to be real human beings. You might assume that it would be impossible to steal a scene from a zombie, especially one with blood dripping from his orifices, but you haven't seen the overacting in this movie. The characters shout their lines from beginning to end, their temples pound with anger, and they use distracting Jamaican and Irish accents, until we are so busy listening to their endless dialogue that we lose interest in the movie they occupy.

Maybe there's a reason for that. Maybe Romero, whose original movie was a genuine inspiration, hasn't figured out anything new to do with his zombies. In his second zombie film, the brilliant *Dawn of the Dead* (1980), he had them shuffling and moaning their way through a modern shopping mall, as Muzak droned in the background and terrified survivors took refuge in the Sears store. The effect was both frightening and satirical. The everyday location made the zombies seem all the more horrible, and the shopping mall provided lots of comic props (as when several zombies tried to crawl up the down escalator).

This time, though, Romero has centered the action in a visually dreary location—an underground storage cavern, one of those abandoned salt mines where they store financial records and the master prints of old movies. The zombies have more or less overrun the surface of America, we gather, and down in the darkness a small team of scientists and military men are conducting experiments on a few captive zombie guinea pigs.

It's an intriguing idea, especially if Romero had kept the semiseriousness of the earlier films. Instead, the chief researcher is a demented butcher with bloodstained clothes, whose idea of science is to teach a zombie named Bub to operate a Sony Walkman. Meanwhile, the head of the military contingent (Joseph Pilato) turns into a violent little dictator who establishes martial law and threatens to end the experiments. His opponent is a spunky woman scientist (Lori Cardille), and as they shout angry accusations at each other, the real drama in the film gets lost.

In the earlier films, we really identified with the small cadre of surviving humans. They were seen as positive characters, and we cared about them. This time, the humans are mostly unpleasant, violent, insane, or so noble that we can predict with utter certainty that they will survive. According to the mad scientist in *Day of the Dead,* the zombies keep moving because of primitive impulses buried deep within their spinal columns—impulses that create the appearance of life long after consciousness and intelligence have departed. I hope the same fate doesn't befall Romero's zombie movies. He should quit while he's ahead.

Dead Man

(Directed by Jim Jarmusch; starring Johnny Depp, John Hurt, Robert Mitchum; 1996)

I once traveled for two days from Windhoek to Swakopmund through the Kalahari Desert, on a train without air conditioning, sleeping at night on a hard leather bench that swung down from the ceiling. That journey seemed a little shorter than the one that opens *Dead Man,* the new film by Jim Jarmusch.

A man named William Blake (Johnny Depp) is traveling from Cleveland, where his parents have just died, to the western town of Machine, where he has been promised a job. He is dressed in a checked suit that looks as if it had been waiting a long time in the menswear store for a sucker to come along. The train drones through the endless prairie. There are shots of the inside of the train. Shots of the view from the train. Shots of the train. Then the train's soot-faced fireman warns Blake that his grave awaits him in Machine.

For some of my readers the name William Blake will have rung a bell, and they will be wondering if there is any connection between this character and the mystical British poet who died in 1827. There is: They both have the same name. Our Blake has not heard of the English Blake, however, but before long he will run into an Indian named Nobody who can quote him by the yard.

We are getting ahead of the story. Blake arrives in Machine, and reports to the Dickinson Steel Works, a dark satanic mill where he expects to be employed as an accountant. The office manager (John Hurt) explains that the job no longer exists. Blake is appalled; he's spent his last dime getting there. He confronts the owner of the mill (Robert Mitchum), who stands between a stuffed bear and a portrait of himself, which frame his fearful symmetry. Mitchum brandishes a shotgun and advises Blake to leave.

Blake befriends a hapless flower girl, and is invited to her room for an encounter between innocence and experience. Then the girl's lover bursts in and shoots her. Blake shoots the man, is shot near the heart, leaps from the window, and flees. We discover the dead man is Dickinson's son, and the mill owner hires men to track and kill Blake.

The next morning Blake regains consciousness in the forest to find his wound being tended by the Indian named Nobody (Gary Farmer), who was raised by white men, educated in England, and treats Blake as if he really is the poet. The two men now undertake an odyssey, pursued by the killers, in search of Blake's ultimate destiny, which is revealed as a pleasing cross between the mysticism of the original Blake and the American Indians.

Dead Man is a strange, slow, unrewarding movie that provides us with more time to think about its meaning than with meaning. The black-and-white photography by Robby Muller is a series of monochromes in which the brave new land of the West already betrays a certain loneliness. Farmer brings to the Indian a sweetness and a curious contemporary air (he talks like a New Age guru), and Depp is sad and lost as the opposite of Nobody—which is, I fear, Everyman. A mood might have developed here, had it not been for the unfortunate score by Neil Young, which for the film's final thirty minutes sounds like nothing so much as a man repeatedly dropping his guitar.

Jim Jarmusch is trying to get at something here, and I don't have a clue what it is. Are the machines of the east going to destroy the nature of the west? Is the white man doomed, and is the Indian his spiritual guide to the farther shore? Should you avoid any town that can't use another accountant? Watching the film, I was reminded of the original William Blake's visionary drawings and haunting poems. Leaving the theater, I came home and took down my Blake and found that the poet had even explained the method of this film: "You never know what is enough until you know what is more than enough."

The Dead Poets Society

(Directed by Peter Weir; starring Robin Williams; 1989)

Peter Weir's *The Dead Poets Society* is a collection of pious platitudes masquerading as a courageous stand in favor of something—doing your own thing, I think. It's about an inspirational, unconventional English teacher and his students at "the best prep school in America," and how he challenges them to question conventional views by such techniques as standing on their desks. It is, of course, inevitable that the brilliant teacher will eventually be fired from the school, and when his students stood on their desks to protest his dismissal, I was so moved, I wanted to throw up.

The film makes much noise about poetry, and there are brief quotations from Tennyson, Herrick, Whitman, and even Vachel Lindsay, as well as a brave excursion into prose that takes us as far as Thoreau's *Walden*. None of these writers are studied, however, in a spirit that would lend respect to their language; they're simply plundered for slogans to exort the students toward more personal freedom. At the end of a great teacher's course in poetry, the students would love poetry; at the end of this teacher's semester, all they love is the teacher.

The movie stars Robin Williams as the mercurial John Keating, teacher of English at the exclusive Welton Academy in Vermont. The performance is a delicate balancing act between restraint and schtick. For much of the time, Williams does a good job of playing an intelligent, quick-witted, well-read young man. But then there are scenes in which his stage persona punctures the character—as when he does impressions of Marlon Brando and John Wayne doing Shakespeare. There is also a curious lack of depth to his character; compared to such other great movie teachers as Miss Jean Brodie and Professor Kingsfield, Keating is more of a plot device than a human being.

The story in *The Dead Poets Society* is also old stuff, recycled out of the novel and movie *A Separate Peace* and other stories in which the good die young and the old simmer in their neurotic and hateful repressions. The key conflict in the movie is between Neil (Robert Sean Leonard), a student who dreams of being an actor, and his father (Kurtwood Smith), a domineering parent who orders his son to become a doctor, and forbids him to go on stage. The father is a strict, unyielding taskmaster, and the son, lacking the will to defy him, kills himself. His death would have had a greater impact for me if it had seemed like a spontaneous human cry of despair, rather than like a meticulously written and photographed set piece.

Other elements in the movie also seem to have been chosen for their place in the artificial jigsaw puzzle. A teenage romance between one of the Welton students and a local girl is given so little screen time, so arbitrarily, that it seems like a distraction. And I squirmed through the meetings of the "Dead Poets Society," a self-consciously bohemian group of students who hold secret meetings in the dead of night in a cave near the campus.

The society was founded, we learn, by Mr. Keating when he was an under-graduate, but in its reincarnate form it never generates any sense of mystery, rebellion, or daring. The society's meetings have been badly written and are dramatically shapeless, featuring a dance-line to Lindsay's "The Congo" and various attempts to impress girls with random lines of poetry. The movie is set in 1959, but none of these would-be bohemians have heard of Kerouac, Ginsberg, or indeed of the beatnik movement at all.

One scene in particular indicates the distance between the movie's manipulative instincts, and what it claims to be about. When Mr. Keating is being railroaded by the school administration (which makes him the scapegoat for his student's suicide), one of the students acts as a fink and tells the old fogies what they want to hear. Later, confronted by his peers, he makes a hateful speech of which not one word is plausible except as an awkward attempt to supply him with a villain's dialogue. Then one of the other boys hits him in the jaw, to great applause from the audience. The whole scene is utterly false, and seems to exist only so that the violence can resolve a situation that the screenplay is otherwise unwilling to handle.

The Dead Poets Society is not the worst of the countless recent movies about good kids and hidebound, authoritarian older people. It may, however, be the most shameless in its attempt to pander to an adolescent audience. The movie pays lip service to qualities and values that, on the evidence of the screenplay itself, it is cheerfully willing to abandon. If you are going to evoke Henry David Thoreau as the patron saint of your movie, then you had better make a movie he would have admired. Here is one of my favorite sentences from Thoreau's *Walden,* which I recommend for serious study by the authors of this film: ". . . instead of studying how to make it worth men's while to buy my baskets, I studied rather how to avoid the necessity of selling them." Think about it.

Death Before Dishonor

(Directed by Tery J. Leonard; starring Fred Dryer, Brian Keith; 1987)
Death Before Dishonor is one of those Far-Off Rattle Movies. You know the kind I mean. The hero is stalking the killer through a large, abandoned warehouse or other interior space, and on the sound track you hear the sound of a Far-Off Rattle. It is usually followed by a series of echoing thumps. Sometimes you then get the sound of a stick on a snare drum, just sort of allowed to fall, so it trails off ominously.

Far-Off Rattle Movies are not necessarily bad. In fact, some of my favorite movies have Far-Off Rattles in them. But they are almost always bad when they are crossbred with Rum-Dum-a-Dum Movies. That's the movie where you get the ersatz military march on the sound track—the canned patriotism with the snare drum keeping marching time, Rum-Dum-a-Dum.

As a general rule, if you get a Rum-Dum-a-Dum and a Far-Off Rattle within five minutes of each other, you're dealing with a creatively bankrupt project. Any movie that has to link clichés that closely is unable to think of anything to go in between them. That's especially true if the movie is a thriller about terrorists and it makes a link between the Myth of the Seemingly Ordinary Day and the Mistake of the Unmotivated Close-up.

For example, in *Death Before Dishonor,* a U.S. official is about to leave his home in a strife-torn Middle Eastern nation. It is a Perfectly Ordinary Day. There is small talk with his family. He makes plans for later in the day. Since these are trivial personal plans, not part of the plot, we know with absolute certainty that the official will be kidnapped or executed. This is not just a possibility but an absolute certainty, because immediately afterward we see the Mistake of the Unmotivated Close-up.

This is a close-up of the official's house servant, a local native whose role in the movie up until now has been utterly insignificant. Suddenly he gets an Unmotivated Close-up, and, of course, his eyes narrow. We do not have time today to discuss the general topic of narrowing eyes, but never mind. We know that the house servant is in on the plot, the official will be kidnapped or killed, and that it will be safe for us to sneak down the aisle for more popcorn or a quick trip to the john and still be back before the next outbreak of Far-Off Rattles and Rum-Dum-a-Dums.

Death Before Dishonor is a fairly pure example of the Ordinary Day/ Narrowed Eyes/Far-Off Rattle/Rum-Dum-a-Dum Movie. There isn't a lick of original thinking in it. The plot: Americans are kidnapped and brave marines blast their way in and free them from their heathen Arab kidnappers. The movie's dramatic high point is when Brian Keith takes an electric drill right through the back of his hand and still won't sign the phony confession. Courage? Maybe. Or maybe it just didn't hurt much. Seconds later, he's barking out orders, and in later scenes he seems to have regained the use of the maimed hand.

Is there anything at all to recommend this movie? Yeah, sort of. For one thing, this is the only movie I have ever seen where an Arab leader is played by an actor named Rockne Tarkington. For another, it sets a modern-day record for the Fruit Cart Rule. That's the rule that says that whenever there is a chase scene in a Third World nation, a speeding car will sooner or later overturn a fruit cart, leaving melons and oranges rolling in its wake. The chase scene in this movie takes out two fruit stands and one fruit cart in less than two minutes. Rum-a-Dum-Dum.

Death Race 2000

(Directed by Paul Bartel; starring David Carradine, Sylvester Stallone; 1975)
My colleague over on the city side, Bob Greene, ran a column not long ago consisting of essays by third- and fourth-graders about what they liked at the movies. To a child they agreed that violence, mayhem, and blood were their favorites. None of them mentioned cowboys, color cartoons, or comedies, which were my favorites when I was growing up in peaceful Downstate.

Greene's column was inspired by my review of *Mandingo,* in which I noted that it was a gruesomely violent R-rated movie to which children, nevertheless, had been admitted. "If I'd been a kid in the audience," I wrote, "I'm sure I would have been terrified and grief-stricken." Greene's point was that the urban kids of today are less easily shocked than I imagine.

To be sure, Greene printed only essays that praised violence (there must have been at least one kid with a high regard for horses, but we didn't hear from him). But Greene's point was provoking, as I was reminded last weekend during *Death Race 2000.* This is a film about a futuristic cross-country race in which the winner is determined, not merely by his speed, but also by the number of pedestrians he kills.

You get 100 points for someone in a wheelchair, 70 points for the aged, 50 points for kids, and so on. The killings are depicted in the most graphic way possible. Giant swords on the fronts of the cars skewer victims. Others are run over several times. In front of an old folks' home, the nurses park the wheelchairs of several patients in the middle of the road and wait for the fun to start—but the driver has his own little joke by swerving off the road and killing the nurses.

Well, the theater was up for grabs. The audience was at least half small children, and they loved it. They'd never seen anything so funny, I guess, and I was torn between walking out immediately and staying to witness a spectacle more dismaying than anything on the screen: the way small children were digging gratuitous bloodshed.

Despite the fact that the movie had a "restricted rating," the vast majority of the kids (and by kids I mean under ten years old) were without parents or guardians. That wasn't a surprise. It's been my observation in several Chicago theaters recently that little or no attempt is made to enforce the R rating. The ratings were intended in the first place to protect kids from violence. But last Saturday I began to wonder who was going to protect us from these kids.

Death Rides a Horse

(Directed by Giullo Petroni; starring Lee Van Cleef, John Phillip Law; 1969)
It's hard to explain the fun to be found in seeing the right kind of bad movie. Pauline Kael had a go at it in an article titled "Trash, Art and the Movies," but I think she set her sights too high. The bad movies she enjoyed *(The Scalphunters, Wild in the Streets)* weren't within a hundred miles of the badness of *Death Rides a Horse,* which is a bad movie indeed.

And yet . . . there's something about surrendering yourself to the dark, womblike security of a large Loop theater on a Saturday afternoon, and hunkering down in your seat, and simply abandoning yourself to a movie like this. From time to time you will laugh, or be thrilled, or distract yourself by noticing that some of the outdoor scenes are shot in a studio with backdrops (at one point, the hero casts a shadow across an entire mountain range).

Or you can try to unravel the puzzles of mistaken or double identity upon which the plots of spaghetti Westerns always seem to depend. The heroes of these films would save a lot of time if they'd accept one simple rule of thumb: Generally speaking, everyone they meet is either (a) the man who killed their families fifteen years ago, (b) a stranger who is after the same villains for mysterious reasons of his own, or (c) their father, brother, or son.

Alas, it generally takes two hours for these connections to be established. But in the meantime, sitting there in the dark, watching this bad Western on a Saturday afternoon, you get an autobiographical feedback. You reestablish contact with yourself at the age of ten, when you sat through dozens of exactly such bad Westerns (only not so violent, although they seemed violent enough). And contemplation of this sort, the mystics assure us, is necessary for psychic well-being.

You can also reflect upon the fates of Lee Van Cleef and John Phillip Law. It is one thing to hurtle into stardom as a result of spaghetti Westerns, as Clint Eastwood did. But it is another thing to remain stuck in them. Van Cleef's face, in close-up, has the lean, hardened, embittered expression of a man who has either (a) been pursuing his lonely vengeance across the plains of the West for thirty years, or (b) realizes he will be making spaghetti Westerns the rest of his life. These two looks are nearly indiscernible.

But Law still retains a certain innocence. His eyes are blue, his face unlined, his cheekbones the sort we expect on a young and stubborn hero. He usually wears suspenders in these movies (just as Eastwood smokes cigars and Van Cleef a pipe), and they give him a naive earnestness. We feel that he will doggedly obtain revenge, wipe out the bad guys, and return to Hollywood some day. We are on his side. He needs us.

The Deathmaster

(Directed by Ray Danton; starring Robert Quarry; 1972)

In the good old days when Roger Corman was producing about two dozen exploitation movies a year for American-International, he had this interesting way of getting the most for his money. He'd go through all the current acting contracts to see who still owed the company a few days of work. And then if, say, Boris Karloff was still on the books for four days, Corman would commission a horror movie that could be about anything. There was only one requirement: The script had to include four shooting days with Karloff. No more.

The Deathmaster, a vampire movie that has moved into neighborhood theaters under cover of darkness (naturally) looks like two Corman specials that ran into one another. Judging by the internal evidence, I'd say the producers were into Robert Quarry for about two weeks of work. They also must have had a batch of unexpired contracts with a team of unemployed beach-party extras. How else to explain the most schizo horror movie since *Schizo?*

Quarry is an old hand at the vampire game by now. The two superstars of the horror genre are Christopher Lee and Peter Cushing, but Quarry has been moving up fast in the last year or two. He was the star of *Count Yorga, Vampire,* a fairly good movie, and of *Return of Count Yorga,* which was not bad as these things go.

Quarry knows all the tricks by now. He can even do this thing with his face so you can't tell he's wearing his false vampire fangs. That's important, because it maintains the element of surprise. Vampire movies all have one thing in common: The people you think you can trust—your best friends— turn out to be vampires at the crucial moment. They've already been bitten.

The hero is always running down musty corridors and through rat-infested wine cellars, shouting "Susan! Thank God, you're still alive!" And then they embrace, and Susan lets him have it in the neck. A moment's thought will reveal that this kind of scene won't work unless the actors involved can conceal their false vampire fangs. If they can't, all the hero can shout is "Susan! Got the mumps?"

Anyway, in *The Deathmaster,* Quarry arrives at dawn in an old coffin that floats up on the beach at Santa Monica. If memory serves, it is the same beach used for the opening scene of *Attack of the Crab Monsters.* Crab monsters would be a relief, in fact, but what with the price of crabmeat these days they have all gone into different lines of work or simply dropped out of circulation. The next time you eat a crabmeat cocktail, reflect that it could be eating you.

Quarry is not, however, eaten by a crabmeat cocktail, which might easily have earned the picture an R rating if there is any decency left in this world. No, he appears mysteriously at a beach house that is inhabited by the beach-party dropouts and a motorcycle bum who looks like a refugee from *She-Devils on Wheels.*

These people are not very bright. They are so dumb, in fact, that they have had to learn to speak the English language by watching old AIP exploitation movies, and their dialogue is eight years out of date. They talk like Frankie

Avalon trying to pass for hip, translated from the German. Count Khorda (for such is his name) makes them a proposition: "Would you like to trade a lifetime of petty passions for an eternity of ecstasy?" They would, I guess. Well, wouldn't you?

What follows is pretty routine. I counted seven chases down the same length of subterranean cavern. It is not a very long length but what they do is photograph a guy running down it one way, and then cut to the other end of the same passage and have him run back. That way, it looks twice as long as it is, which is how the movie feels. Everybody gets turned into a vampire except the hero, who is stuck with his crummy lifetime of petty passions.

Deep Rising

(Directed by Stephen Sommers; starring Anthony Heald, Famke Janssen; 1998)
Deep Rising could also have been titled *Eat the Titanic!* It's about a giant squid that attacks a luxurious cruise ship in the South China Sea. Like all movie monsters, it has perfect timing, and always bursts into the frame just when the characters are least expecting it. And it has an unsavory way of dining. "They eat you?" asks one of the survivors. "No—they drink you."

The mechanics for a movie like this were well established in the *Alien* pictures, and *Deep Rising* clones the same formula. Survivors are trapped inside giant vessel. The creature finds its way around air ducts and sewer pipes, popping out of shaft openings to gobble up minor characters (the first victim is sucked down the toilet).

D'ya think they have meetings out in Hollywood to share the latest twists? I've been seeing the same gimmicks in a lot of different pictures. Evidence: No sooner does the snake in *Anaconda* release a slimy survivor from its innards than the squid in *Deep Rising* does the same thing. No sooner is there an indoor jet-ski chase in *Hard Rain* than there's one in *Deep Rising*. No sooner does a horrible monster crawl out of the air ducts in *Alien Resurrection* than it does so in *Deep Rising*. And last week I saw *Phantoms,* which was sort of *Deep Rising Meets Alien and Goes West.* In that one, the creature emerged from the depths of the earth rather than the sea, but had the same nasty practice of living behind piles of undigested remains.

An effort has been made by Stephen Sommers, writer-director of *Deep Rising,* to add humor to his story, although not even the presence of Leslie Nielsen could help this picture. The hero, Treat Williams, is a freelance power cruiser skipper who hires his craft out to a gang of vile and reprehensible bad guys, led by Wes Studi. They want to hijack a new casino ship on its maiden voyage. The owner of the ship (Anthony Heald) makes several speeches boasting about how stable it is; it can stay level in the water even during a raging tempest. I wonder if those speeches were inserted after the filmmakers realized how phony their special effects look. Every time we see the ship, it's absolutely immobile in the midst of churning waves.

No matter; the creature from the deep attacks the ship, and by the time Williams delivers the pirates, it seems to be deserted. All except for the evil owner, of course, and also a jewel thief (Famke Janssen) who was locked in the brig and survived the carnage.

A movie like this depends much upon the appearance of the monster, which has been designed by f/x wizard Rob Bottin. There is a vast evil squid head, and lots of tentacles (which seem to have minds of their own, and lots of mouths with many teeth). So vicious is the squid, indeed, that only the cynical will ask how it can survive for long periods out of water, or how and why it emits its piercing howl, which goes reverberating through the air shafts.

There's comic relief from Williams's engine room man, Pantucci (Kevin J. O'Connor), who plays the Donald O'Connor role and is always wisecracking in the face of adversity. And an effective supporting performance by Djimon Hounsou, as one of the more fanatic members of the pirate gang (he played Cinque in *Amistad,* and shows a powerful screen presence once again, although on the whole I'll bet he wishes the giant squid movie had come out *before* the Spielberg film).

Bemusing, how much money and effort goes into the making of a movie like this, and how little thought. It's months of hard work—for what? The movie is essentially an *Alien* clone with a fresh paint job. You know something's wrong when a fearsome tentacle rears up out of the water and opens its mouth, and there are lots of little tentacles inside with their own ugly mouths, all filled with nasty teeth, and all you can think is, been there, seen that.

The Devils

(Directed by Ken Russell; starring Oliver Reed, Vanessa Redgrave; 1972)

A burning at the stake, an afternoon in the rack, headscrews, a douche with boiling water, nails into hands, induced vomiting, ripped tongues, dead babes, human target practice, possession by devils, rape, transvestism, nude orgies in the nunnery. Put them all together and they spell Committed Art—because these are modern times and I certainly hope none of us is opposed to truth.

Now truth, as I've explained before, is what's real. If it isn't real, it isn't true, which is why a stone is better than a dream. If it isn't reality, who needs it? Or could lay hands on it, anyway? And everything on the list above really happened, yes it did. All the events and persons depicted in *The Devils* are intended to be confused with actual events and persons. How do I know? Ken Russell tells me so.

And so I stood in line the other night, my shoulders hunched against a nasty wind off Lake Michigan, waiting to get into the Cinema Theater so that I, too, could ascertain that unspeakable atrocities had occurred in the seventeenth century. I didn't want to be the only member of my generation unaware of the terrible events of 1634, a year that will live in infamy. Like everyone who's committed, I found it my duty to bear witness against the moral outrages of, if not my time, then at least somebody's time. I mean, you can't just sit around.

And Ken Russell has really done it this time. He has stripped the lid of respectability off the Ursuline convent in Loudon, France. He has exposed Cardinal Richelieu as a political schemer. He has destroyed our illusions about Louis XIII. We are filled with righteous indignation as we bear witness to the violation of the helpless nuns; it is all the more terrible because, as Russell fearlessly reveals, all the nuns, without exception, were young and stacked.

It is about time that someone had the courage to tell it like it was about Loudon, a seemingly respectable provincial town beneath the façade of which seethed simmering intrigues, unholy alliances, greed, fear, lust, avarice, sacrilege, and nausea. The story has gone untold for too long. Aldous Huxley wrote a book about it, and John Whiting wrote a play about it, but only Ken Russell has made a movie about it.

And make no mistake. *The Devils* has a message for our time. For we learn from the mistakes of the past. We live in a time of violence, and it is only by looking in the mouth of the Devil that we can examine his teeth. In a time when our nation is responsible for violence on a global scale, it is only by bearing witness to violence on a personal scale that we can bring the war home.

I don't know about anyone else, but frankly, I left the Cinema Theater feeling like a new, a different, and, yes, a better person. The poisons of our political system had been drained from me. I entered the theater as an unwitting participant in the atrocities of our time. But believe me, that's all behind me now. It took courage for me to go see *The Devils,* just like it took courage for Ken Russell to make it.

And it took courage for all those folks to congregate in the lobby and lounge of the Cinema Theater before, during, and after the performance. They were ordinary people—kids, students, young folks mostly—you might find living next door. And yet they had gone out into the night to see for themselves, so that the martyrs of Loudon might not go unmourned.

Now they spoke quietly among themselves of the atrocities they had witnessed, or hoped to witness soon. Listening to them, I felt we could all sleep a little sounder from now on. If the movie industry had more hard-nosed, tell-it-like-it-is artists like Ken Russell, Loudon might never happen again.

The Devil's Rain
(Directed by Robert Fuest; starring Ernest Borgnine; 1975)
I walked into *The Devil's Rain* a few minutes late and thought maybe I'd stumbled onto a Sergio Leone Western.

Vast empty spaces baked under the midday sun. There were distant whistles and moans on the sound track, the desert shimmered, and there was eerie music sounding vaguely like the wails of a short-winded harmonica player. A ghost town stood starkly outlined in the wasteland, and the steeple of its church reached for the lowering sky. All that was missing was Clint Eastwood shooing flies.

But, no, here came a new Chevy. At the wheel, one of the men of the Preston clan. His mission: To track down a cult of the Undead, test his faith against their satanist ceremonies, and rescue his kidnapped mother.

She'd been taken in the latest chapter of a feud going back 300 years, when men of the Preston family stole the book all of the Undead had signed with blood. Until the chief satanist (Ernest Borgnine) could get the book back, he wouldn't truly control the souls under his command.

But he doesn't just want the book. No, he wants the Prestons, too: He won't rest until all of them have embraced Satan and given him their souls. Then they'll be able to spend eternity standing outside in the devil's rain.

But . . . what *is* the devil's rain? This is a question frequently asked in *The Devil's Rain* and, believe me, frequently answered. Picture it this way: All the good things of life are on one side of a sheet of plate glass, and you're on the other, and it's raining on your side, Bunky. You pass the time by scratching the glass and pleading to be allowed back in.

All of this would be good silly fun if the movie weren't so painfully dull. The problem is that the material's stretched too thin. There's not enough here to fill a feature-length film. No doubt that's why we get so many barren landscapes filled with lonely music and ennui.

There are, however, a few good scenes, especially those in which Ernest Borgnine appears. He wears his official satanist suit, all red velvet and quite a contrast to the hooded black robes of his disciples. They have empty eye sockets, and when you shoot them, it turns out they're full of a milky green substance that looks like gelatin that didn't set.

Borgnine occasionally disappears in great puffs of smoke, only to reappear as the devil himself, complete with goat's horns, a beard, and fierce eyes. One imagines Borgnine reading the script and telling his agent: "This is a part I must make my own!" He works up a fine fiendish cackle and a passable obscene growl and goes out in style, falling down a manhole into Hell.

Then there's a big explosion, the devil's rain starts to fall, and the Undead all start to melt. Five minutes later, we're wondering if they'll ever finish. The filmmakers apparently spent a lot of money on the special effects, and to justify their investment they have the Undead melt, and melt, and melt, until if we get one more shot of green ooze, we'll feel like an exorcised popsicle. If only they'd melted just a little, just enough to give us the idea.

But, no, we have to wait about five minutes for the surprise ending, in which guess who doesn't have sense enough to come in out of the devil's rain?

Diary of Forbidden Dreams
(Directed by Roman Polanski; starring Marcello Mastroianni,
Hugh Griffith, Roman Polanski; 1976)

There's probably a level of competence beneath which bad directors cannot fall. No matter how dreary their imaginations, how stupid their material, how inept their actors, how illiterate their scripts, they've got to come up with something that can at least be advertised as a motion picture, released, and forgotten.

But a talented director is another matter. If he's made several good films, chances are that sooner or later someone will give him the money to make a supremely bad one. I wonder how much Carlo Ponti gave Roman Polanski to make *Diary of Forbidden Dreams.* Ten cents would have been excessive.

This is a movie so incredibly bad that I ask you to ponder the following facts. Even though (a) it stars Marcello Mastroianni, Hugh Griffith, and Polanski himself, and (b) provides us with almost ninety minutes during which the attractive Sydne Rome wears little more than a table napkin, and (c) is almost exclusively concerned with that surefire box-office winner, sex, it (d) was completed in 1973 and has not been released until now because almost every distributor who saw it fled the screening room in horror, clutching at his wallet.

The movie's original title was *What?* That is reportedly what Carlo Ponti said (in Italian, no doubt, and appropriately embellished) after Polanski showed it to him. In its original version, it looked like the work of a madman, of a crazed cinematic genius off the deep end. Ponti, in desperation, had all of Polanski's outtakes printed up (outtakes are versions of a shot that the director decides not to use). With the aid of skilled editors, Ponti attempted to substitute various outtakes in an attempt to construct a film that resembled, well, a film.

No luck. When Polanski makes a bad movie, he does it with a certain thoroughness. Even the shots he didn't use were bad. And so here we have it, Roman Polanski's *Diary of Forbidden Dreams.* It concerns (I think) the adventures of the young and shapely Miss Rome, a hitchhiker who stumbles upon a bizarre country villa that also functions as a private hospital.

Among the inmates are Mastroianni, who keeps repeating "What would be nice, I think, would be for us to meet for dinner" until we want to mash a plate of lasagna in his face. He walks about in a bathrobe, smoking a cigarette and inspiring us to wonder how in the world he got into the movies. Really. Mastroianni, one of the most charismatic actors in the world, reduced to a cipher. Hugh Griffith, wearing his usual ferocious whiskers, plays an old tyrant who is forever about to drop dead of a heart attack. Polanski plays another inmate who's a Ping-Pong buff. Mastroianni and, finally, Miss Rome keep stepping on his Ping-Pong balls and crushing them, which leads to no end of ill feeling. I would desperately like to believe no symbolism is intended.

Miss Rome loses most of her clothes soon after arriving at the villa, and spends half an hour wearing the above-mentioned table napkin around her neck before stealing the tops of Hugh Griffith's pajamas. Hugh Griffith is provided with dialogue like "Who is that girl wearing my pajama tops?" Another of the residents of the villa paints Miss Rome's left leg blue. There are a lot of shots of her walking around in pajama tops with a blue leg.

These and other shots confirm my long-held suspicion that, when it comes right down to it, there's a nasty streak of misogynism in Polanski. "What we have in mind, dear," I imagine him telling Sydne Rome when he was casting the picture, "is for you to walk around mostly nude for ninety minutes with your left leg painted blue." What she replied I cannot imagine, but she took the job. Some people will do anything to work for a top director.

You will notice that I have awarded *Diary of Forbidden Dreams* one half star. There is a principle at work here, and now's the time to explain it. No movie, no matter how bad, gets no stars at all in the *Sun-Times* unless it is, in addition to being bad, also meretricious and evil. *Diary* doesn't even have the wit to go that extra step.

Dice Rules

(Directed by Jay Dubin; starring Andrew Dice Clay; 1991)
Dice Rules is one of the most appalling movies I have ever seen. It could not be more damaging to the career of Andrew Dice Clay if it had been made as a documentary by someone who hated him. The fact that Clay apparently thinks this movie is worth seeing is revealing and sad, indicating that he not only lacks a sense of humor, but also ordinary human decency.

Andrew Dice Clay comes billed as a comedian, but does not get one laugh from me in the eighty-seven minutes of this film. I do not find it amusing to watch someone mock human affliction, and I don't find it funny, either, for him to use his fear of women as a subject for humor. Of course any subject can theoretically be *made* funny, but just to stand and point is not the same thing as developing a humorous point of view.

An example. We have all known someone who has undergone a tracheotomy, having their voice box removed because of cancer. Sometimes these people are still able to speak through controlling the air stream in their throat, or by using small battery-powered devices that magnify their whispers. Andrew Dice Clay finds their speech funny, and mocks it in this film. I imagine that tracheotomy patients themselves use morbid humor as one way of dealing with their condition, but Clay is not using humor at all—he is simply pointing and making fun, like a playground bully.

He has many other targets. The handicapped. The ill. Minorities. Women. Homosexuals. Anyone, in fact, who is not exactly like Andrew Dice Clay is fair game for his cruel attacks. His material about women constitutes verbal rape. Using obscenity as punctuation, he describes women as essentially things to masturbate with.

I think his approach to women is based on fear of them. It is too painful and too consistent to be explained otherwise. Everything that he says about women is based on the kind of ignorant dirty jokes told by insecure teenage boys among themselves, as they try to conceal their misinformation and bolster their courage by objectifying women into creatures who can be dismissed with the usual crude obscenities. Even then, if he were mocking or kidding this attitude, it could perhaps be funny. But not a single word in Clay's film indicates that he has been able to deal with the fact that women are living, thinking beings. He sees only their sexual organs, fears them, and must punish or conquer them to reassure himself.

Dice Rules was filmed in concert (what a word) at Madison Square Garden, which the comedian was able to fill two nights in a row. It is eerie, watching the shots of the audience. You never see anyone just plain laughing, as if they'd heard something that was funny. You see, instead, behavior more appropriate at a fascist rally, as his fans stick their fists in the air and chant his name as if he were making some kind of statement for them. Perhaps he is. Perhaps he is giving voice to their rage, fear, prejudice, and hatred. They seem to cheer him because he is getting away with expressing the sick thoughts they don't dare to say.

Comedians have long been a lightning rod for society, drawing down the dangers and grounding them. Some of the most brilliant comics of recent years—Lenny Bruce, Richard Pryor, George Carlin—have dealt with taboo words and concepts. But they bring insight and an attitude to them. They help us see how we regard them. They provide a form of therapy, of comic relief. Not Clay. Strutting and sneering, lacking the graceful timing of the great stand-up talents, reciting his words woodenly, he creates a portrait of the comedian as sociopath.

Crowds can be frightening. They have a way of impressing low, base taste upon their members. Watching the way thousands of people in his audience could not think for themselves, could not find the courage to allow their ordinary feelings of decency and taste to prevail, I understood better how demagogues are possible.

Dirty Dingus Magee

(Directed by Burt Kennedy; starring Frank Sinatra, George Kennedy; 1970)
Dirty Dingus Magee is as shabby a piece of goods as has masqueraded as a Western since, oh, *A Stranger Returns.* It's supposed to be a comedy, and it was directed by Burt Kennedy, who is supposed to be a director of Western comedies (*Support Your Local Sheriff* wasn't bad), but its failure is just about complete.

I lean toward blaming Frank Sinatra, who in recent years has become notorious for not really caring about his movies. If a shot doesn't work, he doesn't like to try it again; he might be late getting back to Vegas. What's more, the ideal Sinatra role requires him to be in no more than a fourth of the scenes, getting him lots of loot and top billing while his supporting cast does the work.

This time, as usual, the supporting cast is good. We get George Kennedy as a cigar-chewing sheriff; Anne Jackson as a madam of sorts; Lois Nettleton as a sympathetic nymphomaniac, and Jack Elam, naturally, as the villain. They're fun to watch, but where's Sinatra? In Vegas?

The movie loosely concerns Sinatra as a con man who. . . . But never mind what the movie's about; that's hardly the issue. I want to hurry on to a statement by one Charlie Blackfeet, president of the IFTP (Indians for Truthful Portrayal). Blackfeet is quoted at great length in MGM press releases as saying *Dirty Dingus Magee* has his organization's "first unqualified stamp of approval for Hollywood stories dealing with Indians in twenty years."

Blackfeet, who talks amazingly like an MGM press agent, allows that "Hollywood's version of the average American Indian has been as artificial as a toupee." Not a tactful statement where Frank Sinatra is involved. But Blackfeet likes this movie, because it avoids "make-believe jargon that makes Indians sound like a cross between Tarzan and a man making a phone call underwater." End of press release quotes.

Well, with all due respect, sir, I didn't much dig Paul Fix's dialogue as Chief Crazy Blanket ("If I'm crazy, you're crazy"), or the scene where four old squaws and George Kennedy (disguised by a blanket and, naturally, mistaken as a squaw) watch while Sinatra makes out with the chief's lithe daughter, at the chief's insistence. "Paleface take-um Injun girl," indeed, Mr. Blackfeet.

The Doom Generation
(Directed by Gregg Araki; starring James Duval, Rose McGowan; 1995)
Words like "disaffected," "distanced" and "deadpan" flew from my mind onto my notepad while I was watching *The Doom Generation*. This is the kind of movie where the filmmaker hopes to shock you with sickening carnage and violent amorality, while at the same time holding himself carefully aloof from it with his style. He would be more honest and probably make a better movie if he got down in the trenches with the rest of us.

There is an attitude in Gregg Araki's film that I've sensed in a lot of work recently: The desire by the filmmaker to have his cake and eat it too. He wants to make a blood-soaked, disgusting, disturbing movie about characters of low intelligence and little personal worth, but he's not willing to cop to that, and so by giving them smarmy pop-culture references and nihilistic dialogue, and filling the edges of his frame with satirical in-jokes and celebrity walk-ons (Margaret Cho, Heidi Fleiss), he's keeping himself at arm's length. Hey, if we're dumb enough to be offended by his sleazefest, that's our problem; Araki is, you see, a stylist, who can use concepts like iconography and irony to weasel away from his material.

Note carefully that I do not object to the content of his movie, but to the attitude. Content is neutral until shaped by approach and style. This is a road picture about Amy and Jordan, young druggies who get involved with a drifter named Xavier who challenges their ideas about sex, both gay and straight, while involving them on a blood-soaked cross-country odyssey. The movie opens as the drifter "inadvertently" (Araki's word, in the press kit) blows off the head of a Korean convenience store owner. The head lands in the hot dog relish and keeps right on screaming. Ho, ho,

It continues as the "enigmatic Xavier" (I am again quoting from the wonderfully revealing press kit) "has such rotten karma that every time they stop the car for fries and Diet Cokes, someone ends up dying in one gruesome way or another." Wait, there's more: "As the youthful band of outsiders continue their travels through the wasteland of America, Amy finds herself screwing both Jordan and Xavier, forging a triangle of love, sex, and desperation too pure for this world."

Now let's deconstruct that. The correct word is "its," not "their." (1) "Band of outsiders" is an insider reference to "A Band Apart," the name of Quentin Tarantino's production company, which itself is a pun on the title of a film by Godard. (2) Is it remotely possible that America is a "wasteland" because Amy, Jordan, and Xavier kill someone every time they stop for fries and a soda? That wouldn't have occurred to this movie. (3) The usage "someone ends up dying" employs the passive voice to avoid saying that the three characters *kill* them. This is precisely the same construction used by many serial killers and heads of state, who use language to separate themselves from the consequences of their actions.

Finally, (4) the notion that the threesome is "too pure for this world," which presumably gives them the right to kill store owners and other bystanders, is in its classic form pure fascist twaddle about the *ubermensch,* or superman, whose moral superiority gives him the right to murder. Araki may not have been thinking of Leopold and Loeb when he made his movie, but I was when I watched it.

Two of the best movies I've seen in recent years covered material similar to *The Doom Generation*. They were *Kalifornia* and *Natural Born Killers*. Both were about cross-country odysseys involving young lover/killers. Both dealt thoughtfully with their characters, and the consequences of their actions. Both had a point of view and a moral position. *Bonnie and Clyde* (1967),

Terence Malick's *Badlands* (1972), and both versions of *Gun Crazy* also had doomed young lovers on the run. All of these films were honest enough to be about what they were about—to acknowledge their subject matter.

But Gregg Araki has maybe seen too many movies, and is eager to have us know that he is above his subject matter. He's like the sideshow impresario whose taste is too good to enter his own tent. For him, I recommend several viewings of *Henry: Portrait of a Serial Killer,* a brilliant film that deals with a character very much like Xavier, and is not too shy to *deal* with him—to see him as he is, and accept the consequences.

Was I unfair to quote so liberally from the press kit? I used it because it praises the film so openly in terms that reveal its underlying dishonesty. Directors may not write their press kits, but they are responsible for them. Further reading from the kit: "*The Doom Generation* is the Alienated Teen Pic to End All Alienated Teen Pics—and, oh yeah, it's a comedy and a love story, too."

Oh, yeah.

Dracula A.D. 1972
(Directed by Alan Gibson; starring Christopher Lee; 1972)

The friendly folks at Hammer Films Ltd., the British specialists in horror flicks, have this thing about tiny glass vials. They'll use a vial or two in almost every movie they make. Sometimes they have crystal vials, but mostly just your ordinary glass vial.

The vials are handy for storing dehydrated blood from Count Dracula, who left so much blood behind him when he died that, alive, he would have been a godsend to the blood bank, had his blood not been overrun with vampire germs.

Public prejudice against vampires still runs at a fairly high level, unfortunately, and that is why you never hear of a vampire donating his services when an emergency call goes out for a rare blood type. With a bit of organization and a list of rare-blood donors, a competent team of vampires should be able to come back with the necessary plasma in no time. This is not the unsavory prospect it would have been in the eighteenth or nineteenth century; the widespread use of toothpaste among vampires has removed one of the age-old barriers to their acceptance.

In any event, *Dracula A.D. 1972* opens with a striking testimonial to the staying power of Dracula's blood. We remember from *Taste the Blood of Dracula,* an earlier Hammer endeavor, that when his dried blood is mixed with a little water and taken orally in medicinal amounts, the user becomes infected with the count's evil spirit. That's more or less what happens again this time.

A young man who looks curiously like Alex (Stanley Kubrick's hero in *A Clockwork Orange*) wants to be a vampire. He hangs around all day in a strange coffeehouse that looks curiously like the milk bar in *A Clockwork Orange,* and he looks out from under a lowered brow, just like Alex in *A Clockwork Orange.* He seems to be a symbol of the general decay at Hammer Films, which, having brought the horror film to a peak of perfection and created the first new horror superstar in years (Christopher Lee), now seems willing to follow the artistic leads of violence-come-latelies like Kubrick. Alas.

Anyway, the novice lays hands on some dehydrated Dracula blood, liquefies it during a bizarre ritual in a bombed-out church, and sets into motion a complex chain of forbidden rituals designed to display Stephanie Beacham's cleavage to the greatest possible advantage. This isn't a terrific rationale for another horror flick but, given Miss Beacham's ability to heave, and her bosom to heave with, it will have to do. On leaving the theater, I was given an honorary membership card in the Count Dracula society, and a lapel pin that I inadvertently stuck myself with. And not a vial in sight.

EEEE**E**EEEE

⭐ **Emmanuelle—the Joys of a Woman**
(Directed by Francis Giacobetti; starring Sylvia Kristel; 1976)
Let me, Emmanuelle, teach you the secret joys of love. I will show you how to live for pleasure . . . let me take you to a new world.—Advertisement

And on and on. Emmanuelle was a pristine innocent at the beginning of her first film, but the kid was a quick study, and now here she is in the sequel as a sort of combination sex therapist and hidden garden of desires. She's married, but that hasn't slowed her down; if her husband explains once, he explains a dozen times that Emmanuelle's life is her own to lead, and that he doesn't possess her (more than about twice a day).

The two of them live in Hong Kong now, in a vast mansion filled with potted palms and slowly revolving fans and white wicker furniture and servants who assist them in and out of states of undress. Life is pleasant. Emmanuelle's husband has no apparent line of work, although he maintains a little office at home—primarily, I suspect, because one scene requires a desk for Emmanuelle to crawl under. Such are the demands of sexual liberation.

One day a young aviator comes to call. He was just flying through, you see, on his way to Australia, when he developed a little engine trouble. He sleeps with his propellor. During waking hours, he polishes the propellor while sitting on the lawn. We wait for two hours to discover what additional purposes the propellor will be put to, but we never learn; some secrets are not to be revealed. The aviator gets the guest room.

Then there's the lovely Anna-Marie, whose father throws sophisticated dinner parties after which exotic dancers perform. Anna-Marie doesn't get along with dad, and so she moves in with the Emmanuelles, too. Poor thing, it's so hot out that she can hardly move, and so Emmanuelle and her husband take her to a bathhouse, where they receive what is advertised in the free weekly papers as a full body massage.

Emmanuelle's search for the most distant shores of love is a demanding one, and during the course of *Joys of a Woman* she also (a) surprises a tattooed polo player in a dressing room and is most cruelly treated by him, (b) has her clothing interfered with by Anna-Marie's dancing teacher, (c) is seduced in the women's dormitory of a steamer bound for Hong Kong from Thailand, and (d) achieves orgasm by acupuncture, while the aviator looks on, propellorless for once. We wait in vain for her to discover the missionary position, but such relief is denied her.

The attractive elements of the original *Emmanuelle* are present here, too: the pretty Sylvia Kristel, the languorous color photography, the exotic locations, the outrageous fantasies. But somehow the characters seem to have lost track of their sanity; they wander from one encounter to another like wifeswappers at a postlobotomy ball. They have glazed looks in their eyes and think with their mouths open. And they lose track of time, of things. The aviator never does go on to Australia, and dad doesn't come looking for Anna-Marie, and Emmanuelle and her husband never do decide whether he should shave off his mustache, and dinner's not served . . . yawn . . . and. . . .

End of Days

(Directed by Peter Hyams; starring Arnold Schwarzenegger, Kevin Pollack; 1999)
There are forces here you couldn't possibly comprehend. —Dialogue
You can say that again. *End of Days* opens with a priest gazing out his window at the Vatican City and seeing a comet arching above the moon like an eyebrow. He races to an old wooden box, snatches up a silver canister, pulls out an ancient scroll, unrolls it and sees—yes! A drawing of a comet arching above the moon like an eyebrow! For verily this is the dreaded celestial display known as the "Eye of God."

The priest bursts into an inner chamber of the Vatican, where the pope sits surrounded by advisers. "The child will be born today!" he gasps. Then we cut to "New York City, 1979" and a live childbirth scene, including of course the obligatory dialogue, "Push!" A baby girl is born, and a nurse takes the infant in its swaddling clothes and races to a basement room of the hospital, where the child is anointed with the blood of a freshly killed rattlesnake before being returned to the arms of its mother.

Already I am asking myself, where is William Donohue when we need him? Why does his Catholic League attack a sweet comedy like *Dogma* but give a pass to *End of Days*, in which we learn that once every one thousand years a woman is born who, if she is impregnated twenty years later by the Prince of Darkness during the hour from eleven to twelve P.M. on the last day of the millennium, will give birth to the anti-Christ, who will bring about, yes, the end of days? While meanwhile an internal Vatican battle rages between those who want to murder the woman, and the pope, who says we must put our faith in God?

The murder of the woman would of course be a sin, but perhaps justifiable under the circumstances, especially since the humble instrument chosen by God to save the universe is an alcoholic bodyguard named Jericho Cane, played by Arnold Schwarzenegger. Jericho and his partner (Kevin Pollack) find themselves investigating a puzzling series of events, including a man with his tongue cut out who nevertheless screams a warning and is later nailed to the ceiling of his hospital room.

Movies like this are particularly vulnerable to logic, and *End of Days* even has a little fun trying to sort out the reasoning behind the satanic timetable. When Jericho has the Millennium Eve scheduling explained to him, including the requirement that the Prince of Darkness do his dirty deed precisely between eleven P.M. and midnight, he asks the very question I was asking myself: "Eastern Standard Time?"

The answer, Jericho is told, is that the exact timing was meticulously worked out centuries ago by the Gregorian monks, and indeed their work on this project included, as a bonus spin-off, the invention of the Gregorian Calendar. Let's see. Rome is six hours ahead of New York. In other words, those clever monks said, "The baby will be conceived between five and six A.M. on January 1, Rome time, but that will be between eleven and twelve A.M. in a city that does not yet exist, on a continent we have no knowledge of, assuming the world is round and there are different times in different places as it revolves around the sun, which of course it would be a heresy to suggest." With headaches like this, no wonder they invented Gregorian Chant to take the load off.

End of Days involves a head-on collision between the ludicrous and the absurd, in which a supernatural being with the outward appearance of Gabriel Byrne pursues a twenty-year-old woman named Christine (Robin Tunney) around Manhattan, while Jericho tries to protect her. This being a theological struggle Schwarzenegger style, the battle to save Christine involves a scene where a man dangles from a helicopter while chasing another man across a rooftop, and a scene in which a character clings by his fingertips to a high window ledge, and a scene in which a runaway subway train explodes, and a scene in which fireballs consume square blocks of Manhattan, and a scene in which someone is stabbed with a crucifix, and . . .

But the violence raises another question. How exactly do the laws of physics apply to the Byrne character? Called "The Man" in the credits, he is Satan himself, for my money, yet seems to have variable powers. Jericho shoots him, and he pulls up his shirt so we can see the bullet holes healing. But when Jericho switches to a machine gun, the bullets hurl The Man backward and put him out of commission for a time, before he attacks again. What are the rules here? Is he issued only so much anti-injury mojo per millennium?

The movie's final confrontation is a counterpoint to the Times Square countdown toward the year 2000. Only a churl would point out that the new millennium actually begins a year later, on the last day of 2000. Even then, *End of Days* would find a loophole. This is the first movie to seriously argue that "666," the numerical sign of Satan, is actually "999" upside down, so that all you have to do is add a "1" and, whoa! You get "1999."

Endless Summer II

(Directed by Bruce Brown; starring Robert Weaver, Pat O'Connell; 1994)
Endless Summer II is the kind of movie that observes, quite seriously, that if you had money enough and time, you could spend the rest of your life traveling around the world, surfing on perfect waves. And those waves, it observes, have been rolling ashore for "tens of thousands of years" (or even longer, I'll bet), "just to give us pleasure."

One of the charms of the movie is that it adheres so rigorously to this worldview. Man exists to surf, and waves exist to allow him to. Ultimate bliss is a "sixty-second ride," after which, "no matter how many times it happens," the lucky surfer feels "stoked."

The documentary stars two young surfers, Robert "Wingnut" Weaver, twenty-six, and Pat O'Connell, twenty, who set out on an around-the-world odyssey to find the perfect wave. For O'Connell, that must not be difficult, since he is famous for finding "the greatest wave of my life" every single day. We know this from the movie's narration, spoken by Bruce Brown, the director, since O'Connell is never heard on the sound track except to emit a creepy, high-pitched giggle.

Endless Summer II is a sequel to a movie made before either Weaver or O'Connell were born. The original *Endless Summer* came out, according to Brown, in 1964, although reference books cite the year 1966 and I recall meeting Brown when the movie opened in Chicago in 1967. None of this is of the slightest importance, but all through the movie I kept being distracted by Brown's insistence on the year 1964—maybe because there was so little else for me to think about.

The movie is wonderfully photographed. Right at the beginning, we see fabulous shots of waves and surfers. Some of the shots even go inside the "barrel," so we can see the wave curling over the head of the surfer. What a way to get stoked. These are terrific shots. We see them again, and again, and again. The operative word in the title is *endless,* not *summer.*

Seeking perfect waves, we follow the lads on their odyssey from southern California to Costa Rica to France to South Africa to the Fiji Islands to Australia and back home again, with some footage of Hawaii even though Pat and Wingnut inexplicably did not visit there. On their travels they meet the bronzed veterans of the first *Endless Summer* movie, all of them now thirty (or twenty-eight, or twenty-seven) years older, but still hanging out on the beach. Occasionally there is a small nugget of information, for example: "There are eight million Zulus in South Africa, but only one of them is a surfer." Uncannily, the filmmakers have found that very Zulu, and interview him on the one subject he cannot discuss with his 7,999,999 fellow Zulus. This is a movie with tunnel vision.

Although the movie runs ninety-five minutes, it contains nothing much in the way of information about surfing. It observes that in 1964 surfers mostly used long boards, but today they use short boards. There is no mention of the differences between the two boards, or the reasons why one might use one, or the other. Nor do we discover how you learn to surf or what techniques and skills are useful. We do find out that there is a "pro tour," but there's no information about how the sport is scored, or how competition is held. Brown seems basically interested just in finding great waves, surfing them, and getting "stoked."

He intercuts his surfing scenes with various bits of local color, as when Pat and Wingnut drive through a game reserve in a beach buggy and are pursued by lions. That's risky, but not nearly so disturbing as the topless beaches of France, where the lads encounter several breasts, and ask the advice of local surfers about where to look during such an emergency.

There is such a harmless innocence about all of this that it's seductive. Surfers, like all hobbyists, have a certain madness: They see the world through the prism of their specialty. Nothing else matters. "If you spent one day at every place where surfers ride the waves," the movie tells us wistfully, "it would take you fifty years to visit all of them." But boy, would you be stoked.

Eric the Viking

(Directed by Terry Jones; starring Tim Robbins, Lena Horne, Mickey Rooney; 1989)

Every once in a while a movie comes along that makes me feel like a human dialysis machine. The film goes into my mind, which removes its impurities, and then it evaporates into thin air. *Eric the Viking* is a movie like that, an utterly worthless exercise in waste and wretched excess, uninformed by the slightest spark of humor, wit, or coherence.

Movies like this show every sign of having gotten completely out of hand at an early stage of the production. Perhaps everybody was laughing so hard at the jokes they thought they were telling that they forgot to tell any. The movie looks obscenely expensive, but the money is spent on pointless scenes without purpose or payoff, as for example an interminable storm sequence in which the actors hold onto masts and say inane things to one another while water is splashed in their faces.

The basic comic technique in *Eric the Viking* is the use of the deliberate anachronism. There is a scene, for example, in which Vikings attack and pillage a village, and Eric the Viking (Tim Robbins) finds himself required to assault one of the townswomen. But his tastes do not run toward rape, and so they engage in a discussion on the economic realities of pillaging, and then he asks her to shout "Rape!" as a courtesy, so the other Vikings will think he has done his part.

If you can master the comic logic of that scene, you have exhausted 90 percent of the comic invention in this movie, which is based on Vikings speaking as if they were twentieth-century satirists of themselves. The other 10 percent of the movie consists of guest appearances by such stars as Lena Horne and Mickey Rooney, who demonstrate convincingly that Michael Todd exhausted the possibilities of cameo appearances when he made *Around the World in 80 Days* many, many years ago. (That was the movie where the piano player turned round to grin at the camera, and you shouted, "Look! It's Frank Sinatra!" More than thirty years later, a little Viking grins at the camera, and we are expected to shout "Look! It's Mickey Rooney!")

Erik the Viking was written and directed by Terry Jones, whose previous film, *Personal Services,* was a splendid and intelligent slice-of-life about a notorious London madam who ran a genteel brothel for elderly gents. The two films could not be less similar. I assume *Eric the Viking* represents some kind of comprehensive lack of judgment on Jones's part, and that he will be back among the competent in no time at all.

The Evening Star
(Directed by Robert Harling; starring Shirley MacLaine, Juliette Lewis; 1996)
The Evening Star is a completely unconvincing sequel to *Terms of Endearment* (1982). It tells the story of the later years of Aurora Greenway (Shirley MacLaine), but fails to find much in them worth making a movie about. It shows every evidence, however, of having closely scrutinized the earlier film for the secret of its success. The best scenes in *Terms* involved the death of Aurora's daughter, Emma, unforgettably played by Debra Winger. Therefore, *The Evening Star* has no less than three deaths. You know you're in trouble when the most upbeat scene in a comedy is the scattering of the ashes.

The movie takes place in Houston, where Aurora lives with her loyal housekeeper Rosie (Marion Ross) and grapples unsuccessfully with the debris of her attempts to raise her late daughter's children. The oldest boy (George

Newbern) is in prison on his third drug possession charge. The middle boy (Mackenzie Astin) is shacked up with a girlfriend and their baby. The girl, Melanie (Juliette Lewis) is on the brink of moving to Los Angeles with her boyfriend, a would-be actor. (The absence of their father, Flap, played in the first movie by Jeff Daniels, is handled with brief dialogue.)

Aurora has broken up with the General (Donald Moffat), who lives down the street, but he is still a daily caller, drinking coffee in the kitchen with Rosie and offering advice. The next-door neighbor, in the house that used to be owned by the astronaut (Jack Nicholson), is now the genial Arthur (the late Ben Johnson), who also pays Rosie a great deal of attention. And still on the scene is Patsy (Melanie Richardson), Emma's best friend, now one of Aurora's confidantes.

All of these people live together in the manner of 1950s sitcoms, which means they constantly walk in and out of each other's houses and throw open the windows to carry on conversations with people in the yard. I don't know about you, but if I had to live in a neighborhood where all of my friends and neighbors were hanging out in the kitchen drinking my coffee and offering free advice and one-liners all day long, I'd move. Let them go to Starbucks.

Rosie, a lovable busybody, notices that Aurora has fallen into a depression, and tricks her into seeing a therapist, Jerry (Bill Paxton). Aurora tells him that she is still seeking "the great love of my life." Anyone who has slept with an astronaut played by Jack Nicholson and can still make that statement is a true optimist. Soon, amazingly, the much-younger Jerry violates all the rules of his profession and asks her out, and we get one of those patented movie scenes designed to show how a rich older lady is the salt of the earth: She takes him to a barbeque joint named the Pig Stand, where she knows everybody by name (this is probably one of the danger signals of alcoholism). Now we're in for a series of scenes showing how colorful Aurora is, and sure enough, before long she actually crawls in through Jerry's window.

Developments. Melanie, the granddaughter, wants to move to L.A. with her boyfriend, Bruce. Rosie and old Arthur start dating. The General gets into a snit because Aurora is dating Jerry. Rosie decides to marry Arthur ("Nobody else has ever told me they loved me. Besides, I'll just be next door"). When Rosie gets sick, Aurora reveals her credentials as a control freak by actually going into Arthur's house and carrying Rosie back to her own house, in the rain.

As a counterpoint to these events, Aurora rummages in a closet and comes up with a roomful of diaries, photo albums, old dance cards, theater programs, and journals, which collectively suggest set decorators and prop consultants on an unlimited budget. And the astronaut (Nicholson) turns up again, briefly, adding a shot in the arm. "I'm still looking for my true love," Aurora tells him, and he replies, with the movie's best line, "There aren't that many shopping days until Christmas."

Terms of Endearment was about a difficult relationship between two strong-willed women, the MacLaine and Winger characters. Juliette Lewis, as the granddaughter, is available for similar material here, and indeed her performance is the most convincing in the movie, but the script marginalizes her, preferring instead a series of Auntie Mame–like celebrations of Aurora, alternating with elegiac speeches and clunky sentiment.

Sequels are a chancy business at best, but *Evening Star* is thin and contrived. Even the music has no confidence in the picture: William Ross's score underlines every emotion with big nudges, and ends scenes with tidy little flourishes. The title perhaps comes from *Crossing the Bar,* by Tennyson, who wrote:

> *Sunset and evening star,*
> *And one clear call for me!*
> *And let there be no moaning of the bar,*
> *When I put out to sea . . .*

His bar, of course, was made of sand, and is not to be confused with the Pig Stand. In *Evening Star,* however, there is a great deal of moaning when anyone puts out to sea.

Exit to Eden

(Directed by Garry Marshall; starring Dana Delaney, Rosie O'Donnell, Dan Aykroyd; 1994)

There is a scene in *Exit to Eden* in which the hero butters Dana Delany's breast, sprinkles it with cinnamon, and licks it before taking bites from a croissant. I'm thinking: The breast or the croissant, make up your mind.

The whole movie is like that. It's supposed to be a kinky sex comedy, but it keeps getting distracted. On the first page of my notes, I wrote *Starts slow.*

On the second page, I wrote *Boring*. On the third page, I wrote *Endless!* On the fourth page, I wrote: *Bite-size shredded wheat, skim milk, cantaloupe, frozen peas, toilet paper, salad stuff, pick up laundry.*

The movie is based on a novel by Anne Rice, who is said to know a lot about bizarre sexual practices. Either she learned it all after writing this book, or the director, Garry Marshall, just didn't have his heart in it. The movie is not only dumb and ill constructed, but tragically miscast. The actors look so uncomfortable they could be experiencing alarming intestinal symptoms.

You know me. I'm easy on actors. These are real people with real feelings. When I see a bad performance, I'm inclined to blame anyone but the actors. In the case of *Exit to Eden* I'm inclined to blame the actors. Starting with Rosie O'Donnell. I'm sorry, but I just don't get Rosie O'Donnell. I've seen her in three or four movies now, and she has generally had the same effect on me as fingernails on a blackboard. She's harsh and abrupt and staccato and doesn't seem to be having any fun. She looks mean.

In *Exit to Eden,* she has the misfortune to star in a subplot involving an unnecessary, stupid, boring police investigation. The movie acts as if we care about this dumb case, involving a suspect who may be hiding out in an island resort devoted to S&M. I was reminded of those old nudist camp movies that pretended to be documentaries about volleyball.

Rosie and her partner, played by Dan Aykroyd, turn up on the island, which is managed by a woman named Lisa (Dana Delaney). Oh, it's quite a place. They have a merry-go-round with humans instead of wooden horses. A sticky buns booth. Dialogue like, "Baking *and* bondage? I could do both?!" The male customers look like Chippendale dancers. The female customers look like mud wrestlers. Here is a typical exchange:

"Wow! You're a CEO!"

"Yes, I am."

Come on, Garry Marshall, what's going on here? You're a smart guy. You made *Flamingo Kid* and *Pretty Woman*. Didn't you realize (a) that the whole police plot had to go, and O'Donnell and Aykroyd along with it? And (b) that sex is funny when it's taken seriously, but boring when it's treated as funny? What were your thoughts the first time Rosie turned up in the leather dominatrix uniform? Did you have maybe slight misgivings that you were presiding over one of the more misguided film projects of recent years?

I don't know what kinds of people would sign up for a vacation resort that specializes in sadomasochism, bondage, and discipline, but I imagine they'd want their money's worth. The lifeless, listless charades presided over by Delaney are practically family entertainment. The late Harriett Nelson could have attended this camp with only the occasional "Oh, my!"

And of all the actresses I can imagine playing the role of boss dominatrix, Dana Delaney is the last. She's a cute, merry-faced type—perfect for the dominatrix's best friend. For the lead, let's see. How about Faye Dunaway? Linda Fiorentino? Sigourney Weaver? See what I mean?

Anne Rice recently took out two-page spreads in *Variety* and the *New York Times* to announce that she has seen the film of her novel *Interview with the Vampire,* and thinks it is a masterpiece. I don't think we should look for her ad about *Exit to Eden,* not even in the classifieds.

FFFFFFFFFF

Father's Day
(Directed by Ivan Reitman; starring Robin Williams, Billy Crystal, Julia Louis-Dreyfus; 1997)

Father's Day is a brainless feature-length sitcom with too much sit and no com. It stars two of the brighter talents in American movies, Robin Williams and Billy Crystal, in a screenplay cleverly designed to obscure their strengths while showcasing their weaknesses.

The story is recycled out of a 1983 French film named *Les Comperes,* as part of a trend in which Hollywood buys French comedies and experiments on them to see if they can be made in English with all of the humor taken out. The discussion about this one seems to have been limited to who got to play the Gérard Depardieu role.

Billy Crystal won, I think. At least he's the one who is a master of the sudden, violent head-butt, which is supposed to be amusing because he's a high-powered lawyer and so nobody expects him to be good at head-butting. As the movie opens, he gets an unexpected visit from a woman (Nastassja Kinski) he knew seventeen years ago. She's now happily married, but needs to tell him something: They had a son, the son has disappeared, she's desperate, and she needs his help in finding him.

Robin Williams plays an unsuccessful performance artist from San Francisco who is at the point of suicide when his phone rings. It's Kinski, with the same story: Seventeen years ago, they had a son, who is now missing, and so on. She tells both men to be on the safe side, in case one doesn't want to help. But both men are moved by her story and by the photograph she supplies, of a lad who looks born to frequent the parking lots of convenience stores.

At this point, it is inconceivable that the following events will not transpire: (1) The two men will discover they're both on the same mission. (2) They'll team up, each one secretly convinced he's the real father. (3) They'll find the son, who doesn't want to be saved. (4) They'll get involved in zany, madcap adventures while saving him, preferably in San Francisco, Reno, and places like that. (5) The married one (Crystal) will lie to his wife about what he's doing, and she'll get suspicious and misread the whole situation.

Will the movie get all smooshy at the end, with the kind of cheap sentimentality comedians are suckers for, because they all secretly think they embody a little of Chaplin? You betcha. This movie could have been written by a computer. That it was recycled from the French by the team of Lowell Ganz and Babaloo Mandel is astonishing, given the superior quality of their collaborations like *Parenthood* and *City Slickers.*

Williams and Crystal are pretty bad. You can always tell a lazy Robin Williams movie by the unavoidable scene in which he does a lot of different voices and characters. This time, nervous about meeting his son, he tries out various roles in front of a mirror. All right, already. We know he can do this, We've seen him do it in a dozen movies and on a hundred talk shows. He's getting to be like the goofy uncle who knows one corny parlor trick and insists on performing it at every family gathering. Crystal is more in character most of the time—more committed to the shreds of narrative that lurk beneath the movie's inane surface.

The kid, played by Charlie Hofheimer, is another weak point. He's not much of an actor—not here, anyway, in material that would have defeated anybody—but the movie doesn't even try to make his character interesting. That would upstage the stars, I guess. An indication of the movie's lack of ambition is its decision to surround the runaway clichés: His girlfriend has run off with a rock singer, he follows her, Crystal and Williams follow him into the mosh pits of rock concerts and to the band's engagement in Reno, etc. There's even a gratuitous drug dealer, hauled into the plot so he can threaten the kid about a missing $5,000. Would it have been too much to motivate the kid with something besides sex, drugs, and rock and roll? Do we need a drug dealer in this innocuous material?

And what about poor Julia Louis-Dreyfus? She has the thankless role of Crystal's wife. When Crystal and Williams drag the kid into a hotel room for a shower, she misunderstands everything she hears on the phone and thinks her husband is showering with strange men and boys. Later she turns up while he's telephoning her, and he talks into the phone, not realizing her answers are coming from right behind him. This will be hilarious to anyone who doesn't know how telephones work.

Firewalker

(Directed by J. Lee Thompson; starring Chuck Norris, Lou Gossett; 1986)
Where to start with this movie? Where to end? Even more to the point, in which order to show the reels? J. Lee Thompson's *Firewalker* is a free-form anthology of familiar images from the works of Steven Spielberg, subjected to a new process that we could call discolorization. All of the style and magic are gone, leaving only the booby-trapped temples, the steaming jungle, and such lines as, if I remember correctly, "Witch, woman, harlot—I've been called them all!"

Firewalker borrows its closing images from the Indiana Jones movies, but its press notes optimistically claim the movie is "in the tradition" of *Romancing the Stone.* In literature, it's called plagiarism. In the movies, it's homage. The movie stars Chuck Norris, Lou Gossett, and Melody Anderson in a romp through Central America in search of a lost temple filled with gold. Norris and Gossett are professional adventurers and best pals; Anderson is a rich girl who walks into a bar and asks for two men who are strong, brave, and not too smart. She's got an old treasure map and wants them to help her find the gold.

We know Norris and Gossett are just the guys she's looking for, because we were observing closely during the title sequence, when they were not too smart. The two men are staked faceup in the desert and left to die. And as a special torture, Norris is given a full bottle of Perrier to hold in his right hand, so that water will be tantalizingly close as the hot sun bakes him. Norris breaks the bottle and uses a shard of glass to cut the rope, which is terrific, except that we can clearly see that all either one of them has to do is simply slip the rope off the top of the stake.

Once they're in the jungle with Anderson, the movie turns into one of those blood-soaked travelogues in which enemies pop up like targets in a shooting gallery. The bad guys include mercenary soldiers, Indians, rebel troops, crazed would-be dictators, and a man who is named Cyclops because he wears a patch over one eye.

Cyclops was my inspiration to play the game of Continuity with this movie. That's the game where you count all the mistakes, such as that his patch is over his right eye the first time we see him and his left eye the other times. Also, Norris and Anderson are in a VW bug that sinks while fording a river. It's two feet from shore, but when they escape from it, they have to swim at least twenty-five yards. Later, they find Gossett suspended above a pool of boiling water by a rope tied around his hands. Norris leaps out to embrace Gossett, and they swing back and forth until the rope frays and allows them to land on a ledge, where Gossett's hands are miraculously free.

Continuity is a game you play only during a movie that gives you little else to think about. Although Norris and Gossett are capable of better things, nothing in this movie gives that away. They never really seem to feel anything. For example, Gossett disappears, apparently eaten by an alligator, and the most Norris can work up is a case of vexation. Anderson seems to be in the movie mostly so that Norris has someone to drag out of danger.

There are, of course, the obligatory karate fights, in which Norris flies through the air and aims his magic heels at the villains, killing or disabling dozens of them. Karate scenes always inspire the same question: Why doesn't somebody just shoot the guy dead while he's whirling around?

Firewalker was directed by J. Lee Thompson, whose credits include *The Guns of Navarone*. He has recently labored in the Cannon stable, turning out weary action retreads such as the Richard Chamberlain version of *King Solomon's Mines*. This time he has directed by rote, failing his actors by letting them appear blasé in the moments when they should be excited, and, even worse, excited when they should be blasé. This effectively short-circuits all the potential moments of humor. For example, Gossett is more excited at the sight of the treasure map than he is at the sight of the treasure.

On second thought, maybe Gossett simply got a good look at the treasure. The temple contains a room roughly as big as Citizen Kane's warehouse, filled with gold objects. Once or twice, the camera strayed too close, and I was able to see that some of the priceless treasures of the ancients included spray-painted Tupperware.

Consumer note: Nobody walks on fire in this movie.

Food of the Gods

(Directed by Bert I. Gordon; starring Marjoe Gortner, Ida Lupino; 1976)
"Most guys who play pro ball, they get racked up every once in a while," observes the hero's buddy in *Food of the Gods*. "But not old Joe. Seven years in the major leagues and he never got carried off the field even once. And then

this had to happen to him. It really makes you think." It sure does. Old Joe has just gone and gotten himself stung to death by a giant killer wasp.

Joe's friends load him into a Jeep, drive the body back to the mainland, and then return to the island where the attack took place. "There's something strange going on out there," one observes sagely. "I don't know if I should go back," says the other. "I gotta be in Chicago on Tuesday. . . ." Meanwhile, poor Mr. Skinner has stopped to change a tire and has been eaten alive by gigantic mutant rats. In a way, that was simple justice; it was Mr. Skinner's doing that got the whole plague of giant rats started. He found some of this funny stuff oozing up out of the ground on the back forty, you see. Creamy-like, and about the color of skimmed milk. For some fool reason he mixed it with the chicken feed and fed it to the chickens. It made the baby chicks grow taller than a man. It also had an effect on the adult chickens: Their babies ate them.

This is obviously a case for Marjoe Gortner, playing a pro football team-mate of poor old Joe. He loads up some shotguns and drives back to the island in his Jeep, and not a moment too soon, because Mrs. Skinner has just had her arm chewed up by gigantic mutant worms and a young couple has busted the back axle on their Winnebago camper just as the girl has started labor pains. Meanwhile, the wasps have built hives twenty feet high, the rats are repro-ducing like crazy, and the venal businessman, Bensington, has gone out to the island determined to get the patents on the stuff oozing out of ground: "In five years, no one will be hungry—and we'll be rich!"

What happens next is a cross between *Night of the Living Dead, The Birds,* and a disaster movie, if you follow me. The little band of people are marooned in the Skinner cabin. Rats sniff around outside. Marjoe and the others fire at them with shotguns and throw Molotov cocktails into their midst. Pamela Franklin falls down into a rat hole and Marjoe falls in trying to help her. They get lost and almost eaten before they find a tunnel to safety. Killer wasps attack again and are driven back. Marjoe electrifies the fence that cuts the island in two, but the rats sabotage the electrical generator. The pregnant girl (did I forget to mention her?) says her labor pains are becoming more closely spaced.

"I'll bet those rats can't swim," Marjoe speculates. "When you're a rat and suddenly you weigh 150 pounds, you got to learn all over again how to swim." He dashes to his Jeep, races over to the dam, blows it up with two well-placed charges, and drives so quickly that he gets back to the house before (a) the floodwaters, and (b) before we ask ourselves what a dam could be holding back on a small island with no apparent heights.

Anyway, the floodwaters surround the house, and Marjoe leads the survivors upstairs and out onto a small second-floor balcony that did not exist in any of the earlier shots of the house and will have disappeared in all of the later shots but is mighty handy just at the moment. The rats drown. The baby is delivered. It's a boy. Everybody agrees that Mr. Skinner sure shouldn't have fed that oozy stuff to the chickens.

Fools

(Directed by Tom Gries; starring Jason Robards, Katharine Ross; 1971)
How can I possibly describe how awful *Fools* is, and in how many different ways? The task approaches impossibility. The only way to fully understand how transcendently bad this movie is would be to see it for yourself—an extreme measure I hope, for your sake, you'll avoid. Let me just sort of hint at the depth of my feeling by saying *Fools* is the worst movie in 1971, a statement that springs forth with serene confidence even though here it is only February. Happy Valentine's Day, by the way.

The movie is about love. Now the one thing we all know about love is that it's more important than money, position, respectability, age, anything. When people fall in love, they're supposed to abandon all caution, embrace the moment, be true to Life, run through the park, sing songs, cluck at swans, blow dandelion pods, and in general flout convention. *Fools* is a movie like that.

Jason Robards once again plays the fiftyish Free Spirit with a feather in his hat and spring in his step. He falls in love with Katharine Ross, who has been repressed by her rich, constipated husband, the most successful young lawyer in San Francisco despite the fact that he is a paranoid closet queen with a nasty homicidal streak and a Napoleonic fixation, and likes to play with guns. He's the kind of lawyer that ambulances chase.

Okay, so Jason and Katharine fall in love. They are then set upon by cops, the FBI, the San Francisco pornography epidemic, neon signs, smog, hate, bigotry, exhibitionists, fierce dogs, and freeways. That's what the middle part of the film is about: how people can't be in love because of our materialistic, capitalist, fascist society, which invades privacy and is not, ever, tender. Then at the movie's end Katharine runs into a church during a baptism and is shot dead by her husband, who drives off in his Rolls-Royce.

By now you should be getting the idea that *Fools* is the most cynically "idealistic" exploitation movie in some time. It is for life and love, against fascism and firearms in private hands. It also has countless songs trying to out-banal each other during at least seven Semi-Obligatory Lyrical Interludes. *Fools* sets a new Semi-OLI ground speed record. When in doubt, throw in a song and a sunset. Right?

On top of all this, we get dialogue so inept that I will provide a free ticket to *The Vengeance of She* (the next time it plays town) to the first person who can convince me that any two English-speaking human beings ever talked remotely like these characters at any time during the present century. I commend the dialogue, however, to local comedy groups getting up satires on love, if the satires don't have to be too good.

The only mystery about *Fools* is how Tom Gries could have directed it. He is the tasteful director of *Will Penny,* where the situation and dialogue rang absolutely true, and he demonstrated a genuine narrative gift in *The Hawaiians.* Now we get *Fools.* How?

Henri Bollinger, the film's coproducer, was in town last week for interviews. I declined the opportunity, to save embarrassment all around, but he telephoned me to explain that the film had been made with "absolute sincerity" and the "best intentions." Could be. Nobody sets out deliberately to make a bad film. When I gently suggested to Bollinger that his film was the worst of the year, he gently suggested back that since I was obviously "violently prejudiced" against it, the *Sun-Times* should provide "the other side." I demurred. I said my judgment was sober, impartial, and fair: *Fools* stinks.

Forces of Nature

(Directed by Bronwen Hughes; starring Sandra Bullock, Ben Affleck; 1999)
So I'm sitting there, looking in disbelief at the ending of *Forces of Nature,* and asking myself—if this is how the movie ends, *then what was it about?* We spend two endless hours slogging through a series of natural and man-made disasters with Sandra Bullock and Ben Affleck, and then . . . that's it?

Bronwen Hughes's *Forces of Nature* is a romantic shaggy dog story, a movie that leads us down the garden path of romance, only to abandon us by the compost heap of uplifting endings. And it's not even clever enough to give us the right happy ending. It gives us the *wrong* happy ending.

By then, of course, any ending is good news. The movie is a dead zone of boring conversations, contrived emergencies, unbelievable characters, and lame storytelling. Even then it might have worked at times if it had generated the slightest chemistry between Ben Affleck and Sandra Bullock, but it doesn't. She remains winsome and fetching, but he acts like he's chaperoning his best friend's sister, as a favor.

The movie combines at least five formulas, and probably more: The Meet Cute, the Road Movie, the Odd Couple, Opposites Attract, and Getting to Know Yourself. It also cuts back and forth between a journey and the preparations for a marriage, and it tries to keep two sets of parents in play. With so much happening it's surprising that the movie finds a way to be boring, but it does, by cross-cutting between one leaden scene and another.

Affleck stars as an ad man who is flying from New York to Savannah, Georgia, for his wedding. On the plane, he's strapped in next to Bullock, who has held a lot of jobs in her time: flight attendant, wedding photographer, exotic dancer, auto show hostess. The flight crashes on takeoff, and they end up driving to Georgia together, amid weather reports of an approaching hurricane.

Of course circumstances conspire to make him pretend to be a doctor, and them to pretend they're married, and a motel to put them in the same room, and his best man to see him with this strange woman even though he tries to hide by holding his breath in a swimming pool, and so on. Rarely does the artificial contrivance of a bad screenplay reveal itself so starkly on the screen. And when the contrivances stop the revelations begin, and we learn sad things about Bullock's past that feel exactly as if Marc Lawrence, the writer, supplied them at random.

They have a lot of adventures. Arrests, crashes, trees falling on their car, hospitalizations. They take a train for a while (standing on top of one of the cars in a shamelessly pandering shot). And they take a bus (with condo-shopping oldsters). And a Spinning Sombrero ride. At one point they both find themselves performing onstage in a strip club—not quite the kind of club you have in mind. This scene would seem to be foolproof comedy, but the timing is off and it sinks.

Despite my opening comments, I have not actually revealed the ending of the movie, and I won't, although I will express outrage about it. This movie hasn't paid enough dues to get away with such a smarmy payoff. I will say, however, that if the weatherman has been warning for three days that a hurricane is headed thisaway, and the skies are black and the wind is high and it's raining, few people in formal dress for a wedding would stand out in the yard while umbrellas, tables, and trees are flying past. And if they did, their hair would blow around a little, don't you think?

Friday the 13th, Part 2

(Directed by Steve Miner; starring Betsy Palmer, Amy Steel, John Furey; 1981)
I saw *Friday the 13th, Part 2* at the Virginia Theater, a former vaudeville house in my hometown of Champaign-Urbana, Illinois. The late show was half-filled with high school and college students, and as the lights went down I experienced a brief wave of nostalgia. In this very theater, on countless Friday nights, I'd gone with a date to the movies. My nostalgia lasted for the first two minutes of the movie.

The pretitle sequence showed one of the heroines of the original *Friday the 13th,* alone at home. She has nightmares, wakes up, undresses, is stalked by the camera, hears a noise in the kitchen. She tiptoes into the kitchen. Through the open window, a cat springs into the room. The audience screamed loudly and happily: It's fun to be scared. Then an unidentified man sunk an ice pick into the girl's brain, and, for me, the fun stopped.

The audience, however, carried on. It is a tradition to be loud during these movies, I guess. After a batch of young counselors turns up for training at a summer camp, a girl goes out walking alone at night. Everybody in the audience imitated hoot-owls and hyenas. Another girl went to her room and started to undress. Five guys sitting together started a chant: "We want boobs!"

The plot: In the original movie, a summer camp staff was wiped out by a demented woman whose son had been allowed to drown by incompetent camp counselors. At the end of that film, the mother was decapitated by the young woman who is killed with an ice pick at the beginning of *Part 2.* The legend grows that the son, Jason, did not really drown, but survived, and lurks in the woods waiting to take his vengeance against the killer of his mother . . . and against camp counselors in general, I guess.

That sets up the film. The counselors are introduced, very briefly, and then some of them go into town for a beer and the rest stay at the camp to have sex with each other. A mystery assailant prowls around the main cabin. We see only his shadow and his shoes. One by one, he picks off the kids. He sinks a machete into the brain of a kid in a wheelchair. He surprises a boy and a girl making love, and nails them to a bunk with a spear through both their bodies. When the other kids return to the camp, it's their turn. After almost everyone has been killed in a disgusting and violent way, one girl chews up the assailant with a chain saw, after which we discover the mummies in his cabin in the woods, after which he jumps through a window at the girl, etc.

This movie is a cross between the Mad Slasher and Dead Teenager genres; about two dozen movies a year feature a mad killer going berserk, and they're all about as bad as this one. Some have a little more plot, some have a little less. It doesn't matter.

Sinking into my seat in this movie theater from my childhood, I remembered the movie fantasies when I was a kid. They involved teenagers who fell in love, made out with each other, customized their cars, listened to rock and roll, and were rebels without causes. Neither the kids in those movies nor the kids watching them would have understood a worldview in which the primary function of teenagers is to be hacked to death.

Friends & Lovers

(Directed by George Haas; starring Stephen Baldwin, Claudia Schiffer, Robert Downey, Jr.; 1999)

I don't want to review *Friends & Lovers,* I want to flunk it. This movie is not merely bad, but incompetent. I get tapes in the mail from tenth graders that are better made than this.

Last week I hosted the first Overlooked Film Festival at the University of Illinois, for films that have been unfairly overlooked. If I ever do a festival of films that deserve to be overlooked, here is my opening-night selection. The only possible explanation for the film being released is that there are stars in the cast (Stephen Baldwin, Claudia Schiffer, Alison Eastwood, Robert Downey, Jr.). They should speak sternly with their agents.

The story involves a group of friends spending the holidays in a Park City ski chalet. They're involved in what an adolescent might think were adult relationships. Much time is spent in meaningless small talk. We also get the ultimate sign of writer desperation: characters introducing themselves to each other.

If I were marking this as a paper, I would note:

- Director George Haas often lines up actors so they awkwardly face the camera, and have to talk sideways to one another.
- Much of the dialogue is handled by cutting to each character as he speaks. This is jarring because it reveals that the movie knows when each character will speak. Professional movies overlap sound and image, so that dialogue begins offscreen, before a cut to the speaker.
- The characters frequently propose toasts, as if the movie is a social occasion.
- Pregnant girl looks like she has a pillow stuffed down her dress. Self-consciously holds her belly with both hands in many scenes.
- Dad puts tin can in microwave. Can explodes, and whole chalet is plunged into darkness. I am not surprised that a character in this movie would be stupid enough to microwave an unopened can, but why would the explosion blow every fuse?
- Characters gossip that one character has a big penis. Everyone strips for the Jacuzzi. Movie supplies close-up of penis. Since this is the first nudity of any kind in the movie, audience is jolted. In a light comedy, a close-up of a penis strikes a jarring note. An amazed reaction shot might help, but represents a level of sophistication beyond the reach of this film.
- The general preoccupation with sex and size reminds me of conversations I had when I was eleven. One guy says a female character has two-inch nipples. No one questions this theory. I say two-inch nipples are extremely rare among bipeds.
- Dad says, "My generation thought that working was the best way to support a family." Dad doesn't even know what generation he belongs to. Dad is in his fifties, so is a member of the sixties generation. He is thinking of his parents' generation.

- All dialogue on ski slopes involves ludicrous echoing effects. Yes, a yodel will echo in the Alps. No, conversational levels will not echo in Utah.
- David seems to be a virgin. Friend asks: "You have never done the dirty deed?" David asks, "How exactly would you define that?" Friend makes circle with thumb and finger, sticks another finger through it. Most twenty-something movie characters have advanced beyond this stage.
- Automobile scenes are inept. One "crash" is obviously faked to avoid damaging either vehicle. In a scene that cuts between girl walking by road while a guy drives beside her and talks through open window, the girl is walking at a slower rate of speed than car.

I have often asked myself, "What would it look like if the characters in a movie were animatronic puppets created by aliens with an imperfect mastery of human behavior?" Now I know.

Frogs for Snakes

(Directed by Amos Poe; starring Barbara Hershey, Harry Hamlin; 1999)
Amos Poe's *Frogs for Snakes* is not a film so much as a filmed idea. That could be interesting, but alas, it is a very bad idea. The film is about a group of Manhattan actors who support themselves between roles by working as gangsters and hit men, and as the film opens they turn their guns on one another. This is a movie that gives new meaning to the notion of being willing to kill for a role.

Barbara Hershey stars, as a waitress and debt collector who used to be married to crime kingpin Al (Robbie Coltrane), who doubles as a theater producer and is preparing a production of Mamet's *American Buffalo*. She and several other characters spend much of their time hanging out in a diner and talking about absent friends. So much time is spent in the diner, indeed, that *Frogs for Snakes* begins to resemble a one-set play, until there are excursions to pool halls, apartments and even a theater.

Sample dialogue, from a pool hall:

"What are you doing here?"

"We heard you were doing *True West*."

"Well, you heard wrong. We're doing *American Buffalo*."

[Shoots him]

Not a single one of the characters is even slightly convincing as anything other than an artificial theatrical construction. Is that the point? I haven't a clue. Much of their dialogue is lifted intact from other movies, sometimes inappropriately. Lisa Marie plays a buxom sex bomb who recites Harry Lime's speech about cuckoo clocks from *The Third Man*. Other speeches come from *Night and the City, Sex, Drugs and Rock and Roll, The Hustler, The Apartment, Repo Man, I Am a Fugitive from a Chain Gang,* and several more. (The film ends by crediting the screenplays, just as most films end with a scroll of the songs on the sound track.)

"Today they write dialogue about cheeseburgers and big special effects," one of the characters says, contrasting the quoted classics with *Pulp Fiction*. Yes, but Tarantino's cheeseburger dialogue is wonderful comic writing, with an evil undercurrent as the hit men talk while approaching a dangerous meeting; no dialogue in this movie tries anything a fraction as ambitious, or risks anything.

Seeing the cast of familiar actors (not only Hershey and Robertson but Harry Hamlin, Ian Hart, Debi Mazar, John Leguizamo, and Ron Perlman), I was reminded of *Mad Dog Time* (1996), another movie in which well-known actors engaged in laughable dialogue while shooting one another. Of that one, I wrote: "*Mad Dog Time* is the first movie I have seen that does not improve on the sight of a blank screen viewed for the same length of time." Now comes *Frogs for Snakes,* the first movie I have seen that does not improve on the sight of *Mad Dog Time*.

Frozen Assets
(Directed by George Miller; starring Shelley Long, Corbin Bernsen, Dody Goodman; 1992)

I didn't feel like a viewer during *Frozen Assets*. I felt like an eyewitness at a disaster. If I were more of a hero, I would spend the next couple of weeks breaking into theaters where this movie is being shown, and leading the audience to safety. And if I'd been an actor in the film, I would wonder why all of the characters in *Frozen Assets* seem dumber than the average roadkill.

This is a comedy (not the right word) about a business executive (Corbin Bernsen) whose corporation sends him to a small town to run the bank. Only when he gets there does he discover it's a sperm bank. Ho, ho. In the lobby, he meets a customer (Paul Sand) and their conversation goes like this:

Sand: "I've been making two deposits a week for the last seven years. I keep a lot on hand in case of an emergency."

Bernsen: "That's a smart move for the small depositor."

"Well, it's not that small."

"A jumbo, huh? My door is open if you need a hand."

Ho, ho, ho. Bernsen quickly (well, not that quickly) discovers his error, after meeting Shelley Long, who plays the nurse at the sperm bank. Among other local denizens is a strange young man named Newton (Larry Miller), who seems seriously troubled, and lives at home (in the local castle) with his mother (Dody Goodman). He invites Bernsen over to dinner and Bernsen ends up bunking with him, in the twin bed in Newton's bedroom.

Meanwhile, the sperm count rises. The town's population includes a large number of hookers and the usual assortment of salt-of-the-earth types, who rise, in various ways, to the challenge when the sperm bank gets an emergency order for 10,000 donations. How to inspire the laggard population to such an effort? Bernsen dreams up a big lottery with a $100,000 prize, and the local males line up to take their chances, while we get lots of condom jokes.

And so on. This movie is seriously bad, but what puzzles me is its tone. This is essentially a children's movie with a dirty mind. No adult could possibly enjoy a single frame of the film—it's pitched at the level of a knock-knock joke—and yet what child could enjoy, or understand, all the double entendres about sperm, and what goes into its production? This movie, as nearly as I can tell, was not made with any possible audience in mind.

Movies like *Frozen Assets* are small miracles. You look at them and wonder how, at any stage of the production, anyone could have thought there was a watchable movie here. Did the director find it funny? Did the actors know they were doomed? Here is a movie to watch in appalled silence.

GGGGG**G**GGGGG

Gator

Directed by Burt Reynolds; starring Burt Reynolds, Jack Weston, Lauren Hutton; 1976)

Gator is yet another Good Ol' Movie, and not, I fear, the summer's last. It stars that archetypal Good Ol' Boy himself, Burt Reynolds, along with Lauren Hutton, who is a plenty good enough Good Ol' Girl for me, and Jack Weston, who plays a Good Ol' New York cop. If only it had a Good Ol' Plot worth a damn, it might have even been a halfway tolerable ol' movie.

But it never quite connects, even though a summary of its key scenes is like a laundry list of action-'n'-romance clichés. It contains (a) a chase through the mango swamps featuring boats and a helicopter; (b) several chases through town in which the hapless cops once again get their own squad car stolen from them; (c) our ol' friend the Semi-Obligatory Lyrical Interlude, in which Lauren Hutton and Burt Reynolds snuggle up real close and then run on the beach; (d) one tearful parting and one tearful reunion, and (e) a colorful villain with a weirdo sidekick.

The villain is Jerry Reed, the country-and-western singer, who runs a protection racket and has the whole county in his back pocket. He looks mean enough to chew up Waylon Jennings and spit him out, and that ain't nothing compared to his sidekick.

The sidekick is named Bones and is played by a man named William Engesser, who looks as if all his width went into height. He's so tall that he has to drive a car with a sunroof, so he can roll back the sunroof and sit with his head sticking through the top of the car. At chase speeds, he no doubt gets a lot of bugs in his teeth, and he has to watch the clearance in parking garages. "Tell 'em why they call you Bones, Bones," says Jerry Reed. "Cause I tell 'em to," Bones explains.

Reynolds plays a two-time loser who joins forces with the law so that his Pappy won't have to go on welfare and his darlin' little nine-year-old daughter won't be shipped to a foster home. He's teamed up with Weston, the New York cop, who is supposed to be undercover but sticks out, as Reynolds observes, like a bagel in a bowl of grits. Not too many Good Ol' Boys have ever heard of bagels, but Reynolds has spent a lot of time on talk shows and has picked up cross-cultural references.

Anyway, Reynolds and Weston go after Jerry Reed and Bones, and there is a lot of scheming, especially after Reed signs up Reynolds as his bagman. Along the way, Reynolds falls for Lauren Hutton, a local TV reporter. (They fall in love in a cinematic tribute to the biggest 1940s romantic cliché: Their eyes meet and lock, they exchange tremulous close-ups, the background dialogue fades away, music plays.)

After a number of scenes in which violence is alternated in baffling fashion with in-jokes, love, down-home wit, pathos, slapstick, chases, desperation, arson, relief, murder, intrigue, and tears, retribution is achieved and the remaining relationships brought to bittersweet conclusions while Bobby Goldsboro sings "For a Little While." This is a movie, you might say, that was intended to have something for everyone. I'm sometimes accused of giving away the endings; I'm afraid that's the only way they'll get rid of the one in *Gator.*

The Ghost and the Darkness
(Directed by Stephen Hopkins; starring Val Kilmer, Michael Douglas; 1996)
The Ghost and the Darkness is an African adventure that makes the Tarzan movies look subtle and realistic. It lacks even the usual charm of being so bad it's funny. It's just bad. Not funny. No, wait . . . there is one funny moment. A bridge builder takes leave of his pregnant wife to go to Africa to build a bridge, and she solemnly observes, "You must go where the rivers are."

The bridge man, named Patterson, is played by Val Kilmer in a trim modern haircut that never grows an inch during his weeks in the bush. He is soon joined by a great white hunter named Remington (Michael Douglas), whose appearance is that of a homeless man who has somehow got his hands on a rifle. If this were a comic strip, there would be flies buzzing around his head.

The men meet up in Uganda, where a big push is on to complete a railroad faster than the Germans or the French. The owner of the rail company is a gruff tycoon who boasts, "I'm a monster. My only pleasure is tormenting those people who work for me." He is too modest. He also torments those who watch this movie.

Work on the railroad bridge is interrupted by a lion attack. Patterson spends the night in a tree and kills the lion. There is much rejoicing. Then another lion attacks. Eventually it becomes clear that two lions are on the prowl. They are devilishly clever, dragging men from their cots and even invading a hospital to chew on malaria patients. "Maneaters are always old, and alone, but not these two," Remington intones solemnly.

The rest of the movie consists of Patterson and Remington sitting up all night trying to shoot the lions, while the lions continue their attacks. At the end we learn that these two lions killed 135 victims in nine months. The movie only makes it seem like there were more, over a longer period.

Many scenes are so inept as to beggar description. Some of the lion attacks seem to have been staged by telling the actors to scream while a lion rug was waved in front of the camera. Patterson eventually builds a flimsy platform in a clearing, tethers a babboon at its base, and waits for the lions. Balanced on a wooden beam, he looks this way. Then that. Then this. Then that. A competent editor would have known that all this shifting back and forth was becoming distracting. Then a big bird flies at him and knocks him off the beam, and right into a lion's path. Lesson number one in lion hunting: Don't let a big bird knock you into the path of a lion.

A narrator at the beginning of the film has informed us, "This is a story of death and mystery." The mystery is why these particular lions behaved as they did. I don't see why it's a mystery. They had reasons anyone can identify with. They found something they were good at, and grew to enjoy it. The only mystery is why the screenwriter, William Goldmen, has them kill off the two most interesting characters so quickly. (They are Angus, the chatty man on the spot, and an African with a magnificently chiseled and stern face.)

In the old days this movie would have starred Stewart Granger and Trevor Howard, and they would have known it was bad but they would have seemed at home in it, cleaning their rifles and chugging their gin like seasoned bwanas. Val Kilmer and Michael Douglas never for a second look like anything other than thoroughly unhappy movie stars stuck in a humid climate and a doomed production. I hope someone made a documentary about the making of this film. Now *that* would be a movie worth seeing.

God Told Me To

(Directed by Larry Cohen; starring Tony LoBianco, Sandy Dennis, Sylvia Stanley; 1976)

I wasn't going to see *God Told Me To*—God, indeed, seemed to be telling me not to—but then I read the press release and knew immediately this was a movie I had to see. It had been too long, I decided, since I'd seen a film in which the leading character was, and I quote, "the only man alive who can make the choice to help or destroy a mysterious force which has begun to unleash its dread power upon the earth." Not since *Godzilla vs. the Smog Monster* had a press release promised so much.

The movie, alas, doesn't quite live up to the billing. It never even quite identifies the Dread Power, although from the brief glimpses I got of it, it seemed to be a hippie who glowed yellow. But the movie does achieve greatness in another way: This is the most confused feature-length film I've ever seen.

There were times when I thought the projectionist was showing the reels in random order, as a quiet joke on the hapless audience. But, no, apparently the movie *was* supposed to be put together this way, as a sort of fifty-two-card pickup of cinema. The story's so random, indeed, that by the time Sandy Dennis made her second appearance, I'd forgotten she was in the film.

The plot concerns a New York detective (Tony LoBianco) who investigates a series of murders in which the killers claimed God told them to kill. It turns out they're under the hypnotic sway of the child of visitors from outer space. LoBianco's assignment, if he chooses to accept it: Help or destroy this mysterious force that has begun to unleash its dread power, etc.

As I left the theater, dazed, I saw a crowd across the street. A young man in a straitjacket (try not to get ahead of the story, please) was preparing to be suspended in midair hundreds of inches above the ground, and to escape, Houdini style. At the moment he was still standing on the sidewalk—but, believe me, it was still a better show.

Godzilla

Directed by Roland Emmerich; starring Matthew Broderick,
Hank Azaria; 1998)

Cannes, France—Going to see *Godzilla* at the Palais of the Cannes Film Festival is like attending a satanic ritual in St. Peter's basilica. It's a rebuke to the
faith that the building represents. Cannes touchingly adheres to a belief that
film can be intelligent, moving, and grand. *Godzilla* is a big, ugly, ungainly
device to give teenagers the impression they are seeing a movie. It was the
festival's closing film, coming at the end like the horses in a parade, perhaps
for the same reason.

It rains all through *Godzilla,* and it's usually night. Well, of course it is:
That makes the special effects easier to obscure. If you never get a clear look
at the monster, you can't see how shoddy it is. Steven Spielberg opened
Jurassic Park by giving us a good, long look at the dinosaurs in full sunlight,
and our imaginations leapt up. *Godzilla* hops out of sight like a camera-shy
kangaroo.

The makers of the film, director Roland Emmerich and writer Dean
Devlin, follow the timeless outlines of many other movies about Godzilla,
Rodan, Mothra, Gamera, and their radioactive kin. There are ominous attacks
on ships at sea, alarming blips on radar screens, and a scientist who speculates that nuclear tests may have spawned a mutant creature. A cast of stereotyped stock characters is introduced and made to say lines like, "I don't
understand—how could something so big just disappear?" Or, "Many people
have had their lives changed forever!" And then there are the big special-
effects sequences, as Godzilla terrorizes New York.

One must carefully repress intelligent thought while watching such a film.
The movie makes no sense at all except as a careless pastiche of its betters
(and, yes, the Japanese Godzilla movies are, in their way, better—if only because they embrace dreck instead of condescending to it). You have to absorb
such a film, not consider it. But my brain rebelled, and insisted on applying
logic where it was not welcome.

How, for example, does a 300-foot-tall creature fit inside a subway tunnel? How come it's sometimes only as tall as the tunnel, and at other times
taller than high-rise office buildings? How big is it, anyway? Why can it
breathe fire but hardly ever makes use of this ability? Why, when the heroes
hide inside the Park Avenue tunnel, is this tunnel too small for Godzilla to

enter, even though it is larger than a subway tunnel? And why doesn't Godzilla just snort some flames down there and broil them?

Most monster movies have at least one bleeding-heart environmentalist to argue the case of the monstrous beast, but here we get only Niko Tatopoulos (Matthew Broderick), an expert on the mutant earthworms of Chernobyl, who seems less like a scientist than like a placeholder waiting for a rewrite ("insert more interesting character here"). It is he who intuits that Godzilla is a female. (You would think that if a 300-foot monster were male, that would be hard to miss, but never mind.) The military in all movies about monsters and aliens from outer space always automatically attempts to kill them, and here they fire lots of wimpy missiles and torpedoes at Godzilla, which have so little effect we wonder how our tax dollars are being spent. (Just once, I'd like a movie where they train Godzilla to do useful tasks, like pulling a coaxial cable across the ocean floor, or pushing stuck trains out of tunnels.)

In addition to the trigger-happy Americans there is a French force, too, led by Jean Reno, a good actor who plays this role as if he got on the plane shouting "I'm going to Disneyland!" All humans in monster movies have simpleminded little character traits, and Reno's obsession is with getting a decent cup of coffee. Other characters include a TV newswoman (Maria Pitillo) who used to be the worm man's girlfriend, a determined cameraman (Hank Azaria), a grim-jawed military leader (Kevin Dunn), and a simpering anchorman (Harry Shearer). None of these characters emerges as anything more than a source of obligatory dialogue.

Oh, and then there are New York's Mayor Ebert (gamely played by Michael Lerner) and his adviser, Gene (Lorry Goldman). The mayor of course makes every possible wrong decision (he is against evacuating Manhattan, etc.), and the adviser eventually gives thumbs-down to his reelection campaign. These characters are a reaction by Emmerich and Devlin to negative Siskel and Ebert reviews of their earlier movies *(Stargate, Independence Day)*, but they let us off lightly; I fully expected to be squished like a bug by Godzilla. Now that I've inspired a character in a Godzilla movie, all I really still desire is for several Ingmar Bergman characters to sit in a circle and read my reviews to one another in hushed tones.

There is a way to make material like *Godzilla* work. It can be campy fun, like the recent *Gamera, Guardian of the Universe.* Or hallucinatory, like *Infra-Man.* Or awesome, like *Jurassic Park.* Or it can tap a certain elemental dread, like the original *King Kong.* But all of those approaches demand a certain sympathy with the material, a zest that rises to the occasion.

In Howard Hawks's *The Thing,* there is a great scene where scientists in the Arctic spread out to trace the outlines of something mysterious that is buried in the ice, and the camera slowly pulls back to reveal that it is circular—a saucer. In *Godzilla,* the worm expert is standing in a deep depression, and the camera pulls back to reveal that he is standing in a footprint—which he would obviously have already known. There might be a way to reveal the astonishing footprint to the character and the audience at the same time, but that would involve a sense of style and timing, and some thought about the function of the scene.

There is nothing wrong with making a Godzilla movie, and nothing wrong with special effects. But don't the filmmakers have some obligation to provide pop entertainment that at least lifts the spirits? There is real feeling in King Kong fighting off the planes that attack him, or the pathos of the monster in *Bride of Frankenstein,* who was so misunderstood. There is a true sense of wonder in *Jurassic Park.*

Godzilla, by contrast, offers nothing but soulless technique: A big lizard is created by special effects, wreaks havoc, and is destroyed. What a cold-hearted, mechanistic vision, so starved for emotion or wit. The primary audience for *Godzilla* is children and teenagers, and the filmmakers have given them a sterile exercise when they hunger for dreams.

The Good Son
(Directed by Joseph Ruben; starring Macaulay Culkin, Elijah Wood; 1993)
Who in the world would want to see this movie? Watching *The Good Son,* I asked myself that question, hoping that perhaps the next scene would contain the answer, although it never did. The movie is a creepy, unpleasant experience, made all the worse because it stars children too young to understand the horrible things we see them doing.

The story begins with the death of the hero's mother. His father needs to go to Japan urgently on business, and so young Mark (Elijah Wood) goes to spend a couple of weeks with his aunt and uncle's family in Maine. They've had tragedy, too: A baby boy drowned in his bath some time ago. Now young

Henry (Macaulay Culkin) has the house all to himself—except for his sister, who may not last long.

The two boys seem to be about nine or ten. They are allowed to roam freely all over the island, which seems to be have been designed as a series of death traps for kids. Mark almost falls out of a towering tree house, and then, led by Henry, stands on the edges of cliffs, walks around the rim of a deep well, runs down the railroad tracks, and eventually watches with horror as Henry kills a dog and later causes a highway crash by dropping a human form off a bridge.

This is a very evil little boy; the movie could have been called *Henry, Portrait of a Future Serial Killer.* But what rings false is that the Macaulay Culkin character isn't really a little boy at all. His speech is much too sophisticated and ironic for that, and so is his reasoning and his cleverness. He would be more frightening, perhaps, if he did seem young and naive. This way, he seems more like a distasteful device by the filmmakers, who apparently think there is a market for glib one-liners by child sadists.

Young Mark quickly realizes how evil Henry is, but no one will listen to him—not his uncle, not his aunt, not even the friendly local child psychiatrist. Everything leads up to a cliff-hanging climax that somehow manages to be unconvincing, contrived, meretricious, and manipulative, all at once. I don't know when I've disliked the ending of a movie more.

The screenplay is by Ian McEwan, that British master of the macabre (*The Comfort of Strangers* was based on one of his novels). But don't blame him. He has already published an article in a London newspaper complaining that once the Culkin family came aboard the movie, the original screenplay was the last of anyone's considerations. The story was shaped to fit Macaulay, he charges. Strange. You'd imagine that the tyke's parents and managers would have paid good money to keep him out of this story.

One of the reasons the movie feels so unwholesome is that Macaulay seems too young and innocent to play a character this malevolent. At times, hearing the things he's made to say, you want to confront the filmmakers who made him do it, and ask them what they were thinking of.

For that matter, what were Culkin's parents thinking of when they pushed him into a movie where he drowns his baby brother, tries to drown his little sister, and wants to push his mother off a cliff? If this kid grows up into another one of those pathetic, screwed-up former child stars who are always spilling their guts on the talk shows, a lot of adults will share the blame.

The movie is rated "R." Market surveys indicate that kids want to see it, probably because it stars their *Home Alone* hero. This is not a suitable film for young viewers. I don't care how many parents and adult guardians they surround themselves with. And somewhere along the line, a parent or adult guardian should have kept Macaulay out of it, too.

The Good Wife

(Directed by Ken Cameron; starring Rachel Ward, Sam Neill; 1987)

It gets lonely out there in the country. Sometimes it gets so lonely a woman just doesn't know what to do. "I just wish something would happen to me," Marge complains to her husband. "Anything." But it always seems like things happen to someone else. Just this morning, for example, she assisted in the delivery of a child. Tonight she will go to bed with her brother-in-law. You see how it is.

The Good Wife is slow, solemn, and boring, and so I assume it is meant to be a serious study of Marge and her problems, recycled D. H. Lawrence, maybe. But this material is so dead that maybe having fun with it was the only hope; it needed a David Lynch or a John Cleese to make it work.

The movie stars Rachel Ward as Marge, the repressed young wife, and Bryan Brown as Sonny, her loving and long-suffering husband. They live on a farm in Australia where, as already noted, nothing much seems to happen, not even after Sugar, Sonny's brother, comes to live with them.

Sugar is a total loser who asks Marge if he can sleep with her. Marge advises him to ask her husband. The husband generously gives his permission, but about three seconds later Marge is more bored than ever, if you get what I mean. Meanwhile, the hotel in town hires a new bartender, a slick Clark Gable type played by Sam Neill.

Sexual conduct must have been more permissive in Australia in 1939 than it is these days. Neill gets off the train, sees Marge standing in the station, walks two blocks with her, shoves her up against a hedge, and sexually assaults her. She fights him off, and he says bitterly, "One chance is all you'll get with me."

Marge returns to her lonely farm and begins to develop an obsession about the bartender. She can think of nothing else. She goes into town and gets drunk and shouts lewd suggestions at him in front of the whole barroom. Her husband comes and takes her home in the truck. And so on.

There are some murky minor characters, such as Marge's sluttish mother, who are no doubt supposed to provide some psychological insights. But basically what we have here is a sad woman who is mentally ill, and a husband who is incredibly patient with her. Or, as the movie's press release phrases it, "She is bored, hot, and in trouble—a dangerous combination." Out in the audience, I was bored and hot, an even more dangerous combination.

Goodbye, Lover

(Directed by Roland Joffe; starring Patricia Arquette, Dermot Mulroney; 1999)
I've just transcribed no less than eleven pages of notes I scribbled during *Goodbye, Lover,* and my mind boggles. The plot is so labyrinthine that I'd completely forgotten the serial killer named The Doctor, who murders young women by injecting curare into their veins with a syringe. When a character like The Doctor is an insignificant supporting character, a movie's plate is a little too full, don't you think?

Goodbye, Lover is not so much a story as some kind of a board game, with too many pieces and not enough rules. The characters career through the requirements of the plot, which has so many double-reverses that the real danger isn't murder, it's being disemboweled by G-forces. There's no way to care about the characters, because their fates are arbitrary—determined not by character, not by personality, but by the jigsaw puzzle constructed by the screenwriters (there are three of them—which for this material represents a skeleton crew).

And yet the film does have a certain audacity. It contains a character played by Patricia Arquette who is the most enthusiastic sexual being since Emmanuelle, and another, played by Don Johnson, who just plain gets tuckered out by her demands. (At one point, they've taken the collection in church and are walking down the aisle with the offering, and she's whispering that he should meet her for sex tomorrow, or else.) There's also a droll supporting role for Ellen DeGeneres, as a police detective who keeps picking on her partner, a Mormon man who doesn't, I hope, understand most of her jokes. One of her key clues comes with the discovery of a *Sound of Music* tape, which arouses her suspicions: "I don't trust anybody over the age of ten who listens to *The Sound of Music.*"

The movie opens with phone sex and never looks back. We meet Sandra (Arquette), a Realtor who memorizes Tony Robbins self-help tapes, treasures *The Sound of Music* as her favorite movie, and likes to whisper, "I'm not wearing any underwear." She is having an affair with Ben (Johnson), and at one point handcuffs him with some sex toys she finds in a house she's selling. When the clients return unexpectedly, poor Ben barely has time to release himself and hide the cuffs in his pants pocket. (The Foley artists, concerned that we may have missed the point, cause the cuffs to rattle deafeningly, as if Ben had a tambourine concealed in his underwear.)

Sandra is married to Jake (Dermot Mulroney), who is Ben's brother. Ben is the straight arrow who runs an ad agency, and Jake is the unkempt alcoholic who nevertheless is a brilliant copywriter. Why is Sandra cheating on Jake? The answer is not only more complicated than you might think—it's not even the real answer. This is one of those plots where you might want to take a night school class about double-indemnity clauses in insurance policies before you even think about buying a ticket.

My space is limited, but I must also mention the GOP senator who is caught with a transvestite hustler; the struggle on the condo balcony; the motorcycle-car chase; the sex scene in a church's organ loft; the black leather mask; the Vegas wedding chapel ploy; Mike, the professional killer (not to be confused with The Doctor); and Peggy, Ben's secretary, who is played by Mary-Louise Parker as the kind of woman who would be a nymphomaniac in any other movie, but compared to Sandra is relatively abstentious.

There is a part of me that knows this movie is very, very bad. And another part of me that takes a guilty pleasure in it. Too bad I saw it at a critic's screening, where professional courtesy requires a certain decorum. This is the kind of movie that might be materially improved by frequent hoots of derision. All bad movies have good twins, and the good version of *Goodbye, Lover* is *The Hot Spot* (1990), which also starred Don Johnson, along with Virginia Madsen and Jennifer Connolly, in a thriller that was equally lurid but less hyperkinetic. *Goodbye, Lover* is so overwrought it reminds me of the limerick about that couple from Khartoum, who argued all night, about who had the right, to do what, and with which, and to whom.

The Guardian

(Directed by William Friedkin; starring Jenny Seagrove; 1990)

Of the many threats to modern man documented in horror films—the slashers, the haunters, the body snatchers—the most innocent would seem to be the Druids. What, after all, can a Druid really do to you, apart from dropping fast-food wrappers on the lawn while worshiping your trees?

That's what I would have said, anyway, until I saw *The Guardian,* a movie about a baby-sitter whose goal is to capture babies and embed them in a vast and towering old sacred druidical tree, which she appaently carts around with her from state to state and aeon to aeon.

The Druid, who is probably immortal but takes the human form of a foxy British governess, is played by Jenny Seagrove. Even the people who hire her observe that she's too pretty to be a governess. They are a Chicago couple (Dwier Brown and Carey Lowell) who move to Los Angeles after he gets a better job in the advertising business. A lot better: In Chicago they lived in a two-bedroom flat, but in L.A., despite the higher real estate prices, they're able to rent a house by a famous architect (Brad Hall), who even drops in personally to repair the doors. The house is right on the edge of one of those vast deep green forests that we all know are such a feature of Los Angeles topography.

The nanny brings good references with her, and has one of those British accents that costs a lot to acquire and maintain. She also knows a lot about children. She knows, for example, that after thirty days the "baby-cells" in the bloodstream are replaced by grown-up cells. This seems to be particularly important to her.

Having established these facts, *The Guardian* then bolts headlong into the thickets of standard horror film clichés: Ominous music, curtains blowing in the wind, empty baby cribs, dire warnings from strange women, manifestations of savage canines, and the lot. The architect comes to a gruesome end, the husband suspects the nanny's vile scheme, and about the only original touch in the movie is that, for the first time in horror film history, a chain saw is used against its intended target, a tree.

The Guardian was directed by William Friedkin, sometimes a great film-maker *(The Exorcist, The French Connection).* His most recent previous film, based on a true crime case, was named *Rampage* and was not even properly released. I saw it and admired it. Now this. Maybe after years of banging his head against the system Friedkin decided with *The Guardian* to make a frankly commercial exploitation film. On the level of special effects and photography, *The Guardian* is indeed well made. But give us a break.

Gunmen

(Directed by Deran Sarafian; starring Christopher Lambert, Mario Van Peebles, Patrick Stewart; 1994)

The opening sequence of *Gunmen* begins with a shot of a sweaty, unshaven face with a fly crawling upon it. Not long after, a prisoner is astonished when the wall of his cell is blown away and he is beckoned to freedom by a man standing outside. Both of these visuals are recycled from famous spaghetti Westerns.

This is a bad omen. Most directors have at least one or two original ideas when they start a film, and they tend to put them right at the beginning, as audience grabbers. When Deran Sarafian borrows well known ideas from famous movies right at the get-go, it doesn't bode well for what's to follow. Nor should it.

Gunmen is a movie without plan, inspiration, or originality—and to that list I would add coherence, except that I am not sure this movie would place much value on a plot that hangs together. The film's ambitions are simple: To give us a lot of action, a lot of violence, a few ironic lines of dialogue, and some very familiar characters. To call the characters in *Gunmen* clichés would be a kindness; my notion is that they've been wandering in actionpic cyberspace for years, occasionally surfacing in our dimension as B-movie heroes.

The movie stars Christopher Lambert (he eats the fly in the opening scene) and Mario Van Peebles, in a murky tale of drugs and revenge south of the border. Van Peebles plays Cole, a New York–based drug enforcement agent, who is in an unnamed South American country to mop up illegal drug profits and avenge his father's death. Lambert plays Servigo, a drug runner who may have information that can help him.

The idea is that these two men will have a love-hate relationship throughout the movie, and we will find it amusing. I can't argue with the first half of the idea. In one of the movie's less plausible developments, they actually shoot each other in the leg, and then we get allegedly hilarious scenes in which they limp in unison. Anyone who has ever been shot in the leg and tried to walk immediately afterward was not hired as the technical consultant on this movie.

The dialogue is hard to describe. Imagine the worst spaghetti Western you ever saw, shot in Italian and then dubbed into English by actors familiar only with the most basic movie clichés. Now imagine a film shot in English in which people talk the same way. You've got it. Then imagine them talking that way while inhabiting familiar moments from old movies. Not just the scenes I've already mentioned, but the jump off the cliff from *Butch Cassidy and the Sundance Kid* and the gag about being handcuffed together from *The Defiant Ones,* among many other films.

Several years ago, in *Ebert's Little Glossary of Movie Terms,* I first formulated the Cole Rule. This is the motion picture production rule that states: *No movie made since 1977 containing a character with the first name "Cole" has been any good.* There may, of course, be exceptions to that rule. *Gunmen* is not one of them.

Guyana—Cult of the Damned
(Directed by Rene Cardona, Jr.; starring Stuart Whitman, Gene Barry, Joseph Cotten; 1980)

Guyana—Cult of the Damned has crawled out from under a rock and into local theaters, and will do nicely as this week's example of the depths to which people will plunge in search of a dollar. The movie is a gruesome version of the Jonestown massacre of 1978, so badly written and directed it illustrates a simple rule of movie exhibition: If a film is nauseating and reprehensible enough in the first place, it doesn't matter how badly it's made—people will go anyway.

The film was produced, directed, and cowritten by one Rene Cardona, Jr., whose credits in the movie's press release portray him as a ghoulish retailer of human misery. He is the producer of *Survival,* about the cannibalism of the Andes survivors, and of *The Bermuda Triangle,* and now of the disquieting story of the Guyana massacre. "At least fifteen film producers went after the story," the release says, "but Cardona got there first."

Good old Cardona. He got there first with a film that mixes fact, fiction, and speculation with complete indifference, and that contains an amazing absence of any real curiosity about the bizarre deaths in Jonestown. It presents them as a horror story, but it doesn't really probe for reasons or motivations.

"This story is true," we're promised at the outset. "Only the names have been changed." The story may be true, but the research sure isn't original; the screenplay seems to have been written at typing speed and based on wire service stories of the massacre. The movie's held together with a voice-over narration (handy if you're planning to dub into several languages), and the characters are almost always seen from the outside: We get no scenes attempting to probe the personalities of the cult members.

Instead, there are lots of sermons in which Stuart Whitman, as "Reverend James Johnson," seems to be trying to cross Hitler with Elmer Gantry, as he exhorts his cult members to follow him from San Francisco to Guyana—and to permit his dictatorship there. Whitman plays the cult leader as so rabid and fanatic—such a complete bad guy—that it's difficult to believe anyone would have followed him anywhere. Surely the real Jim Jones must have been somewhat more charismatic?

The scenes in Guyana show crowds of extras herded here and there in the jungle camp and forced to listen to more fanatic sermons. For variety, we get scenes showing cult members being publicly humiliated and tortured; one scene involves electric shocks to the genitals of a young boy. Meanwhile, the narrator introduces such supporting characters as Whitman's mistress (Jennifer Ashley), public relations expert (Yvonne De Carlo), and lawyer (Joseph Cotten). They all appear in a few scenes, look thoroughly ill at ease and embarrassed, and are dispensed with.

During all the garbage that precedes it, we're waiting uncomfortably for the film's climax, the massacre with the cyanide in the soft drink. The movie spares no details. The cult members line up and drink their poison or have it forced down their throats, and then they stagger around, clutch their stomachs, and scream in pain. Later, the film shows actual photographs of the real victims, while we are solemnly reminded that "those who forget the past are condemned to repeat it." So remember: Don't drink cyanide.

All of this is disgusting, and all of it is sad. Why did a reputable studio (Universal) pick up this vile garbage for national release? Because there is money to be made from it, I suppose. The movie brings absolutely no insights to Guyana. It exploits human suffering for profit. It is a geek show. Universal and its exhibitors should be ashamed.

Gymkata

(Directed by Robert Clouse; starring Kurt Thomas, Richard Norton; 1985)
I'm not sure *Gymkata* is the movie it was intended to be—not if they intended to make a straightforward action picture. You know you're in trouble when you get to the big scene and the audience is supposed to scream and it laughs. This is one of the most ridiculous movies I've seen in a while, but make of this what you will: I heard more genuine laughter during the screening than at three or four so-called comedies I've seen lately. I was even toying with praising the movie as a comedy, but I'm not sure the filmmakers would take that as a compliment.

The movie stars Kurt Thomas, in real life a world-champion gymnast, as a young man who is recruited by the U.S. government to break into the obscure Asian mountain kingdom of Parmistan and bring out his father, who is a captive there. Here's the catch: To enter Parmistan, all foreigners have to play The Game, which means running a deadly obstacle course. "In the last 900 years, no foreigner has survived The Game," the lad is informed ominously. In that case, how did the father get into Parmistan? Never mind. Logic will get you nowhere with this movie. That becomes apparent when we meet the Khan of Parmistan, who is played by Buck Kartalian as a cross between a used-car salesman and a counterman in a deli. This man is roughly as Asian as Groucho Marx. The Khan has a beautiful daughter (Tetchie Agbayani) who does indeed look Asian, and one of the several inexplicable lines of dialogue about her is, "Don't worry—her mother is Indonesian." What a relief.

The Kurt Thomas character meets the beautiful princess, who is to be his guide to Parmistan, and falls in love with her. Back in her native land, alas, she is engaged to marry the evil Zamir (Richard Norton), who is the Khan's chief henchman. Thomas is chased by various bands of thugs, and saves himself by using his gymnastic ability. For example, running down a narrow street, he spies a parallel bar between two buildings, starts swinging from it, and smashes the thugs with his deadly feet. Good thing that bar was there.

Halloween: H20

(Directed by Steve Miner; starring Jamie Lee Curtis; 1998)

Notes jotted down while watching *Halloween H20:*

• Medical science should study Michael Myers, the monster who has made the last two decades a living hell for Laurie Strode. Here is a man who feels no pain. He can take a licking and keep on slicing. In the latest *Halloween* movie he absorbs a blow from an ax, several knife slashes, a rock pounded on the skull, a fall down a steep hillside, and being crushed against a tree by a truck. Whatever he's got, mankind needs it.

• How does Michael Myers support himself in the long years between his slashing outbreaks? I picture him working in a fast-food joint. "He never had much to say, but boy, could he dice those onions!"

• I have often wondered why we hate mimes so much. Many people have such an irrational dislike for them that they will cross the street rather than watch some guy in whiteface pretending to sew his hands together. Examining Michael Myers's makeup in *Halloween H20,* I realized he looks so much like Marcel Marceau as to make no difference. Maybe he is a mime when he's not slashing. Maybe what drove him mad was years and years of trying to make a living in malls while little kids kicked him to see if he was real. This would also explain his ability to seem to walk while somehow staying in the same place.

• I happen to know Jamie Lee Curtis is one of the smartest people in Hollywood. I cannot wait for the chapter on horror movies in her autobiography.

• There is a scene in the movie where a kid drops a corkscrew down a garbage disposal. Then the camera goes *inside* the garbage disposal to watch while he fishes around for it. Then the camera cuts to the electric switch on the wall, which would turn the disposal on. I am thinking, if this kid doesn't lose his hand, I want my money back.

• Michael Myers may also have skills as an electrician. All of the lights and appliances in every structure in this movie go on or off whenever the plot requires him to. I can imagine Myers down in the basement by the fuse box, thinking, "Gotta slash somebody. But first . . . geez, whoever filled in the chart on the inside of this fuse box had lousy handwriting! I can't tell the garage door from the garbage disposal!"

• I think Jamie Lee Curtis shouts "Do as I say!" twice in the movie. I could be low by one.

• Yes, the movie contains the line "They never found a body."

• Michael Myers, described in the credits as "The Shape," is played by Chris Durand. There is hope. Steve McQueen started his career in (but not as) "The Blob."

• Half of the movie takes place in an exclusive private school, yet there is not a single shower scene.

• Speaking of shower scenes: Janet Leigh, Jamie Lee's mother, turns up in a cameo role here, and she started me thinking about what a rotten crock it is that they're remaking *Psycho.* I imagined Miss Leigh telling her friends, "They wanted me to do a cameo in the remake of *Psycho,* but I said, hell, I'd do *Halloween H20* before I'd lower myself to that."

Happy Gilmore
(Directed by Dennis Dugan; starring Adam Sandler, Carl Weathers; 1996)
Happy Gilmore tells the story of a violent sociopath. Since it's about golf, that makes it a comedy. The movie, the latest in the dumber and dumbest sweepstakes, stars Adam Sandler as a kid who only wants to play hockey. He hits the puck so hard he kills his father, who is in the act of filming a home movie. Actually, he kills his father's camera, but it's a small point.

Happy can't skate very well, and when he's not chosen for the hockey team, he beats up the coach. Life seems to hold no future for him. After his father's death he is taken in by his beloved grandmother (Francis Bay), and then a crisis strikes: The IRS seizes Grandma's house and possessions. How can Happy possibly earn $275,000 to pay all of the back taxes?

During a visit to a golf-driving range, he discovers a hidden talent. He can hit the ball hundreds of yards, straight as an arrow. He's taken under the arm of a veteran golf pro named Chubbs (Carl Weathers), who tries to teach him the game, but it's Happy's tendency to explode and pound his clubs into the ground when he misses a shot. (Chubbs retired from the Tour when a one-eyed alligator bit off his hand in a water trap; he is now forced to use a flimsy wooden hand, which he grasps with his real hand, which is clearly outlined beneath his shirt sleeve. No prizes for guessing that the alligator will turn up again.)

Happy's long game is great but his short game stinks. He goes on the Tour, where the defending champion, Shooter McGavin (Christopher McDonald), becomes his archenemy. They go mano á mano for weeks, in a series of golf scenes that are too heavy on golf for nongolfers, and too irrelevant to the ancient and honorable game for those who follow it. At a Pro-Am tourney, Happy teams up with Bob Barker, whose fight scene seems longer in the preview trailer than in the movie.

The Happy Gilmore character is very strange. I guess we are supposed to like him. He loves his old grandma, and wins the heart of a pretty P.R. lady (Julie Bowen), who tries to teach him to control his temper. Yet, as played by Sandler, he doesn't have a pleasing personality: He seems angry even when he's not supposed to be angry, and his habit of pounding everyone he dislikes is tiresome in a PG-13 movie. At one point, he even knocks the bottom off a beer bottle and goes for Shooter.

It was a Heineken's beer, I think. The label was a little torn. Maybe nobody paid for product placement. *Happy Gilmore* is filled with so many plugs it looks like a product placement sampler in search of a movie. I probably missed a few, but I counted Diet Pepsi, Pepsi, Pepsi Max, Subway sandwich shops, Budweiser (in bottles, cans, and Bud-dispensing helmets), Michelob, Visa cards, Bell Atlantic, AT&T, Sizzler, Wilson, *Golf Digest,* the ESPN sports network, and Top-Flite golf balls.

I'm sure some of those got in by accident (the modern golf tour has ads plastered on everything but the grass), but I'm fairly sure Subway paid for placement, since they scored one Subway sandwich eaten outside a store, one date in a Subway store, one Subway soft-drink container, two verbal mentions of Subway, one Subway commercial starring Happy, a Subway T-shirt, and a Subway golf bag. Halfway through the movie, I didn't know which I wanted more: laughs, or mustard.

The Happy Hooker
(Directed by Nicholas Sgarro; starring Lynn Redgrave,
Jean-Pierre Aumont; 1975)

If Horatio Alger were alive today, he would no doubt be appalled by *The Happy Hooker*, the story of a girl who gets started off on the right foot in life but, through pluck and endurance, makes bad. The movie's a success story in reverse, starting with its heroine being named Secretary of the Year in her native Holland and ending with her imprisonment in New York on charges of operating a disorderly house.

What all of this is supposed to prove is beyond me, unless it's that America is still the land of opportunity, until you get caught. The film's based on the autobiography of Xaviera Hollander, the former hooker who now writes a column for *Penthouse* in which readers can obtain the most astonishing advice about vacuum cleaners, household pets, and cold baths. I have no way of knowing if the book was based on fact—nor can the movie, being R-rated, give me many clues.

That's not to say I would have preferred an X-rated porno flick like *The Life and Times of Xaviera Hollander,* which opened here during the summer to little or no acclaim. No, I like the R rating for *The Happy Hooker.* It gives the movie a certain restraining charm. What was the last bordello epic you saw in which all the most interesting scenes were set in the parlor? The movie at times makes Miss Hollander's enterprise seem so wholesome, so much of a spirit with such other moneymakers as commodity futures and the franchising game, that it's a wonder the postal service hasn't commemorated the industry by now.

That's largely due to the charm of Lynn Redgrave, in the title role. Miss Redgrave is the distinguished British actress, daughter of Sir Michael, sister of Vanessa, who vowed when *The Happy Hooker* started filming that it would be a tasteful comedy and wouldn't embarrass the family. By and large, she's right. The movie's got a sort of innocence to it, and when Xaviera pedals between clients on her ten-speed bike she seems to be hooking just for the fresh air.

She's lured to New York in the first place by a marriage proposal, but the would-be suitor turns out to be a twerp, and she gets a job as a secretary and translator. In walks a Frenchman with a charming stutter (Jean-Pierre Aumont), and she falls for him. They indulge in unspecified offscreen bliss long enough for her to meet the Frenchman's friends, who include New York's top madam, and then the Frenchman exits after giving her a large envelope filled with currency.

He has, she announces tearfully, made her feel like a whore—but she counts the money and her tears dry. And from then until the final calamitous police raid (which is only revenge by a cop who tried and failed to rape her, you understand), Xaviera services a growing clientele of New York's top businessmen, opens her own brothel, and learns such profundities as that "all men are really little boys." The movie has a happy ending—she and her girls get out on bail—and all that's left for next time is a sequel showing her writing her magazine advice column. Maybe it could be called "Miss Lonelytarts."

Hard Rain
(Directed by Mikael Salomon; starring Morgan Freeman, Christian Slater; 1998)

Hard Rain is one of those movies that never convince you their stories are really happening. From beginning to end, I was acutely aware of actors being paid to stand in cold water. Suspension of my disbelief in this case would have required psychotropic medications.

Oh, the film is well made from a technical viewpoint. The opening shot is a humdinger, starting out with a vast floodplain, zooming above houses surrounded by water, and then ending with a close-up of a cop's narrowing eyes. But even then, I was trying to spot the effects—to catch how they created the flood effect, and how they got from the flood to the eyes.

Funny, how some movies will seduce you into their stories while others remain at arm's length. *Titanic* was just as artificial and effects driven as *Hard Rain,* and yet I was spellbound. Maybe it was because the people on the doomed ship had no choice: The *Titanic* was sinking, and that was that.

In *Hard Rain,* there is a bad guy (Morgan Freeman) who *has* a choice. He wants to steal some money, but all during the film I kept wondering why he didn't just give up and head for dry ground. How much of this ordeal was he foolish enough to put up with? Water, cold, rain, electrocutions, murders, shotguns, jet-ski attacks, drownings, betrayals, collisions, leaky boats, stupid and incompetent partners, and your fingertips shrivel up: Is it worth it?

The film opens in a town being evacuated because of rising floodwaters. There's a sequence involving a bank. At first we think we're witnessing a robbery, and then we realize we are witnessing a pickup by an armored car. What's the point? Since the bankers don't think they're being robbed and the armored-truck drivers don't think they're robbing them, the sequence means only that the director has gone to great difficulty to fool us. Why? So we can slap our palms against our brows and admit we were big stupes?

By the time we finally arrived at the story, I was essentially watching a documentary about wet actors at work. Christian Slater stars, as one of the armored-truck crew. Randy Quaid is the ambiguous sheriff. Morgan Freeman is the leader of the would-be thieves, who have commandeered a powerboat. Ah, but I hear you asking, why was it so important for the armored car to move the cash out of the bank before the flood? So Freeman's gang could steal it, of course. Otherwise, if it got wet, hey, what's the Federal Reserve for?

Minnie Driver plays a local woman who teams up with Slater, so that they can fall in love while saving each other from drowning. First Slater is in a jail cell that's about to flood, and then Driver is handcuffed to a staircase that's about to flood, and both times I was thinking what rotten luck it was that *Hard Rain* came so soon after the scene in *Titanic* where Kate Winslet saved Leonardo Di Caprio from drowning after he was handcuffed on the sinking ship. It's bad news when a big action scene plays like a demonstration of recent generic techniques.

Meanwhile, Morgan Freeman's character is too darned nice. He keeps trying to avoid violence while still trying to steal the money. This plot requires a mad dog like Dennis Hopper. Freeman's character specializes in popping up suddenly from the edge of the screen and scaring the other characters, even though it is probably pretty hard to sneak up on somebody in a powerboat. Freeman is good at looking wise and insightful, but the wiser and more insightful he looks, the more I wanted him to check into a motel and order himself some hot chocolate.

Hard Rain must have been awesomely difficult to make. Water is hard to film around, and here were whole city streets awash, at night and in the rain. The director is Mikael Salomon, a former cameraman, who along with cinematographer Peter Menzies, Jr., does a good job of making everything look convincingly wet. And they stage a jet-ski chase through school corridors that's an impressive action sequence, unlikely though it may be.

I was in Los Angeles the weekend *Hard Rain* had its preview, and went to talk to the cast. I found myself asking: Wasn't there a danger of electrocution when you were standing for weeks in all that water with electrical cables everywhere? That's not the sort of question you even think about if the story is working. Hey, how about this for a story idea? An actor signs up for a movie about a flood, little realizing that a celebrity stalker, who hates him, has been hired as an electrician on the same picture.

Hav Plenty

(Directed by Christopher Scott Cherot; starring Christopher Scott Cherot, Chenoa Maxwell; 1998)

I've grown immune to the information that a movie is "a true story," but when a movie begins with that promise *and* a quote from the Bible, I get an uneasy feeling. And when it starts with a "true story," a Bible quote, *and* clips from home movies, *and* photos of several main characters, I wonder if I'm watching a movie or a research project. Amateur writers love to precede their own prose with quotations. I don't know whether they think it's a warm-up or a good luck charm.

Hav Plenty is basically an amateur movie, with some of the good things and many of the bad that go along with first-time efforts. Set in a comfortable milieu of affluent African Americans, it's ostensibly the autobiographical story of its writer-director, Christopher Scott Cherot, who plays a homeless writer named Lee Plenty. As the movie opens, he's cat-sitting for a woman named Havilland Savage (Chenoa Maxwell), who has just broken up with a famous musician. She's with her family in Washington for New Year's Eve, invites him to come down and join them, and he does. (So much for the cat.) At the end of the movie, there's a thank-you to "the real Havilland Savage," and I gather most of the things in the movie actually happened, in one way or another. How else to account for an episode involving the offscreen explosion of a toilet?

Cherot plays Lee Plenty as a smart young man of maddening passivity. The plot essentially consists of scenes in which Havilland's best friend Caroline throws herself at Plenty, who rebuffs her. Then Havilland's sister, who has only been married for a month, throws herself at Plenty, but he rebuffs her, too. Then Havilland herself throws herself at Plenty, and he does his best to rebuff her. Although we see the beginning of a sex scene, he eventually eludes her, too. The movie ends with a scene at a film festival, at which Plenty speaks after the premiere of a film that is a great deal like this one.

As a young man I would have been quite capable of writing and starring in a movie in which three beautiful women threw themselves at me. I would have considered this so logical that I would not have bothered, as Cherot does not bother, to write myself any dialogue establishing myself as intelligent, charming, seductive, etc. I would assume that the audience could take one look at me and simply intuit that I had all of those qualities. So I can accept that the homeless Lee Plenty character is irresistible, even to a newlywed and to a beautiful, rich, ex-fiancée of a big star. What I cannot accept is that he fights them all off with vague excuses and evasions. "He's not gay," the women assure each other. That I believe. But either he's asexual or exhibiting the symptoms of chronic fatigue syndrome.

Hav Plenty is not a film without charm, but, boy, does it need to tighten the screws on its screenplay. The movie's dialogue is mostly strained, artificial small talk, delivered unevenly by the actors, who at times seem limited to one take (how else to account for fluffed lines?). There are big setups without payoffs, as when Hav's grandmother insists, "You're going to marry him!" And nightmare dream sequences without motivation or purpose. And awkward scenes like the one where the newlywed sister tells her husband that something went on between her and Plenty. The husband enters the room, removes his jacket to reveal bulging muscles, and socks poor Plenty in the stomach. This scene illustrates two of my favorite obligatory clichés: (1) The husband is told only enough of the story to draw exactly the wrong conclusion, and (2) all muscular characters in movies always take off outer garments to reveal their muscles before hitting someone.

Hav Plenty is basically a three-actress movie; Cherot, as the male lead, is so vague and passive he barely has a personality (listen to his rambling explanations about why he "doesn't date"). All three actresses (Chenoa Maxwell as Hav, Tammi Katherine Jones as Hav's best friend, and Robinne Lee as the married sister) have strong energy and look good on the screen. With better direction and more takes, I suspect they'd seem more accomplished in their performances. But *Hav Plenty* is more of a first draft than a finished product.

Heartbreak Hotel

(Directed by Chris Columbus; starring David Keith, Tuesday Weld, Charlie Schlatter; 1988)

Here it is, the goofiest movie of the year, a movie so bad in so many different and endearing ways that I'm darned if I don't feel genuine affection for it. We all know it's bad manners to talk during a movie, but every once in a while a film comes along that positively requires the audience to shout helpful suggestions and lewd one-liners at the screen. *Heartbreak Hotel* is such a movie. All it needs to be perfect is a parallel sound track.

The film tells the story of an Ohio high school kid (Charlie Schlatter), back in 1972, who has his own rock and roll band. But the fuddy-duddys on the high school faculty don't like rock and roll, so they ban the band from the school talent show. Meanwhile, the kid has problems at home. His divorced mother (Tuesday Weld) is an alcoholic who sleeps with a guy who works at the junkyard. She's also a diehard Elvis Presley fan. Things are not so great at home for Schlatter and his kid sister, who live upstairs over mom's business, a fleabag motel. And things get worse when Weld is hospitalized after a traffic accident.

What to do? Well, Elvis himself is going to appear in Cleveland on Saturday night, and so Schlatter and the members of his band concoct a desperate plot to kidnap Presley and bring him home, to cheer up mom. How are they going to get him away from his cocoon of security guards? They come up with a brainstorm. Rosie, the local pizza cook, looks exactly like Elvis's beloved dead mother. So they'll give her a black wig, adjust her makeup, and convince Elvis that she has returned from the grave for one last visit with her son. Rosie, portrayed by Jacque Lynn Colton in a role the late Divine was born to play, sends Elvis flowers and lures him outside his hotel at three A.M., and then the high school kids chloroform him and whisk him away in a pink Cadillac.

Once Elvis enters the plot, the movie ascends to new heights of silliness. Elvis, played in the film by David Keith (a good actor who doesn't look one bit like Elvis), is mad at first, of course. But then he begins to listen when this teenage punk tells him he's lost his sense of danger and is playing it safe for his fans, who are mostly blue-haired old ladies. Elvis also sort of falls for Tuesday Weld, and he takes a special liking in his heart for her little daughter Pam (Angela Goethals), who is afraid to sleep with the lights out. The tender bedside scenes between Elvis and the young girl are hard to watch with a straight face, especially if you've read Albert Goldman's muckraking biography *Elvis,* with its revelations about the King's taste in pubescent adolescents.

I don't know what Chris Columbus, the writer and director of this film, had in mind when he made it. One of my fellow critics, emerging from the screening and wiping tears of incredulous laughter from his eyes, said maybe they were trying to make a Frank Capra film—*Mr. Presley Goes to Ohio.* Elvis gives Schlatter tips on picking up women and holds lessons in pelvis-grinding, before agreeing to make a guest appearance at the high school talent show. Any resemblence between this behavior and the real Presley exists only in the realm of fantasy.

And yet Elvis fans are a special lot, and will enjoy some of the small touches in the film, such as the name of Weld's motel (the "Flaming Star") and the way the movie reproduces the famous juke box dance and fight scene from one of Presley's aging classics. Some scenes are tongue-in-cheek send-ups of hoary old B-movie clichés, as when Elvis grabs a paintbrush and helps Weld redecorate her motel, or when he says a tearful good-bye at the airport before flying back to reality in his private jet (he reserves an especially fond pat on the head for the young daughter).

I never know how to deal with movies like *Heartbreak Hotel.* Sure, it's bad—awesomely bad, contrived, awkward, and filled with unintentional laughs. And yet I was not bored. The movie finds so many different approaches to its badness that it becomes endearing. The organizers of Golden Turkey film festivals have been complaining lately that they don't make truly great bad movies anymore. *Heartbreak Hotel* is proof that the genre is not completely dead.

Heaven's Gate

(Directed by Michael Cimino; starring Kris Kristofferson, Christopher Walken, Jeff Bridges, John Hurt, Sam Waterston, Mickey Rourke, Willem Dafoe; 1980)

We begin with a fundamental question: Why is *Heaven's Gate* so painful and unpleasant to look at? I'm not referring to its content, but to its actual visual texture: This is one of the ugliest films I have ever seen. Its director, Michael Cimino, opens his story at Harvard, continues it in Montana, and closes it aboard a ship. And yet a grim industrial pall hangs low over everything. There are clouds and billows of dirty yellow smoke in every shot that can possibly justify it, and when he runs out of smoke he gives us fog and such incredible amounts of dust that there are whole scenes where we can barely see anything. That's not enough. Cimino also shoots his picture in a maddening soft focus that makes the people and places in this movie sometimes almost impossible to see. And then he goes after the colors. There's not a single primary color in this movie, only dingy washed-out sepia tones.

I know, I know: He's trying to demystify the West, and all those other things hotshot directors try to do when they don't really want to make a Western. But this movie is a study in wretched excess. It is so smoky, so dusty, so foggy, so unfocused, and so brownish yellow that you want to try Windex on the screen. A director is in deep trouble when we do not even enjoy the primary act of looking at his picture.

But Cimino's in deeper trouble still. *Heaven's Gate* has, of course, become a notorious picture, a boondoggle that cost something like $36 million and was yanked out of its New York opening run after the critics ran gagging from the theater. Its running time, at that point, was more than four hours. Perhaps length was the problem? Cimino went back to the editing room, while a United Artists executive complained that the film had been "destroyed" by an unfairly negative review by *New York Times* critic Vincent Canby. Brother Canby was only doing his job. If the film was formless at four hours, it is insipid at 140 minutes. At either length it is so incompetently photographed and edited that there are times when we are not even sure which character we are looking at. Christopher Walken is in several of the initial Western scenes before he finally gets a close-up and we see who he is. John Hurt wanders through various scenes to no avail. Kris Kristofferson is the star of the movie, and is never allowed to generate enough character for us to miss him, should he disappear.

The opening scenes are set at Harvard (they were actually shot in England, but never mind). They show Kristofferson, Hurt, and other idealistic young men graduating in 1870 and setting off to civilize a nation. Kristofferson decides to go west, to help develop the territory. He explains this decision in a narration, and the movie might have benefited if he'd narrated the whole thing, explaining as he went along. Out west, as a lawman, he learns of a plot by the cattlebreeders' association to hire a private army and assassinate 125 newly arrived European immigrants who are, it is claimed, anarchists, killers, and thieves. Most of the movie will be about this plot, Kristofferson's attempts to stop it, Walken's involvement in it, and the involvement of both Kristofferson and Walken in the private life of a young Montana madam (Isabelle Huppert).

In a movie where nothing is handled well, the immigrants are handled very badly. Cimino sees them as a mob. They march onscreen, babble excitedly in foreign tongues, and rush off wildly in all directions. By the movie's end, we can identify only one of them for sure. She is the Widow Kovach, whose husband was shot dead near the beginning of the film. That makes her the emblem of the immigrants' suffering. Every time she steps forward out of the mob, somebody respectfully murmurs "Widow Kovach!" in the subtitles. While the foreigners are hanging on to Widow Kovach's every insight, the cattlemen are holding meetings in private clubs and offering to pay their mercenaries $5 a day plus expenses and $50 for every other foreigner shot or hung. I am sure of those terms because they are repeated endlessly throughout a movie that cares to make almost nothing else clear.

The ridiculous scenes are endless. Samples: Walken, surrounded by gunmen and trapped in a burning cabin, scribbles a farewell note in which he observes that he is trapped in the burning cabin, and then he signs his full name so that there will be no doubt who the note was from. Kristofferson, discovering Huppert being gang-raped by several men, leaps in with six-guns in both hands and shoots all the men, including those aboard Huppert, without injuring her. In a big battle scene, men make armored wagons out of logs and push them forward into the line of fire, even though anyone could ride around behind and shoot them. There is more. There is much more. It all adds up to a great deal less. This movie is $36 million thrown to the winds. It is the most scandalous cinematic waste I have ever seen, and remember, I've seen *Paint Your Wagon.*

Hell Night

(Directed by Tom DeSimone; starring Linda Blair,
Vincent Van Patten; 1981)

It was that legendary Chicago film exhibitor Oscar Brotman who gave me one of my most useful lessons in the art of film watching. "In ninety-nine films out of a hundred," Brotman told me, "if nothing has happened by the end of the first reel . . . nothing is going to happen." This rule, he said, had saved him countless hours over the years because he had walked out of movies after the first uneventful reel.

I seem to remember arguing with him. There are some films, I said, in which nothing happens in the first reel because the director is trying to set up a universe of ennui and uneventfulness. Take a movie like Michelangelo Antonioni's *L'Avventura,* for example.

"It closed in a week," Brotman said.

"But, Oscar, it was voted one of the top ten greatest films of all time!"

"They must have all seen it in the first week."

I was running this conversation through my memory while watching *Hell Night.*

I had waited through the first reel, and nothing had happened. Now I was somewhere in the middle of the third reel, and still nothing had happened. By "nothing," by the way, I mean nothing original, unexpected, well crafted, interestingly acted, or even excitingly violent.

Hell Night is a relentlessly lackluster example of the Dead Teenager Movie. The formula is always the same. A group of kids get together for some kind of adventure or forbidden ritual in a haunted house, summer camp, old school, etc. One of the kids tells a story about the horrible and gruesome murders that happened there years ago. He always ends the same way: ". . . and they say the killer never died and is still lurking here somewhere." That was the formula of *The Burning* and the *Friday the 13th* movies, and it's the formula again in *Hell Night.*

This time, the pretext is a fraternity-sorority initiation stunt. The venue is an old mansion. We learn that the hapless Garth family once lived there and had four deformed and handicapped children. The misfortunes of the children are described in great detail, with dialogue in very bad taste. But then, of course, *Hell Night* is in bad taste. The only child that need concern us is the youngest Garth, who was named Andrew and was born, we are told, a "gork."

None of the dictionaries at my command include the word "gork," but for the purposes of *Hell Night* we can define "gork" thus:

Gork (n.) Deformed, violent creature that lurks in horror movies, jumping out of basement shadows and decapitating screaming teenagers.

I have now of course, given away the plot of *Hell Night.* As the fraternity and sorority kids creep through passageways of the old house, their candle flames fluttering in the wind, Andrew the Gork picks them off, one by one, in scenes of bloody detail. Finally only Linda Blair is left. Why does she survive? Maybe because she's a battle-hardened veteran, having previously more or less lived through *The Exorcist, Exorcist II: The Heretic,* and *Born Innocent.* At least in those movies, something happened in the first reel.

Hellbound: Hellraiser II
(Directed by Tony Randel; starring Ashley Laurence, Clare Higgins; 1988)
Generally speaking, there are two kinds of nightmares, the kind that you actually have, and the kind they make into movies. Real nightmares usually involve frustration or public embarrassment. In the frustrating ones, a loved one is trying to tell you something and you can't understand them, or they're in danger and you can't help them. In the embarrassing ones, it's the day of the final exam and you forgot to attend the classes, or you're in front of a crowd and can't think of anything to say, or you wandered into the hotel lobby without any clothes on, and nobody has noticed you yet—but they're about to.

Those are scary nightmares, all right, and sometimes they turn up in the movies. But *Hellbound: Hellraiser II* contains the kinds of nightmares that occur *only* in movies, because our real dreams have low budgets and we can't afford expensive kinds of special effects. The movie begins a few hours after the original *Hellbound* ended. A young girl named Kirsty has been placed in a hospital after a night in which she was tortured by the flayed corpses of her parents, who were under the supervision of the demons of hell. What this girl needs is a lot of rest and a set of those positive-thinking cassettes they advertise late at night on cable TV.

But no such luck. The hospital is simply another manifestation of the underworld, hell is all around us, we are powerless in its grip, and before long Kirsty and a newfound friend named Tiffany are hurtling down the corridors of the damned. Give or take a detail or two, that's the story. *Hellbound: Hellraiser II* is like some kind of avant-garde film strip in which there is no beginning, no middle, no end, but simply a series of gruesome images that can be watched in any order.

The images have been constructed with a certain amount of care and craftsmanship; the technical credits on this movie run to four single-spaced pages. We see lots of bodies that have been skinned alive, so that the blood still glistens on the exposed muscles. We see creatures who have been burned and mutilated and twisted into grotesque shapes, and condemned for eternity to unspeakable and hopeless tortures. We hear deep, rasping laughter, as the denizens of hell chortle over the plight of the terrified girls. And we hear their desperate voices calling to each other.

"Kirsty!" we hear. And "Tiffany!" And "Kirsty!!!" and "Tiffany!!!" and *"Kirstieeeeeee!!!!!"* And *"Tiffanyyyyyyy!!!!!"* I'm afraid this is another one of those movies where they violate the First Rule of Repetition of Names, which states that when the same names are repeated in a movie more than four times a minute for more than three minutes in a row, the audience breaks out into sarcastic laughter, and some of the ruder members are likely to start shouting "Kirsty! and "Tiffany!" at the screen.

But this movie violates more rules than the First Rule of Repetition. It also violates a basic convention of story construction, which suggests that we should get at least a vague idea of where the story began and where it might be headed. This movie has no plot in a conventional sense. It is simply a series of ugly and bloody episodes, strung together one after another like a demo tape by a perverted special-effects man. There is nothing the heroines can do to understand or change their plight, and no way we can get involved in their story. That makes *Hellbound: Hellraiser II* an ideal movie for audiences with little taste and atrophied attention spans, who want to glance at the screen occasionally and ascertain that something is still happening up there. If you fit that description, you have probably not read this far, but what the heck, we believe in full-service reviews around here. You're welcome.

Her Alibi

(Directed by Bruce Beresford; starring Tom Selleck, Paulina Porizkova; 1989)
You know a movie is in trouble when you start looking at your watch. You know it's in bad trouble when you start shaking your watch because you think it might have stopped. *Her Alibi* is a movie in the second category—endless, pointless, and ridiculous, right up to the final shot of the knife going through the cockroach. This movie is desperately bankrupt of imagination and wit, and Tom Selleck looks adrift in it.

He plays a detective-novelist named Blackwood, who has run out of inspiration. So he goes to criminal court for fresh ideas, and there he falls instantly in love with Nina (Paulina Porizkova), a Romanian immigrant who is accused of murdering a young man with a pair of scissors. Blackwood disguises himself as a priest, smuggles himself into jail to meet Nina, and offers to supply her with an alibi: She can claim they were having an affair at his country home in Connecticut at the time of the crime.

These developments, and indeed the entire movie, are narrated by Blackwood in the language of a thriller novel he is writing as he goes along. One of the minor curiosities of the movie is why the Selleck character is such a bad writer. His prose is a turgid flow of cliché and stereotype, and when we catch a glimpse of his computer screen, we can't help noticing that he writes only in capital letters. Although the movie says he's rich because of a string of best-sellers, on the evidence this is the kind of author whose manuscripts are returned with a form letter.

If the plot of his novel is half-witted, the plot of the movie is lame-brained. Blackwood and Nina move to Connecticut to make the alibi look good, and they're shadowed by a band of Romanian spies who make several murder attempts against them, including one in which they blow up Blackwood's house. The movie betrays its desperation by straying outside the confines of even this cookie-cutter plot for such irrelevant episodes as the one where Blackwood shoots himself in the bottom with an arrow, and is rushed to the hospital by Nina in one of those cut-and-dried scenes where the racing vehicle scares everyone else off the road before arriving safe and sound.

In a movie filled with groaningly bad moments, the worst is no doubt the dinner party at which Blackwood becomes convinced that Nina has poisoned him and everybody else at the table. Why does he think so? Because the cat is dead, next to a bowl filled from the same casserole. We are treated to the sight of eight characters doing the dry heaves, and then another visit to the hospital, after which we learn it's all a false alarm and the cat was accidentially electrocuted in a neighbor's basement and returned by the solicitous neighbor to a resting place beside the suspicious bowl. Uh-huh.

The explanation for the whole story is equally arbitrary and senseless, and the big reconciliation scene between the two lovers is not helped by taking place at a clown's convention, with Selleck wearing a red rubber ball on his nose. But for a full appreciation of just how much contempt *Her Alibi* has for the audience, reflect for a moment on the movie's last scene, in which Blackwood and Nina are back home again at last in the snug Connecticut farmhouse, for a big love scene and a fade-out. The people who made this movie apparently actually forgot that they blew the house up half an hour earlier.

Highlander 2: The Quickening
(Directed by Russell Mulcahy; starring Sean Connery, Christopher Lambert; 1991)

This movie has to be seen to be believed. On the other hand, maybe that's too high a price to pay. *Highlander 2: The Quickening* is the most hilariously incomprehensible movie I've seen in many a long day—a movie almost awesome in its badness. Wherever science fiction fans gather, in decades and generations to come, this film will be remembered in hushed tones as one of the immortal low points of the genre.

The story opens in the year 1999, and then we get the title card "25 years later," following not long after by the title card "The Planet Zeist, 500 Years Ago." Uh, are those Earth years or Zeist years? Apparently Zeist, which has a sun so close it takes up a quarter of the visible sky, revolves around that orb so slowly that a Zeist year is exactly the same as an Earth year, which accounts for the fact that one of the Immortals sent to Earth 500 years ago found himself in medieval Scotland, also 500 years ago.

Now about the Immortals. They led a rebellion on Zeist, and were banished to the planet Earth, under a sentence of eternal life. They cannot die. In a sense. Actually, they can, but it depends. Or, as one of the characters explains it more helpfully, "You will live forever here, until you return to Zeist, where you can die, or, under certain circumstances, you can die here, but not on Zeist."

The immortals are played by Sean Connery and Christopher Lambert, and they have both been on Earth 500 (Earth) years, and will be here a lot longer, looks like. Meanwhile, in the year 1999, the disappearing ozone layer is causing global panic on Earth. The ozone has finally been destroyed by billions of deodorized armpits, and people are dying like flies, until a corporation headed by Lambert devises a shield to save the planet. This shield, known as the Shield, involves using all of the energy on the planet, concentrated into a laser beam that is shot up to an Earth satellite, whereupon Earth is saved from excess solar radiation, but there's a catch: It will always be night, and the temperature and humidity will both hover around 99.

Flash forward twenty-five years, as the older Lambert goes to an opera, wearing a tuxedo, which people still wear despite the heat wave and the 99 percent humidity. Life in big cities has grown dangerous and criminal, although people are still alive and should not complain, considering that you would *think* that the total blackout on earth might have curtailed food production, since nothing could grow.

For that matter, why isn't everything covered with a carpet of fungus? And for *that* matter, *why* is the humidity 99 percent—after all, the lack of sunlight should have (a) ended the process of cloud formation, so that, without rain, all of the water would end up in the oceans and the land would be a desert, and (b) without warmth from the sun, a new Ice Age should have begun.

Never mind. Earth is in the grip of an evil cartel which manages the Shield, until a brave underground scientist (Virginia Madsen) hacks into the computers of the Shield's owners and discovers, as she breathlessly reports: "The solar radiation above the Shield is normal!!!" She explains that the ozone layer has "repaired itself."

Meanwhile, Sean Connery, still a creature of the medieval Scotland where he first arrived from Zeist, appears in the twenty-first century wearing a kilt and talking in a thick brogue, and gets himself suited up in modern dress before there are several sword fights and some byplay involving bad guys on the planet Zeist. If there is a planet somewhere whose civilization is based on the worst movies of all time, *Highlander 2: The Quickening* deserves a sacred place among their most treasured artifacts.

Film note: "Quickening" is a process by which two people touch each other and are surrounded by special effects making it look as if one of them is standing in a puddle and the other had just stuck his finger into a light socket.

The Hindenburg

(Directed by Robert Wise; starring George C. Scott, Anne Bancroft; 1975)
The Hindenburg is a disaster picture, all right. How else can you describe a movie that makes people laugh out loud at all the wrong times? Why else would they film a story with an ending everybody knows and then try to build up suspense about it?

The movie's so bad I've made a little list. You just can't dismiss it; you linger over it. People stand in the lobby afterward like the survivors of a traffic accident.

First on my list is the movie's fundamental flaw, a lack of understanding of what makes disaster movies interesting. We go to see the characters in the *process* of experiencing the disaster. As the disaster develops, so do the characters. The skyscraper in *The Towering Inferno* catches on fire in the first fifteen minutes and burns for two hours. The good ship *Poseidon* is hit by a tidal wave ten minutes after we walk into the theater; it turns over, and the characters spend the rest of the movie fighting fire and flood. The airplanes in the two *Airport!* movies fly for ninety minutes after things go wrong, with George Kennedy wringing his hands on the ground and Dean Martin and Karen Black fighting the controls.

But in *The Hindenburg* almost nothing of consequence happens until the last few minutes of the movie. How can you thrill people with the saga of a dirigible floating across the Atlantic Ocean? We know it's going to blow up over Lakehurst, New Jersey—but we also know that it's not going to blow up before then. And so George C. Scott searches his conscience, and Anne Bancroft camps it up as a mysterious German countess, and the captain peers confidently out over the wheel, and for nearly two hours little of any consequence happens.

Meanwhile (no. 2 on my list) the movie has to deal with the fact that Nazi Germany used giant dirigibles like the *Hindenburg* as propaganda devices. They were the symbols of Hitlerism, floating in the sky past the Empire State Building, the queens of the air. Their crews were German. Their makers were German. Their sponsors were Nazis.

And so, while nothing else is happening except that the characters are making inane conversation with each other in futile attempts to piece together vignettes of human nature, the good Germans and the bad Germans and the in-between Germans climb through the rigging of the airship playing a cat-and-mouse game with sabotage.

George C. Scott is an in-between German. He's deeply disturbed, you see, because the Nazi youth movement enlisted his teenage son, and the poor lad was misled by bad company: While climbing up onto a synagogue to paint a swastika on it, the hapless youth fell off and broke his neck. This forces George C. Scott into a crisis of agonizing indecision. Meanwhile, we laugh, because the information has been imparted so artlessly, so awkwardly, it seems like a sick joke. Moviemakers talk about "bad laughs." That's when the audience laughs when it's not supposed to. This is conceivably the first movie which is in its entirety a bad laugh.

Meanwhile (third and last point) the *Hindenburg* drifts toward its rendezvous with destiny. And here the director, Robert Wise, uses actual newsreel footage. There's not much of it; the *Hindenburg* went down pretty fast. So he keeps stopping the footage to give us ground-and-air developments, as people race about in flames and fall to their deaths. This isn't fun. We go to disaster movies for fun. We know a few supporting players are going to catch their lunch, but we figure Paul Newman and Steve McQueen will come out all right. And here are all these people burning up and falling out of the *Hindenburg*. Well, at least we stop laughing.

The Hitcher
(Directed by Robert Holman; starring Rutger Hauer,
Jennifer Jason Leigh; 1986)
The Hitcher begins and ends with the same sound: a match being struck, flaring into flame. At the beginning of the film, the sound is made by the villain, a hitchhiker who is a mass murderer. At the end of the film, the sound is made by the hero, a young man whose life has been spared so that he can become the special victim of the hitchhiker.

The movie seems to be telling us, by the use of the sounds and in several other ways, that the killer and the hero have developed some kind of deep bond through their shared experiences.

The victim's identification with his torturer is not a new phenomenon. In many of the hostage cases in recent years, some of the captives have adopted the viewpoints of their jailers. What is particularly sick about *The Hitcher* is that the killer is not given a viewpoint, a grudge, or indeed even a motive.

He is deliberately presented as a man without a past, without a history, who simply and cruelly hurts and kills people. Although he spares the movie's young hero, he puts him through a terrible ordeal, framing him as a mass murderer and trapping him in a Kafkaesque web of evidence.

At the end of the movie, there is, of course, a scene of vengeance in which the two men meet in final combat. And yet this showdown does not represent a fight between good and evil, because the movie suggests that there is something sadomasochistic going on between the two men. The death of the villain is not the hero's revenge, but the conclusion that the villain has been setting up for himself all along.

This unhealthy bond between the young hero (played by C. Thomas Howell) and the older killer (the cold-eyed Rutger Hauer) is developed in a movie that provides a horrible fate for its only major female character. As Howell flees down empty desert highways from the violence of Hauer, he is befriended by a young waitress (Jennifer Jason Leigh). She believes that he is innocent and goes on the run with him.

But the movie does not develop into a standard story of teenagers in love. And the Leigh character's death—she is tied hand and foot between two giant trucks and pulled in two—is so grotesquely out of proportion with the main business of this movie that it suggests a deep sickness at the screenplay stage.

There are other disgusting moments, as when a police dog feasts on the blood dripping from its master's neck, and when Howell finds a human finger in his french fries.

The Hitcher grants the Hauer character almost supernatural powers. Although that makes the movie impossible to accept on a realistic level, it didn't bother me. I could see that the film was meant as an allegory, not a documentary.

But on its own terms, this movie is diseased and corrupt. I would have admired it more if it had found the courage to acknowledge the real relationship it was portraying between Howell and Rutger, but no: It prefers to disguise itself as a violent thriller, and on that level it is reprehensible.

Home Alone 2: Lost in New York

(Directed by Chris Columbus; starring Macaulay Culkin, Joe Pesci, Daniel Stern; 1992)

I have a feeling that *Home Alone 2: Lost in New York* is going to be an enormous box-office success, but include me out. I didn't much like the first film, and I don't much like this one, with its sadistic little hero who mercilessly hammers a couple of slow-learning crooks. Nor did I enjoy the shameless attempt to leaven the mayhem by including a preachy subplot about the Pigeon Lady of Central Park. Call me hard-hearted, call me cynical, but please don't call me if they make *Home Alone 3*.

I know, I know—the violence is all a joke. Some of the gags are lifted directly from old color cartoons, and in spirit what we're looking at here are Road Runner adventures, with the crooks playing the role of Wile E. Coyote. As the two hapless mopes fall down ladders, are slammed by bricks and 500-pound bags of cement, and covered with glue and paint and birdseed, you can hear the cackling of the old Looney Tunes heroes in the background. And just like in the cartoons, the crooks are never *really* hurt; they bounce back, dust themselves off, bend their bones back into shape, and are ready for the next adventure. When little Kevin (Macaulay Culkin) taunts them ("Hey! Up here!") he sounds like Bugs Bunny, and when they chase him (always unwisely) they're in the tradition of Elmer Fudd.

The problem is, cartoon violence is only funny in the cartoons. Most of the live-action attempts to duplicate animation have failed, because when flesh-and-blood figures hit the pavement, we can almost hear the bones crunch, and it isn't funny. Take, for example, the scene in *Home Alone 2* where Kevin lures the crooks into trying to crawl down a rope from the top of a four-story town house. He has soaked the rope in kerosene, and when they're halfway down he sets it on fire. Ho, ho.

The movie repeats the formula of the best-selling original film. Once again, Kevin's forgetful family leaves home without him (he gets on the plane to New York instead of Miami), and once again they fret while he deals effortlessly with the world. He checks into the Plaza Hotel on his dad's credit card, and has time for heartwarming conversations with a kindly old toy shop owner (Eddie Bracken) and a homeless bird lover (Brenda Fricker), not to mention Donald Trump, before running into his old enemies, the crooks (Joe Pesci and Daniel Stern). When he discovers they plan to rob the toy store, whose receipts are destined for a children's hospital, he knows he has his work cut out for him ("Messing with kids on Christmas Eve—that's going too far!").

The kid outsmarts the usual assortment of supercilious adults, including hotel clerk Tim Curry, before setting a series of ingenious traps for the crooks. As before, he seems to have a complete command of all handyman skills, including rigging ladders and wiring appliances for electrical shocks—and, of course, he finds all the props he needs, even for rigging the exploding toilet and setting that staple gun to fire through the keyhole.

In between the painful practical jokes, there's his treacly relationship with Fricker, as the Pigeon Lady, who shows him her hideaway inside the ceiling of Carnegie Hall. Christmas carols swell from the concert below as the sanctimonious little twerp lectures the old lady on the meaning of life. If he believes half of what he says, he'd give the crooks a break.

Is this a children's movie? I confess I do not know. Millions of kids will go to see it. There used to be movies where it was bad for little kids to hurt grown-ups. Now Kevin bounces bricks off their skulls from the rooftops, and everybody laughs. The question isn't whether the movie will scare the children in the audience. It's whether the adults will be able to peek between their fingers.

Home Fries

(Directed by Dean Parisot; starring Drew Barrymore, Catherine O'Hara; 1998)
There is a moment about halfway through *Home Fries* when one of the characters is snaking a rubber tube up through the toilet of a house trailer, in order to pump in carbon monoxide and asphyxiate the woman inside—who he mistakenly thinks is the mistress of the stepfather he has earlier frightened to death. And I'm thinking—you know, this scene requires a *whole* lot more setup. And then I'm thinking, no, a scene like this only works if there is no setup at all.

The whole movie is kind of like that. The leaden plot hangs heavy on the characters, who could take flight if they could only break free from it. This is one of those movies where you wish you could just beam all of the characters up into another movie. I especially liked the work done by Drew Barrymore and Catherine O'Hara, but lord, the mileage they have to cover, slogging through the inane byways of the story line.

The movie opens with a key piece of information. A doctor steers his car past the drive-thru window of a Burger-Matic, and says to the window girl, "My wife knows about us!" The girl (Barrymore) says, "Did you tell her about this?" and thrusts forward her pregnant belly. "Do you want a ride home?" asks the miserable doc. The girl is contemptuous: "I don't need a ride home. I need a father for my baby."

Now in a screenplay class this would be a good opening for a movie. But a wise teacher, asking his students to write more, would add, "And, please— no helicopters!" Because, yes, later that night, the doctor's car is attacked by a combat helicopter, and is literally frightened to death.

The helicopter is piloted by two brothers in the Air National Guard. They are Dorian and Angus (Luke Wilson and Jake Busey), the sons of Mrs. Lever (O'Hara) by a first marriage. Her current marriage, of course, is to the doctor, and she has ordered the attack by her sons in revenge because she knows the doc is fooling around.

She does not know, however, that Sally, the Barrymore character, is the other woman. Nor, after Dorian comes to work at the Burger-Matic, does Sally know Dorian is the stepson of her dead lover. Nor does Dorian know Sally was fooling around with the doc. He takes the burger job at Angus's urging, because they suspect that radio emissions from the helicopter were picked up on Sally's radio earphones in the drive-thru line.

Sometimes it really would be easier to just write about the damn characters.

Vince Gilligan, who wrote the original screenplay, at least gets credit for writing the opposite of an Idiot Plot. The Idiot Plot, you will recall, is a plot in which the secrets are so obvious, and are concealed through such a convoluted chain of contrivances, that if one character were to blurt out one piece of information, everything would instantly be solved. In *Home Fries,* the situation is so complex that even though people constantly blurt out almost everything they can think of, the mystery still persists, and even at the end the puzzled characters are still trying to explain it to one another.

The Catherine O'Hara character is the one person who holds most of the threads (although she only belatedly figures out who Sally the burger girl is). Her relationship to her sons puts one in mind of Greek tragedy (shouldn't those boys realize it's time to move away from home?). But at least she's consistent: You cheat, you pay. And she defends her sons with ferocious intensity.

Drew Barrymore, as Sally, focuses on what her character knows and how she feels about it, and succeeds in creating a pure performance that sort of stands outside the movie. This same burger girl, looking this way, talking this way, could be carefully packed and moved intact into a better film. Even the inevitable childbirth scene is more or less effective in her hands, despite the fact that the insecure screenplay doesn't take any chances and combines it with a chase scene.

Another problem is that the filmmakers haven't decided how relatively smart the people in the movie can be. All movies have some people who are smarter than others, of course, but at some point a movie has to decide what the parameters are. O'Hara, as Mrs. Lever, is so much smarter than her dimwit sons that if we were going to pack them up, we'd have to ship them to a Pauly Shore movie. It's not that a woman that smart can't have sons that dumb. It's that they couldn't get into the Air National Guard.

Howling II

(Directed by Philippe Mora; starring Christopher Lee, Sybil Danning; 1986)
There is a moment in *Howling II* when Sybil Danning and two other werewolves revert to their native state. Fangs grow from their mouths, their nails turn into claws, and they are covered with fur. Then they have a ménage à trois, snarling and snapping at each other and raking each other with their claws, in what must be the most unintentionally funny movie scene of the week.

You do not see scenes like this in other movies. You do not see a lot of well-known actresses appearing in them. Let us therefore speak in praise of Sybil Danning. I have interviewed her three times, and have always found her with one of the best senses of humor in Hollywood. She appears in movies like this for the money, of course, but also (I suspect) because she laughs out loud when she reads the scripts.

I'd like to check out Danning's closets at home. If they let her keep the costumes from her movies, I'll bet she has quite a collection. For example, the cloak that Lou Ferrigno made her wear in *Hercules and the 7 Gladiators,* because her muscles were distracting from his.

From this movie alone, not counting the wolf fur, there's her Flash Gordon outfit, with the low-cut bronze breastplates and the pushup armor. And then there's the slightly more formal leather gear she wears to receive Christopher Lee, who has come to do battle with her. It's only suitable to dress up for Christopher Lee, who has been in so many vampire and werewolf movies that a Hollywood traffic cop once pulled him over and asked him if he should be driving in the daylight.

In *Howling II,* which is not the worst movie Danning has made (though it is close), she plays Stirba, bisexual queen witch of Transylvania. Transylvania consists of a special-effects drawing of a castle on a hill, and a single street set showing some painted backdrops, a few doors, and what looks like an ethnic food fair—the Taste of Transylvania.

Into this dread kingdom venture the heroes of the movie. There's Christopher Lee as the expert werewolf killer, and Red Brown as the brother of a TV anchorwoman who turned into a werewoman during a newscast and attacked a cameraman. This was, of course, a great tragedy for the TV station: It didn't take place during a Nielsen ratings period.

Anyway, the heroes get involved in the strange rituals of the cult of Stirba. Although the rituals, like the rest of the movie, are impenetrable and amazingly inept, I have to concede that no one presides over a ritual quite as well as Sybil Danning, especially when she is savagely ripping open the bodice of her dress. She rips the dress so dramatically, in fact, that the shot is repeated twice during the closing credits, providing the movie with its second and third interesting moments.

IIIIIIII I IIIIIII

I Am Curious (Yellow)

(Directed by Vilgot Sloman; starring Lena Nyman; 1969)

If your thing is shelling out several bucks to witness a phallus (flaccid), then *I Am Curious (Yellow)* is the movie for you. But if you hope for anything else (that it might be erotic, for example, or even funny), forget it. *I Am Curious (Yellow)* is not merely not erotic. It is antierotic. Two hours of this movie will drive thoughts of sex out of your mind for weeks. See the picture and buy twin beds.

It is possible, of course, to manufacture an elaborate defense of the movie. I could do it myself with one hand tied behind my back. I could talk about the device of the film-within-a-film and the director's autobiographical references, and all that. But the movie is boring, stupid, and slow.

I wondered at times, during my long and restless ordeal while the picture ground out at roughly the rate of three feet every seven years, whether it was perhaps intended as a put-on. But I doubt it. I think there actually is a director in Sweden who is dull enough to seriously consider this an act of movie-making. There is a dogged earnestness about the "significant" scenes in the movie that suggests somebody moved his lips when he wrote the script and had to use a finger to mark his place.

Beyond that, there's also a pudgy girl with an unpleasant laugh (she thinks she's so cute). And a boy who looks like Archie rolled into Jughead. They do not exactly talk about current political and social problems, but they recite words associated with them. You can hear words like class structure, labor union, Vietnam, racism, Franco, nonviolence and, of course, the Bomb. But these words are never quite assembled into sentences.

There are also, of course, the celebrated sex scenes. They may not be sexy, but they are undeniably scenes. The boy and the girl perform in these scenes with the absorption and determination of a Cub Scout weaving a belt.

The one interesting aspect is that the hero succeeds in doing something no other man has ever been able to do. He makes love detumescently. The hell with the movie; let's have his secret.

I Know What You Did Last Summer
(Directed by Jim Gillespie; starring Jennifer Love Hewitt, Sarah Michelle Gellar, Ryan Phillippe, Freddie Prinze, Jr.; 1997)
The best shot in this film is the first one. Not a good sign. *I Know What You Did Last Summer* begins dramatically, with the camera swooping high above a dark and stormy sea, and then circling until it reveals a lonely figure sitting on a cliff overlooking the surf. The shot leads us to anticipate dread, horror, and atmospheric gloominess, but, alas, it is not to be.

Like so many horror films, this one is set on a national holiday—the Fourth of July. (Christmas and Graduation Day are also popular, although Thanksgiving now seems reserved for movies about dysfunctional families.) In a small North Carolina town, a beauty pageant ends with Helen (Sarah Michelle Gellar) being crowned the Croaker Queen. (The reference is to a fish, but the pun is intended, I fear.) Blinking back tears of joy, she announces her plans: "Through Art, I shall serve my country."

We meet her friends: Her obnoxious rich boyfriend Barry (Ryan Phillippe), her brainy best friend Julie (Jennifer Love Hewitt), and Julie's boyfriend Ray (Freddie Prinze, Jr.). Barry is a jerk who likes to get in fights and drive while drunk ("Can you say 'alcoholic'?" Julie asks him). They build a bonfire on the beach and debate the old urban legend about the teenage couple who found the bloody hook embedded in their car door. And then, on the way home, they strike a shadowy figure walking in the road.

In a panic, they dump him into the sea, even though he is not quite dead at the time. They're afraid to go to the police and risk reckless manslaughter charges. ("This is your future, Julie," Barry screams at her.) Helen then goes off to New York for her showbiz career, and Julie heads for college, but by the next summer they're back home again, pale, chastened, and racked by guilt.

That's when one of them gets a note that says, "I know what you did last summer." As they panic and try to find out who sent it—who knows what they did—the movie loses what marginal tension it has developed, and unwinds in a tedious series of obligatory scenes in which nonessential characters are murdered with a bloody hook wielded by The Fisherman, a macabre figure in a long slicker and a rubber rain hat.

"This is a fishing village," one of the friends says. "Everybody has a slicker." Yes, but not everybody wears it ashore, along with the hat, during steamy July weather. Only The Fisherman does. And since the movie doesn't play fair with its Fisherman clues, we're left with one of those infuriating endings in which (danger! plot spoiler ahead!) the murders were committed by none of the above.

The ads make much of the fact that *I Know What You Did Last Summer* is from "the creators of *Scream*." That means both scripts are by Kevin Williamson. My bet is that he hauled this one out of the bottom drawer after *Scream* passed the $100 million mark. The neat thing about *Scream* was that the characters had seen a lot of horror films, were familiar with all the conventions, and knew they were in a horror-type situation. In *I Know*, there's one moment like that (as the two women approached an ominous house, they observe ominously, "Jodie Foster tried this . . ."). But for the rest of the movie they're blissfully unaware of the dangers of running upstairs when pursued, walking around at night alone, trying to investigate the situation themselves, going onto seemingly empty fishing boats, etc.

After the screening was over and the lights went up, I observed a couple of my colleagues in deep and earnest conversation, trying to resolve twists in the plot. They were applying more thought to the movie than the makers did. A critic's mind is a terrible thing to waste.

I Spit on Your Grave
(Directed by Meir Zarchi; starring Camille Keaton, Eron Tabor; 1980)
I Spit on Your Grave is sick, reprehensible, and contemptible. Attending it was one of the most depressing experiences of my life. This is a film without a shred of artistic distinction. It lacks even simple craftsmanship. There is no possible motive for exhibiting it, other than the totally cynical hope that it might make money. Perhaps it will make money: When I saw it on a Monday morning, the theater contained a larger crowd than usual.

It was not just a large crowd, it was a profoundly disturbing one. I do not often attribute motives to audience members, nor do I try to read their minds, but the people who were sitting around me on Monday morning made it easy for me to know what they were thinking. They talked out loud. And if they seriously believed the things they were saying, they were vicarious sex criminals.

The story of *I Spit on Your Grave* is told with moronic simplicity. A girl goes for a vacation in the woods. She sunbathes by a river. Two men speed by in a powerboat. They harass her. Later, they tow her boat to a rendezvous with two of their buddies. They strip the girl, beat her, and rape her. She escapes into the woods. They find her, beat her, and rape her again. She crawls home. They are already there, beat her some more, and rape her again.

Two weeks later, somewhat recovered, the girl lures one of the men out to her house, pretends to seduce him, and hangs him. She lures out another man and castrates him, leaving him to bleed to death in a bathtub. She kills the third man with an ax and disembowels the fourth with an outboard engine. End of movie.

These horrible events are shown with an absolute minimum of dialogue, which is so poorly recorded that it often cannot be heard. There is no attempt to develop the personalities of the characters—they are, simply, a girl and four men, one of them mentally retarded. The movie is nothing more or less than a series of attacks on the girl and then her attacks on the men, interrupted only by an unbelievably grotesque and inappropriate scene in which she enters a church and asks forgiveness for the murders she plans to commit.

How did the audience react to all of this? Those who were vocal seemed to be eating it up. The middle-aged, white-haired man two seats down from me, for example, talked aloud. After the first rape: "That was a good one!" After the second: "That'll show her!" After the third: "I've seen some good ones, but this is the best." When the tables turned and the woman started her killing spree, a woman in the back row shouted: "Cut him up, sister!" In several scenes, the other three men tried to force the retarded man to attack the girl. This inspired a lot of laughter and encouragement from the audience.

I wanted to turn to the man near me and tell him his remarks were disgusting, but I did not. To hold his opinions at his age, he must already have suffered a fundamental loss of decent human feelings. I would have liked to talk with the woman in the back row, the one with the feminist solidarity for the movie's heroine. I wanted to ask if she'd been appalled by the movie's hour of rape scenes. As it was, at the film's end I walked out of the theater quickly, feeling unclean, ashamed, and depressed.

This movie is an expression of the most diseased and perverted darker human natures. Because it is made artlessly, it flaunts its motives: There is no reason to see this movie except to be entertained by the sight of sadism and suffering. As a critic, I have never condemned the use of violence in films if I felt the filmmakers had an artistic reason for employing it. *I Spit on Your Grave* does not. It is a geek show. I wonder if its exhibitors saw it before they decided to play it, and if they felt as unclean afterward as I did.

In Dreams

(Directed by Neil Jordan; starring Annette Bening, Aidan Quinn; 1999)
In Dreams is the silliest thriller in many a moon, and the only one in which the heroine is endangered by apples. She also survives three falls from very high places (two into a lake, one onto apples), escapes from a hospital and a madhouse, has the most clever dog since Lassie, and causes a traffic pile-up involving a truck and a dozen cars. With that much plot, does this movie really need the drowned ghost town, the husband's affair with an Australian woman, the flashbacks to the dominatrix mom, and the garbage disposal that spews apple juice?

All of this goofiness is delivered with style and care by a first-rate team; this is a well-made bad movie. The heroine, named Claire, is portrayed by Annette Bening as a woman in torment. She begins to dream of horrible things, and realizes an evil killer is causing her nightmares ("He's inside my head!"). Her husband (Aidan Quinn) goes to the cops with her premonitions, but gets the brush-off. A frequent dream involves harm to a child; it turns out to be her own.

Eventually she falls into the hands of a psychiatrist (Stephen Rea) who is wise, kindly, and patient, and locks her up in two cruel institutions. One has a padded cell and is guarded by a Nurse Ratchet clone. The other looks like the original snake pit crossed with a dorm at summer camp. The psychiatrist isn't even the villain.

In Dreams is the kind of movie where children's nursery rhymes and sayings are underscored like evil omens. "Mirror, mirror, on the wall . . ." we hear, while the sound track vibrates with menace, and a mother, a daughter, and their dog walk on the banks of a reservoir which was, we learn, created in 1965 by flooding a village that still lurks beneath the waters, a ghost town.

Scuba divers explore it, and we see that the napkin dispensers are still on the counters in the diner, while holy statues float around the church.

Was the villain (Robert Downey, Jr.) drowned in this town? It's not that simple. The explanation of this movie contains more puzzles than the plot itself. Let's say we grant the premise that the villain can indeed project his dreams into the mind of poor Claire. In addition to being clairvoyant, is he also telekinetic? Can he make children's swings move on their own, turn on boom boxes at a distance, project words onto a computer screen, and control garbage disposals?

And does he control the family dog, which has an uncanny ability to find its masters anywhere, anytime? (This is such a clever dog it should know better than to lure Claire into the middle of that highway—unless of course, its dreams are also under remote control.) And what does the buried village have to do with anything? And although the killer was abused as a child by his mother, whose high heels supply a central image, what does that have to do with the nursery rhyme about how "My father was a dollar"?

I dunno. The movie was directed by Neil Jordan, who has done a whole lot better *(Mona Lisa, The Crying Game, Interview with the Vampire)*. Here he navigates uncertainly through a script that is far too large for its container. Whole subplots could have been dumped; why even bother with the other woman in Australia? Although the drowned village supplies some vivid images, wasn't it a huge expense just for some atmosphere? And how many viewers will be able to follow the time-shifted parallels as Claire's escape from a hospital is intercut with the killer's?

In *my* dreams, I'm picturing Tony Lawson's first day on the job. He was the editor of this picture. His survey of the unassembled footage must have been the real horror story.

In Praise of Older Women
(Directed by George Kaczender; starring Tom Berenger, Karen Black, Susan Strasberg; 1977)
In all your amours you should prefer old women to young ones . . . because they have greater knowledge of the world.

So says noted kite-flyer Benjamin Franklin, quoted on the first page of Stephen Vizinczey's novel *In Praise of Older Women*. He may be right. He invented bifocals, after all. But his advice has a built-in male chauvinist flaw, since it assumes that the greater knowledge possessed by older women is not sufficient to warn them away from younger men. This is (we must be fair) a movie clearly inspired by its title. It is in favor of older women, with a top age, I should judge, of about forty. Maybe forty-three. The women pass through the life of Tom Berenger, who plays a Hungarian philosophy teacher who emigrates to Canada. Both Hungary and Canada have their share of older women, who emigrate to Berenger as if he were going out of style, if he had any. He's a kinda pleasant kid, soft-spoken, with a grateful grin that he has to employ again and again in this movie. Older women can't get enough of him.

And that's the problem with the movie: It's not *about* sexual encounters with older women, it's simply the record of them. He keeps running into older women, and having affairs with them, and moving on, and learning nothing. It may well be, as Ben Franklin promises, that older women have greater knowledge of the world, but in this movie, they're canny, and keep it to themselves. The Berenger character isn't a young student of life that they can tutor; he's a heaven-sent one-night stand.

This whole business of older women and younger men is a big deal right now. Another quickly forgettable new movie, *Players,* also deals with the theme. But it cheats: Ali MacGraw may sleep with Dean-Paul Martin in the movie, and she may be, according to the screenplay, twelve years older than he is, but she isn't an older woman, for Pete's sake—she's Ali MacGraw.

Same problem with *In Praise of Older Women.* The older women include Karen Black and Susan Strasberg and a Canadian actress named Helen Shaver. Older women? Big deal. I had a pizza with Helen Shaver at last year's Cannes Film Festival, and she wasn't an older woman then. The movie's basically just a series of soft-core sex scenes tied together by the hero's gratitude. It's not about anything. Berenger has a neat way with his licentious grin, something like Albert Finney's in *Tom Jones,* and that's about it. There are no insights into the relationships involved, no efforts to make the characters into people, no mornings after. No wonder he's so filled with praise.

And yet the movie's doing business, maybe because the title is sensational. I saw it up near the Loyola campus, where the students no doubt consider thirty-three-year-olds to be older women, and I had the benefit of a running commentary from the two jocks sitting behind me. "She's neat," they agreed, after Susan Strasberg appeared on the screen. "She's cool," they agreed about Alexandra Stewart. "She's nice," they agreed about Marilyn Lightstone. "She's neat," they agreed about Marianne McIsaac. That's the trouble with younger men. They're so quick to praise.

In the Army Now

(Directed by Daniel Petrie, Jr.; starring Pauly Shore, Andy Dick; 1994)
We were about halfway into *In the Army Now* when I realized the movie's secret ambition, which is to be nice. It's a movie about a misfit who finds himself in the army—the kind of setup that lends itself to the barbed satire of the Bill Murray movie *Stripes*. I was waiting for the barbs and they weren't coming and to my amazement I realized the movie wanted basically to be an innocent, childlike adventure.

The star is Pauly Shore, a curly-haired comedian who comes across like a skinny Richard Simmons and whose characters are never the slightest bit brighter than the screenplay absolutely demands. He plays an incompetent clerk in an electronics store who gets fired and decides, with his buddy Jack (Andy Dick) to join the Army Reserves—because, hey, after all, they like pay you money for like doing practically nothing, right?

The movie comes to life during a basic training sequence in which the boys draw a sexy female drill sergeant (Lynn Whitfield). The biggest laugh comes after she adjusts a trainee's uniform and Shore quickly dishevels his own, so she'll tug on his pants, too. The scene doesn't have a payoff, but, hey, the setup is fun. Shore and Dick join Lori Petty and David Alan Grier on a water purification team, and are amazed when a crisis breaks out in Liberia, and they find themselves in the middle of a potentially deadly situation.

The screenplay, work by five writers, based on a story by three others, is by a committee and about a committee; the most-used phrase of dialogue is, "Hey, you guys!" The bad guys are of course all Arabs, Hollywood's flavor of the year in villains. But they aren't really bad, because the movie doesn't care that much. Most of the war scenes consist of the four heroes slogging through the sand enchanging rueful one-liners and low-key observations. I was waiting for comedy and got whimsy.

The movie clocks in at ninety-two minutes, not time enough to explain why the Arabs didn't notice anything when U.S. troops parachuted two dune buggies, machine guns, and supplies to Shore and his buddies, immediately outside an enemy camp. Nor time enough to explain such strange details as the Petty character's conviction that if you tear off a shirtsleeve you can use it to carry water in.

I guess maybe the point of the Pauly Shore character is that he's cool and unengaged most of the time. Bombs are exploding all around him, but he's laid-back and doesn't let anything get to him. Instead of laughs, we get to see him having a good time. Lost in the desert, he has lines like, "We are the few, the proud, the water boys." As they slog through the sand, a vulture follows them, and eventually I began to identify with the vulture, which seemed to be hanging around in case anyone thought of any vulture jokes.

Instinct

(Directed by Jon Turteltaub; starring Cuba Gooding, Jr., Donald Sutherland, Anthony Hopkins; 1999)

If there's anything worse than a movie hammered together out of pieces of bad screenplays, it's a movie made from the scraps of good ones. At least with the trash we don't have to suffer through the noble intentions. *Instinct* is a film with not one but four worthy themes. It has pious good thoughts about all of them, but undermines them by slapping on obligatory plot requirements, thick. Nothing happens in this movie that has not been sanctioned by long usage in better films.

This is a film about (1) why Man should learn to live in harmony with Nature; (2) how prison reform is necessary; (3) how fathers can learn to love their children; and (4) why it is wrong to imprison animals in zoos. It doesn't free the beasts from their cages, but it's able to resolve the other three issues— unconvincingly, in a rush of hokey final scenes.

Instinct, directed by John Turteltaub *(Phenomenon),* is all echoes. It gives us Anthony Hopkins playing a toned-down version of Hannibal Lector, Cuba Gooding, Jr., reprising his nice-guy professional from *As Good As It Gets,* Donald Sutherland once again as the wise and weary sage, and John Ashton (you'll recognize him) as a man who is hateful for no better reason than that the plot so desperately needs him to be. Oh, and the settings are borrowed from *Gorillas in the Mist* and *One Flew Over the Cuckoo's Nest.*

The movie's just so darned uplifting and clunky, as it shifts from one of its big themes to another while groaning under the weight of heartfelt speeches. The photography labors to make it look big and important, and the music wants to be sad and uplifting at the same time, as if to say it's a sad world but that's not entirely our fault.

Hopkins stars as Ethan Powell, an anthropologist who went missing in 1994 in an African jungle, and surfaced two years later while murdering two rangers and injuring three others. After a year in chains, he's returned to the United States and locked up in a brutal psycho ward. His interrogation is set to be conducted by an eminent psychiatrist (Donald Sutherland), who instead assigns his famous prisoner to Theo Caulder (Gooding), a student just completing his final year of residency. Why give this juicy patient to a kid who admits he wants to write a best-seller about him? Because Cuba Gooding is the star of the movie, that's why, and Donald Sutherland, who cannot utter a word that doesn't sound like God's truth, always has to play the expert who waits in an oak-paneled study, passing around epigrams and brandy.

Powell's hair and beard make him look like the wild man of Borneo— with reason, since he lived with a family of gorillas in the jungle. He has been mute since the murders, but Caulder thinks he can get him to talk—and can he ever. Hopkins faces one of his greatest acting challenges, portraying a character who must seem reluctant to utter a single word while nevertheless issuing regular philosophical lectures. "I lived as humans lived 10,000 years ago," he explains. "Humans knew how to live then." Even 10,000 years ago, don't you suppose humans were giving gorillas lots of room?

Caulder believes that if he can get Powell to talk about what he did, and why, he can "get him out of there." No matter that Powell *did* kill two men; to understand is to forgive. In his struggle to comprehend his patient, Caulder meets Powell's bitter daughter (Maura Tierney, in a good performance). She is angry with her father. Her father doesn't want to talk about her. "Leave it," he snaps, menacingly. What dire issues stand between them? The movie disappoints us with a reconciliation that plays like a happy ending on the Family Channel. One should always have time for one's children, Powell learned (from the gorillas).

The prison is a snake pit of brutality, run by cruel guards and presided over by a sadistic warden and a weak psychiatrist. Each man is supposed to get thirty minutes a day outdoors. Because this is too much trouble, the guards hand out cards, and the man with the Ace of Diamonds gets to go outside. The toughest prisoner beats up anyone who won't give him the card. Dr. Caulder sees that this is wrong, and institutes a fair lottery, over the objections of the sadistic guards, but with the prisoners chanting their support. The entire business of the Ace of Diamonds, which occupies perhaps twenty minutes, is agonizingly obvious, contrived, and manipulative; the prison population, colorful weirdos of the *Cuckoo's Nest* variety, responds with enthusiastic overacting.

Ethan Powell, of course, sees through the entire system. Superhumanly strong and violent, he puts Caulder through a brief but painful education in the laws of the wild. What he is able to do at the end of the film, and where he is finally able to do it, I leave you to explain, since the film certainly cannot. I also have the gravest doubts about the thank-you note from Powell, which reads not like something that would be written by a man who had lived with the gorillas and killed two men, but by a marketing expert concerned that audiences feel real good when they leave the theater.

Ishtar

(Directed by Elaine May; starring Warren Beatty, Dustin Hoffman; 1987)
It's hard to play dumb. There's always the danger that a little fugitive intelligence will sneak out of a sideways glance and give the game away. The best that can be said for *Ishtar* is that Warren Beatty and Dustin Hoffman, two of the most intelligent actors of their generation, play dumb so successfully that on the basis of this film there's no evidence why they've made it in the movies.

Ishtar is a truly dreadful film, a lifeless, massive, lumbering exercise in failed comedy. Elaine May, the director, has mounted a multimillion-dollar expedition in search of a plot so thin that it hardly could support a five-minute TV sketch. And Beatty and Hoffman, good soldiers marching along on the trip, look as if they've had all wit and thought beaten out of them. This movie is a long, dry slog. It's not funny, it's not smart, and it's interesting only in the way a traffic accident is interesting.

The plot involves the two stars as ninth-rate songwriters who dream of becoming Simon and Garfunkel. They perform bad songs badly before appalled audiences. Their agent gets them a gig in Morocco, and once in Northern Africa, they become involved in the political intrigues of the mythical nation of Ishtar. Isabelle Adjani plays the sexy rebel who leads them down the garden path, and dependable Charles Grodin supplies the movie's only laughs as the resident CIA man.

The movie cannot be said to have a plot. It exists more as a series of cumbersome set pieces, such as the long, pointless sequence in the desert that begins with jokes about blind camels and ends with Hoffman and Beatty firing machine guns at a helicopter. It probably is possible to find humor in blind camels and helicopter gunfights, but this movie leaves the question open.

As I was watching *Ishtar*, something kept nagging at the back of my memory. I absorbed Hoffman and Beatty, their tired eyes, their hollow laughs, their palpable physical weariness as they marched through situations that were funny only by an act of faith. I kept thinking that I'd seen these performances elsewhere, that the physical exhaustion, the vacant eyes, and the sagging limbs added up to a familiar acting style.

Then I remembered. The movie was reminding me of the works of Robert Bresson, the great, austere French director who had a profound suspicion of actors. He felt they were always trying to slip their own energy, their own asides, their own "acting" into his movies. So he rehearsed them tirelessly, fifty or sixty times for every shot, until they were past all thought and caring. And then, when they were zombies with the strength to do only what he required, and nothing more, he was satisfied.

That's what I got out of Beatty and Hoffman in *Ishtar*. There's no hint of Hoffman's wit and intelligence in *Tootsie*, no suggestion of Beatty's grace and good humor in *Heaven Can Wait*, no chemistry between two actors who should be enjoying the opportunity to act together. No life.

I don't know if *Ishtar* was clearly a disaster right from the first, but on the evidence of this film, I'd guess it quickly became a doomed project and that going to the set every morning was more like a sentence than an opportunity. It's said this movie cost more than $40 million. At some point, maybe they should have spun off a million each for Hoffman and Beatty, supplied them with their own personal camera crews, and allowed them to use their spare time making documentaries about what they were going through.

J

⭐ **Jack Frost**

(Directed by Troy Miller; starring Michael Keaton, Joseph Cross, Kelly Preston; 1998)

Jack Frost is the kind of movie that makes you want to take the temperature, if not feel for the pulse, of the filmmakers. What possessed *anyone* to think this was a plausible idea for a movie? It's a bad film, yes, but that's not the real problem. *Jack Frost* could have been codirected by Orson Welles and Steven Spielberg and still be unwatchable, because of that damned snowman.

The snowman gave me the creeps. Never have I disliked a movie character more. They say state-of-the-art special effects can create the illusion of anything on the screen, and now we have proof: It's possible for the Jim Henson folks *and* Industrial Light and Magic to put their heads together and come up with the most repulsive single creature in the history of special effects, and I am not forgetting the Chucky doll or the desert intestine from *Star Wars*.

To see the snowman is to dislike the snowman. It doesn't look like a snowman, anyway. It looks like a cheap snowman suit. When it moves, it doesn't exactly glide—it walks, but without feet, like it's creeping on its torso. It has anorexic tree limbs for arms, which spin through 360 degrees when it's throwing snowballs. It has a big, wide mouth that moves as if masticating Gummi Bears. And it's this kid's dad.

Yes, little Charlie (Joseph Cross) has been without a father for a year, since his dad (Michael Keaton) was killed—on Christmas Day, of course. A year later, Charlie plays his father's magic harmonica ("If you ever need me . . .") and his father turns up as the snowman.

Think about that. It is an *astounding fact*. The snowman on Charlie's front lawn is a living, moving creature inhabited by the personality of his father. It is a reflection of the lame-brained screenplay that despite having a sentient snowman, the movie casts about for plot fillers, including a school bully, a chase scene, snowball fights, a hockey team, an old family friend to talk to mom—you know, stuff to keep up the interest between those boring scenes when *the snowman is talking.*

What do you ask a snowman inhabited by your father? After all, dad's been dead a year. What's it like on the other side? Is there a heaven? Big Bang or steady state? When will the NBA strike end? Elvis—dead? What's it like standing out on the lawn in the cold all night? Ever meet any angels? Has anybody else ever come back as a snowman? Do you have to eat? If you do, then what? Any good reporter could talk to that snowman for five minutes and come back with some great quotes.

But Charlie, self-centered little movie child, is more concerned with how Jack Frost (his father's real name) can help *him.* His dad has been dead for a year and comes back as a snowman and all he can think of is using the snowman to defeat the school bully in a snowball fight. Also, the kid tries to keep dad from melting. (What kind of a half-track miracle is it if a snowman can talk, but it can't keep from melting?) Does the snowman have any advice for his son? Here is a typical conversation:

Jack Frost: "You da man!"

Charlie: "No, *you* da man!"

Jack: "No, I da *snowman!*"

Eventually the snowman has to leave again—a fairly abrupt development announced with the cursory line, "It's time for me to go . . . get on with your life." By this time the snowman's secret is known not only to his son but to his wife (Kelly Preston), who takes a phone call from her dead husband with what, under the circumstances, can only be described as extreme aplomb. At the end, the human Jack Frost materializes again, inside swirling fake snow, and tells his wife and son, "If you ever need me, I'm right here." And Charlie doesn't even ask, "What about on a hot day?"

The Jackal

(Directed by Michael Caton-Jones; starring Bruce Willis, Richard Gere, Sidney Poitier; 1997)

The Jackal is a glum, curiously flat thriller about a man who goes to a great deal of trouble in order to create a crime that anyone in the audience could commit more quickly and efficiently. An example: Can you think, faithful reader, of an easier way to sneak from Canada into the United States than by buying a sailboat and entering it in the Mackinaw-to-Chicago race? Surely there must be an entry point somewhere along the famous 3,000-mile border that would attract less attention than the finish line of a regatta.

To be sure, the Jackal (for it is he) has the money to buy the boat. He is charging $70 million to assassinate the head of the FBI—half now, half payable on completion. He's hired by the head of the Russian Mafia, who, like many a foreigner with extra change in his pocket, doesn't realize he is being overcharged. There are guys right here in town, so I have heard, who would do a whack for ten grand and be happy to have the business.

The Jackal is based on the screenplay of Fred Zinnemann's 1973 classic *The Day of the Jackal.* That was a film that impressed us with the depth of its expertise: We felt it knew exactly what it was talking about. *The Jackal,* on the other hand, impressed me with its absurdity. There was scarcely a second I could take seriously.

Examples: In the Washington, D.C., subway system, the Jackal jumps across the tracks in front of a train, to elude his pursuers. The train stops, exchanges passengers, and pulls out of the station. Is it just possible, do you suppose, that in real life after a man jumps across the tracks, the train halts until the situation is sorted out?

Or, how about the scene where the Jackal parks his van in a garage, and paints the hatch handle with a deadly poison? One of his enemies touches the handle, convulses, and dies an agonizing death. Is that a good way to avoid attention? By being sure there's a corpse on the ground next to your van?

Or, how about the scene early in the film where a fight breaks out on cue, and then stops immediately after a gunshot is fired? Bad handling of the extras here by the assistant director: Everybody in a bar doesn't start or stop fighting at once. Even in the movies, there are always a few guys who delay before joining in, or want to land one last punch at the end. These barflies are as choreographed as dancing Cossacks.

The Jackal is played by Bruce Willis, as a skilled professional killer who hires a man to build him a remote-controlled precision gun mount. The man unwisely asks the kinds of questions that, in his business, are guaranteed to get you killed. Hint: If you should find yourself doing business with a man who wants to pay cash for a device to hold, move, and aim a rifle capable of firing 100 explosive rounds before the first one hits its target—hey, don't go into a lot of speculation about what he may be planning to do with it.

On the Jackal's trail is the deputy head of the FBI (Sidney Poitier), who enlists the help of an IRA terrorist (Richard Gere). The IRA man is a federal prisoner, released into Poitier's custody to lead them to his lover, a Basque terrorist (Mathilda May), who knows what the Jackal looks like. The other major character is a Russian-born agent named Valentina (Diane Venora), whose character trait (singular) is that she lights a cigarette every time she is not already smoking one. I kept waiting for her to be killed, so that a last puff of smoke could drift from her dying lips as her fingers relaxed their grip on her lighter.

There was never a moment in *The Jackal* where I had the slightest confidence in the expertise of the characters. The Jackal strikes me as the kind of overachiever who, assigned to kill a mosquito, would purchase contraband insecticides from Iraq and bring them into the United States by hot-air balloon, distilling his drinking water from clouds and shooting birds for food.

Without giving away too much of the plot, I would like to register one dissent on the grounds of taste. There is a scene making a target out of a character clearly intended to be Hillary Clinton (hints: She is blonde, fiftyish, the wife of the president, and is dedicating the New Hope Children's Hospital). The next time Bruce Willis or Richard Gere complains about the invasion of their privacy by the media, I hope someone remembers to ask them why their movie needed to show the first lady under fire.

Jaws the Revenge
(Directed by Joseph Sargent; starring Lorraine Gary, Michael Caine, Lance Guest; 1987)
Jaws the Revenge is not simply a bad movie, but also a stupid and incompetent one—a ripoff. And that's a surprise, because the film is the fourth in a series that has served Universal Pictures long and well, and it stars Lorraine Gary, the wife of the studio's chief executive officer. Wasn't there someone in charge of assuring that the film was at least a passable thriller, however bad? I guess not.

The plot centers on the character of Ellen Brody, who, you may recall, was the wife of the Roy Scheider character in the first and second *Jaws* movies. Now she is a widow, and her son has his dad's old job at the police department. The story opens at Christmas, as the son is eaten by a shark right off Martha's Vineyard, while a children's choir drowns out his screams with Christmas carols.

Mrs. Brody (Gary) flees in horror to the Bahamas, where her other son (Lance Guest) works as, you got it, a marine biologist. She pleads with him not to go into the water, but he argues that the great white shark has never been seen in warm waters. Not long after, the shark is seen, having made the trip from Martha's Vineyard to the Bahamas in three days.

Mrs. Brody, meanwhile, falls in love with a local pilot (Michael Caine), and there is a subplot about how her son is jealous of this new man in his mother's life. This jealousy, like every other plot device in the movie, is left unresolved at the end, but so what? The screenplay is simply a series of meaningless episodes of human behavior, punctuated by shark attacks.

Since we see so much of the shark in the movie, you'd think they would have built some good ones. They've had three earlier pictures for practice. But in some scenes the shark's skin looks like canvas with acne, and in others all we see is an obviously fake shark head with lots of teeth. The shark models have so little movement that at times they seem to be supporting themselves on boats, instead of attacking them. Up until the ludicrous final sequence of the movie, the scariest creature in the film is an eel.

What happens at the end? Ellen Brody has become convinced that the shark is following her. It wants revenge against her entire family. Her friends pooh-pooh the notion that a shark could identify, follow, or even care about one individual human being, but I am willing to grant the point, for the benefit of the plot.

I believe that the shark wants revenge against Mrs. Brody. I do. I really do believe it. After all, her husband was one of the men who hunted this shark and killed it, blowing it to bits. And what shark wouldn't want revenge against the survivors of the men who killed it?

Here are some things, however, that I do not believe:

• That Mrs. Brody could be haunted by flashbacks to events where she was not present and that, in some cases, no survivors witnessed.

• That the movie would give us one shark attack as a dream sequence, have the hero wake up in a sweat, then give us a second shark attack, and then cut to the hero awake in bed, giving us the only thing worse than the old "it's only a dream" routine, which is the old "is it a dream or not?" routine.

• That Mrs. Brody would commandeer a boat and sail out alone into the ocean to sacrifice herself to the shark, so that the killing could end. That Caine's character could or would crash-land his airplane at sea so that he and two other men could swim to Mrs. Brody's rescue.

• That after being trapped in a sinking airplane by the shark and disappearing under the water, Caine could survive the attack, swim to the boat, and climb on board—not only completely unhurt but wearing a shirt and pants that are *not even wet.*

• That the shark would stand on its tail in the water long enough for the boat to ram it.

• That the director, Joseph Sargent, would film this final climactic scene so incompetently that there is not even an establishing shot, so we have to figure out what happened on the basis of empirical evidence.

There is one other thing I can't believe about *Jaws the Revenge,* and that is that on March 30, 1987, Michael Caine passed up his chance to accept his Academy Award in person because of his commitment to this movie. Why? Well, as the marine biologist in the movie explains, if you don't go right back in the water after something terrible happens to you, you might be too afraid to ever go back in again. Maybe Caine was thinking that if he ever left the set, he could never bring himself to return.

The Jazz Singer
(Directed by Richard Fleischer; starring Neil Diamond, Lucie Arnaz, Laurence Olivier; 1980)

The Jazz Singer has so many things wrong with it that a review threatens to become a list. Let me start with the most obvious: This movie is about a man who is at least twenty years too old for such things to be happening to him. *The Jazz Singer* looks ridiculous giving us Neil Diamond going through an adolescent crisis.

The movie is a remake, of course, of Al Jolson's 1927 *The Jazz Singer,* which was the first commercially successful talking picture. The remake has played with time in an interesting way: It sets the story in the present, but it places the characters in some kind of time warp. Their behavior seems decades out of date, and some scenes are totally inexplicable in any context.

For example: In the film, Diamond plays a young Jewish cantor at his father's synagogue. He is married, he has apparently settled down to a lifetime of religion. But he also writes songs for a black group. When one of the quartet gets sick, Diamond takes his place, appearing in a black nightclub in blackface. Oh yeah? This scene is probably supposed to be homage to Jolson's blackface performance of *Mammy* in the original, but what it does in 1980 is get the movie off to an unintentionally hilarious start.

The bulk of the movie concerns Diamond's decision to leave New York, his father, and his wife and go to Los Angeles, where he hopes to break into the music industry. This whole business of leaving the nest, of breaking the ties with his father, seems strange in a middle-aged character: Diamond is just too old to play these scenes. But no matter; the movie is ridiculous for lots of other reasons.

When he arrives in LA, for example, he's instantly "discovered" in a recording studio by Lucie Arnaz, who plays an agent and is filled with energy and spunk—she's the best thing in the movie. She thinks he has promise, so she gets him a job as the opening act for a comic. This gives Diamond a chance to sing, and his onstage appearances, I guess, are supposed to be the big deal in this movie. Because of that, the film sacrifices any attempt to present them realistically: For his West Coast debut as a warm-up for a comic, Diamond is backed up by dozens of onstage musicians, which look like the LA Philharmonic and, at union scale, would cost upward of $80,000. Sure.

The plot plods relentlessly onward. Laurence Olivier plays the aging father in the film, in a performance that seems based on that tortured German accent he also used in *The Boys from Brazil, Marathon Man,* and *A Little Romance:* Is it too much to hope that Sir Laurence will return to the English language sometime soon? Father and son fight, split, grudgingly meet again, hold a tearful reunion—all in scenes of deadly predictability.

One sequence that is not predictable has Neil Diamond abandoning the (now pregnant) Lucie Arnaz in order to hit the highway and become a roadshow Kristofferson. This stretch of the film, with Diamond self-consciously lonely and hurting, is supposed to be affecting, but it misfires, it drips with so much narcissism.

But then Diamond's whole presence in this movie is offensively narcissistic. His songs are melodramatic, interchangeable, self-aggrandizing groans and anguished shouts, backed protectively by expensive and cloying instrumentation. His dramatic presence also looks overprotected, as if nobody was willing to risk offending him by asking him to seem involved, caring, and engaged.

Diamond plays the whole movie looking at people's third shirt buttons, as if he can't be bothered to meet their eyes and relate with them. It's strange about the Diamond performance: It's not just that he can't act. It's that he sends out creepy vibes. He seems self-absorbed, closed off, grandiose, out of touch with his immediate surroundings. His fans apparently think Neil Diamond songs celebrate worthy human qualities. I think they describe conditions suitable for treatment.

Jennifer 8

(Directed by Bruce Robinson; starring Andy Garcia, Lance Henrickson, Uma Thurman; 1992)

Jennifer 8 promises a plot of excruciating complexity, but the story line turns relentlessly dumb. By the end the characters might as well be wearing name tags: "Hi! I'm the serial killer!" This is the kind of movie where everybody makes avoidable errors in order for the plot to wend its tortuous way to an unsatisfactory conclusion. Somebody should have taken a hard look at the screenplay and decided that it wasn't finished.

The movie stars Andy Garcia as a big-city detective who is recovering from a bad marriage with a cheating wife, and returns to the smaller city where his brother-in-law (Lance Henriksen) is a cop. Within minutes of his arrival, he's digging through a garbage dump in search of body parts, and in no time flat he's on the trail of a serial killer.

Deducing that a severed hand belonged to a blind person (yes, the fingertips are worn down from reading Braille) and that it was in a freezer for a long time, Garcia runs a computer search and discovers a pattern: Eight blind women have been killed and mutilated, all with .22 revolvers, within a 300-mile radius. (The fact that it takes a computer to discern this trend reminds me of the classic line from *Fargo*, "I'm not sure I agree with you a hundred percent on your police work there, Lou.") This is obviously the work of a serial killer, Garcia announces, only to arouse the fury of the local cop (Graham Beckel) who was on the case of the original missing woman.

The movie turns into a police procedural as Garcia interviews the blind roommate (Uma Thurman) of one of the missing women. Before long they have fallen into a particularly unconvincing love affair; I didn't believe it because Thurman, usually so alive in her roles, here interprets her character as a soggy zombie who occasionally musters a smile. At Christmas she gets all dressed up to go to a party, but retreats in tears to the bedroom after she loses her way and everybody talks loud at the same time. That wouldn't stop any of the blind party animals I've known.

The movie has no insights about the blind, other than they benefit greatly from talking alarm clocks and don't need any lightbulbs in their bedrooms. Blindness is simply another plot gimmick in a movie with so many it can hardly remember what corner it's currently cutting. Like many needlessly complicated movies, it plays long—real long—and it's a relief when John Malkovich appears, at about the ninety-minute mark, playing an FBI man (I think) who accuses Garcia of murder.

The murder in question has to be seen to be believed. One cop climbs a fire escape into a building where he suspects the killer is hiding. He tells his partner, "If anyone comes down this fire escape but me, shoot." Somebody else comes down the fire escape, shining a flashlight into the eyes of the other cop, who of course stands in full view to make himself a better target, and does not shoot. Even movie cops should be smarter than that.

And then there is the big climax, a red herring of truly startling proportions, indicating that the movie is willing to cheat, lie, and defraud to get a cheap thrill. The audience simply laughed in disbelief. *Jennifer 8* has aspirations to be a cross between the murderer-next-door thriller and the Pathology Picture, so named because everybody stands around making hard-boiled comments about body parts (my favorite: A cop, examining a corpse at the dump, asks, "How long has he been feeling like this?").

The cast in this movie has been outstanding in other movies; in addition to Garcia, Thurman, Malkovich, and Henriksen *(The Stepfather),* there's Kathy Baker as the sister-in-law, plucky and determined, and even Kevin Conway as a police chief. It was quite an achievement to assemble them into one picture, but my guess is they'll skip the reunions.

Joe's Apartment

(Directed by John Payson; starring Jerry O'Connell, Megan Ward, Robert Vaughn; 1996)

I am informed that 5,000 cockroaches were used in the filming of *Joe's Apartment*. That depresses me, but not as much as the news that none of them were harmed during the production. I do not like cockroaches, and I wonder if they even like themselves. Although it is said that after a nuclear holocaust they would inherit the earth, my guess is they would still scurry out of sight even when there was no one left to see them.

Joe's Apartment would be a very bad comedy even without the roaches, but it would not be a disgusting one. No, wait: I take that back. Even without the roaches, we would still have the subplot involving the pink disinfectant urinal cakes. Not everybody's cup of tea.

My standards are not inflexible. There is a scene in *Trainspotting* in which the hero dives headfirst into the filthiest toilet in Scotland, and I actually enjoyed that scene (you would have to see the movie to understand why). But when we arrived at the tender little scene in *Joe's Apartment* where the roaches were tugging at his eyelashes to wake him up, I easily contained my enthusiasm.

The movie is a feature-length version of a 1992 short film made for MTV by John Payson. Less is more. The idea of singing, dancing cockroach buddies can easily be explored in all of its manifestations, I am sure, in a film much briefer than eighty minutes, which is how long *Joe's Apartment* runs, illustrating my principle that no good film is too long and no bad film is short enough.

The plot has been recycled out of many another Manhattan comedy about the evil property developer who wants to tear down the colorful little brownstone and put up some architectural monstrosity. The rent-controlled apartment building in this film is occupied by a little old lady, who is tripped by hidden wires and in other ways forced out of her flat by the nephews of the evil slumlord (played by Don Ho; yes, Don Ho). But then the hero, Joe (Jerry O'Connell) moves into the apartment, posing as her heir, and so the nephews start on him. The real tenants of the apartment are tens of thousands of cockroaches, who at first dislike Joe but eventually become his friend and gang up on the slumlord.

I am not sure I need to go into all of the details involving Joe's new girlfriend Lily (Megan Ward), or how hard she works on her garden, or how well Joe collects manure from the carriage horses of Central Park to help her, or how her dad is a senator (played by Robert Vaughn; yes, Robert Vaughn). If you want to know how the pink scented urinal cakes come into the story, send me a stamped, self-addressed postcard. On second thought, don't stamp it.

The roaches are the real centerpiece of the movie. These are not ordinary roaches. They sing and dance. Some people will be reminded of the singing mice in *Babe,* but singing mice are one thing and a roach quintet is quite another. The insects have obnoxious piping little voices and sound like the Chipmunks if they had inhaled helium.

Some of the roaches are given names, but I must say none of them really emerged as individuals for me. They were more of a large squirming mass, and when several hundred of them crawled across Joe's face, I for one was happy to be sitting in the back row, lest a fellow moviegoer be moved to hurl. The special effects are very good, I suppose. You can see every detail of the carefully articulated armor on their little tummies, if you want to.

Jonathan Livingston Seagull
(Directed by Hall Bartlett; 1973)

At the point when I walked out of *Jonathan Livingston Seagull*—some forty-five minutes into the movie—the hero had learned to avoid garbage and fly high, but the film, alas, had not. I hardly ever walk out of movies, and in fact I sometimes make a point of sitting through bad ones, just to get ammunition for a juicy review. But this one was too much.

It is based, to begin with, on a book so banal that it had to be sold to adults; kids would have seen through it. *The Little Engine That Could* is, by comparison, a work of some depth and ambition. Consider that the movie made from the book has now been made the object of a lawsuit by the book's author and you have some measure of the depths to which we sink as Jonathan dives.

Jonathan not only dives, and perfects his aeronautical ability, and makes his name as the flocks leading nonconformist, but he also talks. Allowing him to talk is perhaps the movie's basic strategic error. Jonathan talks under his breath with great gasping urgency: He talks to himself about how if only he could hold his wings a little different, etc., he, too, could dive for fish and not have to scavenge garbage.

And then there's the problem of the birds. The movie uses real birds, and it's a little sickening to show them being knocked out and batted around in the interest of the story line. I left when Jonathan had dragged himself, groggy and bleeding, onto some flotsam. Who wants to pay to see birds bleed?

Jungle 2 Jungle

(Directed by John Pasquin; starring Tim Allen, Sam Huntington; 1997)
There is a scene early in *Jungle 2 Jungle* that indicates how brainless the movie is. Before I explore its delights, I must make you familiar with the premise. A Manhattan commodities broker journeys up the Amazon to obtain a divorce from the wife he has not seen in many years. She works now among the Indians. The broker is astonished to find that he has a son, who has been raised by his estranged wife in the jungle. The son now wants to return to New York with his father, because he has promised the tribal chief he will bring back the fire from the torch atop the Statue of Liberty.

Now, as we rejoin our story, the broker (Tim Allen) and his son (Sam Huntington) arrive at Kennedy Airport, and here is the brainless part: The boy, who is about thirteen, is still dressed for the jungle. He wears only a loincloth and some feathers and suchlike; no shirt or shoes. If memory serves, he carries his deadly dart blowgun, which is the sort of thing you're not allowed to have on an aircraft, but never mind: Did either of this child's parents stop to consider that perhaps the lad should have jeans and a sweatshirt for a 3,000-mile air journey? Such garments are available in Brazil. I know; I've been there. I flew upstream in a plane with pontoons, and landed on the Amazon above Belim without seeing a single person in a loincloth, although I saw many Michael Jordan T-shirts.

But no, the parents didn't stop to think, and that is because they *don't think*. Why don't they think? Because no one is allowed to think in this movie. Not one single event in the entire plot can possibly take place unless every character in the cast has brains made of Bac-O-Bits.

The plot of *Jungle 2 Jungle* has been removed from a French film called *Little Indian, Big City*. The operation is a failure and the patient dies. The only reason I am rating this movie at one star while *Little Indian, Big City* got "no stars" is that *Jungle 2 Jungle* is too mediocre to deserve no stars. It doesn't achieve truly awful badness, but is sort of a black hole for the attention span, sending us spiraling down into nothingness.

Most of the comic moments come from the "fish out of water" premise, or "FOW," as Hollywood abbreviates it (you know a plot's not original when it has its own acronym). The kid has been raised in the jungle, and now, in the city, he tries to adapt. There are many jokes involving his pet tarantula, which he has brought along with him, and his darts, which Allen uses to accidentally put his fiancée's cat to sleep.

The fiancée is played by Lolita Davidovich, who is supposed to be a successful businesswoman, but dresses as if she aspires to become a lap dancer. The joke is that she doesn't like the idea of her future husband having a jungle boy. Additional jokes involve Martin Short, who plays Allen's associate and has stolen Jim Jarmusch's hairstyle, although not his wit. There are also some Russian Mafia guys, who march in and out like landlords in a *Three Stooges* comedy.

Little Indian, Big City (1996) got many if not most of the year's worst reviews, but when I heard it was being remade with Tim Allen, I must confess I had some hope: Surely they would see how bad the premise was, and repair it? Not a chance. This movie has not learned from the mistakes of others, and like a lemming follows *Little Indian* over the cliff and into the sea.

KKKKKKKKKKK

Kazaam

(Directed by Paul M. Glaser; starring Shaquille O'Neal, Francis Capra; 1996)

Kazaam is a textbook example of a filmed deal, in which adults assemble a package that reflects their own interests and try to sell it to kids. How else to explain a children's movie where the villains are trying to steal a bootleg recording so they can sell pirated copies of it? What do kids know, or care, about that?

The movie stars Shaquille O'Neal, the basketball player, as Kazaam, a genie who is released from captivity in an old boom box, and has to perform three wishes for a little kid (Francis Capra). Right there you have a wonderful illustration of the movie's creative bankruptcy. Assigned to construct a starring vehicle for Shaq, the filmmakers looked at him, saw a tall bald black man, and said, "Hey, he can be a genie!" At which point, somebody should have said, "Okay, that's level one. Now let's take it to level three."

Shaq has already proven he can act (in *Blue Chips,* the 1994 movie about college basketball). Here he shows he can be likable in a children's movie. What he does not show is good judgment in his choice of material; this is a tired concept, written by the numbers. Kids old enough to know about Shaq as a basketball star will be too old to enjoy the movie. Younger kids won't find much to engage them. And O'Neal shouldn't have used the movie to promote his own career as a hopeful rap artist; the sound track sounds less like music to entertain kids than like a trial run for a Shaq album.

The plot: A wrecking ball destroys an old building, releasing a genie who is discovered by a kid named Max (Capra). The rules are, he gets three wishes. The twist is, the genie doesn't much like people, having made no friends in 5,000 years and having spent most of that time cooped up in bottles, lamps, radiators, etc. The other twist is, the kid doesn't much trust people, because his father has disappeared.

The genie, however, helps the kid find his father, only to find out the father is involved in an illegal music pirating operation. The father is not quite ready to go straight, but eventually, after some action sequences involving an evil gang, he realizes that his future depends on living up to his son's expectations.

Uncanny, how much this plot resembles *Aladdin and the King of Thieves,* a Disney made-for-video production. In that one, Aladdin has never known his father, but an oracle in an old lamp tells him where the father is to be found, and the helpful blue genie helps him go there. His father is the King of the Thieves, it turns out, and may not be entirely ready to go straight. But after some action sequences involving the evil gang of thieves, the father realizes that he must live up to his son's expectations, etc.

Did anybody at Disney notice they were making the same movie twice, once as animation, once as live action? Hard to say. The animated movie at least has the benefit of material that fits the genre, much better songs, a colorful graphic style, and another outing for the transmogrifying genie with the voice by Robin Williams. *Kazaam,* on the other hand, by being live action, makes the bad guys too real for the fantasy to work, and the action sequence feels just like the end of every other formula movie where the third act is replaced by fires and fights.

There are several moments in the movie when fantasy and reality collide. One comes when the genie astonishes the kid with a roomful of candy, which cascades out of thin air. I was astonished, too. Astonished that this genie who had been bottled up for most of the last 5,000 years would supply modern off-the-shelf candy in its highly visible commercial wrappers: M&M's, etc. Does the genie's magic create the wrappers along with the candy, or does the genie buy the candy at wholesale before rematerializing it?

There is also the awkwardness of the relationship between the genie and the kid, caused by the need to make Kazaam not only a fantasy figure, but also a contemporary pal who can advise the kid, steer him straight, and get involved in the action at the end. Genies are only fun in the movies if you define and limit their powers. That should have been obvious, but the filmmakers didn't care to extend themselves beyond the obvious commercial possibilities of their first dim idea. As for Shaquille O'Neal, given his own three wishes the next time, he should go for a script, a director, and an interesting character.

Lair of the White Worm

(Directed by Ken Russell; starring Amanda Donohue, Hugh Grant; 1988)
Let this much be said for Ken Russell's *The Lair of the White Worm:* This
movie provides you with exactly what you would expect from a movie named
The Lair of the White Worm. It has a lair, it has a worm, the worm is white,
and there is a sufficient number of screaming victims to be dragged down into
the lair by the worm.

Russell provides you with your money's worth. Why he would have
wanted to make this film is another matter. This is the kind of movie that
Roger Corman was making for American-International back in the early
1960s, when AIP was plundering the shelves of out-of-copyright horror tales,
looking for cheap story ideas. Corman would have found *The Lair of the
White Worm* on the shelf right next to *Dracula;* both books were written by
the same strange man, Bram Stoker.

In losing a juicy early-1960s AIP horror movie, we have gained a juicy
late-1980s horror movie that would probably seem better if Russell's name
were not connected to it. People expect something special from Ken Russell,
whose inflamed filmography includes such items as *Women in Love, The
Music Lovers, The Devils, The Boyfriend, Tommy, Altered States, Crimes of
Passion,* and *Salome's Last Dance.* Every one of Russell's films have been an
exercise in wretched excess. Sometimes it works. Russell loves the bizarre,
the Gothic, the overwrought, the perverse. The strangest thing about *The Lair
of the White Worm* is that, by his standards, it is rather straight and square.

The movie begins on an archaeological dig in the wilds of Scotland,
where a curious fossil is discovered, a fossil that seems neither man nor beast,
nor reptile, for that matter, and yet contains aspects of more than one species.
What does the skull represent? That is an assignment for young Angus Flint,
who has the perfect name for an archaeologist, and who has made his find in
the barnyard of the Trent sisters, Mary and Eve. Eventually, Flint discovers

some of the family history. The Trent girls lost their father when he disappeared during a spelunking expedition in a nearby cave. And local tradition has it that the medieval lord of the area once slew a giant dragon.

Anyone who has ever seen a horror film can carry on unassisted from here; no prizes for reaching the end before Ken Russell. The skull obviously belongs to a race of giant dragons, or worms, and one of them quite possibly devoured the late Mr. Trent down in that cave. Russell introduces us to two more characters, and the chase is on. One of them is Lord James D'Ampton, descendant of the dragon-slayer. The other is Lady Sylvia Marsh, who dresses like a tasteful Elvira and lives in the moldering Gothic mansion down the lane.

More than this I will not tell. No, not even to hint that the worm of Stone Rigg Cavern can manifest itself in human form. Certainly not that. What I will say for *The Lair of the White Worm* is that this is a respectable B-grade monster movie, more tame and civilized than the Mad Slasher movies that have all but destroyed the genre. It has everything you want: shadows, screams, feverish scientific speculations, guttering candle flames, flowing diaphanous gowns, midnights, dawns, and worms. Ken Russell was once, and no doubt will be again, considered an important director. This is the sort of exercise he could film with one hand tied behind his back, and it looks like that was indeed more or less his approach.

Lake Placid

(Directed by Steve Miner; starring Bill Pullman, Bridget Fonda; 1999)
"What an animal does in the water is his own business—unless he does it to man." So says Sheriff Keough, one of the crocbusters of *Lake Placid.* I couldn't disagree with him more. The thirty-foot crocodile in this movie stays in the water, contentedly munching on bears and cows, until scuba-diving beaver-taggers invade his domain. It's their own fault that the beast gets mad and eats a scientist and half a game warden.

The croc inhabits Black Lake, in Maine. (There is no Lake Placid in the movie, which may be its most intriguing mystery). It is, we learn, an Asian crocodile. "How did he swim across the sea?" a lawman asks, not unreasonably. "They conceal information like that in books," one of the movie's croc lovers answers sarcastically. I dunno; I thought it was a pretty good question.

As the movie opens, two game wardens are tagging beavers, to study their movements. Suddenly they're attacked by an underwater camera, which lunges at them in an unconvincing imitation of an offscreen threat. It becomes clear that Black Lake harbors more than beavers, although for my money the scenes involving beavers were the scariest in the movie. Can you imagine being underwater, inside a beaver dam, with angry animals the size of footstools whose teeth can chomp through logs?

When it becomes clear that Black Lake harbors a gigantic beast, an oddly assorted crew assembles to search for it. There's fish warden Jack Wells (Bill Pullman), museum paleontologist Kelly Scott (Bridget Fonda), Sheriff Keogh (Brendan Gleeson), and millionaire croc-lover Hector Cyr (Oliver Platt), a mythology professor who believes "crocodiles are divine conduits." Oh, and there's Mrs. Bickerman (Betty White), who lives in a cute little farm cottage on the shores of the lake and lost her husband a few years ago. That's her story, anyway.

Whether the movie was intended at any point to be a serious monster thriller, I cannot say. In its present form it's an uneasy compromise between a gorefest and a comedy—sort of a failed *Anaconda.* One peculiar aspect is the sight of an expensive cast in such a cheap production. We're looking at millions of dollars' worth of actors in the kind of aluminum boat you see on display outside Sam's Club. Given the size of the crocodile, this movie lends a new meaning to the classic *Jaws* line, "We're going to need a bigger boat."

There's tension between the locals and the visitors, between the croc lovers and the croc killers, between the sheriff and the state game officials, between the sexes, and between everybody else and Betty White, who uses language that would turn the Golden Girls green. Almost all of the disagreements involve incredibly stupid decisions (would you go scuba diving in a lake with a hungry giant crocodile?). New meaning is given to the disclaimer "no animals were harmed during the filming of this movie" by a scene where a cow is dangled from a helicopter as bait for the crocodile. I believe the cow wasn't harmed, but I'll bet she was really upset.

Occasional shots are so absurd they're just plain funny. Consider the way thousands of perch jump into the air because they're scared of the crocodile. What's their plan? Escape from the lake? I liked the way the croc's second victim kept talking after he'd lost half his body. And the way the Fonda character was concerned about toilet and tent facilities in their camp; doesn't she know she's an hour's drive from Freeport, Maine, where L. L. Bean can sell her a folding condo?

The movie is pretty bad, all right. But it has a certain charm. It's so completely wrongheaded from beginning to end that it develops a doomed fascination. We can watch it switching tones within a single scene—sometimes between lines of dialogue. It's gruesome, and then camp, and then satirical, and then sociological, and then it pauses for a little witty intellectual repartee. Occasionally the crocodile leaps out of the water and snatches victims from the shore, looking uncannily like a very big green product from the factory where they make Barney dolls. This is the kind of movie that actors discuss in long, sad talks with their agents.

Larger than Life
(Directed by Howard Franklin; starring Bill Murray, Linda Fiorentino, Janeane Garofalo; 1996)

Curious, how in such a disappointing comedy, Bill Murray manages to dash off a hilarious warm-up. The opening scenes of *Larger than Life,* showing him as a third-rate motivational speaker, are right on target, with one zinger after another aimed at after-dinner speakers who promise to remake your life with touchy-feely slogans.

Murray plays Jack Corcoran, whose trademark slogan is "Get Over It!" He shows a banquet crowd how to unleash its hidden abilities by calling for volunteers to make a human pyramid. His clients include the American Motion Upholstery Assn. (reclining chairs), but his agents promise him some bigger fees, real soon. Meanwhile, he's preparing to get married, urged on by his mom (Anita Gillette), who has always told him his father drowned while saving helpless children.

Not true. A telegram arrives informing him of his father's death. "You mean I had a father all these years?" he wails, and his mother explains she left her husband because he was "irresponsible." Maybe he was. The old man was a circus clown. Jack's inheritance includes a pile of bills and a trained elephant named Vera.

Most of *Larger than Life* involves Jack's attempts to move Vera entirely across the United States, to California, where the elephant will end up either as the victim of a sadistic animal trainer (Linda Fiorentino) or as part of a breeding herd being shipped to Sri Lanka by an environmental activist (Janeane Garofalo).

The formula for road movies, even those involving elephants, includes colorful characters encountered along the way, and two of the bright spots in a dim screenplay are provided by an old carny named Vernon (Pat Hingle) and his tattooed wife Luluna (Lois Smith). They knew and loved Jack's father, and teach Jack some commands which (sometimes) make Vera perform an amazing repertory of tricks. They also advise him to avoid the straight life and become a carny, not a rube.

Jack's adventures with transporting Vera include a train journey, followed by an attempt to maneuver a semitrailer truck. And we meet Tip Tucker (Matthew McConaughey), a manic semi owner-operator with weird theories about everything in American society, especially school lunch programs. He pursues Jack and Vera cross-country after they misuse his truck. At the end of the journey, Jack has to decide between the circus and the zoo for Vera—and, in a way, for himself.

The materials are here to make a good comedy, I guess. The screenplay is by Roy Blount, Jr., a funny writer. But the energy isn't there. Murray often chooses to play a laid-back, detached character, but this time he's so detached he's almost absent. He chooses to work in a low key, and the other actors, in matching his energy level, make a movie that drones instead of hums. Comedy is often about people who are passionately frustrated in goals they're convinced are crucial. Here Jack hardly seems to care, as he and Vera mosey along cross-country, bemused rather than bedazzled by their adventures.

The sad thing is, there are the fixings for another comedy, probably a much better one, right there in the opening scenes. Motivational speakers are ripe for satire. The bookshelves groan with self-improvement volumes, all promising to explain the problems of your universe, and their solution, in a few well-chosen rules. An honest bookstore would post the following sign above its "self-help" section: "For true self-help, please visit our philosophy, literature, history, and science sections, find yourself a good book, read it, and think about it."

Murray's portrait of an inspirational speaker is right on target, and filled out with lots of subtle touches of movement and dialogue, and there is humor, too, in the way his audiences will go along with his insane schemes (like the human pyramid), as if being able to balance three people on your back would solve your problems at work. This whole section of the movie is inspired; Murray should star in the movie of *The Dilbert Principle.*

As for the elephant portions of the movie: They say an elephant never forgets, which means that I have an enormous advantage over Tai, who plays Vera, because I plan to forget this movie as soon as convenient.

The Last Movie
(Directed by Dennis Hopper; starring Dennis Hopper, Peter Fonda, Kris Kristofferson; 1972)

Dennis Hopper's *The Last Movie* is a wasteland of cinematic wreckage. There are all sorts of things you can say about it, using easy critical words to describe it as undisciplined, incoherent, a structural mess. But mostly it's just plain pitiful. Hopper hasn't even been able to cover his tracks; the failure of his intentions is nakedly obvious. Near the movie's end there's a pathetic scene in which he sits, half-stoned, dazed, confused, and says the hell with it. It feels like he means it.

In Hollywood, they talk about movies and performances being "saved on the Green Machine." They mean the editing process, when a skilled editor can take mixed-up footage and somehow give a meaning and structure to it. Movies are such a suggestive art form that a good editor can forget about the gaps and chasms in a story line and convince moviegoers—before their very eyes!—that it all somehow fits together.

Based on the evidence in this cut of *The Last Movie,* every possible effort was made to save the project after Hopper finally returned from Peru with his hours of footage. The plan seems to have been to make the movie look like *Easy Rider,* whenever possible, and hope the counterculture would get behind it. Well, that didn't work but I wonder if anything would have worked.

The story line (if you'll permit me to be linear in the face of the movie's fragmentation) concerns a Hollywood cowboy extra who stays behind after a B-Western crew has finished filming a potboiler. He shacks up with a girl he's met, gets involved in a dazed search for gold, passes some time with the local American expatriates, and then he becomes the unwitting star in a "movie" that the local Indians make on the Western sets that were left behind.

It appears from the evidence on the screen that the movie's events were originally intended to unfold in chronological order. But it didn't work out that way. Hopper's gold-mining expedition, for example, is duly announced. But then we get a lyrical sequence of silhouettes against the sunset, trucks driving into the dusk, small figures in a vast landscape, etc., while a suitable song is performed on the sound track. And that is the gold-mining expedition.

After they get back, however, there's a scene where they try to talk the rich Americans into backing them—and this scene is done in a realistic tone, with lots of dialogue and everything. Then, at the movie's end, there's a flash-back to a campfire scene on the gold-hunting expedition. This scene, done in the style and mood of the pot-inspired campfire scene in *Easy Rider,* has the two prospectors reveal that they learned about gold mining by watching Walter Huston in *Treasure of the Sierra Madre.*

Fine. The easy, stoned absurdity of the scene reminds us of Jack Nicholson and his warnings about flying saucers in *Easy Rider.* But if we watch the scene like cinematic archaeologists, we sense the invisible presence of the Green Machine. My notion is that an entire gold-seeking expedition was filmed, and then not used; that the pastoral photography was put in to paper over the hole in the plot, and that the campfire scene was then salvaged and stuck in at the end to give the necessary mood lift before the movie's downer conclusion.

All of this—the fancy photography, the fragmented editing, the series of expensive performers, and high-royalty songs—is just an elaborate rescue attempt. There are also all sorts of guest appearances by Hopper's friends, who flew down to the big doings on the Peru location: *The Last Movie* almost becomes the drug culture's *Around the World in 80 Days.*

The idea, I guess, is that we're supposed to understand that if Peter Fonda and John Phillip Law and everybody had such a dandy time, and if the movie thumbs its nose at making any sense and if Hopper throws us off the scent by using title cards that say "scene missing" and if he leaves in clapboards and puts in a jolly handwritten "The End!" when the movie's over, why, then, *The Last Movie* must exist on many levels, some of them droll, some significant, some intended as kind of an underground telegram to users.

I dunno. Audiences and especially the young audience this movie is aimed for (or at) aren't going for the old razzle-dazzle so much anymore. They've played against too much of it. Hip directors aren't getting away with the fast break and the downcourt pass from nowhere: audiences are playing a more defensive game, and for *The Last Movie* they may even have to go into a man-to-man.

Last Rites
(Directed by Donald P. Bellisario; starring Tom Berenger, Dane Clark; 1988)
This is it, located at last and with only six weeks to spare—the worst film of 1988. *Last Rites* qualifies because it passes both acid tests: It is not only bad filmmaking, but it is offensive as well—offensive to my intelligence. Many films are bad. Only a few declare themselves the work of people deficient in taste, judgment, reason, tact, morality, and common sense. Was there no one connected with this project who read the screenplay, considered the story, evaluated the proposed film, and vomited?

The movie begins with the following premise: Handsome young Father Michael Pace (Tom Berenger) is an assistant priest at St. Patrick's Cathedral in New York. His father, Carlo Pace (Dane Clark) is the godfather of the New York Mafia. The movie opens with Michael's sister, Zena (Anne Twomey) catching her husband with his mistress and shooting him. She's a pretty good shot. The first shot castrates him, the second one kills him. Then she goes to Father Michael to confess her sin.

The sacrament of confession is handled throughout this movie as a cheap gimmick, without the slightest evidence that any of the characters or film-makers understand how it works. But never mind. I mention that the *sister* goes to her *brother* to make a confession because the movie is inept at story-telling. Unless you are very clever or perhaps psychic, you will actually not catch on until late in the movie that Father Michael is even *related* to Don Carlo or to Zena. The movie isn't keeping it a secret; it's simply so slipshod that this crucial information is not clearly supplied.

The husband's mistress is named Angela (Daphne Zuniga). After she escapes from the bloodbath of revenge, she finds herself sheltered and com-forted by none other than Father Michael, who believes her story that she is a simple Mexican girl who got into some very deep water. Zuniga's Mexican accent is so unbelievably bad it wouldn't even qualify for a Taco Bell ad. No one could possibly believe she is really a Mexican—except perhaps in this movie, which is so witless that you're inclined to give the accent the benefit of the doubt. (The linguistic depths of the movie are murky indeed; Don Carlo pronounces his name, Pace, to sound like "pa-chay," but young Michael makes it rhyme with "race." Thus, of course, at a crucial moment a character does not realize they are related.)

Michael and Angela fall in love, after Michael moves her into his bachelor quarters inside St. Patrick's Cathedral. You might ask how a priest could live with a woman inside a cathedral without being noticed, but the cathedral seems to be severely understaffed, and the only other priest in view is genial old Father Freddie (Paul Dooley), who stutters a lot and waxes philosophical. In order to handle the tricky challenge of a love scene between the priest and the young woman, the writer-director, Donald P. Bellisario, gives us an extended erotic sequence and then reveals it was only a dream. Of course, after the "dream," both characters subsequently change in their behavior toward each other as if they had really made love, the movie being so dishonest that it eats its cake and has it, too.

There are "secrets" in this movie that will gnaw at your credibility, "revelations" that are either (a) not surprises, or (b) completely implausible. The plot is a feverish scavenger hunt through lurid melodrama, impossible coincidence, shocking exploitation of the religious material, utter disregard for the audience, and a cheerful contempt for the talented actors—who have the right, I think, not to be made fools of.

Although Bellisario makes pious bleats in his press releases about the moral crisis faced by his hero in the movie, let's face it: This movie was *made* in order to give us a love affair between a priest and a sexy woman. The other stuff—making the Mafia look noble, putting in lots of bloody special effects— are bonuses. Ask yourself this simple question: Would *Last Rites* have been financed if the priest had resisted all temptations and remained chaste until the end? Are there stars in the sky? Does a bear shine his shoes in the woods?

Lawn Dogs

(Directed by John Duigan; starring Mischa Barton,
Christopher McDonald, Kathleen Quinlan; 1998)

John Duigan's *Lawn Dogs* is like a nasty accident at the symbol factory. Pieces are scattered all over the floor, as the wounded help each other to the exits. Some of the pieces look well made, and could be recycled. We pick up a few of them, and them together, to see if they'll fit. But they all seem to come from different designs.

The movie isn't clear about what it's trying to say—what it wants us to believe when we leave. It has the form of a message picture, without the message. It takes place in an upscale Kentucky housing development named Camelot Gardens, where the $300,000 homes sit surrounded by big lawns and no trees. It's a gated community; the security guard warns one of the "lawn dogs"—or yard workers—to be out of town by 5 P.M.

In one of the new houses lives ten-year-old Devon (Mischa Barton), who has a scar running down her chest after heart surgery. Her insipid parents are Morton (Christopher McDonald) and Clare (Kathleen Quinlan). Trent plans to run for office. Clare has casual sex with local college kids. And Trent (Sam Rockwell) mows their lawn.

Devon is in revolt, although she doesn't articulate it as interestingly as the heroine of *Welcome to the Dollhouse*. She wanders beyond the gates, finds Trent's trailer home in the woods, and becomes his friend. There are unrealized undertones of sexuality in her behavior, which the movie never makes overt, except in the tricky scene where she asks Trent to touch her scar. He has a scar, too; here's a new version of you show me yours and I'll show you mine.

The people inside Camelot Gardens are all stupid pigs. That includes the security guard, the parents, and the college kids, who insult and bully Trent. Meanwhile, Trent and Devon spend idyllic afternoons in the woods, being friends, until there is a tragic misunderstanding that leads to the death of a dog and even more alarming consequences.

Nobody makes it into the movie just as an average person. Trent's dad is a Korean vet whose lungs were destroyed by microbes in the K rations, and who is trying to give away his American flag collection. Trent is the kind of guy who stops traffic on a one-lane bridge while he strips, drives into the river, and walks back to his pickup boldly nude. Devon is the kind of little girl who crawls out onto her roof, throws her nightgown into the sky, and utters wild dog cries at the moon.

All of these events happen with the precision and vivid detail of a David Lynch movie, but I do not know why. It is easy to make a film about people who are pigs and people who are free spirits, but unless you show how or why they got that way, they're simply characters you've created. It's easy to have Devon say, "I don't like kids—they smell like TV." But what does this mean when a ten-year-old says it? It's easy to show good people living in trailers and awful people living in nice homes, but it can work out either way. It's easy to write a father who wants his little girl to have plastic surgery so her scar won't turn off boys, and then a boy who thinks it's "cool." But where is it leading? What is it saying? Camelot Gardens is a hideous place to live. So? Get out as fast as you can.

Little Giants

(Directed by Duwayne Dunham; starring Ed O'Neill, Rick Moranis; 1994)
Just yesterday I was cleaning out the office and I threw away a paperback by Sid Field, the famous Hollywood screenplay coach. Field is the man who is largely responsible for that strange feeling you may have had lately, that every movie seems to be about the same. The characters, locations, and gimmicks may change—but the story structure is right out of the book.

Field teaches screenwriting workshops. The workshops don't seem able to teach you how to write like yourself, but they sure are able to teach you how to write like everyone else. At a time when Hollywood is bashful about originality, it's a real career asset to be able to write clone screenplays.

Look at *Little Giants,* written by James Ferguson, Robert Shallcross, Tommy Swerdlow, and Michael Goldberg. What do you mean, it's one of the stupidest movies you've seen? It got sold, didn't it? And it got made, didn't it? So that makes it a success, doesn't it?

It's mind-boggling to reflect that this screenplay actually involved work by four writers. It's such a small achievement, their division of labor must have resembled splitting the atom. I don't have any idea if Ferguson, Shallcross, Swerdlow, and Goldberg have ever attended one of Field's workshops. Maybe they didn't need to. Working in two platoons, they have skillfully removed all vestiges of originality from this story, and turned in a perfectly honed retread of every other movie about how a team of losers wins the big game.

Oops! I gave away the ending! The plot stars Ed O'Neill and Rick Moranis as two brothers in the small town of Urbania, Ohio. O'Neill is a football hero and Heisman Trophy winner. Moranis is a nerd who runs a gas station. His daughter Becky (Shawna Waldron) is one of the best football players in town, but when O'Neill chooses a team for the Pop Warner League, he doesn't choose Becky, 'cause she's a girl. He also doesn't choose the fat kid, the skinny kid, the kid who drops every pass, etc.

Moranis thinks it's unfair. So he decides to coach his own team—the Little Giants. At first they are utterly incompetent. Then John Madden and a bunch of pro stars (Emmitt Smith, Bruce Smith, Tim Brown, and Steve Emtman) turn up in town after their bus gets lost. And they give the kids some quick lessons, turning them into only severely incompetent players.

Comes the day for the big game between O'Neill's jocks and the Little Giants. The O'Neill team includes a mountainous kid named Spike, who speaks of himself in the third person, and whose father has the movie's only funny line: "Every night before he goes to bed I massage his hamstrings with evaporated milk." Spike, of course, is the instant enemy of Becky, who has despaired of playing football as a girl, and joined the cheerleading squad. But after the first half ends disastrously, she gets steamed, and runs out on the field wearing her helmet, shoulder pads, jersey—and, of course, cheerleader skirt.

Little kids may like this movie, if they've never seen one like it before. Slightly older kids with good memories will notice that this is not even the first movie this year where a character passes gas to knock out the other team. Even older viewers are likely to bitterly resent the fate that drew them into the theater.

Little Indian, Big City
(Directed by Herve Palud; starring Thierry Lhermitte; 1996)
Little Indian, Big City is one of the worst movies ever made. I detested every moronic minute of it. Through a stroke of good luck, the entire third reel of

the film was missing the day I saw it. I went back to the screening room two days later, to view the missing reel. It was as bad as the rest, but nothing could have saved this film. As my colleague Gene Siskel observed, "If the third reel had been the missing footage from Orson Welles's *The Magnificent Ambersons,* this movie *still* would have sucked." I could not have put it better myself.

Little Indian, Big City is a French film (I will not demean the fine word "comedy" by applying it here). It is not in French with English subtitles, however. It has been dubbed into English, a canny move, since the movie is not likely to appeal to anyone who can read. The dubbing means that awkward, hollow-sounding words emerge from the mouths of the characters while they flap their lips to a different rhythm. In an attempt to make the English dubbing match the length of the French dialogue, sentences are constructed backwards and the passive voice pops up at random. People say things like, "You have a son—you hear?"

The character speaking that last line is the mother (Miou Miou) of a boy of about twelve. She was once married to the film's hero (Thierry Lhermitte), but left him thirteen years ago, when she was pregnant, because he spent too much time on the telephone. She fled to the Amazon, and has raised her child while living with an Indian tribe. Now he has flown to the rain forest to find his wife, so they can be divorced, and he can marry the stupidest woman on earth.

The hero did not know he had a son—you hear? Now he meets him. The son, named Mimi-Siku (Ludwig Briand), wears a cute breechcloth, carries a bow and arrow, has a mask painted on his face, and kills snakes by biting them. His mother is an intelligent, sensitive soul, who loves the environment and the rain forest. She is the only person in the jungle who speaks English (or French, in the original), and so if her son learned to speak it, he learned it from her. I guess it was her idea of a joke to teach him pidgin English, so that he says things like, "Me no able read." I guess she didn't teach him to read, either. She is depicted as kind of a secular saint.

Mimi-Siku is so good at a blowgun that he can kill a fly with a dart, and often does so. He has a hairy pet spider. His father brings him back to Paris, where the movie gets worse. The father has a business partner who never knows what to wear, and so always wears the same thing the father wears. Ho, ho. They go to business meetings in matching ties. Hee, hee. The partner has a daughter, and soon the son is bouncing in a hammock with a nubile twelve-year-old and telling his father, "Me like you—love only one female." I doubt if the relationship will last, since the boy is prettier than the girl.

Later (or perhaps earlier, since it was in the third reel) Mimi-Siku climbs barefoot up the Eiffel Tower. This feat is handled so ineptly by the film that it has neither payoff nor consequence. He does it, and then the movie forgets it. Meanwhile, the father is doing a business deal with some shady Russians, who speak in dubbed accents and drink vodka and seem to be wearing Krushchev's old suits. The father's fiancée (Arielle Dombasle) chants mantras, plans a New Age wedding, and wants her guru to live with them. I think she's in such a hurry to get married because she's afraid the collagen injections in her lips might shift. By the end of the film, father and son have bonded, and cooked a fish by the side of the expressway. And the father has learned to kill a fly with a dart.

There is a movie called *Fargo*. It is a masterpiece. Go see it. If you under any circumstances see *Little Indian, Big City,* I will never let you read one of my reviews again.

The Lonely Lady

(Directed by Peter Sasdy; starring Pia Zadora, Ray Liotta; 1983)

If *The Lonely Lady* had even a shred of style and humor, it could qualify as the worst movie of the year. Unfortunately, it's not that good. It's a dog-eat-dog world out there in Hollywood and it's not enough to be merely awful. You need something to set yourself apart. Pia Zadora tries, and she has pluck, but she's just not bad enough all by herself.

The movie is bad in all the usual ways, and it would be easy enough to simply list them: The overacting, the use of voice-over narration to bridge awkward chasms between scenes, the predictable plot. But why don't we take all of those things for granted and move on to the truly unspeakable things in this movie? We could make a list:

1. I suppose it was necessary to have a scene in which the heroine is cruelly treated by men. But (a) couldn't they have thought of something other than rape by a garden hose? and (b) shouldn't such a traumatic event have had some effect on the character?

2. After the rape, Pia is seen being comforted in bed by her mother and a doctor. A single thread of stage makeup, representing blood, has trickled out of her mouth and dried. It is left in place for the entire scene, suggesting that at no point did the doctor, her mother, or any other medical personnel or family member care enough to disturb the makeup in order to make the scene realistic by wiping away the blood.

3. Proper nouns are missing from this movie. It seems to exist in a generic alternative universe in which nothing has its own name. The Oscars are known as "these awards" or "the awards." After Pia and her first lover leave a movie, they have this conversation: "I liked him better." "I liked her better." No him or her is identified. This is the kind of conversation that results when a screenplay says, "They leave the theater and briefly discuss the movie," but the screenplay doesn't care what movie they saw.

4. The movie has no time for emotional transitions. When Pia marries the successful Hollywood writer, he is attentive and caring in one scene, and a sadist in the next, simply because the plot requires him to act that way. No motivation. When Pia goes crazy, it's not so much in reaction to what's been happening to her (she survived the garden hose with nary a backward glance) but because the script requires it, so that, later, she can pull herself back together again just as arbitrarily.

5. The movie's whole plot hinges on Pia's ability to rewrite a scene better than her jealous writer-husband. When the star of her husband's movie weeps that she can't play a certain graveyard scene, Pia whips out the portable type-writer and writes brilliant new dialogue for the star. What, you may ask, does Pia write? Here's what. She has the grieving widow kneel by the side of the open grave and cry out (are you ready for this?) "Why? Why!!!"

That's it. That's the brilliant dialogue. And it can be used for more than a death scene, let me tell you. In fact, I walked out of this movie saying to myself, "Why? Why!!!"

Look Who's Talking Now

(Directed by Tom Ropelewski; starring John Travolta, Kirstie Alley; 1993)
Look Who's Talking Now is a fairly misleading title for those who paid attention during English class, since the talkers are dogs, and so the title of course

should be *Look What's Talking Now.* Anyone who paid attention during English will also find innumerable other distressing elements in the film, including what teachers used to call "lack of originality and aptness of thought."

The movie revisits John Travolta and Kirstie Alley, who in 1989 made a charming movie named *Look Who's Talking,* and in 1990 a less charming movie named *Look Who's Talking Too.* The first movie was about how Alley, who was pregnant by her no-good boyfriend, met a taxi driver played by Travolta. The baby, with voice by Bruce Willis, took a liking to Travolta, and so, after a while, did Alley.

In the second film, they had a baby daughter together, who spoke in the voice of Roseanne Arnold. Now their dogs speak with the voices of Danny DeVito and Diane Keaton. The children, in the meantime, have grown up enough to speak in their own voices, although not with the wit and insight they possessed as infants.

All of which leads us to an overwhelming question: Why is it necessary for the dogs to speak? They engage in your standard *Lady and the Tramp* repartee, but along about the second reel I realized that there was no earthly reason at all for the dogs to talk except that they were in a sequel made by filmmakers who had lost the nerve to produce another talking baby *(Look Who's Talking Three).*

The first film had maybe a shred of realism to flavor its romantic comedy. This one looks like it was chucked up by an automatic screenwriting machine. Travolta gets a corporate pilot's license, and is hired by sexy bombshell Lysette Anthony, a corporate exec who wants to seduce him. She contrives for him to be away from his family on Christmas Eve, after which Alley packs the kids and the dogs into the taxi and heads off for the North Woods, where Travolta is being held captive in a snowbound cabin by the sex-starved exec. After the taxi skids off the road and savage wolves attack the stranded family and the brave dogs fight them off and the kids unwrap their Christmas presents in the middle of a blizzard. . . .

So help me God, I am not making this up. Suggestions, please, for the fourth movie in the series. How about *Look Who's Talking Back,* in which the audience gets its turn.

Lord of the Flies

(Directed by Harry Hook; starring Balthazar Getty, Chris Furrh; 1990)
William Golding's *Lord of the Flies* is, or used to be, a staple of everyone's
teenage reading experience, a harrowing fable about how ordinary kids revert
to savagery when they are marooned on a desert island. The story is less
poignant nowadays than it once was, if only because events take place every
day on our mean streets that are more horrifying than anything the little monsters do to one another on Golding's island.

When Peter Brook made the first film version of the novel in 1963, most
of the viewers no doubt identified with the character of Ralph, the little liberal
humanist, instead of with Jack, the little free-market economist. These days,
I imagine the audiences are more evenly divided. Of all the films that cry out
to be remade, the call of Brook's *Lord of the Flies* is very faint indeed. But it
has been heard by Harry Hook and Sara Schiff, who have directed and written this new and anemic Classics Illustrated version of the story.

Golding's tale is a parable, a simple one, ideal as the subject for essays
in English class. Schoolboys from a private school are shipwrecked (or, in the
new version, their airplane crashes into the sea), and they swim to a deserted
island where they must fend for themselves. At first they stick together and
act reasonably, but then they divide into two camps: Followers of Ralph, who
believe in decency and civilization, and followers of Jack, who paint their
faces, sharpen their spears, and become militarists. Despairing of ever being
rescued, the boys go to war with one another, with deadly results.

The staging of this story is fairly straightforward. The kids crawl up on
the sand, their clothes gradually grow more tattered, they light a signal fire
and then fight over who will tend it, they fight for possession of the knife and
a pair of glasses that can be used to start fires, and they draw the battle lines
between their two camps.

Hook's visual sense is not acute here; he doesn't show the spontaneous
sense of time and place that made his first film, *The Kitchen Toto* (1988),
so convincing. He seems more concerned with telling the story than showing
it, and there are too many passages in which the boys are simply trading
dialogue. The color photography tends to turn many scenes into travelogues;
this is a film that needs black and white to contain the lush scenery. The "lord
of the flies" itself—the rotting head of a wild boar—never becomes the

focus of horror it is intended as, and the surprise ending of the film is some-how over before we have the opportunity to be surprised. The acting is work-manlike.

Because this material is so obviously constructed to bear a message, a film made from it will work best if it concentrates on the story elements and lets the symbolism take care of itself. Hook's version does neither. The sym-bolism is right up front and unmissable, and the story part—the events that in theory should cause our throats to tighten and our pulses to quicken—is pretty lame. Once you understand what is going to happen (and even the viewer who has never heard of the book will not take long), there are few sur-prises. It happens.

The reviews of Brook's 1963 film version were not glowing ("Semi-professional . . . crude and unconvincing"—Halliwell; "Patched together"—Kauffmann). But I recall it having at least a certain force, maybe because in 1963 it was still shocking that ordinary schoolkids could be killers—that they had the seeds of evil in them, and, given the opportunity and freedom from the restraints of society, the seeds would grow.

Golding's novel is the sort of fable that could shock only those who believe in the onwardness and upwardness of civilization, as some still did in those days. At the time of its publication (1954) attempts were made to find political messages in it, but today it seems more like a sad, literal prophecy of what is happening in neighborhoods ruled by drugs. What week goes by with-out another story of a Ralph gunned down by a Jack?

Lord Shango

(Directed by Raymond Marsh; starring Marlene Clark, Lawrence Cook; 1975)
The story thus far:

A black church is holding a fundamentalist baptism by complete immer-sion. The ceremony is interrupted by a young man who belongs to a voodoo sect. In an attempt to prevent his girlfriend from being baptized, he leaps into the water, whereupon the three church brethren baptize him so thoroughly that he drowns.

His body is buried after a ritual held by the voodoo group, who smear him with the blood of a chicken and adjure his spirit to "look out for his friends, relatives, and associates." His girlfriend suffers a nervous breakdown and is seduced by her mother's second husband. The mother has a nervous breakdown because she cannot conceive a child by her second husband. The girl runs away from home.

The mother, frantic with grief, refuses to believe that her daughter's boyfriend was drowned by accident during the baptismal ceremony, despite reassurances from the church elders, including those who held him under a little too long.

She seeks out the voodoo sect at its next meeting, held by the light of the full moon, and after several chants, recitations, and virtuoso solos on the bongo drums, she is invited to step forward and express (a) her loyalty to the voodoo god, Manubeesa, and (b) her desires.

She expresses the desire to have either (a) a child, or (b) her child. This is going to cause some confusion later. The voodoo priest asks who will be sacrificed to attain this (these) goal(s). She doesn't answer, but she must have been thinking the right thoughts, because after the voodoo priest ceremoniously slices a sweet potato in two, one of the church elders collapses of a heart attack while walking home from the grocery store.

The mother's devotion to Manubeesa is sealed in an ancient supernatural dance bearing an uncanny resemblance to the Twist as performed by Chubby Checker in ads for top hits of the 1960s. The mother goes home, tosses in her sleep, utters the name "Manubeesa" several times, and in the morning is overjoyed to discover that (a) her daughter has returned, and (b) her daughter is pregnant. It would also appear that (c) the mother is pregnant as well, Manubeesa having come through with all the children any mother could possibly have desired, even in her fondest dreams.

Next time, if I am able to sit through the second half of *Lord Shango,* we will discover whether the other church elders catch their lunch on the way home from the A&P; whether the dead boyfriend is brought back to life by further applications of chicken, which is at least worth a try; whether the children were conceived by mortal fathers, and whether Manubeesa is having his own little joke or is simply cursed with an overly literal imagination.

Lost & Found

(Directed by Jeff Pollack; starring David Spade, Sophie Marceau, Patrick Breuel; 1999)

Lost & Found is a movie about characters of limited intelligence, who wander through the lonely wastes of ancient and boring formulas. No one involved seems to have had any conviction it could be great. It's the kind of movie where the hero imitates Neil Diamond—and he's not making fun of him, he's serious.

In asking us to believe David Spade as a romantic lead, it miscalculates beyond all reason. Spade is wrong by definition for romantic leads, because his persona is based on ironic narcissism and cool detachment. A girl has to be able to believe it when a guy says she loves her more than anything else in the world. When Spade says it, it means he doesn't love anything else in the world, either.

Spade plays the owner of an Italian restaurant in Los Angeles. Like not very many owners of Italian restaurants, his name is Dylan. I have three hints for Dylan. (1) Unless you know them very well, customers do not like to be caressed on their arms as you pass their tables. (2) Although waiters must touch plates while serving them, it is bad form for the owner to put his thumb on a plate while it is being eaten from. (3) During renovations, do not seat customers directly below drywall with holes ripped in it.

Most LA restaurant owners do not live in colorful apartment buildings where all the neighbors know each other, and little old ladies play strip poker. But the screenplay throws in the colorful rental units as a way of supplying recycled sitcom characters, and to place Dylan near the apartment of Lila (Sophie Marceau), a French cellist. She has a former boyfriend named Rene (Patrick Breuel), whose function is to look pained and supply straight lines to Dylan. And she has a dog named Jack, who is treated as much like the dog in *There's Something About Mary* as is possible without actually including clips from the other movie.

Dylan and Lila have a Meet Cute. She runs into him and knocks him flat, with her landing on top, which is about the cheapest Meet Cute you can buy at the Movie Cliché Store. He falls in love with Lila, gets nowhere, and steals her dog so that he can claim to have found it and thus win her love. Lila is so unobservant that Dylan often carries the dog past her windows, and even walks it in a nearby park, without Lila ever seeing them together. When the dog needs to poop, Dylan wears one of those tool belts you see on power company linemen, with eight or nine bright plastic pooper-scoopers dangling from it. Supplying a character with too much equipment is a creaky comedy wheeze; in a good movie, they'd give him one pooper scooper and think of something funny to do with it.

Anyway. Dylan has an employee at the restaurant named Wally (Artie Lange), who is tall, fat, and dumb, sleeps over one night, and ends up in Dylan's bed because he gets scared. As they leap to attention in the morning, they can't even think of a funny payoff (such as Steve Martin in *Planes, Trains & Automobiles,* shouting at John Candy, "That wasn't a pillow!"). Instead, when Lila rings the doorbell, they both answer the door in their underpants and she assumes they're gay. Ho, ho.

Meanwhile, Jack the dog eats junk food and throws up. When Dylan comes home, we get a nauseated-dog's-eye-view of an optically distorted Dylan dressed in 1970s disco gear while dancing to a record on the sound track. Don't ask how a dog could have this hallucination; be thankful instead that the dog's fantasies are more interesting than any other visual in the movie.

Lost & Found ends at a big lawn party for rich people, which in movies about people over twenty-one is the equivalent of the Senior Prom scene in all other movies. There is a role for Martin Sheen, as Mr. Millstone, the tight-fisted banker who wants to fly in Neil Diamond as a surprise for his wife. In 1979, Martin Sheen starred in *Apocalypse Now.* In 1999, he plays Mr. Millstone. I wish he had taken my advice and gone into the priesthood.

As for the Neil Diamond imitation, my best guess is that David Spade secretly thinks he could have a parallel career as a Las Vegas idol, and is showing us how he can do Neil Diamond better than Diamond himself. All that's lacking is for Spade to take that hank of hair that hangs in front of his eyes, and part it, so that it hangs over his ears.

Truth in Criticism: The movie has one funny scene, starring Jon Lovitz, as a Dog Whisperer.

Lost Horizon

(Directed by Charles Jarrott; starring Peter Finch, Liv Ullmann, Sally Kellerman, John Gielgud; 1973)

I don't know how much Ross Hunter paid Burt Bacharach and Hal David to write the music for *Lost Horizon,* but whatever it was, it was too much. Not that the movie would have been better if the music were better; no, the movie is awful on its own. But the music is really bad. About two hours into the movie, Bobby Van has a birthday party and they sing "Happy Birthday" to him. That's the one you'll come out humming.

The movie is a remake of the 1937 Ronald Colman classic, which was fun because it maintained its sense of humor. I mean, how seriously can you take this stuff? The story involves a group of political and social refugees whose airplane is mysteriously hijacked and taken to Shangri-la. There they discover a civilization where nobody ever gets tired, nobody ever grows old, there's gold in every stream and the coolies have not yet been organized by Cesar Chavez. The movie more or less follows the earlier version, with a few twists. For example, the prostitute in the 1937 movie has now become a *Newsweek* correspondent.

What I don't understand is why the remake had to be a musical in the first place. Just a nice, quiet new version of the good old story would have been enough. The material is so slight it can hardly bear the weight of music, and it sinks altogether during a series of the most incompetent and clumsy dance numbers I've ever seen.

There's one production number, for example, in which the people of Shangri-la celebrate the solidarity of the family. A young man (symbolic of a young man) and a young woman (symbolic of a young woman) solemnly hand a baby back and forth in order to symbolize how neither one holds the baby all the time. Meanwhile, several other young men twirl orange scarves. I mention this particular number because, if you go to the movie, I want you to look out for it. You wouldn't want to spend all that money and miss the worst single piece of choreography you've ever seen in your life. The dancers march about and twirl their scarves as if Leni Reifenstahl's *Triumph of the Will* had been gotten pregnant by Busby Berkeley.

Meanwhile, several love affairs get under way. See, the people of Shangri-la are sort of happy that the strangers have arrived, since some of them have been waiting eighty years for their first love affairs. Good thing you don't age in Shangri-la. Anyhow, Peter Finch falls in love with Liv Ullmann, Michael York falls in love with Olivia Hussey, George Kennedy falls in love with Sally Kellerman, and Bobby Van teaches the children of the valley how to dance (God knows the valley could use a good choreographer).

These pairings are celebrated by Bacharach-David songs that I absolutely cannot remember. Between songs, the Shangri-la philosophy is unveiled. In the valley, you see, if you love a woman more than her lover does—why, you just cleave her to your side. And the lover understands. But if *he* loves her more than *you* do, he gets to keep her. You see how fair it is, especially for the woman, who is relieved of the bother of choice. On the other hand (as that guy in the back row used to shout in cold war jokes), what about the workers?

Well, they're happy, too. They get to carry water and do odd jobs, work in their field, that sort of thing. On holidays they get to twirl their scarves. Don't worry about them; they're happy. They get a new bucket and a new scarf every Bastille Day. We have a saying in the valley that I hope you'll remember. It goes like this: When the strong wind bends the mighty tree, the tree stands all the straighter when the wind stops blowing. Remember that; it'll be on the final.

Lost in Space

(Directed by Stephen Hopkins; starring William Hurt, Heather Graham, Lacy Chabert, Matt LeBlanc, Gary Oldman; 1998)

Lost in Space is a dim-witted shoot-'em-up based on the old (I hesitate to say "classic") TV series. It's got cheesy special effects, a muddy visual look, and characters who say obvious things in obvious ways. If it outgrosses the brilliant *Dark City,* the previous s-f film from the same studio, then audiences must have lost their will to be entertained.

The TV series was loosely modeled on the novel *The Swiss Family Robinson,* about a family shipwrecked far from home and using wit and ingenuity to live off the land. I loved that book, and especially its detailed description of how the family made tools, machines, and a home for themselves, and trained the local animals.

The movie doesn't bother with such details. After a space battle that is the predictable curtain-raiser, and a quick explanation of why and how the Robinson family is setting off for a planet called Alpha Prime, the film takes place mostly on board their saucer-shaped ship, and involves many more space battles, showdowns, struggles, attacks, hyperspace journeys, and exploding planets. In between, the characters plow through creaky dialogue and exhausted relationship problems.

Imagine the film that could be made about a family marooned on a distant planet, using what they could salvage from their ship or forage from the environment. That screenplay would take originality, intelligence, and thought. *Lost in Space* is one of those typing-speed jobs where the screenwriter is like a stenographer, rewriting what he's seen at the movies.

The story: Earth will not survive another two decades. Alpha Prime is the only other habitable planet mankind has discovered. Professor John Robinson (William Hurt) and his family have been chosen to go there and construct a hypergate, to match the gate at the Earth end. Their journey will involve years of suspended animation, but once the other gate is functioning, humans can zip instantaneously to Alpha Prime.

There needs to be a hypergate at both ends, of course, because otherwise there's no telling where a hyperdrive will land you—as the Robinsons soon find out. Also on board are the professor's wife Maureen (Mimi Rogers), their scientist daughter, Judy Robinson (Heather Graham), their younger daughter, Penny (Lacey Chabert), and their son Will (Jack Johnson), who is the brains of the outfit. The ship is piloted by ace space cadet Don West (Matt LeBlanc), and includes an intelligent robot who will help with the tasks at the other hand.

Oh, and lurking below deck is the evil Dr. Zachary Smith (Gary Oldman), who wants to sabotage the mission, but is trapped on board when the ship lifts off. So he awakens the Robinsons, after which the ship is thrown off course and seems doomed to fall into the sun.

Don West has a brainstorm: They'll use the hyperdrive to zap right *through* the Sun! This strategy of course lands them in a galaxy far, far away, with a sky filled with unfamiliar stars. And then the movie ticks off a series of crises, of which I can enumerate a rebellious robot, an exploding planet, mechanical space spiders, a distracting romance, and family issues of trust and authority.

The movie might at least have been more fun to look at if it had been filmed in brighter colors. Director Stephen Hopkins and his cinematographer, Peter Levy, for some reason choose a murky, muted palate. Everything looks like a drab brown suit, or a cheap rotogravure. You want to use some Windex on the screen. And Bruce Broughton's musical score saws away tirelessly with counterfeit excitement. When nothing of interest is happening on the screen, it just makes it worse when the music pretends it cares.

Of the performances, what can be said except that William Hurt, Gary Oldman, and Mimi Rogers deserve medals for remaining standing? The kids are standard-issue juveniles with straight teeth and good postures. And there is a monkeylike little alien pet who looks like he comes from a world where all living beings are clones of Felix the Cat. This is the kind of movie that, if it fell into a black hole, you wouldn't be able to tell the difference.

Love Always

(Directed by Jude Pauline Eberhard; starring Marisa Ryan, Moon Zappa, Beverly D'Angelo; 1997)

"You are like a cluster bomb that explodes in a thousand different ways at once," the heroine is told in *Love Always.* As opposed to a cluster bomb that doesn't? I dunno. This movie is so bad in so many different ways you should see it just to put it behind you. Let's start with the dialogue. Following are verbatim quotes:

- "Someday you'll love somebody with all the intensity of the Southern Hemisphere."
- "There's a Starbuck-free America out there!"
- "To be young and in love! I think I'm gonna head out for some big open spaces."
- "Like sands in an hourglass, these are the days of our lives. That's the way the cookie crumbles."
- "Watch your back."

And my favorite, this advice from the heroine's girlfriend (Moon Zappa), as she sets out on her hitchhike odyssey across America: "Follow your intestines."

Does Jude Pauline Eberhard, the writer and director, intend these lines to be funny? Does this film belong in one of those funky festivals where they understand such things? Alas, I fear not. *Love Always* is sincere in addition to its other mistakes.

The movie tells the story of Julia Bradshaw (Marisa Ryan), an intrepid San Diego woman who finds herself in a series of situations that have no point and no payoff, although that is the screenplay's fault, not hers. Early in the film, for example, she goes to the race track and her horse comes in, and she says "Yes!" and rides her bike home along the beach, and we never really find out why she was at the track, but no matter, because before long the film goes to visit an amateur theatrical and we see an *entire* "rooster dance," from beginning to end, apparently because film is expensive and since they exposed it they want to show it.

The rooster dance also has nothing to do with the film, which properly gets under way when Julia gets a postcard from her onetime lover Mark, asking her to come to Spokane so he can marry her. This information is presented by filling the screen with a big close-up of the postcard, which Julia then reads aloud for us. Soon we find her in the desert with a bedroll on her back, posing photogenically on the windowsill of a deserted house so that interesting people can brake to a halt and offer her rides.

Her odyssey from San Diego to Spokane takes her via a wedding in Boston. That's a road movie for you. At one point along the way she shares the driving with a woman who is delivering big ceramic cows to a diary. Julia drops a ceramic calf and breaks it, drives the truck to Vegas to get another calf, but when she gets there the ceramic cow lady's husband tells her the dairy canceled the order, so Julia wanders the Strip in Vegas, no doubt because the Road Movie Rule Book requires at least one montage of casino signs.

Back on the road, Julia meets a band of women in a van. They are the Virgin Sluts. They dress like models for ads for grunge clubs in free weeklies in the larger cities of smaller states. She is thrilled to meet them at last. She also meets a makeout artist, a sensitive photographer, and a guy who is convinced he has the movie's Dennis Hopper role. On and on her odyssey goes, until finally she gets to Spokane, where she finds out that Mark is a louse, as we knew already because he didn't send her bus fare.

M

Mad Dog Time

(Directed by Larry Bishop; starring Richard Dreyfuss, Jeff Goldblum, Diane Lane, Ellen Barkin; 1996)

Mad Dog Time is the first movie I have seen that does not improve on the sight of a blank screen viewed for the same length of time. Oh, I've seen bad movies before. But they usually made me *care* about how bad they were. Watching *Mad Dog Time* is like waiting for the bus in a city where you're not sure they have a bus line.

The plot: A gangster boss (Richard Dreyfuss) is released from a mental hospital, and returns to a sleazy nightclub to take over control of his organization. He has been gone long enough that a long list of gangsters would like to have his job, led by (Jeff Goldblum), who has been conducting an affair with Dreyfuss's girlfriend (Diane Lane) and her sister (Ellen Barkin). The girls share the last name of Everly, so they're the Everly Sisters—get it? Ho, ho, ho. God, what rich humor this movie offers!

Other candidates for Dreyfuss's throne include characters played by Gabriel Byrne, Kyle McLachlan, Gregory Hines, Burt Reynolds, and Billy Idol. The way the movie works is, two or three characters will start out in a scene and recite some dry, hard-boiled dialogue, and then one or two of them will get shot. This happens over and over.

"Vic's gonna want everybody dead," a character says at the beginning, in what turns out to be a horrible prophecy. Vic is the Dreyfuss character. Goldblum is named Mick, and Larry Bishop, who directed this mess, is Nick. So we get dialogue that thinks it's funny to use Vic, Nick, and Mick in the same sentence. Oh, hilarious.

I don't have any idea what this movie is about—and yet, curiously, I don't think I missed anything. Bishop is the son of the old Rat Packer Joey Bishop, who maybe got him a price on the songs he uses on the sound track, by Dean Martin, Sammy Davis, and Frank Sinatra (Paul Anka sings "My Way," which was certainly Bishop's motto during the production).

What were they thinking of? Dreyfuss is the executive producer. He's been in some good movies. Did he think this was a script? (Not a bad script—a script at all?) The actors perform their lines like condemned prisoners. The most ethical guy on the production must have been Norman Hollyn, the editor, because he didn't cut anybody out, and there must have been people willing to do him big favors to get out of this movie.

Mad Dog Time should be cut up to provide free ukulele picks for the poor.

Magic in the Water
(Directed by Rick Stevenson; starring Mark Harmon, Joshua Jackson, Sarah Wayne; 1995)

Now that the Loch Ness monster has been unmasked as a trick photograph, is there a future for legendary creatures of the deep? *Magic in the Water* hopes so. It's about a couple of kids and their preoccupied dad, who visit a Canadian lake said to be inhabited by a mysterious creature named Orky.

The creature has been drummed up into a local tourist industry by the go-getters down at the chamber of commerce, who stretch banners across Main Street proclaiming the town to be the "Home of Orky." For Josh and Ashley, the two kids, Orky is not much harder to spot than their dad, Jack (Mark Harmon), who is so busy with business calls on his cellular phone that he pays little attention to them.

Better communication between parent and children is but one of the up-lifting themes of *Magic in the Water,* which also introduces a wise old Indian (Ben Cardinal), who spends much time chanting and explaining to the kids that at one time, men and animals could trade places. (The Indian's name, Joe Pickled Trout, may help explain why animals grew disenchanted with men.)

Josh (Joshua Jackson) is obsessed by vehicles of any kind; his catch-phrase is "I bet I could drive that," so we know with absolute certainty that sooner or later he will be called upon to drive something. Ashley (Sarah Wayne) spends much time looking at the water, where Orky seems to mani-fest itself as ripples, waves, heaves, and spouts. Even more proof Orky exists: When Ashley leaves her Oreos on the dock, Orky takes the cookies, eats the white stuff in between, and returns the outsides, still dry. That can't be easy if you don't have hands and live underwater. Try it yourself.

We meet a local psychiatrist named Dr. Wanda Bell (Harley Jane Kozak), who runs group therapy for several local people who all share the same conviction that their minds and bodies have been inhabited by Orky. Jack falls for Wanda, and is soon a member of her group—because, yes, Orky inhabits him, too, and makes him a better dad for the experience.

Meanwhile, bad guys lurk around the fringes of the story, and it's revealed that they are secretly turning the lake into a hazardous waste dump. Could it be that Orky is trying to tell the locals something? Josh and Ashley, who are easily as clever as the Hardy Boys and maybe even Nancy Drew, soon discover the evil secret, and then it's up to them, and Orky, to save the day.

One of the problems with the first two-thirds of *Magic in the Water* is that we don't see Orky. One of the problems with the last third is that we do. Orky turns out to be singularly uncharismatic, looking like an ashen Barney on downers.

The underlying inspiration for *Magic in the Water* is, of course, the *Free Willy* pictures, with kids making friends of noble aquatic creatures while bad guys scheme to kill the whales and pollute the waters of the earth. *Magic in the Water* is innocuous fun, but slow, and not distinguished in the special-effects department. And about those two one-armed brothers, who both allegedly lost an arm to Orky: I'll bet they could find those missing arms if they'd look closely inside their shirts.

Marie Baie des Anges

(Directed by Manuel Pradal; starring Vahina Giocante, Frederic Malgras; 1998)
At the height of the storm over *Last Tango in Paris,* Art Buchwald, who had lived in Paris for years, weighed in with some common sense: The movie, he explained, is really about real estate. Both characters want the same apartment, and are willing to do anything to get it.

Marie Baie des Anges is not really about real estate. It is about sex. But I thought a lot about real estate while I was watching it. It takes place on the French Riviera, which is pictured here as an unspoilt Eden in which the film's adolescent lovers gambol and pose, nude much of the time, surfacing only occasionally for the dangers of the town.

Anyone who has visited the French Riviera knows that it has more in common with Miami than with Eden. It is a crowded, expensive perch for ugly condos and desperate beachgoers, and the only place where teenage lovers can safely gambol is in their bathtubs. *Marie Baie des Anges* is as realistic as *Blue Lagoon,* although without any copulating turtles.

The movie stars Vahina Giocante as Marie, a fifteen-year-old who spends her vacations on the Riviera, picking up American sailors and sleeping under the stars. No mention of her parents, home, income, past, experience, etc. She is the pornographer's dream, an uncomplicated nubile teenager who exists only as she is. Giocante has been billed as "the new Bardot," and she's off to a good start: Bardot didn't make many good films, either.

On the beach, she meets Orso (Frederic Malgras), a sullen lout who lurks about looking like a charade with the answer, "Leonardo DiCaprio." Together, they run, play, boat, swim, eat strawberries, and flirt with danger, and inevitably a handgun surfaces, so we will not be in suspense about the method used to bring the film to its unsatisfactory conclusion. "Get me the best-looking gun you can find," Orso tells Marie, who steals it from a one-night stand.

The movie is yet one more evocation of doomed youth, destined for a brief flash of happiness and a taste of eroticism before they collide with the preordained ending. All of these movies end the same way, with one form of death or another, which casts a cold light on the events that went before, showing you how unlucky these young people were to be in a story written by a director who lacked the wit to think of anything else that might happen.

The filmmaker is Manuel Pradal, who in addition to recycling exhausted clichés also fancies himself at the cutting edge of narrative. He tells his story out of sequence, leaving us to collect explanations and context along the way; one advantage of this style is that only at the end is it revealed that the story was not about anything. We get glimpses and fragments of actions; flashforwards and flashbacks; exhausting self-conscious artiness.

Yes, there is beautiful scenery. And nice compositions. Lots of pretty pictures. Giocante and Malgras are superficially attractive, although because their characters are empty vessels there's no reason to like them much, or care about them. The movie is cast as a tragedy, and it's tragic, all right: Tragic that these kids never developed intelligence and personalities.

The Master Gunfighter

(Directed by "Frank Laughlin," aka Tom Laughlin; starring Tom Laughlin; 1975)
A film archaeologist could have fun with *The Master Gunfighter,* sifting among
its fragments of plot and trying to figure out what the hell happened to this
movie on the way to the theater. The movie opens with a long-winded narration, in a hapless attempt to orient us, but not long afterward the narrator has
to break in again—we're lost already. It's all to little avail. I don't think there's
any way an intelligent moviegoer could sit through this mess and accurately
describe the plot afterward.

On the basis of the available evidence, I'd say the director and star, Tom
Laughlin, began with a badly confused screenplay (one that never did clearly
establish the characters and the main story line) and then shot so much film
that he had to cut out key scenes in order to edit everything down to a reasonable playing time.

The movie opens, for example, with Laughlin leaving the California hacienda of his wife, for obscure reasons (and not only the reasons are obscure—
I had to read the synopsis to figure out the woman was his wife). Then there's
a title card—"Three Years Later"—and he decides to go *back* to the hacienda,
for more compelling reasons. This is pretty dizzying exposition.

The movie has ambitions to look like one of Sergio Leone's Italian
Westerns—it has the eerie music and the vast landscapes and the irritating
habit of opening and closing scenes with zooms as dramatic as they're arbitrary. Watching it, we reflect that Leone was never too strong on plotting
either (what actually happened in *The Good, the Bad and the Ugly* remains a
matter of great controversy). But Leone at least was the master of great
moments—stretches of film that worked, even if they meant nothing.

Laughlin has moments, too, but he has no flair for timing or development
or surprise. We leave *The Master Gunfighter* remembering very long, very
pointless conversations in which the characters seemed to be referring to
events in another film. These yawn-inducing dialogues are occasionally interrupted by swordplay, so badly staged and photographed we're not even sure
Laughlin could handle a steak knife. In one of his predicaments, he is surrounded by enemy swordsmen—so he backs up against an old shed. But wait
a minute, you're thinking: If he's surrounded, how does he back up against
that shed? What about the guys behind him? Aha!

The opening narration provides some nonsense about samurai training that's supposed to explain the sword, as well as the MG's revolver, which can fire twelve shots. After we've seen the MG nail all kinds of bad guys with the pistol, only to use the sword in his next emergency, we're reminded of John Carter of Mars, the Edgar Rice Burroughs hero who kept getting sliced up in swordplay when he could have just pulled out his atomic ray gun. But nothing as simple as logic is going to explain this movie.

Maxie

(Directed by Paul Aaron; starring Glenn Close, Mandy Patinkin, Ruth Gordon; 1985)

Jan is an absolutely normal San Francisco woman. She lives in a big landmark Victorian house, she's married to a librarian, and she works as the secretary to the local Catholic bishop. (So far, all that's wrong with this picture is the landmark Victorian house, which Jan and her husband, Nick, could not afford unless he owned the library and she were the bishop.)

One day they are stripping wallpaper from the walls, and they discover a message that was left more than sixty years ago by Maxie, a flapper who once lived in the house. We know the message is from Maxie because Ruth Gordon, the next-door neighbor, drops in and tells them Maxie once had a bit role in a silent film and then died tragically at a young age.

Jan and Nick do what any normal couple would do. They rent a videocassette of the old silent film. And apparently their act of seeing Maxie's old performance, in Maxie's old house, causes the psychic energies to flow in such a way that Maxie appears and possesses Jan's body. Jan begins to talk in Maxie's penetrating nasal screech and she starts using a lot of 1920s slang. But she still looks exactly like Glenn Close, who plays both Jan and Maxie.

Nick (played by Mandy Patinkin) does not at first figure out what is happening. This leads to some embarrassment, as when Maxie suddenly occupies Jan's body during an office party and throws her drink down the dress of Nick's boss (Valerie Curtin, as a sex-mad harridan). There are other horrible moments, as when Jan becomes Maxie at bedtime, and when Maxie forces Jan to audition for a TV commercial. Maxie can be shocking, but she is not anywhere near as shocking as the utter, complete lack of wit and intelligence in this movie, which goes its entire length without producing one single clever twist on its boring premise.

As a service to the screenwriter and director, I herewith supply some ideas they might have used:

(1) Jan becoming Maxie during sex, to Nick's consternation;

(2) The bishop turning out to be Maxie's old beau, before he went into the seminary;

(3) Maxie in a San Francisco leather bar;

(4) Nick preferring Maxie to boring old Jan;

(5) Nick being possessed by Maxie's old boyfriend, who goes after her, only to find the boring yuppie, Jan, in his arms;

(6) Maxie enlisting her friends from the Other Side to possess everyone else at the office party, so that W. C. Fields is talking with Calvin Coolidge, etc.

I offer these possibilities only to illuminate the fact that *Maxie* does as little with its original inspiration as is humanly possible. This is the sort of movie where, if Maxie had any brains, she'd appear in Jan's body, take one look at the script, and decide she was better off dead.

Medicine Man

(Directed by John McTiernan; starring Sean Connery, Lorraine Bracco; 1991)
All of the elements are here for a movie I would probably enjoy very much, but somehow they never come together. *Medicine Man,* which is shot on location in the rain forests of the Amazon, has the great, grizzled Sean Connery as its star, doing research countless miles up an anonymous river with Lorraine Bracco, a tough-talking scientist from the Bronx. If this had been some dumb adventure movie it would probably have been terrific. Alas, it is a "relationship" movie, told along lines of timeworn weariness, and since that is not dreary enough it also throws in several Serious Issues for the characters to discuss.

Connery, first seen wearing an Indian headdress while thoroughly marinated in an intoxicating jungle potion, is an eccentric Scotsman who has been doing research by himself for so long that he has almost forgotten what pajamas look like. Bracco reminds him of them, and other things. She's the head of the organization that is financing him, and responds to his call for a research assistant because she wants to find out what he's doing out there in the jungle.

It goes, I think, almost without saying that Connery will resent a "girl" turning up as his helper, that Bracco will be a liberated woman, that they will fight, that together they will overcome great odds, and that eventually they will find themselves in each other's arms. It also goes without saying that there will be a lot of snakes and ants in the jungle (and one mosquito—announced with a loud buzz on the sound track).

The ads for the movie have already revealed the story line (which, to be fair, is so elementary it can be summarized in a sentence). Connery has found the cure for cancer, but the mercenary villains who are burning and bulldozing the rain forest will soon destroy the only place on Earth where the ingredients for his rare cancer drug can exist. The plot is thickened because, once having concocted a miraculous overnight anticancer serum, Connery cannot repeat his experiment. His failure has him stumped, and Bracco, too, although not the audience, which is able to figure out what he's doing wrong because of two clues that are as subtle as blows to the head.

There are some beautiful moments in *Medicine Man*. I enjoyed the freedom of the rope-and-pulley arrangement by which Connery is able to journey to the treetops. And the drollery of his dialogue, although it is interrupted by the screenwriter's bizarre ideas of how Bracco should talk ("No boat! No boat!" she keeps shouting at one juncture, when Connery wants to send her home). The movie also has a perfect closing line ("Unbutton your shirt"), although it is typical of the filmmakers that they fail to recognize it as the closing line, and keep going.

Meet the Deedles
(Directed by Steve Boyum; starring Steve Van Wormer, Paul Walker, John Ashton; 1998)
The cult of stupidity is irresistible to teenagers in a certain mood. It's a form of rebellion, maybe: If the real world is going to reject them, then they'll simply refuse to get it. Using jargon and incomprehension as weapons, they'll create their own alternate universe.

All of which is a tortuous way to explain *Meet the Deedles,* a movie with no other ambition than to create mindless slapstick and generate a series in the tradition of the *Bill & Ted* movies. The story involves twin brothers Stew and Phil Deedle (Steve Van Wormer and Paul Walker), slackers from Hawaii who find themselves in the middle of a fiendish plot to sabotage Old Faithful in Yellowstone National Park.

As the movie opens, Stew and Phil are hanging beneath a balloon being towed above the Hawaiian surf, while being pursued by a truant officer on a jet-ski. Soon they're called on the carpet before their millionaire father (Eric Braeden), who snorts, "You will one day take over the entire Deedles empire—and you are surf bums!" His plan: Send them to Camp Broken Spirit, a month-long experience in outdoor living that will turn them into men.

Through plot developments unnecessary to relate, the Deedles escape the camp experience, are mistaken for Park Ranger recruits, come under command of Ranger Pine (John Ashton), and stumble onto the solution to a mysterious infestation of prairie dogs.

Now prairie dogs can be cute, as anyone who has seen Disney's *The Living Prairie* nature documentary can testify. But in large numbers they look alarmingly like herds of rats, and the earth trembles (slightly) as they scurry across the park. Why so many prairie dogs? Because an evil ex-Ranger named Slater (Dennis Hopper) has trained them to burrow out a cavern around Old Faithful, allowing him to redirect the geyser's boiling waters in the direction of New Faithful, to which he plans to sell tickets.

Hopper lives in the cavern, relaxing in his E-Z-Boy recliner and watching the surface on TV monitors. His sidekicks include Nemo, played by Robert Englund, Freddy of the *Nightmare on Elm Street* pictures. At one point he explains how he trained the prairie dogs, and I will add to my permanent memory bank the sound of Dennis Hopper saying, "Inject kibble into the dirt, and a-tunneling they would go." Study his chagrin when the Deedles employ Mentholatum Deep-Heat Rub as a weapon in this war.

While he schemes, the Deedles fumble and blunder their way through Ranger training, and Phil falls for Jesse (A. J. Langer), the pretty stepdaughter of Ranger Pine. There are a lot of stunts, involving mountains, truck crashes, and river rapids, and then the big showdown over Old Faithful. The Deedles relate to everything in surfer terms (plowing into a snowbank, they cry, "We've landed in a Slurpy!").

I am prepared to imagine a theater full of eleven-year-old boys who might enjoy this movie, but I can't recommend it for anyone who might have climbed a little higher on the evolutionary ladder. The *Bill & Ted* movies had a certain sly self-awareness that this one lacks. Maybe that's a virtue. Maybe it isn't.

Mercury Rising

(Directed by Harold Becker; starring Bruce Willis, Alec Baldwin; 1998)
Mercury Rising is about the most sophisticated cryptographic system known to man, and about characters considerably denser than anyone in the audience. Sitting in the dark, our minds idly playing with the plot, we figure out what they should do, how they should do it, and why they should do it, while the characters on the screen strain helplessly against the requirements of the formula.

The movie begins with the two obligatory scenes of most rogue lawman scenarios: (1) Opening hostage situation, in which the hero (Bruce Willis) could have saved the situation if not for his trigger-happy superiors; (2) the Calling on the Carpet, in which his boss tells the lawman he's being pulled off the job and assigned to grunt duty. "You had it—but the magic's gone," the boss recites. Willis's only friend is a sidekick named Bizzi Jordan (Chi McBride), who has, as is the nature of sidekicks, a wife and child, so that the hero can gaze upon them and ponder his solitude.

Experienced moviegoers will know that in the course of his diminished duties, Willis (playing an FBI man named Jeffries) will stumble across a bigger case. And will try to solve it single-handedly, while he is the object of a police manhunt. And will eventually engage in a hand-to-hand struggle with the sinister man behind the scheme. This struggle will preferably occur in a high place (see "Climbing Villian," from *Ebert's Bigger Little Movie Glossary*). Plus, it's a safe bet the hero will enlist a good-looking woman who will drop everything for a chance to get shot at while at his side.

The new twist this time is explained by the evil bureaucrat (Alec Baldwin) in one of several lines of dialogue he should have insisted on rewriting: "A nine-year-old has deciphered the most sophisticated cipher system ever known—and he's autistic!?!" Yes, little Simon (Miko Hughes) looks at a word game in a puzzle magazine, and while the sound track emits quasi-computeristic beeping noises, he figures out the code concealed there, and calls the secret phone number, causing two geeks in a safe room to leap about in dismay.

Agents are dispatched to try to kill the kid and his parents, who live in Chicago. FBI agent Jeffries comes late to the scene, eyeballs the dead parents, immediately intuits it wasn't really a murder-suicide ("How's a guy that's so broke afford a $1,500 handgun?"), and then finds Simon hiding in a crawl space. Putting two and two together (without beeping noises), he deduces that Simon knows a secret, and powerful people want to destroy him.

The movie then descends into formula again, with obligatory scenes in which the police guard is mysteriously pulled off duty in a hospital corridor (see *The Godfather*), and Jeffries runs down corridors with the kid under his arm while evil agents demonstrate that no marksman, however well trained, can hit anyone important while there's still an hour to go. (The David Mamet movie *The Spanish Prisoner*, which is as smart as *Mercury Rising* is dumb, has the hero ask a markswoman: "What if you had missed?" and supplies her with the perfect answer: "It would be back to the range for me!")

The movie's greatest test of credibility comes when Jeffries, object of a citywide manhunt, walks into a restaurant in the Wrigley Building, meets a complete stranger named Stacy (Kim Dickens), and asks her to watch the kid for him while he goes on a quick mission. Of course Stacy agrees, and cooperates again when the agent and the kid turn up at her house in the middle of the night and ask for a safe place to stay. Before long, indeed, she's blowing off a business trip to Des Moines because, well, what woman wouldn't instinctively trust an unshaven man in a sweaty T-shirt with an autistic kid under his arm and a gun in his belt—especially if the cops were after him?

What is sad is that the performances by Willis, Dickens, and young Miko Hughes are really pretty good—better than the material deserves. Willis doesn't overplay or overspeak, which redeems some of the silly material, and Dickens somehow finds a way through the requirements of her role that allows her to sidestep her character's wildly implausible decisions.

But what happened to Alec Baldwin's bullshit detector? Better replace those batteries! His character utters speeches that are laughable in any context, especially this one. "You know," he says, "my wife says my people skills are like my cooking skills—quick and tasteless." And listen to his silky speech in the rain as he defends his actions.

Here are the two most obvious problems that sentient audiences will have with the plot. (1) Modern encryption cannot be intuitively deciphered, by rainmen or anyone else, without a key. And, (2) if a nine-year-old kid can break your code, don't kill the kid, kill the programmers.

Message in a Bottle

(Directed by Luis Mandoki; starring Kevin Costner, Paul Newman, Robin Wright Penn; 1999)

Message in a Bottle is a tearjerker that strolls from crisis to crisis. It's curiously muted, as if it fears that passion would tear its delicate fabric; even the fights are more in sorrow than in anger, and when there's a fistfight, it doesn't feel like a real fistfight—it feels more like someone thought the movie needed a fistfight round about then.

The film is about a man and a woman who believe in great true love. The man believes it's behind him; the woman hopes it's ahead of her. One of their ideals in life is "to be somebody's true north." Right away we know they're in trouble. You don't just find true love. You team up with somebody, and build it from the ground up. But *Message in a Bottle* believes in the kind of love where the romantic music comes first, trembling and sweeping under every scene, and the dialogue is treated like the lyrics.

Yet it is about two likable characters—three, really, since Paul Newman not only steals every scene he's in, but puts it in the bank and draws interest on it. Robin Wright Penn plays Theresa, a researcher for the *Chicago Tribune,* who finds a letter in a bottle. It is a heartbreaking love note to "Catherine," by a man who wants to make amends to his true north.

Theresa, a divorced mother of one, is deeply touched by the message, and shares it with a columnist named Charlie (Robbie Coltrane), who of course lifts it for a column. Theresa feels betrayed. (If she thinks she can show a letter like that to a guy with a deadline and not read about it in tomorrow's paper, no wonder she's still a researcher.) The column leads to the discovery of two other letters, on the same stationery. Charlie has the bottle, the cork, the stationery, and the handwriting analyzed, and figures the messages came from the Carolinas. A few calls to gift shops, and they know who bought the stationery.

It's Garret Blake (Kevin Costner). Theresa is sent out on a mission to do research about him. She meets his father (Newman), and then the man himself, a shipwright who handcrafts beautiful vessels. He takes her for a test sail. The wind is bracing and the chemistry is right. "You eat meat?" he asks her. "Red meat? I make a perfect steak. It's the best thing I do." With this kind of build-up, Linda McCartney would have tucked into a T-bone.

Soon it's time for Theresa to return home (where after she writes one column, the paper promotes her and gives her an office with a window view; at that rate, in six weeks she'll be using Colonel McCormick's ancestral commode). Of course she wants him to come and see her—to see how she lives. "Will you come and visit me?" she asks. His reply does not represent the proudest moment of the screenwriter: "You mean, inland?"

Sooner or later he's going to find out that she found his letter in a bottle and is not simply a beautiful woman who wandered onto his boat. That his secrets are known in those few places where the *Tribune* is still read. Yes, but it takes a long time, and when his discovery finally comes, the film handles it with a certain tact. It's not just an explosion about betrayal, but more complicated—partly because of the nature of the third letter. (Spoiler: It's a bit of a stretch that Garret's dying wife coincidentally hit on the idea of writing a note in a bottle to him on the same typewriter and stationery he was using, especially since she presumably didn't know about the first two notes.)

As morose and contrived as the movie is, it has a certain winsome charm, because of the personal warmth of the actors. This is Robin Wright Penn's breakthrough to a different kind of acting, and she has a personal triumph; she's been identified with desperate, hard-as-nails characters, but no more. Costner finds the right note of inarticulate pain; he loves, but doesn't feel he has the right to. Paul Newman handles his role, as Costner's ex-drunk father, with the relaxed confidence of Michael Jordan shooting free-throws in your driveway. It is good to see all three of them on the screen, in whatever combination, and the movie is right to play down the sex scenes and underline the cuddling and the whispers.

But where, oh where, did they get the movie's ending? Is it in the original novel, *The Notebook,* by Nicholas Sparks? Don't know. Haven't read it. The climactic events are shameless, contrived, and wildly out of tune with the rest of the story. To saddle Costner, Penn, and Newman with such goofy melodrama is like hiring Fred Astaire and strapping a tractor on his back.

Meteor

(Directed by Ronald Neame; starring Sean Connery, Natalie Wood, Henry Fonda, Trevor Howard; 1979)

Movie critics are always complaining the special effects are bad, but do they ever say why? Not usually. They satisfy themselves with a snappy one-liner ("Godzilla's opponent looks like a large, runny blob of Gorgonzola cheese") and then race on to the sociological implications of the work in review.

Well, the special effects in *Meteor* are bad, and let's take ourselves a nice, leisurely conducted tour of their various shortcomings. We can indulge that luxury because the story of *Meteor* (apart from the special effects) hardly inspires discussion. This basic plot has already been filmed nineteen times. It wasn't any good before and it's not any good now.

1. The Meteor. Apparently a very large, false rock, photographed from just above its top surface as it occupies the foreground and rolls toward the camera. The problem here is that since the camera doesn't seem to move in relation to the background, the meteor appears to be rolling in place on its axis—rather than toward us.

2. Outer Space. In his classic film *2001,* Stanley Kubrick revolutionized the way we visualize objects in space by photographing them moving slowly in relationship to one another, while a Strauss waltz filled the sound track. Fine, if the objects are delicately rendezvousing while their speeds are synchronized in the same plane—as his were. *Meteor* also gives us majestic outer space ballets of space objects, but is guilty of an oversight: Its objects are hurtling toward each other from opposite directions and thus would be perceived as moving at the sum of their speeds—in this case, tens of thousands of miles an hour. You'd have to look fast.

3. Reaction Time. After an explosion, a piece of meteor hits an American space probe. Just before it does, the crew members throw up their arms in horror and recoil. Impossible. At the speeds involved, they wouldn't have the slightest chance of realizing what was going to happen—let alone see the meteor approach—before they were blasted to smithereens.

4. The Disasters. I'll be kind here. I won't mention the unspeakably incompetent obligatory shots of tidal waves and cities in flame. But here are two laughable scenes that didn't even have to be in the picture:

Scene One: An Eskimo or Mongolian (I didn't catch the accent) looks up in the sky and gasps as a small meteor flashes down and explodes. Where does it land? Just on the other side of a handy nearby mountain, of course, so its glow can light up the sky. Since it is obvious that in a fiction film the director can place his Mongolians anywhere, why pinch pennies and put him on the wrong side of the mountain?

Scene Two: my favorite. The heartrending incident of the 12,000 dead Olympic cross-country skiers, who are all crushed by a massive avalanche. Hold on! you say. Do we really see all 12,000 skiers? Yes, as a matter of fact, we do: The movie fools us. We see all 12,000 skiers cheerfully speeding past the camera, and then the announcer on a newscast breathlessly breaks the tragic news: "Just minutes after these scenes were shot, the skiers were all killed!! . . . Luckily, our camera crew escaped by helicopter just in time!" What luck.

5. The Case of the Anamorphic Intergalactic Objects. Here we have the ultimate El Cheapo Sleazo effect, but first let me explain "anamorphic." To make widescreen movies, the images are first squeezed, and then projected through a special lens that stretches them out to lifelike dimensions. But, if you take ordinary, everyday images and then project them through an anamorphic lens, they will look really stretched out. Example: The ads at intermissions with those squatty and fat Coke bottles.

Meteor uses anamorphic effects in a desperate and truly sleazy attempt to make its explosions look bigger. Ordinary explosions and glowing meteors are shot (badly) in regular ratio and run through the lens. Result? All the meteors in this movie are wider than they are high.

Enough. Do the people who made *Meteor* take us all for total fools? And, if so, could that possibly be because they're looking for company?

Milk Money

(Directed by Richard Benjamin; starring Melanie Griffith, Ed Harris; 1994)
Sometimes they produce a documentary about the making of a movie. You know, like *The Making of "Jurassic Park."* I would give anything within reason to see *The Making of "Milk Money,"* or, for that matter, to simply listen to recordings of the executive story conferences. In fact, it's funny . . . as I sit here in a late-summer reverie . . . why, it's almost as if I can hear the voices now. . . .

* * *

Studio Executive A: So what's the premise?

Studio Executive B: We got kids, we got sex, we got romance, all in a family picture

A: Can't have sex in a family picture.

B: Depends. Nobody actually *has* sex. Sure, you got a hooker, but she's a *good* hooker, with a heart of gold. Melanie Griffith is gonna play her.

A: Kind of like *Working Girl Turns a Trick*?

B: Cuter than that. We start with three twelve-year-old boys. They're going crazy because they've never seen a naked woman.

A: Whatsamatter? They poor? Don't they have cable?

B: Ever hear of the concept of "the willing suspension of disbelief?" I know the audience will find it hard to believe but it's true: These kids don't know what a naked woman looks like. So they pool their pocket money and ride their bikes into the big city, and ask women on the street if they're hookers, until they find one who is. That's Melanie.

A: How much they got?

B: More'n a hundred bucks. So she shows them.

A: She strips? This has got to get a PG-13 rating.

B: Like I say, it's a family movie. She only strips to the waist. And we only see her from the back.

A: (slightly disappointed): Oh. So that's ten minutes. Where do we go from here?

B: There's more to the plot. Melanie is in danger from the evil gangsters who control prostitution, and after her pimp is killed they think she has all of his money. So she needs to hide out. And one of the kids thinks she'd make an ideal wife for his dad. So he invites her out to the suburbs.

A: The dad's not married?

B: We got a nice touch here. The kid's mother died in childbirth. So all his life he's had this single father. He wants to fix up dad with the hooker, see? He thinks she'd make a great mom.

A: So we get a Meet Cute?

B: Yeah. See, the kid moves the hooker into his tree house, and then tells his dad that she's his buddy's math tutor.

A: What's she wearing?

B: A kind of clingy minidress with a low neckline. High heels.

A: Is that what a math tutor wears?

B: You ever see *My Tutor*? *Private Lessons*? Any of those Sybil Danning or Sylvia Kristel pictures?

A: You got a point. So dad doesn't catch on.

B: Naw. He falls for her. Also, this is a nice angle, he's a high school science teacher who is fighting to save the wetlands near the school from an evil developer who wants to pave it and turn it into a shopping center. Dad is played by Ed Harris.

A: (nods approvingly) Ecology. Very good.

B: So the hooker is in the tree house, dad thinks she's a math tutor, and meanwhile the evil gangster is cruising the streets of the suburb with another hooker, looking for her. While dad fights against the encroachment of the wetlands and chains himself to his automobile so the bulldozers can't come in. And meanwhile we throw in some of those cute conversations where one person means one thing and another person means something else. You know, so that all of the people in the town know she's a hooker except for dad, who takes her out to eat and scandalizes your standard table of gossiping local biddies.

A: This is nice, this is original.

B: We put in some nice Normal Rockwell touches. Like, the way the kid communicates between his bedroom and the hooker in the tree house is with one of those old tin-can telephones? You know, where you attach two tin cans with a string?

A: I was never able to get one of those to work when I was a kid.

B: Neither was I. But don't worry. No kid today has ever seen one before, so they won't know. Today's kids use cellular phones and beepers.

A: Good point.

B: And then we get the big climax.

A: What happens?

B: I don't want to spoil it for you, but let's just say the gangster doesn't get what he wants, and true love saves the day.

A: What about the wetlands?

B: The wetlands? Let me just say, from the point of view of the ultimate significance of this picture, the message for the family audience sort of thing, the wetlands are what this picture is all about.

A: Saving the wetlands. A good cause.

B: Of course, you don't mention the wetlands in the ads.

A: No, you mention the hooker in the ads. So what's the picture called? *Pocket Money*?

B: No, it's called *Milk Money.*

A: Why *Milk Money*?

B: You'll understand when you see the ads.

Mr. Magoo
(Directed by Stanley Tong; starring Leslie Nielsen; 1997)

Magoo drives a red Studebaker convertible in *Mr. Magoo,* a fact I report because I love Studebakers and his was the only thing I liked in the film. It has a prescription windshield. He also drives an eggplantmobile, which looks like a failed wienermobile. The concept of a failed wienermobile is itself funnier than anything in the movie.

Mr. Magoo is transcendently bad. It soars above ordinary badness as the eagle outreaches the fly. There is not a laugh in it. Not one. I counted. I wonder if there *could* have been any laughs in it. Perhaps this project was simply a bad idea from the beginning, and no script, no director, no actor, could have saved it.

I wasn't much of a fan of the old cartoons. They were versions of one joke, imposed on us by the cantankerous but sometimes lovable nearsighted Magoo, whose shtick was to mistake something for something else. He always survived, but since it wasn't through his own doing, his adventures were more like exercises in design: Let's see how Magoo can walk down several girders suspended in midair, while thinking they're a staircase.

The plot involves Magoo as an innocent bystander at the theft of a jewel. Mistaken as the thief, he is pursued by the usual standard-issue CIA and FBI buffoons, while never quite understanding the trouble he's in. He's accompanied on most of his wanderings by his bulldog and his nephew, Waldo, of which the bulldog has the more winning personality.

Magoo is played by Leslie Nielsen, who could at the very least have shaved his head bald for the role. He does an imitation of the Magoo squint and the Magoo voice, but is unable to overcome the fact that a little Magoo at six minutes in a cartoon is a far different matter than a lot of Magoo at ninety minutes in a feature. This is a one-joke movie without the joke. Even the out-takes at the end aren't funny, and I'm not sure I understood one of them, un-less it was meant to show stunt people hilariously almost being drowned.

I have taken another look at my notes, and must correct myself. There is one laugh in the movie. It comes after the action is over, in the form of a foolish, politically correct disclaimer stating that the film "is not intended as an accurate portrayal of blindness or poor eyesight." I think we should stage an international search to find one single person who thinks the film is intended as such a portrayal, and introduce that person to the author of the dis-claimer, as they will have a lot in common, including complete detachment from reality.

Mr. Payback
(Directed by Bob Gale; starring Billie Warlock; 1995)
The armrest of your seat contains a little console with red, orange, and green buttons. You do a test run, clicking them. The lights go down, the "Interfilm" trademark appears on the screen, and an announcer encourages you to talk, scream, shout, and snort during the following film: "Feel free to generally behave as if you were raised in a barn."

Mr. Payback, the first "interactive movie," is supposed to inspire these reactions because you, the lucky audience member, will be able to make key decisions affecting the progress of the story. The first "interfilm" opens this weekend in forty-four specially equipped theaters around the country, and you can see for yourself.

If you feel, for example, that the headmistress of a private school should torture the handcuffed hero with a cattle prod, you will want to push the red button. Other choices include a paddle or a rod. I was for the paddle, but the majority voted for the cattle prod, after which the hero was given electric shocks to the genitals (thankfully below screen level) and then dropped in a Dumpster while a subtitle cheerfully assured us that his "family jewels" had survived intact.

I went to see *Mr. Payback* with an open mind. I knew it would not be a "movie" as I understand that word, because movies act on you and absorb you in their stories. An "interfilm," as they call this new medium, is like a cross between a video game and a CD-ROM game, and according to Bob Bejan, president and CEO of Interfilm, Inc., "suspension of disbelief comes when you begin to believe you're in control."

I never believed I was in control. If I had been in control, I would have ended the projection and advised Bejan to go back to the drawing board. While an interactive movie might in theory be an entertaining experience, *Mr. Payback* was so offensive and yokel-brained that being raised in a barn might almost be required of its audiences.

Few adults are going to find the process bearable. The target audience is possibly children and younger adolescents. That's why I found it surprising that *Mr. Payback* shovels as much barnyard material into its plot as possible. The movie seems obsessed with scatology: with excrement, urination, enemas, loudly passing gas, stepping in dog messes, etc. It also involves a great deal of talk about sexual practices, not to mention every possible rude four-letter word except, to be sure, the ultimate one. The movie bends over backward to be vulgar. It's the kind of film where horrified parents might encourage the kids to shout at the screen, hoping the noise might drown out the flood of garbage.

Hey, I'm not against four-letter words—in context, and with a purpose. But why did *Mr. Payback* need to be gratuitously offensive? Nonstop? Knowing there would be young children in the audience?

Now what about the process itself? True, you can "influence" events. You sit through the movie once, choosing villains, choosing "paybacks," choosing fates, even choosing celebrity guests (Paul Anka, Ice T) for a final game show. That takes twenty minutes. Then you're allowed to sit through the movie again, and this time of course you choose different villains, paybacks, etc. In one version, you can force that evil headmistress to be strapped into a leather bondage uniform and walked on all fours. In another version, the villain might be forced to eat monkey brains. Ho, ho.

How are these choices conveyed to the screen? Four laserdisc players with various plot choices are standing by in the control booth, and double-brightness video projectors are suspended from the theater ceiling. The image is acceptable and the sound is excellent; there is no perceptible delay between the audience vote and the scene it has chosen.

It was clear after two viewings that most of the movie remains essentially the same every time, and that the "choices" provide brief detours that loop back to the main story line. Choose a different villain, and he or she still gets gassed in the backseat of the limousine. It's said that two hours of material are shot for every twenty-minute movie. Nothing on Earth could induce me to sit through every permutation of *Mr. Payback.*

Is there a future for "interfilms"? Maybe. Someday they may grow clever or witty. Not all of them will be as moronic and offensive as *Mr. Payback.* What they do technically, they do pretty well. It is just that this is not a *movie.* It is mass psychology run wild, with the mob zealously pummeling their buttons, careening downhill toward the sleaziest common denominator.

There were lots of small children in the audience. I thought about asking one little girl if she had voted for the paddle, the rod, or the cattle prod. Because she must have voted for one of them. I saw her pushing her buttons.

The Mysterious Island of Captain Nemo

(Directed by Juan Antonio Bardem and Henri Colpi; starring Omar Sharif; 1975)

Lots of movies have been inspired by their special effects, but *The Mysterious Island of Captain Nemo* may be the first movie inspired by its lack of special effects. Here's a kiddie movie with a nihilistic, suicidal ending—because there wasn't enough money to show Nemo's famous submarine, the *Nautilus,* actually moving under water. Nemo, faced with doom and lacking the expensive special effects necessary to make his escape, chooses to go down with his ship and save the producers money.

We do, however, get the inside of the *Nautilus,* as well as a cheap set alleged to show its conning tower and upper deck (the rest of the vast vessel is underwater, and, as the saying goes, out of sight is out of mind and also not out of pocket). It's inhabited by Nemo himself, played by the sad-eyed Omar Sharif, who gets star billing for his approximately ten minutes on screen.

The plot involves a group of shipwrecked balloonists (or balloon-wrecked sailors) and their dog, who are stranded on a strange island guarded by devices that look like a cross between Chinese dragons and death rays. They set up housekeeping in a cave, stay away from the death rays, float to a nearby island to rescue another shipwreck victim, and spend an inordinate amount of time following their dog, who is as clever as, and vastly more humorous than, the rest of the cast.

There are also some pirates who turn up, apparently looking for Nemo, and there are several inconclusive gun battles for no very good reason. The most inexplicable scene (in a movie full of them) is one involving a pet chimpanzee who arrives unannounced, does its stuff, and then is shot by the pirates and buried. Never introduce a chimpanzee in the first act unless you're going to shoot it in the third?

After adventures too boring to mention, our heroes wind up in Captain Nemo's grotto and on board the *Nautilus*. He gives them an illustrated slide lecture of his background and early years, and meanwhile the island is blowing up. That's our chance to see stock footage of lava flowing from volcanoes. In fear that we may miss the point (after all, this is rented footage), the producers show it to us, not once, but twice. That's not necessary since we saw the identical stock footage in last month's *The Island at the Top of the World*. That volcano gets around.

Movies like this have an obligatory structure (or used to) that requires a climax at the end. We can reasonably expect that our heroes will assist Captain Nemo in freeing himself and his submarine from the grotto, but, no, they don't. They climb out of the grotto and make their way to the beach. The *Nautilus* goes down in an orgy of trick photography. A ship steams into sight to rescue the survivors. The movie's last line of dialogue is one of regret that rescue has arrived "since now our adventures are over." That's assuming they ever began.

The Myth of Fingerprints

(Directed by Bart Freundlich; starring Blythe Danner, Roy Scheider, Julianne Moore, Noah Wylie; 1997)

Some families cannot be saved. The family in *The Myth of Fingerprints* is one of them. There have been a lot of movies where dysfunctional families return home for uneasy Thanksgiving weekends (*Home for the Holidays* and *The Ice Storm* come to mind), but few in which the turkey has less to complain about than anyone else at the table.

The film takes place in chilly light at a farmhouse somewhere in New England, where angry and sullen grown children return for Thanksgiving, bringing along apprehensive lovers and angry memories. Waiting to welcome them is their mother, Lena (Blythe Danner), whose relative cheer under these circumstances is inexplicable but welcome, and their father, Hal (Roy Scheider), who, like so many WASP fathers in recent films, is by definition a monster (aware of his pariah status, he walks and talks like a medieval flagellant).

The family drags itself together like torture victims returning to their dungeons. The dialogue, wary and elliptical, skirts around remembered wounds. Angriest of all is Mia (Julianne Moore), who glowers through the entire film, nursing old grudges, and lashes out at her hapless fiancée Eliot (Brian Kerwin), a psychotherapist who, if he were any good at all, would prescribe immediate flight for himself. Mia's younger sister, Leigh (Laurel Holloman) seems relatively unscathed by the family experience, maybe because her siblings exhausted the family's potential for damage before she grew into range.

Also in the family are two sons. Warren (Noah Wylie) is interested to learn that the great love of his life, Daphne, is back in town. Jake (Michael Vartan) has brought along his fiancée, Margaret (Hope Davis), who has an alarming taste for immediate sexual gratification ("anywhere, anytime," as Travis Bickle once said).

During the weekend, two of these characters will meet people from their pasts. For Warren, the reunion with Daphne (Arija Bareikis) will be a chance to explain why he broke off their warm relationship so suddenly and seemed to flee. Mia meets an old schoolmate who now calls himself Cezanne (James Le Gros), and who represents, I think, a life principle the family would be wise to study.

Frequently in the movies, when an alienated, inarticulate, and depressed father starts cleaning his rifle, we can anticipate a murder or a suicide by the end of the film. Here we're thrown off course when Hal, the dad, buys a turkey at the grocery store and then shoots it with his rifle, so his family will think he hunted it down himself. (I would have appreciated a scene where he explained the plastic bag with the gizzards.)

The movie is not unskillful. The acting is much better than the material deserves, and individual scenes achieve takeoff velocity, but the movie ends without resolution, as if its purpose was to strike a note and slink away. *The Myth of Fingerprints* makes one quite willing to see the same actors led by the same director—but in another screenplay. This one is all behavior, nuance, and angst, seasoned with unrelieved gloom. Some families need healing. This one needs triage.

N

●●

Newsies

(Directed by Kenny Ortega; starring Robert Duvall, Ann-Margret; 1992)

Newsies, we are informed as the movie opens, is based on actual events. I do not doubt this. I am sure that shortly before the turn of the century, newsboys organized a strike against the greedy Joseph Pulitzer, and were cheered on by a dance-hall madam with a heart of gold. Nor do I doubt that the lads, some of them boys of nine or ten, hung out in saloons and bought rounds of beer while making their plans, or that the proprietor of an evil city orphanage made himself rich by collecting fees from the city. I don't even doubt that the news-boys printed their own strike paper on an old flat-bed press down in the basement of Pulitzer's building. Of course I believe. Yes, Virginia.

What I find it hard to believe, however, is that anyone thought the screen-play based on these actual events was of compelling interest. *Newsies* is like warmed-over Horatio Alger, complete with such indispensable clichés as the newsboy on crutches, the little kid, and of course the hero's best pal, who has a pretty sister. Nor does the movie lack the standard villains, including Oscar nominee Michael Lerner as the hard-hearted circulation manager.

In the role of New York publisher Joseph Pulitzer, Robert Duvall, wear-ing a beard that makes him look like one of the Smith Brothers, plays a stan-dard fat-cat industrialist, with none of the wit or insight that the original Pulitzer employed while selling the first mass-circulation newspapers to the unwashed masses. The real Pulitzer, who was one of the inspirations for *Citizen Kane,* must have known something about ordinary people; here he seems here to despise them.

Ann-Margret, who plays Madda, the dance-hall star, has a role whose purpose is all but incomprehensible. She acts as a sort of big sister and con-fidante to the striking newsboys, chucking some of them under the chin while talking to others in terms of fairly alarming intimacy. Are we to guess that her dealings with some of the lads have gone beyond buying a paper for a penny?

She performs onstage in her music hall, which functions in the movie primarily as a transparent device for getting an Ann-Margret number into the show.

The newsies themselves are up in arms because Mr. Pulitzer has cut their take by a tenth of a cent. They organize, form a union, and agitate for workers' rights with such articulate energy that we can only wonder what these kids could accomplish if they were high school graduates, instead of street waifs. They sing and dance a lot, too, on olde New York street sets that stretch unconvincingly for hundreds of yards down studio back lots. The music is by Alan Mencken, whose material for *The Little Mermaid* and *Beauty and the Beast* was unforgettable. Here he achieves the opposite result.

I saw the movie at a Saturday morning preview attended by hundreds of children. From what I could see and hear, the kids didn't get much out of it. No wonder. Although the material does indeed involve young protagonists, no effort is made to show their lives in a way today's kids can identify with. This movie must seem as odd to them as a foreign film. The fact that old man Pulitzer once tried to screw newsies out of a tenth of a cent must represent, for many of them, the very definition of the underwhelming.

Nick and Jane

(Directed by Richard Mauro; starring Dana Wheeler-Nichols, James McCaffrey; 1997)

You don't want to watch *Nick and Jane,* you want to grade it. It's like work by a student inhabiting the mossy lower slopes of the bell curve. Would-be filmmakers should see it and make a list of things they resolve never to do in their own work.

The story involves Jane (Dana Wheeler-Nicholson), a business executive, and Nick (James McCaffrey), a taxi driver. She is unaware of the movie rule that requires that whenever a character arrives unannounced at a lover's apartment for a "surprise," the lover will be in bed with someone else. She finds the faithless John (John Dossett) in another's arms, bolts out of the building, and into Nick's cab. Then follow the usual scenes in which they fall in love even though they live in two different worlds.

I call that the story, but it's more like the beard. Inside *Nick and Jane*'s heterosexual cover story is a kinky sex comedy, signaling frantically to be released. Consider. Nick's neighbor in his boardinghouse is Miss Coco Peru (Clinton Leupp), a drag queen. Nick's roommate is Enzo (Gedde Watanabe), whose passion for feet is such that he drops to his knees to sniff the insteps of complete strangers. The friendly black woman at the office is into bondage and discipline with the naughty boss. Carter (David Johansen), the boss's special assistant, is Miss Coco's special friend. Key scenes take place at a drag club where Miss Coco is the entertainer (her act consists of singing "The Lord's Prayer"—in all seriousness, and right down to the "forever and ever, Amen," I fear).

These elements could possibly be assembled into quite another movie (for all I know, they were disassembled from quite another movie). But they don't build into anything. They function simply to show that the filmmakers' minds are really elsewhere—that the romance of Nick and Jane is the bone they're throwing to the dogs of convention. I kept getting the strange feeling that if they had their druthers, director Richard Mauro and writers Neil William Alumkal and Peter Quigley would have gladly ditched Nick and Jane and gone with Miss Coco as the lead.

As for Nick and Jane, they have alarming hair problems. Dana Wheeler-Nicholson goes through the movie wearing her mother's hairstyle, or maybe it's Betty Crocker's. James McCaffrey starts out with the aging hippie look but after an expensive makeover paid for by Jane he turns up with his hair slicked back in the Michael Douglas Means Business mode. I think the idea was to show him ever so slightly streaked with blond, but they seem to have dismissed the stylist and done the job themselves, maybe over Miss Coco's sink with a bottle of something from Walgreen's, and Nick looks like he was interrupted in the process of combing yolks through his hair.

The camera work is sometimes quietly inept, sometimes spectacularly so. Consider the scene involving a heated conversation, during which the camera needlessly and distractingly circles the characters as if to say—look, we can needlessly circle these characters! The dialogue is written with the theory that whatever people would say in life, they should say in a movie ("This is a wonderful view!" "I've never been in the front seat of a cab before!").

There is one scene where Nick bashfully confesses to having studied art and reluctantly lets Jane see some sketches he has done of her. The usual pay-off for such scenes is a drawing worthy of Rembrandt, but what Nick shows her is one of those Famous Artist's School approaches where he drew an egg shape and then some crosshairs to mark where the ears and eyes should line up.

Nick's artistry knows no bounds. Masquerading as a business executive, he effortlessly absorbs the firm's current challenge, which apparently involves saving 25 percent on the importation of scrap metal from Surinam. He dispatches Enzo (wearing those L.A. Gear shoes with heels that light up) to collect lots of scrap metal from a junkyard, after which Nick dons a handy welder's helmet to fashion a sculpture that he hauls into the CEO's office, explaining it is intended "to punctuate the enormity of the idea I'm about to present." Yes. That's what he says.

The Night Porter
(Directed by Liliana Cavani; starring Dirk Bogarde,
Charlotte Rampling; 1975)
The Night Porter is as nasty as it is lubricious, a despicable attempt to titillate us by exploiting memories of persecution and suffering. It is (I know how obscene this sounds) Nazi chic. It's been taken seriously in some circles, mostly by critics agile enough to stand on their heads while describing 180-degree turns, in order to interpret trash as "really" meaningful.

That's not to say I object per se to the movie's subject matter, a sado-masochistic relationship taken up again fifteen years after the war by a former SS concentration camp officer and the inmate he raped and dominated when she was a young girl. I can imagine a serious film on this theme—on the psychological implications of shared guilt and the identification of the slave with the master—but *The Night Porter* isn't such a film; it's such a superficial soap opera we'd laugh at it if it weren't so disquieting.

Fascism and its favorite sexual taste, sadomasochism, have come into a certain degree of fashion in the movies recently, and that's the subject of a scary essay by Susan Sontag in the *New York Review of Books*. She finds films like *The Night Porter* to be, on one level at least, attractive to certain audiences because of their undertones of doom and death. That may be an aspect of the times or it may just be that such movies reach areas of the personality that weren't widely admitted before; she's not sure. But she's worried.

I am, too. For a long time I've defended the belief that what we see in the movies doesn't direct our behavior, if we're more or less normal; that there are infinitely greater influences all around us in society to explain deviant and violent behavior, and that the movies are just a convenient whipping boy. I still believe that, but I'm getting awfully weary of the violence I have to witness week after week as a critic.

It's been years since most movie violence was motivated, explained, or even taken seriously by the characters themselves. In most of the violent exploitation movies I see, the killings and hurtings are just there, a way to get through a few minutes of screen time. The audience laughs, most often. But now here's a movie that's not intended for the action-and-escapism crowd, a movie presumably intended for more intelligent and venturesome audiences, who don't laugh at it (although maybe it would be better if they did). What's going on here?

The Night Porter has a nice, classy visual style, filled with browns and blacks (and blues), and good performances by its romantic leads, Dirk Bogarde and Charlotte Rampling. But it's such nonsense. It gives us, through flashbacks and sketchy hints, the story of the relationship they had years earlier in the concentration camp, where his "little girl" appealed to him in a demented way, and she found herself enjoying the raping, the beating, and cuts and bruises.

Now they meet again in a Vienna hotel. She's the wife of an American conductor, and he's the quiet little night porter. All he wants to do, he says, is live "like a church mouse." From the moment she sees him again, she's bound to him. She stays behind when her husband leaves, then moves into his apartment and the fun and games start again: Chains and broken glass and slaps on the face are their aphrodisiacs, and they make love mostly on the floor.

Meanwhile, there's a subplot so ridiculous it must be intended as fantasy. The Bogarde character is a member of a sort of Nazi encounter group that specializes in expiating past guilt and destroying evidence against itself. The Rampling character, alas, is the last surviving witness against Bogarde and so the Nazis want to kill her. They lay siege to the apartment, and the lovers slowly starve together. There's no reason at all why the couple can't be killed straightaway except that then, of course, the movie would be over.

The director, Liliana Cavani, describes her film as a love story, praises the honesty between her two leading characters, and sees the story as a straightforward handling of one aspect of the concentration camp experience. I see it as a shallow exploitation of that theme, containing no real insight or understanding. Even worse, the movie is now being marketed as a controversial audience-grabber. One theater marquee quotes the *New York Times:* "A kinky turn-on!" I looked up that *Times* review. Its opening sentence was: "Let us now consider a piece of junk."

No Looking Back

(Directed by Edward Burns; starring Edward Burns, Blythe Danner; 1998)
Hobbies. That's what the characters in *No Looking Back* need. Bowling or yard sales or watching the Knicks on television. Anything. Although the movie wants us to feel sympathy for them, trapped in meagre lives and empty dreams, I saw them as boring slugs. There is more to existence than moping about at bars and kitchen tables, whining about unhappiness while endlessly sipping from long-neck Budweiser bottles. Get a life.

The movie is the latest from Ed Burns, who won the Sundance Film Festival in 1995 with his rich and moving *The Brothers McMullen,* but has since made two thin and unconvincing films: *She's the One* (1996) and now this one, in which self-absorbed characters fret over their lives. I have no brief against that subject matter; I simply wish the characters and their fretting were more interesting, or their unhappiness less avoidable.

The film is set in the bleak, wintry landscape of Rockaway Beach, New York, where Claudia (Lauren Holly) works in a diner and lives with Michael (Jon Bon Jovi), a mechanic. They are engaged, in a sense, but with no plans for marriage; Michael wants to marry her, but she's "afraid to wake up ten years from now" still working in the diner.

As the film opens, Charlie (Edward Burns) returns to town on the bus after an absence of three years. He was once Claudia's lover, but ditched her without a farewell. Now he apparently hopes to pick up where they left off. He moves into his mother's house; she has his number, and tells him to get a job. And then Michael, who was his best friend, comes over for more beer and conversation, and explains that he and Claudia are "together" now.

Will Claudia accept the dependable Michael? Or will she be swept off her feet once again by the flashier, more charismatic Charlie? "It's different this time," he tells her. "This time I need you. I love you." He's not the soul of eloquence, but she is willing to be persuaded.

The problem is, Charlie is an enigma. Where was he for three years? Why is he back? What are his skills, his plans, his strategies? His vision for the two of them is not inspiring: They'll leave town and go to Florida, where he has no prospects, and "start over." Still, Charlie paints a seductive picture.

Or does he? The film wants us to see Michael, the Bon Jovi character, as a boring, safe, faithful but unexciting choice. But I sort of liked him; Bon Jovi plays the role for its strengths, which involve sincerity and a certain bottom line of integrity. Charlie, on the other hand, is one of those men who believe that true happiness, for a woman, consists of doing what he wants. He offers Claudia not freedom, but the choice of living in his shadow instead of her own.

The story plays out during overcast days and chilly nights, in lonely barrooms and rented houses. Some small life is provided by Claudia's family, which includes her mother (Blythe Danner) and her sister. The mother is convinced her husband, who has deserted her, will return some day. The sister is dating the local fishmonger. As the three women discuss the comings and goings of the men in their lives, they scheme like some of Jane Austen's dimmer characters, for whom the advent of the right man is about the most a girl can hope for.

It is extremely important to some men that the woman of their choice sleep with them. This is a topic not of much interest to outside observers, and often not even to the woman of their choice. *No Looking Back* is really only about whether Claudia will sleep with Charlie, stay with Michael, or leave town. As the characters unhappily circled those possibilities, I felt like asking Claudia to call me when she made up her mind.

Nomads

(Directed by John McTiernan; starring Leslie-Anne Down, Pierce Brosnan; 1986)

I would like to describe the plot of *Nomads,* but my space is limited. Maybe I can give it a try. A French anthropologist (Pierce Brosnan) moves to Los Angeles with his wife. Their new home is immediately made the target of a roaming band of fierce street people who dress in leather and chains and paint slogans on garage walls.

The anthropologist discovers that these people are not your average, big-city vandals, but an urban version of the Innuat. And, about halfway through the movie, we learn what the Innuat are. According to Eskimo legends, they are nomadic spirits who wander Earth in human form, spreading evil.

That is not the complicated part of the plot. The hard part is what we have to slog through before we find out about Innuats.

The movie starts with Lesley-Anne Down as an emergency-room doctor. A deranged patient (Brosnan) is brought in and handcuffed to the bed. Everybody thinks he's on a bad drug trip, but no, it's simpler than that; he has gone stark raving mad.

He keeps screaming the same phrase in French: *N'y sont pas; sont des Innuat.* This translates as, "They are not there; they are Innuat." But nobody can figure that out, because they don't know "Innuat" is an Eskimo word, you see, and they simply think his French is bad.

That reminds me of a classic story from the Cannes Film Festival a few years back, when Rex Reed got an engraved invitation in French. The only word he could read was "Eskimo."

He had heard that there was a great new Eskimo film in the festival, however, and so at midnight he went bravely out into the rainy night and got a cab and went to the address on the invitation, only to discover that he was a guest at the opening of an Eskimo Pie ice-cream store.

Now you may argue, not unreasonably, that my story has little to do with *Nomads.* True. But it has at least as much to do with *Nomads* as the ancient Eskimo myth of the Innuat.

Nomads is a very confused movie, especially after the berserk Brosnan leaps out of his manacles and bites Lesley-Anne Down on the neck, transferring all of his memories into her head, so that she goes crazy and relives all of Brosnan's traumatic experiences with the Innuat.

This grows very confusing for Brosnan's wife (Anna-Maria Monticelli), who does not understand why Down is telling her things only Brosnan would know. It is also very confusing for the audience, because the movie keeps switching signals on us. Sometimes we see Down and then we get a point-of-view shot that is supposed to be inside her head but looking out through Brosnan's eyes. Sometimes we see Brosnan from the outside. Sometimes that means we are looking at the real Brosnan, and sometimes it doesn't. We'd really be confused, if we cared.

But we don't. The movie tells one of those stories where the characters have only themselves to blame for going out into dark nights and looking for trouble with the Innuat and not getting on the next plane back to France. Everybody in this movie gets what's coming to them, except for Lesley-Anne Down, and even she should have been smart enough not to shine her flashlight into the eyes of a man who was foaming at the mouth.

Nomads does, however, have one great shot. An Innuat on a motorcycle is chasing the two women down a lonely interstate highway. Suddenly, the Innuat turns back, and the camera pans slowly to reveal a highway sign: the California state line. Apparently Nevada is not loony enough for the Innuat. And so the lonely Innuat wheels his motorcycle around, and drives slowly back to Los Angeles, where, in keeping with the ancient Eskimo legend, his spirit will haunt the backlots of Hollywood, waiting for another movie that wouldn't be quite bad enough without him.

North
(Directed by Rob Reiner; starring Elijah Wood, Bruce Willis, Jason Alexander, Dan Aykroyd, Kathy Bates; 1994)
I have no idea why Rob Reiner, or anyone else, wanted to make this story into a movie, and close examination of the film itself is no help. *North* is one of the most unpleasant, contrived, artificial, cloying experiences I've had at the movies. To call it manipulative would be inaccurate; it has an ambition to manipulate, but fails.

The film stars Elijah Wood, who is a wonderful young actor (and if you don't believe me, watch his version of *The Adventures of Huck Finn*). Here he is stuck in a story that no actor, however wonderful, however young, should be punished with. He plays a kid with inattentive parents who decides to go into court, free himself of them, and go on a worldwide search for nicer parents.

This idea is deeply flawed. Children do not lightly separate from their parents—and certainly not on the evidence provided here, where the great parental sin is not paying attention to their kid at the dinner table. The parents (Jason Alexander and Julia Louis-Dreyfus) have provided little North with what looks like a million-dollar house in a Frank Capra neighborhood, all on dad's salary as a pants inspector. And, yes, I knew that is supposed to be a fantasy, but the pants-inspecting jokes are only the first of several truly awful episodes in this film.

North goes into court, where the judge is Alan Arkin, proving without the slightest shadow of a doubt that he should never, ever, appear again in public with any material even vaguely inspired by Groucho Marx. North's case hits the headlines, and since he is such an all-star overachiever, offers pour in from would-be parents all over the world, leading to an odyssey that takes him to Texas, Hawaii, Alaska, and elsewhere.

What is the point of the scenes with the auditioning parents? (The victimized actors range from Dan Aykroyd as a Texan to Kathy Bates as an Eskimo). They are all seen as broad, desperate comic caricatures. They are not funny. They are not touching. There is no truth in them. They don't even work as parodies. There is an idiocy here that seems almost intentional, as if the filmmakers plotted to leave anything of interest or entertainment value out of these episodes.

North is followed on his travels by a mysterious character who appears in many guises. He is the Easter bunny, a cowboy, a beach bum, and a Federal Express driver who works in several product plugs. Funny, thinks North; this guy looks familiar. And so he is. All of the manifestations are played by Bruce Willis, who is not funny, or helpful, in any of them.

I hated this movie. Hated hated hated hated hated this movie. Hated it. Hated every simpering stupid vacant audience-insulting moment of it. Hated the sensibility that thought anyone would like it. Hated the implied insult to the audience by its belief that anyone would be entertained by it.

I hold it as an item of faith that Rob Reiner is a gifted filmmaker; among his credits are *This Is Spinal Tap, The Sure Thing, The Princess Bride, Stand by Me, When Harry Met Sally,* and *Misery.* I list those titles as an incantation against this one. *North* is a bad film, but it is not by a bad filmmaker, and must represent some sort of lapse from which Reiner will recover—possibly sooner than I will.

Nowhere to Run
(Directed by Robert Harmon; starring Jean-Claude Van Damme, Rosanna Arquette; 1993)

I am trying to remember where I saw *Nowhere to Run* before, but I have forgotten—just as, before too much longer, I will have forgotten *Nowhere to Run* itself. This is the kind of movie that is so witlessly generic that the plot and title disappear into a mist of other recycled plots and interchangeable titles.

If you have seen the ads on TV, you already know everything that happens in the movie. A prisoner (Jean-Claude Van Damme) escapes from a prison bus and ends up camping on the farm of a sexy widow (Rosanna Arquette) and her two young children, including Kieran Culkin, brother of the little superstar. At first Arquette wants him to leave, but no sooner has he said nineteen words, which are a lot for him, than attraction begins to grow between them.

Meanwhile, an evil real estate developer (Joss Ackland) has designs on the idyllic valley wherein nestles Arquette's farm. He wants to bulldoze her out, and replace this Eden with suburban sprawl. She resists, and he enlists hired goons and the corrupt local lawman (who is smitten with Arquette) to strong-arm her off the land. Van Damme comes to her rescue, and after assorted barn-burnings, pitchfork stabbings, knife fights, gun battles, motorcycle chases, and bulldozer duels, victory is distributed among the just, while the evil are carted away, sneering, "Don't you know who I am?"

Van Damme has specialized in kickboxing and martial arts pictures up until now, but *Nowhere to Run* gives him a few quiet conversational scenes—almost too quiet, since he seems reluctant to speak up. Rosanna Arquette is rather thanklessly used in the film, but shows a quiet grace that should have served a better script. After Van Damme wins her over by repairing the farm machinery, befriending her children, saving her life, and letting her see him in the shower, the erotic tension builds until she finally cracks and utters the movie's best line: "Want to see what my room looks like?"

The movie's screenplay includes a contribution by Joe Eszterhas, author of *Basic Instinct* and *Jagged Edge*. I have a feeling this one was in the bottom of the desk drawer for a long time.

OOOOOOOOOOO

Oh Heavenly Dog

(Directed by Joe Camp; starring Chevy Chase, Benji, Jane Seymour, Omar Sharif, Robert Morley, Alan Sues; 1980)

Satire has such a curious way of catching up with itself. Just a few short years ago, Chevy Chase was on *Saturday Night Live,* that sworn enemy of our national tendency toward the smarmy. Now Chevy Chase is playing Benji in a movie. Among the great unrecorded conversations in Hollywood history, we must now include the one in which Chevy Chase's agent convinced him that playing Benji would be the right career move.

The conversation itself could no doubt have played on *Saturday Night Live,* and there'd also be endless possibilities for the ads: You'll believe a man can bark! Just when we thought it was safe to go back into the pond!

Oh Heavenly Dog is not, alas, anywhere near as funny as the thoughts it inspires. It's a total miscalculation from beginning to end, inspired by an idiotic decision to increase the average age of the Benji audience by starring him in a movie rated PG. Let's face it. Movie audiences have a certain set of expectations for any movie starring a trained dog, and no mere PG rating is going to inspire hopes for greater wit, sophistication, and maturity. There is only so much you can do with a dog.

And *Oh Heavenly Dog* does most of it. In this movie, you'll see Benji dial a telephone, open drawers, go through files, jump into cars, snuggle up to a beautiful girl, jump into her bubble bath and (oh, you PG!) bury his wet, black little nose in her cleavage. The possibilities for Benji in an R-rated movie are too depressing to consider.

The movie's plot crossbreeds the original *Benji* formula with a whodunit murder mystery and several scenes inspired by *Heaven Can Wait.* The film begins with Chevy Chase in human form, as a London private eye who's called in on a new case. He makes a house call, discovers a corpse, and is immediately stabbed in the back by a mysterious stranger.

The stabbing scene incorporates a movie device I detest: We only see the shoes, pants, coat, etc., of the killer, as he stabs our hero. Since the camera could obviously show us his identity but doesn't, we're being set up for a cheap, dumb revelation scene in the end. Since the thriller genre depends absolutely on the solution of mysteries set up early in the story, it's infuriating to get shots suggesting that the camera knows who did it, but isn't telling.

Anyway. Chevy Chase dies, goes to heaven, and is processed by a Mr. Higgins, who informs him that he can redeem his sinful record on Earth by going back and solving the original murder. The only catch is, he'll have to go back as a dog. So the movie continues with Benji bouncing around while his thoughts are spoken on the sound track in Chevy Chase's voice.

This premise could have been fun if the filmmakers had used imagination in exploring the fantasy of a man in a dog's body: The whole problem of surviving in an out-scale environment has been shown entertainingly in movies such as *The Incredible Shrinking Man.* But no. Benji is such a cute little tyke that realities aren't allowed to intrude, and *Oh Heavenly Dog* becomes another one of those insufferable movies in which the plot grinds to a dead halt while the trained dog does his tricks. You know: A-ha! The dead woman is connected in some way with the art gallery! Now let's watch Benji pick up a pencil in his teeth and dial the telephone!

Every scene in the movie is directed at the same deadening crawl, most of the dialogue is delivered in a dispirited monotone, and the solution to the mystery, when it comes, is shatteringly uninteresting. Even the happy ending isn't so happy. The human female that Benji falls in love with is reincarnated and sent back to Earth as a cat. The music swells on the sound track, and Benji and the cat rub sensuously against each other. My own cat, who knows a great deal about the sex lives of cats, says spending his nights in the sack with a dog is not his idea of a happy ending.

Old Dracula

(Directed by Clive Donner; starring David Niven, Teresa Graves; 1975)
In addition to the other, more distinguished, roles he was born to play, David Niven was all but made for Count Dracula. Who else could summon up quite the same combination of weary charm and seedy elegance? And who else,

rising from the neck of his latest victim, his fangs dripping blood, could observe that it used to be a lot easier to get a decent meal in the old days—you just sent out for something from the neighborhood.

Such reflections lure us into *Old Dracula* with, well, fairly high expectations, anyway. The movie's obviously intended as a rip-off of *Young Frankenstein,* right down to the artwork in the ads. But the presence of David Niven is encouraging, and so is the identity of the director: Clive Donner, who, back in the days of Swinging London, made such films as *What's New, Pussycat?*

So nothing quite prepares us for the mess to follow. Niven does, indeed, keep his cool; he may be slumming but he never acts as if he knows it. But the rest of the cast—and Donner—don't seem to have a clue as to why they're making this movie, or how they want us to respond.

There are laughs, but they come either from isolated lines of dialogue or from the sheer incoherence of the plot. There are thrills—or, more accurately, there is one thrill, a fairly boring one as horror-film thrills go. (Will the heroine get trapped in the well with the rats and the rising water?) And there's a great deal of fang-sinking. (The press booklet informs us that Niven's fangs were supplied by a top London dentist: Were they covered by the National Health Service?)

But for the most part, this is a depressing exercise, because Donner and his colleagues don't seem to have caught on to two of the most obvious developments in recent British cinema: (1) British horror films have gotten to be pretty good recently, especially the horror films from Hammer Films and the Max Rosenberg-Milton Subotsky assembly lines, so you can't get away with schlock, and (2) Swinging London is long since gone and done with and you can no longer entertain an audience by showing lots of what used to be called birds and dollies doing the frug beneath psychedelic lights.

Just at the point where the film's suspense, if any, is going to have to come to its climax, Donner stops everything for a party scene that could have been ripped off from *Blow-Up* or all of those, uh, mod, with-it 1960s British films starring girls who didn't know how to spell Susie. Some attempt has been made to make things contemporary by supplying Count Dracula with a black girlfriend, under the following circumstances. His female companion of the last several centuries, Countess Vampira, fell into a coma some fifty years ago and has been put into a deep-freeze while the Count seeks a cure. "But—aren't vampires supposed to be immortal?" someone asks him. Yes, he explains, but the poor countess had a run of bad luck—ate some poisoned peasant. The count finds the rare triple-O blood group necessary to make a vaccine, injects it into his sleeping vampiress, and sees her turn black as she comes back to life. Something about mixing up the vials of blood. . . .

Well, black is beautiful, and the resurrected countess immediately hits the West End of London, digging the discos and going to black exploitation films and saying "right on" a lot, and the count turns into a bat and flies around looking for an antidote for the vaccine, and the ending is so obvious that I won't tell you, you tell me. But when you think what a truly great bad movie David Niven might have made of all of this, it's a shame he merely made a terrible bad movie. There's a difference.

$1,000,000 Duck
(Directed by Vince McEveety; starring Dean Jones, Sandy Duncan; 1971)
Walt Disney's *$1,000,000 Duck* is one of the most profoundly stupid movies I've ever seen. It is a movie about a duck that gets an overdose of radiation and starts laying golden eggs. It is also about the people who won the duck, and about how greed and avarice appear in their lives, and about the lesson in love and understanding that the father gets when his son runs away with the duck and becomes trapped on a ladder between the ledges of two tall buildings, and about how the father gets a fair trial from the American judiciary system.

The people in this movie inhabit a universe of clean little 1940s bungalows with rose trellises, and there's a mean neighbor next door and some teenagers down the street who are always souping up their hot rod. This universe looks vaguely familiar, and you wonder where you've seen it before. It certainly doesn't exist in the current American space-time continuum, but maybe . . .

And then you recognize the universe. The reason you had trouble before was that you'd never seen the *whole* universe before, but only its laundry room. This is the universe of those sweet, simple folks who live in TV soap ads. They mean well, poor souls, and they dress neatly and keep a cheery smile, but they must have been shortchanged in the smarts department because all they care about in this life is how white their whites get. At night they have surrealistic dreams in which their towels come out whiter and whiter and whiter until the whole laundry room is filled with dazzling metaphysical sunlight, and (at last!) their towels are clean and their sins forgiven.

The woman in the family in the movie has apparently survived nine years of marriage since she has an eight-year-old son, but her survival must have been a matter of blind luck. She makes applesauce with garlic in it because she doesn't know any better, and she takes a golden egg down to the bank when her checking account gets overdrawn. Being married to such a woman would be wearying to her husband, you imagine; he is a young scientist engaged in teaching rabbits and ducks to walk down the ramp and through the maze and push the right button and be rewarded with rabbit food or duck food.

There was a Stan Freberg record once about a rat that was put through this ordeal. Over drawbridges. Up ramps. Through doors. Past dead ends. Across the moat. Up the ladder. And finally, finally . . . when the exhausted rodent reached his objective and punched the right button, do you know what came out of the little door for him to eat? A chlorophyll gumball.

One Woman or Two

(Directed by Daniel Vigne; starring Gérard Depardieu; 1987)
See if you agree with me on this. It is not funny when people in a movie walk around being dumb and making stupid mistakes, unless the people are named Curly, Moe, and Larry. If the characters are allegedly people of normal intelligence, their stupidity isn't funny, it's exhausting—and *One Woman or Two* is the most exhausting movie in many a moon.

The movie is about a French anthropologist who hopes to get a large research grant from a rich American woman. He does not know what she looks like. He goes to meet her plane, and through a comedy of errors he ends up connecting with Sigourney Weaver instead of Dr. Ruth Westheimer. That could happen to anybody. What is amazing is that he persists in his misunderstanding for half of the movie.

There is, of course, a lamebrained plot to explain why Weaver wants to be mistaken for somebody else. There is also a reason why "Dr. Wooth" missed her plane. And a subplot about the controversy over the scientist's belief that the first Frenchman actually was a black woman. Add it all up, and what you've got here is a waste of good electricity. I'm not talking about the electricity between the actors. I'm talking about the current to the projector.

The scientist is played by Gérard Depardieu, everybody's favorite French slob, who shuffles through the movie looking more sheepish than usual. He is provided with one of the most hapless characters of his career—a scientist so lacking in perception that he ignores literally dozens of opportunities to discover that the woman he is looking for is not an American amazon but a little German choo-choo. Once Dr. Ruth arrives, she is equally lax in determining that Weaver has been mistaken for her. The light dawns so slowly that this is one of those movies you wish were on video, so you could watch it at fast-forward.

Is there any redeeming facet to this movie? Anything at all that makes it worth seeing? Maybe some nice scenery, or a small, funny moment, or a flash of charm? Let me think. I'm sitting here. I'm thinking. I'm looking at the list of cast members, to see if anything jogs my memory. Nothing. Tell you what. I'm going to turn off my portable computer and close my eyes and meditate, and if anything at all occurs to me, then this will not be the last sentence of the review.

The Opposite Sex

(Directed by Matthew Meshekoff; starring Courteney Cox; 1993)
The people who made *The Opposite Sex* believe it's about a love affair between a stockbroker and an aide to the mayor of Boston. I believe it's about the fact that two of the most idiotic people in recent movie history were able to find employment.

This is the kind of movie where nothing that is done, said, thought, or performed bears any relationship to anyone you have ever met. No one, not even the people who made this movie, believes people can be this dumb and still tie their shoes. Making *The Opposite Sex* is what can happen to you if you grow up thinking sitcoms are funny.

We could begin with the ungrammatical full title of the movie, which is: *The Opposite Sex and How to Live with Them.* Mrs. Seward, who drummed rhetoric into us at Urbana High School, would have cracked director Matthew

Meshekoff over the knuckles for that one. She would have gone on to describe his script as "trite," which was one of her favorite words, but which I have never used in a review, until now.

The movie stars Ayre Gross as David, a stockbroker who hangs out with his best buddy, Eli (Kevin Pollak). They're regulars in the kind of lower-level singles bar that has a periscope sticking up out of the sidewalk so they can see the babes coming. Yes. They believe their days of happy bachelorhood can last forever, and they explain their theories in "comic" monologues that they deliver while looking straight at the camera, while I found myself looking at my watch. You know a movie is slow when you start looking to see what time it is. You know it's awful when you start shaking your watch to see if it has stopped.

One day David meets Carrie (Courteney Cox), who works, as I have mentioned, in the mayor's office. They come from different worlds, according to the press materials, which describe them as "a Jewish stockbroker and a WASPy mayoral aide." I believe they come from exactly the same world, the twilight zone of sitcomland, where they learned that a conversation consists of straight lines, punch lines, one-liners, and asides to themselves, friends, and/or the audience. It would be madness trying to carry on a conversation with people like this. You'd be wondering why nobody wrote *your* lines.

David and Carrie meet, fall in love, get real serious, and then, according to the ancient laws of formulas that the shameless filmmakers borrow from countless other films, they get cold feet. After All, They Come From Different Worlds. I know I am repeating myself, but the movie offers me nothing new to say.

Then he tries dating around, and she goes out with a sensitive type, but gee, wouldn't you know they miss one another, and so they get back together again, followed by one of those endings in which everything depends on one character being able to find another character at a time and place when no living person could have possibly found him there.

My requirements for movies are so simple. All I ask is that the characters be of reasonable intelligence—at least smart enough so that I could spend half an hour with them with slight interest. If not intelligent, then they should be kooky, or stupid in some original way, or even sexy will do. But if they bring nothing to the party, my response is obvious: Why make a movie about them?

PPPPP**P**PPPP

· ·

Patch Adams

(Directed by Tom Shadyac; starring Robin Williams; 1998)
Patch Adams made me want to spray the screen with Lysol. This movie is shameless. It's not merely a tearjerker. It extracts tears individually by liposuction, without anesthesia. It is allegedly based on the life of a real man named Patch Adams, who I have seen on television, where he looks like Salvador Dali's seedy kid brother. If all of these things really happened to him, they should have abandoned Robin Williams and brought in Jerry Lewis for the telethon.

As the movie opens, a suicidal Patch has checked into a mental hospital. There he finds that the doctors don't help him, but the patients do. On the outside, he determines to become a doctor in order to help people, and enrolls in a medical school. Soon he finds, not to our amazement, that medicine is an impersonal business. When a patient is referred to by bed number or disease, Patch reasonably asks, "What's her name?"

Patch is a character. To himself, he's an irrepressible bundle of joy, a zany live wire who brings laughter into the lives of the sick and dying. To me, he's a pain in the wazoo. If this guy broke into my hospital room and started tap-dancing with bedpans on his feet, I'd call the cops.

The lesson of *Patch Adams* is that laughter is the best medicine. I know Norman Cousins cured himself by watching Marx Brothers movies, but to paraphrase Groucho, I enjoy a good cigar, but not when it explodes. I've been lucky enough to discover doctors who never once found it necessary to treat me while wearing a red rubber nose.

In the movie, Patch plays the clown to cheer up little tikes whose hair has fallen out from chemotherapy. Put in charge of the school welcoming committee for a gynecologist's convention, he builds a papier mâché prop: Enormous spread legs reaching an apex at the entrance to the lecture hall. What a card. He's the nonconformist, humanist, warmhearted rebel who defies the cold and materialist establishment and stands up for clowns and free spirits everywhere. This is a role Robin Williams was born to play. In fact, he was born playing it.

We can see at the beginning where the movie is headed, but we think maybe we can jump free before the crash. No luck. (Spoiler warning!) Consider, for example, the character named Carin (Monica Potter), who is one of Patch's fellow students. She appears too late in the movie to be a major love interest. Yet Patch does love her. Therefore, she's obviously in the movie for one purpose only: to die. The only suspense involves her function in the movie's structure, which is inspired by those outlines that Hollywood writing coaches flog to their students: Will her death provide the False Crisis, or the Real Crisis?

She's only good for the False Crisis, which I will not reveal, except to say that it is cruel and arbitrary, stuck in merely to get a cheap effect. It inspires broodings of worthlessness in Patch, who ponders suicide, but sees a butterfly, and pulls himself together for the False Dawn. Life must go on, and he must continue his mission to save sad patients from their depression. They may die, but they'll die laughing.

The False Dawn (the upbeat before the final downbeat) is a lulu. A dying woman refuses to eat. Patch convinces her to take nourishment by filling a plastic wading pool with spaghetti and jumping around in it. This is the perfect approach, and soon the wretched woman is gobbling her pasta. I hope she got some from the part he hadn't stepped in.

Next comes the Real Crisis. Patch is threatened with expulsion from medical school. I rubbed my eyes with incredulity: *There is a courtroom scene!* Courtrooms are expected in legal movies. But in medical tearjerkers, they're the treatment of last resort. Any screenwriter who uses a courtroom scene in a nonlegal movie is not only desperate for a third act, but didn't have a second act that led anywhere.

What a courtroom. It's like a John Grisham wet dream. This could be the set for *Inherit the Wind.* The main floor and balcony are jammed with Patch's supporters, with a few seats up front for the villains. There's no legalistic mumbo-jumbo; these people function simply as an audience for Patch's narcissistic grandstanding. (Spoiler warning No. 2.) After his big speech, the courtroom doors open up, and who walks in? All those bald little chemotherapy kids that Patch cheered up earlier. And yes, dear reader, each and every one is wearing a red rubber nose. Should these kids be out of bed? Their immune systems are shot to hell. If one catches cold and dies, there won't be any laughing during the malpractice suit.

I have nothing against sentiment, but it must be earned. Cynics scoffed at Robin Williams's previous film, *What Dreams May Come,* in which he went to heaven and then descended into hell to save the woman he loved. Corny? You bet—but with the courage of its convictions. It made no apologies and exploited no formulas. It was the real thing. *Patch Adams* is quackery.

Phantasm II
(Directed by Don Coscarelli; starring Michael Baldwin; 1988)
The silver sphere is about twice the size of a billiard ball. It has a couple of very sharp hooks built into it. It flies through the air, attaches itself to your forehead, and digs in. Then a drill comes out and pierces your skull right above the bridge of the nose, while blood spurts out the other end. I hate it when that happens.

The sphere is the property of the Tall Man. He is an evil mortician who lurks in the ghost town of Paragore, where all of the houses seem empty, and most of the graves seem robbed. "When you die," he tells one of his luckless victims, "you don't go to heaven. You come to us."

Who is us? Or, to phrase the question more elegantly, what's going on here? After having paid close attention to *Phantasm II,* I am not sure I can answer that question. "This time, I'm going to get him," Mike vows early in the film. But unless you have seen *Phantasm,* a low-budget horror film released nine years ago, the reference is likely to be lost. I did see the original *Phantasm,* but the details do not leap into my mind with crystal clarity.

There is a sense in which Mike's history is not so important to this film— a sense in which the plot itself is expendable. *Phantasm II* is like an extended dream, in which characters appear and disappear according to no logical timetable, and a wide-angle lens makes everything look distended and nightmarish.

The images are of corpses and graveyards, spurting blood and severed skulls, rotting flesh and faces filled with terror. Sitting through a film like this, which contains so little of genuine interest, I find myself meditating on such images, wondering who they would appear to, and why.

The target audience for *Phantasm II* is obviously teenagers, especially those with abbreviated attention spans, who require a thrill a minute. No character development, logic, or subtlety is necessary, just a sensation every now and again to provide the impression that something is happening on the screen.

But why would images of death and decay seem entertaining to them? For the same reason, I imagine, that the horror genre has always been attractive to adolescents. They feel immortal, immune to the processes of aging and death, and so to them these scenes of coffins and corpses represent a psychological weapon against adults. Kids will never die. Only adults will die. Kids, of course, eventually become adults, but there is always a new generation of kids, and there perhaps we have our answer to the question of why anyone would want to make a sequel to *Phantasm.*

Phantoms

(Directed by Joe Cahppelle; starring Rose McGowan, Joanna Going; 1998)
Did you know that if a certain kind of worm learns how to solve a maze, and then you grind it up and feed it to other worms, the other worms will then be able to negotiate the maze on their first try? That's one of the scientific nuggets supplied in *Phantoms,* a movie that seems to have been made by grinding up other films and feeding them to this one.

As the movie opens, two sisters arrive by Jeep in a quaint mountain town that seems suspiciously quiet, and no wonder: Everybody in town appears to be dead. Some of them have died rather suddenly. The baker's wife, for example. Her hands still grip the rolling pin. Just her hands. The rest of her is elsewhere.

The sisters (Rose McGowan and Joanna Going) find more ominous signs. A dead deputy sheriff, for example. And phones that don't work—but then one does. The older sister picks it up. "Who are you? What do you want?" she asks. It is a test of great acting to be able to say those ancient lines as if you mean them. A test like many others that this movie fails.

The sheriff turns up. He is played by Ben Affleck, wearing an absurd cowboy hat that looks like the kind of unsold stock they unload on city slickers at the end of the season. He is accompanied by another deputy (Nicky Katt) who wears an identical hat. Don't they know it's a rule in the movies: Hero wears cool hat, sidekick wears funny hat?

Joining the two young women, they search the town, and find a desperate message written in lipstick on a mirror, which (I'm jumping ahead now) leads them to Dr. Timothy Flyte (Peter O'Toole), an editor of the kind of supermarket rag that features babies with nine-pound ears. Dr. Flyte and U.S. Army troops soon arrive in the small town, dressed like ghostbusters, to get to the bottom of the mystery. "What kind of threat are we dealing with here—biological, chemical, or other?" he's asked. "I'm leaning toward 'other,'" he replies, with all the poignancy of a man who once played Lawrence of Arabia and is now playing Dr. Timothy Flyte.

The movie quickly degenerates into another one of those Gotcha! thrillers in which loathsome slimy creatures leap out of drain pipes and sewers and ingest supporting actors, while the stars pump bullets into it. There are a few neat touches. In front of an altar at the local church, the heroes discover a curious pile of stuff: Watches, glasses, ballpoints, pacemakers. At first they think it's an offering to the Virgin Mary. But no: "That's not an offering. Those are undigested remains."

How common are these films getting to be? Two out of the three films I saw today used the formula. With a deep bow (almost a salaam) to *Tremors,* they locate their creatures beneath the surface of the land or sea, so that most of the time, although not enough of the time, you can't see them.

Peter O'Toole is a professional and plays his character well. It takes years of training and practice to be able to utter lines like, "It comes from the deep and secret realms of our earth" without giggling. It is O'Toole who gets to float the educated tapeworm theory. When these creatures eat a human, they learn everything it knows—and even everything it thinks it knows, so that since many humans think they are being eaten by the devil, the creatures think they are the devil, too. If only we could learn to think more kindly of those who digest us, this movie could have ended happily.

Pink Flamingos
(Directed by John Waters; starring Divine; 1972, re-reviewed in 1997)
John Waters's *Pink Flamingos* has been restored for its twenty-fifth anniversary revival, and with any luck at all that means I won't have to see it again for another twenty-five years. If I haven't retired by then, I will.

How do you review a movie like this? I am reminded of an interview I once did with a man who ran a carnival sideshow. His star was a geek, who bit off the heads of live chickens and drank their blood.

"He's the best geek in the business," this man assured me.

"What is the difference between a good geek and a bad geek?" I asked.

"You wanna examine the chickens?"

Pink Flamingos was filmed with genuine geeks, and that is the appeal of the film, to those who find it appealing: What seems to happen in the movie really does happen. That is its redeeming quality, you might say. If the events in this film were only simulated, it would merely be depraved and disgusting. But since they are actually performed by real people, the film gains a weird kind of documentary stature. There is a temptation to praise the film, however grudgingly, just to show you have a strong enough stomach to take it. It is a temptation I can resist.

The plot involves a rivalry between two competing factions for the title of Filthiest People Alive. In one corner: a transvestite named Divine (who dresses like a combination of a showgirl, a dominatrix, and Bozo); her mentally ill mother (sits in a crib eating eggs and making messes); her son (likes to involve chickens in his sex life with strange women); and her lover (likes to watch son with strange women and chickens). In the other corner: Mr. and Mrs. Marble, who kidnap hippies, chain them in a dungeon, and force their butler to impregnate them so that after they die in childbirth their babies can be sold to lesbian couples.

All of the details of these events are shown in the film—oh, and more, including the notorious scene in which Divine actually ingests that least appetizing residue of the canine. And not only do we see genitalia in this movie—they do exercises.

Pink Flamingos appeals to that part of our psyches in which we are horny teenagers at the county fair with fresh dollar bills in our pockets, and a desire to see the geek show with a bunch of buddies, so that we can brag about it at school on Monday. (And also because of an intriguing rumor that the Bearded Lady proves she is bearded all over.)

After the restored version of the film has played, director John Waters hosts and narrates a series of outtakes, which (not surprisingly) are not as disgusting as what stayed in the film. We see long-lost scenes in which Divine cooks the chicken that starred in an earlier scene; Divine receives the ears of

Cookie, the character who costarred in the scene with her son and the chicken; and Divine, Cookie, and her son sing "We Are the Filthiest People Alive" in Pig Latin.

John Waters is a charming man, whose later films (like *Polyester* and *Hairspray*) take advantage of his bemused take on pop culture. His early films, made on infinitesimal budgets and starring his friends, used shock as a way to attract audiences, and that is understandable. He jump-started his career, and in the movie business, you do what you gotta do. Waters's talent has grown; in this film, which he photographed, the visual style resembles a home movie, right down to the overuse of the zoom lens. (Amusingly, his zooms reveal he knows how long the characters will speak; he zooms in, stays, and then starts zooming out before speech ends, so he can pan to another character and zoom in again.)

After the outtakes, Waters shows the original trailer for the film, in which, not amazingly, not a single scene from the movie is shown. Instead, the trailer features interviews with people who have just seen *Pink Flamingos,* and are a little dazed by the experience. The trailer cleverly positions the film as an event: Hey, you may like the movie or hate it, but at least you'll be able to say you saw it! Then blurbs flash on the screen, including one comparing *Pink Flamingos* to Luis Buñuel's and Salvador Dali's *Un Chien Andalou* (1928), in which a pig's eyeball was sliced. Yes, but the pig was dead, while the audience for this movie is still alive.

Note: I am not giving a star rating to *Pink Flamingos,* because stars simply seem not to apply. It should be considered not as a film but as a fact, or perhaps as an object.

Piranha

(Directed by Joe Dante; starring Kevin McCarthy, Bradford Dillman; 1978)
I walked into *Piranha* wondering why the U.S. government would consider the piranha to be a potential secret weapon. After all, I reasoned, you can lead the enemy to water but you can't make him wade. I was, it turns out, naive. *Piranha* is filled with people who suffer from the odd compulsion to jump into the water the very moment they discover it is infested by piranhas.

Consider, for example, the case of Kevin McCarthy. He plays a government scientist who has developed superpiranhas, which can live in salt or fresh water, reproduce with amazing speed, and are smarter than your average fish. If anybody knows how dangerous these piranhas are, Kevin McCarthy does. And yet when a little kid's father falls into the river and is gobbled up, and then the kid is clinging to the top of an overturned canoe, and Kevin McCarthy sees him, what does Kevin McCarthy do? Why, jumps in the water, of course, and swims toward the kid, and is eaten.

He is the first of many victims. By the time this movie is over, half a kids' summer camp and three-quarters of a crowd of potential homesite buyers have been eaten alive. That often happens to potential homesite buyers, but for the kids it's rotten luck.

There they are, the little tykes, splashing about in their inner tubes when the deadly piranhas attack. The kids bleed a lot, and people in the audience cheer a lot, and finally there is this to be said: It is in the nature of a piranha to eat flesh, so the piranha can be forgiven. But why is it in the nature of a movie audience to cheer?

This movie has really bad special effects. We kinda expect that, though, since it's hard to actually show thousands of tiny fish ripping peoples' legs apart. It's a good thing that it's hard, too—because if it were easy the producers would have shown it. Because it's so hard, what we get instead is a weird noise on the sound track, like a window fan being fed Styrofoam. And what we see are dozens of piranhas that share a curious trait: They all swim at exactly the same speed and without moving anything. That's probably because they're phony little models being pulled through the water.

The movie's plot is mostly an excuse for showing people thrashing about in bloody water. When it gets more specific, though, it turns out to be a rip-off of the first two *Jaws* movies. In both of them, you will recall, the danger of shark attacks was concealed by venal real estate speculators who didn't want to scare the buyers away. That's the case this time, too: The Realtor throws a party for prospective homesite buyers and denies that there are piranhas in the lake until most of his would-be customers have been digested. Implausible, you say? Try telling that to the piranhas. Next I am anticipating a movie called *Realtor.*

Pirates

(Directed by Roman Polanski; starring Walter Matthau; 1986)

There hasn't been a pirate movie in a long time, and after Roman Polanski's *Pirates,* there may not be another one for a *very* long time. This movie represents some kind of low point for the genre that gave us Captain Blood. It also gives us a new pirate image to ponder. After Errol Flynn and Tyrone Power—Walter Matthau? Matthau is only partially visible behind his makeup and his costumes, but the part we can see appears to be totally at a loss to answer this question: What is Walter Matthau doing on the bounding main, wearing a peg leg?

The movie stars Matthau as Captain Red, a vile old swashbuckler who eats fishhooks for breakfast. Cast adrift in the open sea, he is picked up by a passing Spanish galleon and soon learns that the ship's cargo is a priceless golden throne. He sets about trying to steal the booty, but not before the movie bogs down in a hopeless quagmire of too much talk, too many characters, and ineptly staged confrontations in which everyone stands around wondering what to do next.

Pirates proves, if nothing else, that Matthau is not an action star and that Polanski is not an action director. We kind of knew that already. Matthau is, however, a very capable comedy actor, and there are times when Polanski seems to be trying for comedy, although search me if you can find a laugh in this movie. One of Polanski's worst films was *The Fearless Vampire Killers,* and again this time, he is totally adrift trying for laughs with an expensive takeoff of a B-movie genre.

The real star of the movie is the *Neptune,* the full-size, functional galleon that was constructed as a set for most of the scenes. It's one of the finest sailing ships I've ever seen in a movie, but I couldn't see much of it, because Polanski steadfastly refuses to give us blood-stirring shots of the *Neptune* plowing through the waves. He begins with a real ship, then treats it like a studio set.

The real tragedy of *Pirates* may be that the movie was more of a deal than an inspiration. Polanski wrote the script twelve years ago, shortly after finishing *Chinatown,* and it languished on his agent's desk until Tarak Ben Ammar, a wealthy Tunisian, finally signed on as producer. Polanski had gone eight years without a movie (his last film was *Tess*), and no doubt he was happy to have the work. But *Pirates* should never have been made, at least not by a director with no instinctive sympathy for the material, and not by an actor whose chief inspiration seems to be the desire to be a good sport.

A Place for Lovers

(Directed by Vittorio De Sica; starring Faye Dunaway,
Marcello Mastroianni; 1969)

A Place for Lovers is the most godawful piece of pseudo-romantic slop I've ever seen. I did see it. Yes. I sat there in the dark, stunned by disbelief. Could Vittorio de Sica possibly have directed it? De Sica? Who made *Bicycle Thief*? Even a director who had made no movies would have a hard time making one as bad as this.

It is about a beautiful woman (Faye Dunaway) who has an incurable disease and takes up with an engineer (Marcello Mastroianni) who designs big plastic bags of water that are supposed to bring an end to racetrack accidents. They go up to a ski lodge and ponder at each other. Ponder, ponder, ponder. When Faye gets all pondered out, she takes the Jeep and drives into town to enigmatically threaten suicide. But she never kills herself, alas.

Instead, she lingers on during some of the most incredibly static scenes ever put on film. There's a byplay involving a stray dog that she rescues from the dogcatcher and then (apparently) abandons. Either she abandons the dog or the script does. The screenplay was written by no less than five writers, who were possibly locked into separate rooms and forbidden to communicate.

One goes to this movie in the same spirit one visits an ancient town buried by lava centuries ago: To try to determine by examining the ruins what made the gods punish man so.

The Postman

(Directed by Kevin Costner; starring Kevin Costner, Olivia Williams; 1997)
There are those who will no doubt call *The Postman* the worst film of the year, but it's too good-hearted for that. It's goofy, yes, and pretentious, and Kevin Costner puts himself in situations that get snickers. And it's way too long. But parables like this require their makers to burn their bridges and leave common sense behind: Either they work (as *Forrest Gump* did), in which case everyone involved is a genius, or they don't—in which case you shouldn't blame them for trying.

In choosing *The Postman* as his new project, however, Kevin Costner should perhaps have reflected that audiences were getting to be overfamiliar with him as the eccentric loner in the wilderness, coming across an isolated community, and then joining their war against evil marauders. He told that story magnificently in *Dances With Wolves* (1990) and then did another version in the futuristic fantasy *Waterworld* (1995). Now he sort of combines them, in a film that takes place in the post-Apocalyptic future like *Waterworld*, but looks and feels like it takes place in a Western.

The movie, based on an award-winning science fiction novel by David Brin, takes place in 2013. The dust clouds have settled after nuclear war, and scattered communities pick up the reins of civilization. There is no central government. Costner is a lone figure in the wilderness, friendly only with his mule, named Bill. They support themselves by doing Shakespeare for bands of settlers. Bill can hold a sword in his mouth, and in *Macbeth* he plays Birnam Wood. His master recites lines like, "Life is a tale told by a moron," not the sort of mistake he'd be likely to make, especially with a woman helpfully prompting him by whispering, "Idiot! Idiot!" Or maybe she's a critic.

Costner is conscripted into a neofascist army run by General Bethlehem (Will Patton). He escapes, stumbles over an abandoned U.S. Mail van, and steals the uniform, cap, and letterbag of the skeleton inside. At the gates of a settlement called Pineview, he claims he's come to deliver the mail. Building on his fiction, he tells the residents of a restored U.S. government in Minneapolis. The sheriff spots him for a fraud, but the people want to believe, and the next morning, he finds letters pushed under his door. Walking outside, he discovers that all the people of the town have gathered in hushed silence in a semicircle around his lodging, to await his awakening and appearance—the sort of thing townspeople do in movies, but never in real life, where some helpful townsman invariably suggests, "Let's just wake the sonuvabitch up."

In a movie that proceeds with glacial deliberation, the postman becomes a symbol for the survivors in their struggling communities. "You give out hope like it was candy in your pocket," a young woman tells him. It's the sort of line an actor-director ought to be wary of applying to his own character, but Costner frankly sees the postman as a messiah, and there is a shot late in the film where he zooms high above a river gorge in a cable car that serves absolutely no purpose except to allow him to pose as the masthead on the ship of state.

That young woman (Olivia Williams), by the way, wants the postman's semen. Her husband is infertile after the "bad mumps," and the couple desire a child. The postman eventually obliges, and she makes love with him in a scene reminiscent of those good Victorian wives who closed their eyes and thought of the empire. Her husband is murdered, and she's kidnapped by General Bethlehem, who has seen *Braveheart* and knows about the feudal system where the lord gets first dibbies on the wedding nights of his vassals. She and the postman eventually escape into the wilderness and spend the winter together while she comes full term. This is some frontier woman; in the spring, she burns down their cottage so they'll be forced to move on, and "we can find someplace nice for the baby."

In his absence, the postman's legendary status has been magnified by young Ford Lincoln Mercury (Larenz Tate), who has named himself after an auto dealership and in the absence of the postman has organized a postal service in exile. It is clear that the postman and Bethlehem will sooner or later have to face each other in battle. When they do, the general produces a hostage he has captured—Ford L. Mercury—and the postman pales and pauses at the prospect of F. L. Mercury's death, even though the postman's army consists mostly of hundreds of women and children he is cheerfully contemplating leading to their slaughter.

The movie has a lot of unwise shots resulting in bad laughs, none more ill-advised than one where the postman, galloping down a country lane, passes a gate where a tow-headed little tyke holds on to a letter. Some sixth sense causes the postman to look back, see the kid, turn around, then gallop back to him, snatching up the letter at full tilt. This touching scene, shot with a zoom lens in slow motion to make it even more fatuous than it needed to be, is later immortalized in a bronze statue, unveiled at the end of the movie. As a civic figure makes a speech in front of the statue, which is still covered by a tarpaulin, a member of the audience whispered, "They've bronzed the postman!" Dear reader, that member was me, and I guess I shouldn't have been surprised that I was right.

Priest
(Directed by Antonia Bird; starring Linus Roache; 1995)
Priest, one critic has written, "vigorously attack(s) the views of the Roman Catholic Church on homosexuality," which is just the way the filmmakers

probably want the film to be positioned. Actually the film is an attack on the vow of celibacy, preferring sexuality of any sort to the notion that men should, could, or would live chastely.

The story takes us into a Liverpool rectory where the senior priest sleeps with the pretty black housekeeper, and the younger priest removes his Roman collar for nighttime soirees to gay bars. When he and his partner are caught in a police sweep, he is disgraced, but the older priest is pleased that the young man has finally gotten in touch with his emotions, and begs him to return to the church to celebrate Mass with him. (The bishop, who advises him to "piss off out of my diocese," is portrayed, like all the church authorities, as a dried-up old bean.)

The question of whether priests should be celibate is the subject of much debate right now. What is not in doubt is that, to be ordained, they have to *promise* to be celibate. Nobody has forced them to become priests, and rules are rules. The filmmakers seem to feel that since they wouldn't want to live that way, of course it is wicked that priests must.

I am aware that the touchy-feely movement is so well established that no commercial film could seriously argue for celibacy. What I object to is the use of the church as a spice for an otherwise lame story; take away the occupations of the two central characters, and the rest of the film's events would be laid bare as tiresome sexual politics. The most obnoxious scene in the film is the one where the young priest, tortured by the needs of the flesh and by another problem we will soon get to, lectures Christ on the cross: "If you were here, you'd . . ." Well, what? Advise him to go out and get laid?

The priest, named Father Greg and played by Linus Roache, picks up Graham (Robert Carlyle) for a night of what he hopes will be anonymous sex, but later Graham recognizes him on the street, and soon they are in love. This is all done by fiat; the two men are not allowed to get to know one another, or to have conversations of any meaning, since the movie is not really *about* their relationship, but about how backward the church is in opposing it.

Instead of taking the time to explore the sexuality of the two priests in a thoughtful way, *Priest* crams in another plot, this one based on that old chestnut, the inviolable secrecy of the confessional. Father Greg learns while hearing a confession that a young girl parishioner is being sexually abused by her father. What to do? Of course (as the filmmakers no doubt learned from Hitchcock's *I Confess*) he cannot break the seal of the confessional—a rule that, for the convenience of the plot, he takes much more seriously than the rules about sex. This dilemma also figures in his anguished monologue to Jesus.

Once again, the church is used as spice. (Can you imagine audiences getting worked up over the confidential nature of a lawyer-client or a doctor-patient relationship?) But here the movie leaves a hole wide enough to run a cathedral through. The girl's father confronts the priest in the confessional, threatens him, and tells the priest he plans to keep right on with his evil practice (we don't simply have a child abuser here, but a spokesman for incest). What the film fails to realize is that this conversation is not protected by the sacramental seal, because the sinner makes it absolutely clear he is not asking forgiveness, does not repent, and plans to keep right on sinning as long as he can get away with it. At this point, Father Greg should pick up the phone and call the cops.

The unexamined assumptions in the *Priest* screenplay are shallow and exploitative. The movie argues that the hidebound and outdated rules of the church are responsible for some people (priests) not having sex although they should, while others (incestuous parents) can keep on having it although they shouldn't. For this movie to be described as a moral statement about anything other than the filmmaker's prejudices is beyond belief.

Prison Girls
(No credits—not listed on the Internet Movie Database; 1973; also includes references to The Devil's Window *and* The Blind Dead*)*
During the past week, I have seen the end of *The Blind Dead,* the beginning of *The Devil's Widow,* and two of the three dimensions of *Prison Girls.* Here is my report.

Prison Girls was the toughest because the right lens fell out of my 3-D glasses and got lost on the floor. That was the whole ball game right there.

From what I could understand of the dialogue, the movie was about a group of girls in prison who were given two-day leaves in order to go home and appear in sex scenes for the movie.

There were very few scenes in the prison itself, I was sorry to see. From what I could determine (it was a little hard with the 3-D images overlapping), there was a scene in the prison psychiatrist's office, and that was about it. Why no prison?

The first explanation that leaps to mind is that the movie was so cheap they couldn't afford prison sets. But, no, that doesn't make sense, because the current wave of prison movies was *invented* to save money on sets. If you shoot a whole movie in a motel room, the audience is going to notice the cheap sets. But if you shoot a whole movie in a prison cell, everybody understands because the characters are locked in anyway. So I guess *Prison Girls* didn't have a lot of prison sets because it was a big-budget exploitation movie. Maybe.

Anyway, I was disappointed, because whenever I go to a prison movie, I always look in the cell next to the cell where the main characters are. Burgess Meredith always used to be the guy in the next cell, and I wanted to see if he ever got out.

The Devil's Widow was a movie I wanted to see because I saw Roddy McDowell, the director, on a TV talk show about three years ago and he was talking about it. He said he made it because he wanted to make a tribute to Ava Gardner, and the movie was a gesture of love. I hope Ava Gardner appreciated it. The movie was finished two years ago but has only been released now because it took the brains in the promotion department all that time to figure out that the movie's original title, *Tam Lin,* sounded like a Cantonese restaurant. *The Devil's Widow,* I am sure you will agree, is a title with a lot more class, although I, for one, did not even know the devil was dead. I guess he got lonely after God passed on.

The Blind Dead is a movie about centuries-old corpses who rise from the dead and chase people around cemeteries and churches. They are blind. After being dead 200 years, I think it's pretty good that they can even walk.

They have to listen for you before they can chase you. Sometimes they ride slow-motion horses. The horses are not blind, but they do have arthritis, and the lead horse suffers from the heartbreak of psoriasis. The way to escape from the blind dead is to keep real quiet. Then they don't know where you are, and the movie would be over. To avoid this, the people in the movie bang on doors, shout, breathe heavily, scream, gasp, cough, clear their throats, snap their fingers, tap their toes, step on twigs, grind their teeth, and ream out their ears. Then the blind dead chase them, catch them, and eat them.

Prom Night

(Directed by Paul Lynch; starring Leslie Nielsen, Jamie Lee Curtis; 1980)
Prom Night is merely an execrable movie—not despicable, like *I Spit on Your Grave*. But the experience of watching it at the Adelphi Theater last week was the worst of my moviegoing career. On one of the hottest nights of the year, the theater had no air conditioning (a fact revealed only after customers had entered). There was no ice for the soft drinks. The management relented and opened the theater's exit doors, and some of the crowd stood outside in the marginally cooler summer night. When a scream went up, they dashed back inside to see what moment of violence they'd just missed.

What's amazing is that despite these subhuman viewing conditions, there was a large crowd, and most stayed until the end. What was the attraction? Well, *Prom Night* was playing on a double bill with *I Spit on Your Grave*—which had been held over after the reviews hailed it as one of the sickest movies of all time.

I arrived early for *Prom Night,* sat through the last twenty-five minutes of *I Spit on Your Grave,* and got a bizarre surprise: The movie had been extensively edited since I'd seen it last, and a great deal of the most offensive violence was missing. In the scene where the heroine castrates the rapist in the bathtub, for example, there was now only one brief shot of the bloody victim. All the shots of him thrashing about in the bloody water were missing, as was a later shot of her mopping up the blood with towels.

How do we interpret the fact that the movie was secretly edited in mid-run? The movie was beneath contempt in the first place. But for exhibitors to hold it over on the basis of its reputation for nauseating violence—and then to show a censored version without that violence—is a species of doublethink too diseased for me to penetrate.

Anyway, back to *Prom Night.* The plot is simple: A bunch of little kids semi-accidentally cause the death of a playmate, and vow to keep the secret all of their lives. Then we flash forward to their senior prom, as a maniac killer stalks and kills them. Who is the killer? The movie makes it painfully obvious very early on—and then insists on boring us with repeated shots of another suspect. It's as if we know who the killer is, but the movie doesn't.

After an endless hour of buildup (with a sound track so muffled and so badly played in the theater that most of the words couldn't be understood), the night for the prom arrives. And the killer, dressed in black and with a ski mask, starts the killing spree. To the terminally bored audience, every killing was an occasion for screams, laughter, and applause. To call such a response cretinous would be generous. One typical killing went this way: bloody murder, followed by a loud disco song and a cut to a bloodred bowl of punch. Barf.

Why do people go to these movies? Probably because they've been browbeaten by the hard-sell advertising exploitation campaign on TV. It's easy to make a great-looking, thirty-second TV spot, so why bother making a good film? As your friendly neighborhood movie critic, I have only one piece of advice. If you have an appetite for violence and the macabre, at least try to satisfy it in a movie done with artistry and craftsmanship—Brian de Palma's *Dressed to Kill,* for example. *Prom Night* should be cut up to make bookmarks.

Psycho

(Directed by Gus Van Sant; starring Anne Heche, Vince Vaughn; 1998 remake)
The most dramatic difference between Alfred Hitchcock's *Psycho* (1960) and Gus Van Sant's "shot by shot" remake is the addition of a masturbation scene. That's appropriate, since this new *Psycho* evokes memories in an attempt to re-create remembered passion.

Curious, how similar the new version is, and how different. If you have seen Hitchcock's version, you already know the characters, the dialogue, the camera angles, the surprises. All that is missing is the tension—the conviction that something urgent is happening on the screen at this very moment. The movie is an invaluable experiment in the theory of cinema, because it demonstrates that a shot-by-shot remake is pointless; genius apparently resides between or beneath the shots, or in chemistry that cannot be timed or counted.

Students of trivia will note the differences. The opening shot is now an unbroken camera move from the Phoenix skyline into the hotel room where Marion Crane (Anne Heche) is meeting with her lover, Sam Loomis (Viggo Mortensen). There is a shot of Loomis's buttocks, and when he turns toward her, a quick downward glance of appreciation by Marion. In the scene where Marion packs while deciding to steal the money, Heche does more facial acting than Janet Leigh did in the original—trying to signal what she's thinking with twitches and murmurs. Not necessary.

The highway patrolman who wakes her from her roadside nap looks much the same as in the original, but has a speaking voice which, I think, has been electronically tweaked to make it deeper—and distracting.* We never get the chilling closer shot of him waiting across the street from the car lot, arms folded on his chest. When Marion goes into the "parlor" of Norman Bates (Vince Vaughn), the stuffed birds above and behind them are in indistinct soft focus, so we miss the feeling that they're poised to swoop. There is a clearer shot of "Mrs. Bates" during the knife attack in the shower. And more blood.

As for the masturbation scene, as Norman spies on Marion through the peephole between the parlor and Room No. 1: Even if Hitchcock was hinting at sexual voyeurism in his 1960 version, it is better not to represent it literally, since the jiggling of Norman's head and the damp offscreen sound effects inspire a laugh at the precise moment when one is not wanted.

All of these details would be insignificant if the film worked as a thriller, but it doesn't. One problem is the casting of Vaughn in the Norman Bates role. He isn't odd enough. Norman's early dialogue often ends in a nervous laugh. Anthony Perkins, in the original, made it seem compulsive, welling up out of some secret pool of madness. Vaughn's laugh doesn't seem involuntary. It sounds as if he intends to laugh. Possibly no actor could have matched the Perkins performance, which is one of the unique creations in the cinema, but Vaughn is not the actor to try. Among actors in the correct age range, my suggestion would be Jeremy Davies, who was the frightened Corporal Upham in *Saving Private Ryan*.

Anne Heche, as Marion Crane, lacks the carnal quality and the calculating detachment that Janet Leigh brought to the original film. She is less substantial. Van Sant's decision to shoot in color instead of black and white completes the process of de-eroticizing her; she wears an orange dress that looks like the upholstery from my grandmother's wingback chair. Viggo Mortensen is also wrong for Sam Loomis, the lover. Instead of suggesting a straight arrow like John Gavin in the original film, he brings an undertow of elusive weirdness. The only new cast members who more or less get the job done are William H.

---

*I was wrong. That's James Remar's real voice.

Macy, as the private eye Arbogast, and Philip Baker Hall, as Sheriff Chambers. By having a psychiatrist (Robert Forster) reproduce a five-minute speech of clinical diagnosis at the end of the film, Van Sant demonstrates that a completely unnecessary scene in the original, if reproduced, will be completely unnecessary in the remake as well.

I viewed Hitchcock's *Psycho* a week ago. Attending this new version, I felt oddly as if I were watching a provincial stock company doing the best it could without the Broadway cast. I was reminded of the child prodigy who was summoned to perform for a famous pianist. The child climbed into the piano stool and played something by Chopin with great speed and accuracy. When the child had finished, the great musician patted it on the head and said, "You can play the notes. Someday, you may be able to play the music."

Puppet on a Chain
(Directed by Geoffrey Reeve; starring Barbara Parkins; 1972)
There must be a wonderful world inside Alistair MacLean's head. I imagine the climate is fair there, and the winters mild. It is a world where there are no cities that do not drip with intrigue, and only the most romantic of those make the grade: Amsterdam, London, Zurich. Between the cities there are continents occupied by fortresses and dragons, neat continents like Africa and Asia. There are no flatlands inside Alistair MacLean's head, no small towns, no marshes, no boring people, and no real people. Just bizarre, fantastical people who eventually find themselves crowded together into too small a space and have to shoot their way out.

But these people are bored, alas. They are bored because they are romantic heroes who work for the CIA or the international heroin trade, and the ordinary stuff of life is too goddamn dreary for them. They would not know how to operate an alarm clock if you gave them one, but they can defuse bombs and drive speedboats. And they devote their lives to doing things in illogical ways. If something has always been done one way, and not another, they will find a new way to do it no matter what the cost or inconvenience.

Take heroin smuggling, for example. They would never dream of flying it in from Mexico or hiding it in a Lincoln Continental as was done in *The*

French Connection. No, that would be too mundane. They must infiltrate a 150-year-old family importing business in Amsterdam and set up a complicated system of helicopter drops, midnight boat rides, hollow dolls, trick grandfather clocks, and phony Bibles.

Why go to all this trouble? For example, there is the problem of getting the heroin out of the warehouse and into the castle where it will be stuffed into the dolls and grandfather clocks. How do they do this? They take the insides out of the Bibles, fill them with heroin, and give the Bibles to phony nuns who carry them to the chapel in the castle, where they trade them for real Bibles. Yes, it's as simple as that. And so subtle, too, that it takes a trained CIA operative like Barbara Parkins to realize that the nuns are wearing diamond rings on their fingers and high-heel shoes and mesh stockings.

All of this reminded me of the final chapters of *Huckleberry Finn,* where Jim is locked in the smokehouse and Huck and Tom want to get him out. You remember. Jim and Huck think the perfectly obvious way to pull off the job is to dig a hole under the smokehouse and let Jim crawl out. Elementary. Too elementary for Tom Sawyer. He wants Jim to play an escaping prisoner role right out of Lord Byron and Sir Walter Scott. He has to tame spiders and make them his pets, and scratch messages on tin plates and throw them outside, and write his name in blood on the wall, and on the day of the escape he has to chain his own leg to his bed. Why? So they can saw it off in order to free him, of course.

Some days it is just easier not to escape. That was the feeling I had about the Amsterdam heroin-smuggling outfit. They put themselves to so much trouble that with just a little more effort they could have made as much money running a franchised chicken operation. When they kill a person, for example, they paint up a doll so it looks like the person and then they hang the person and the doll next to each other.

Dying is very important in the world inside Alistair MacLean's head, you see. A man must die with style or he is not a man—not a stylish man, anyway. Nobody dies in bed except, of course, under unspeakable circumstances. Nobody is shot if he can be garroted, garroted if he can be run down by a speedboat, or ran down by a speedboat if he can be double-crossed by a twenty-two-year-old girl pretending to be a mentally retarded heroin victim with the IQ of a child. You see how it works. These thoughts and others crossed my mind as I was watching *Puppet on a Chain.*

RRRRRRRRR

● ●

Radio Flyer

(Directed by Richard Donner; starring Lorraine Bracco, John Heard; 1992)
Radio Flyer pushes so many buttons that I wanted to start pushing back. One of the things I resisted was the movie's almost doglike desire to please. It seems to be asking, how can anyone dislike a movie that is against child abuse, and believes little red wagons can fly? I found it fairly easy. The movie pushes so many fundamental questions under the rug of its convenient screenplay that the happy ending seems like cheating, if not like fraud.

Radio Flyer begins with the compulsion, common to so much children's literature and film, to place its little heroes in a cruel and heartless world. Like all those cartoon characters who lose their parents, are kidnapped, or have their homes burned down or their families lost at sea, this one begins on a sad note, with a divorce. The central characters, Mike and Bobby, are then taken by their mother to California, where she marries a sadistic, drunken bully who wants to be called The King. When mom isn't around, The King likes to beat little Bobby, who gets black-and-blue welts as a result.

The mother (Lorraine Bracco) is a strange case, an engaging, intelligent, hardworking woman who somehow fails to notice that she is married to a monster. She also misses the welts on Bobby's back, and of course her kids, feeling untrusted and abandoned, do not tell her about the beatings. Instead, they begin to plan an escape for little Bobby by outfitting his Radio Flyer wagon with wings and an engine, so it will fly, and he can leave town and never come back.

They have some reason to think this plan will work. A kid named Fisher once coasted his wagon down a hill and up the slope of a barn, and he flew through the sky so high he was almost able to hitch a ride on the tail of a plane that was taking off from the valley. Of course, Fisher also suffered a terrible fall, and when we finally meet him, late in the picture, he is crippled, but there you have it: Heroes have to take chances.

I will not regale you with the details by which Bobby's maiden flight takes place. I was so appalled, watching this kid hurtling down the hill in his pathetic contraption, that I didn't know which ending would be worse. If he fell to his death, that would be unthinkable, but if he soared up to the moon, it would be unforgivable—because you can't escape from child abuse in little red wagons, and even the people who made this picture should have been ashamed to suggest otherwise.

Who was this movie made for? Kids? Adults? What kid needs a movie about a frightened little boy who is at the mercy of drunken beatings? What adult can suspend so much disbelief that the movie's ending, a visual rip-off from *E.T.,* inspires anything other than incredulity? What hypothetical viewer could they possibly have had in mind?

Radio Flyer was a famous screenplay by David Mickey Evans before it was a movie. It was one of the hottest screenplays in town, maybe because of the incongruity of its elements. If somebody at a story conference didn't describe this movie as "child abuse meets Peter Pan," they were missing a bet. It is utterly cynical from beginning to end, and never more cynical than in its contrived idealism. Was the screenplay so sought-after, so expensive, that no sane voice was heard, raising fundamental objections? Hollywood fought tooth and nail to spend a fortune on this screenplay. Was the movie launched in some kind of mass hysteria?

I know that the voice-over narration suggests that maybe this wasn't the way the story really happened, and is only the way Mike, the older brother, now remembers it as an adult. Okay, but then what *did* really happen? Did Bobby fall to his death? Did the cops haul away The King? Did mom wise up? *Radio Flyer* is a real squirmarama of unasked and unanswered questions. At the end, there's an 800 number you can call if you want information on child abuse. I imagine the volunteers at the other end would have some pithy observations about this movie.

Rapa Nui

(Directed by Kevin Reynolds; starring Jason Scott Lee, Sandrine Holt; 1994)
Rapa Nui slips through the *National Geographic* Loophole. This is the Hollywood convention that teaches us that brown breasts are not as sinful as white

ones, and so while it may be evil to gaze upon a blonde *Playboy* centerfold and feel lust in our hearts, it is educational to watch Polynesian maidens frolicking topless in the surf. This isn't sex; it's geography.

For years in my liberal youth I thought this loophole was racist, an evil double standard in which white women were protected from exposure while "native" women were cruelly stripped of their bras, not to mention the equal protection of the MPAA. Watching *Rapa Nui,* in which there are dozens if not hundreds of wonderful bare breasts on view, I have changed my mind. Since female breasts are the most aesthetically pleasing part of the human anatomy, it is only a blessing if your culture celebrates them.

The movie, which is sublimely silly, takes place in the South Seas in the carefree days before missionaries and other visitors arrived to distribute brassieres, smallpox, and VD. The action takes place on Easter Island, "the navel of the world," whose inhabitants languish under a senile king. The king is of the Long Ear tribe, which has enslaved the Short Ears and impoverished the island by building dozens of giant stone faces. The purpose of the faces is to attract the great White Canoe that the king believes will carry him off to heaven. No face can be big enough. "Build another one," he tells the slaves at one point. "Then take the rest of the day off."

This is a king, played with superb comic timing (by Eru Potaka-Dewes), who has lots of good lines. "Tell me you won't make fishhooks of my thigh bones," he tearfully implores his high priest. The priest, however, has the movie's best line: "I'm busy! I've got chicken entrails to read!" Meanwhile, sweating slaves pull giant sledges and plot rebellion.

The plot stars Jason Scott Lee as Noro, a young Long Ear who has fallen in love with a Short Ear girl, the breathtakingly lovely Ramana. He goes to the chief for permission to marry her, which is granted—but on two conditions. (1) He must win the annual competition among the young men of the island; (2) she must spend six months locked in the darkness of the Cave of the White Virgin.

This is a lot better deal for him than her. The competition, sort of a Polynesian triathlon, requires the young men to climb down a cliff to the sea, swim to an offshore peak, climb the peak, steal the first eggs of spring from birds' nests, swim back with them, climb the cliff, and present the eggs to the chief. Break an egg, and you're an omelet. Meanwhile, the bride-to-be slowly goes blind in the Cave of the White Virgin, so called because that's what you become after you lose your tan in the dark—always assuming, of course, that you were a virgin to begin with.

Concern for my reputation prevents me from recommending this movie. I wish I had more nerve. I wish I could simply write, "Look, of course it's one of the worst movies ever made. But it has hilarious dialogue, a weirdo action climax, a bizarre explanation for the faces of Easter Island, and dozens if not hundreds of wonderful bare breasts." I am, however, a responsible film critic and must conclude that *Rapa Nui* is a bad film. If you want to see it anyway, of course, that's strictly your concern. I think I may check it out again myself.

Rape Squad

(Directed by Robert Kellichien; starring Peter Brown; 1975)
Sitting through *Rape Squad* is a fairly weird experience because the audience doesn't know how to take it: A lot of the knee-jerk movie responses are challenged. It's not an old-style sexist movie, but it's not a feminist movie, either. The men in it are creeps at best and sex maniacs at worst, so the audience can't get off on the usual macho punch lines. But the women, who organize an antirapist guerrilla unit, get the idea while floating completely nude in a whirlpool bath. So while they're doing their rewrite of Betty Freidan, they're putting on a skin show at the same time.

The whole movie's like that, and we're not surprised to learn that it was directed by a man but its principal author was a woman. The dialogue adopts a militantly feminist position, but the actresses recite it wearing miniskirts and see-through blouses (on those occasions, indeed, when they bother to dress at all).

In a typical scene, one of the squad members distributes antirape leaflets in a parking lot, which requires her to lean over the hoods of cars and display an expanse of thigh to truck drivers eating their lunch nearby. When they make rude remarks, she counterattacks fiercely, getting so angry that it's necessary for her to lean forward and display some cleavage. We don't know whether to look or listen. The story involves a rapist with the nickname "Jingle Bells," who's been terrorizing young women with his attacks. His disguise includes a goaltender's mask, so he can't be identified in lineups. Five of his victims, dissatisfied with the police work on the case, decide to form their own rape crisis program and take karate lessons. The karate instructor is a compact young woman who could no doubt demolish Bruce Lee single-handed; she has the girls practice hitting a dummy in the groin with night-sticks.

Once trained, the rape squad turns into a feminist vigilante unit. They're everywhere, like Batman and Robin. A black pimp, for example, is mistreating one of his girls in a parking lot. A squad member calls in. The entire karate class piles into a VW bus and races to the rescue. The pimp is kicked unconscious while the girls bang up his Thunderbird with sledgehammers. Mission accomplished, they leave. The pimp groggily wakes up, only to be knocked unconscious by the hooker, who has instantaneously had her consciousness raised.

Wouldn't you know, though, that when the chips are down, our heroines make all the dumb mistakes women do in movies where they're mere sex objects (instead of liberated sex objects). Jingle Bells lures them into an abandoned zoo at night. The girls walk along single file. One decides to return to the car. Bells picks her off. Another one loses the heel from her shoe. He gets her, too. The other three turn around and there are frantic cries of "Where's Gloria?" Where do you think? Haven't you seen any Westerns lately, with the Indians picking off the stragglers?

There's also a certain amount of entrapment, which the movie apparently approves of. Rape squad members wear their sexiest dresses to a nightclub where the manager is an alleged rapist. One of the girls allows herself to be picked up and taken to the guy's apartment to see flicks of his last ski holiday in Switzerland. Uh, huh. Astoundingly, no such film is there to be shown. Why, the beast wants to make out! The victim screams, the rape squad breaks through the door, the karate instructor sends the depraved monster flying through the air, the girls wreck his apartment and then they pour indelible blue dye (labeled "sulphuric acid"—their little joke) on his genitals. That way, I guess, the next time he tries to get fresh with a sister she'll know him by his true colors.

Rapid Fire

(Directed by Dwight H. Little; starring Brandon Lee, Powers Boothe; 1992)
Rapid Fire is a movie weary almost unto death with the sameness of its genre. It's yet another mindless slog through the familiar materials of drug dealing, the Mafia, and the martial arts. The star is Brandon Lee, son of the legendary Bruce Lee, who, like James Dean, did something original and then died, inspiring hordes of feeble imitations. The costars include Powers Boothe, who has an uncanny ability to appear in movies that are beneath his talent, and Nick Mancuso, also talented, but oddly miscast as a Mafia don.

The plot has been pieced together from countless other movies, and involves Mancuso's determination to get his hands on a piece of the action in a major heroin-smuggling operation that brings drugs from an unnamed Asian nation to Chicago. Brandon Lee is an innocent Chicago art student who, coincidentally, witnessed the massacre at Tienanmen Square and is a ranking martial arts champion. After he accidentally witnesses Mancuso committing murder during a fund-faiser for Chinese dissidents, Lee becomes the object of a four-way tug-of-war involving the Mafia, the drug smugglers, the good police, and the corrupt police.

If this sounds perhaps a mite ludicrous, it's because the filmmakers consider the plot only a clothesline on which to hang five major martial arts sequences, all of which illustrate three ancient standbys from my *Bigger Little Movie Glossary:* The Talking Killer Syndrome (in which the bad guys talk when they should be shooting), the Principle of Evil Marksmanship (no bad guy can hit anything with a gun, while no good guy ever misses), and the One-at-a-Time Attack Rule (in martial arts movies, the enemies obligingly approach the hero one by one).

Brandon Lee is an adequate martial arts performer, if not a particularly riveting actor, although he has his work cut out for him in a movie where the drugs are smuggled in as starch in bed linens, and then removed in a laundry. But what can we make of the rest of the film?

The screenplay is so absentminded that it provides a love scene between Lee and Kate Hodge (as a good Chicago cop) without remembering that up to that point their only relationship consisted of Lee taking her hostage during a shoot-out. Powers Boothe, as the movie's other good cop, has such deathless lines as "Why don't you take your fists of fury and get out of here?" And Mancuso, who informs Lee he is going to break his fingers one at a time, seems to run a Mafia empire that consists of a lot of guys who are always sitting around in an Italian restaurant, eating.

Where is the audience for a movie like this? It's out there, I guess. Martial arts movies generally make their money back and then some, perhaps because their fans are connoisseurs who evaluate the fight scenes and don't mind that the dialogue is brainless. Truly inspired action scenes do, of course, have a special energy of their own. *Rapid Fire* is not truly or any other kind of inspired.

Reach the Rock

(Directed by William Ryan; starring Allesandro Nivola, Bruce Norris; 1998)
Reach the Rock plays like an experiment to see how much a movie can be slowed down before it stops. It was produced and written by John Hughes, who should have donated his screenplay to a nearby day-care center for use by preschoolers in constructing paper chains. How can the man who made *Plains, Trains and Automobiles* have thought this material was filmable?

The story involves an unhappy young man named Robin (Allesandro Nivola), who in the opening scene uses a flagpole to break the window of a hardware store. When Ernie the small-town cop (Bruce Norris) arrives, he finds Robin seated in a beach chair before the window, cooling himself with an electric fan. Robin is returned to the station, where the only other cop on the overnight shift is Sergeant Phil Quinn (William Sadler).

Robin is well known to the officers. His arrest sheet lists such offenses as loitering, disturbing the peace, vandalism, and so on. The sergeant and the kid dislike one another, and the actors demonstrate this with various reliable techniques, including the always dependable flaring of the nostrils.

The cops lock Robin in a cell. He steals the keys to the cell, lets himself out, steals a squad car, drives downtown, fires a shotgun through a coffee-shop window, returns, and locks himself back in. This is a pattern that will repeat itself many times during the long night. "How are you gettin' out of here?" asks Sergeant Quinn, convinced that Robin is the culprit. It never occurs to him to search the prisoner for the keys. I can't say much for his police work. (That line is borrowed from *Fargo,* a movie I thought of during this one as a drowning man will think of an inflatable whale.)

Robin's sneaky activities unfold with the velocity of sleepwalking. There are two cells in the jail, and at various times Robin is locked in both, Ernie is locked in one, Quinn is locked in the other, a bunk catches fire, Robin's old girlfriend is locked in with him, and Quinn is locked out of the building. Sounds like a maelstrom of activity with all those cell doors banging open and shut, but imagine the stateroom scene in *A Night at the Opera,* enacted in slow motion and with sadness.

Yes, *Reach the Rock* is very sad. Halfway through the film we learn that Sergeant Quinn blames Robin for the drowning death of his nephew. Even later, we learn that Robin has been moping and pining for four years because a rich local girl (Brooke Langton) dated him in high school but dropped him when she went to college—except of course for summers, when she comes home and resumes their sexual relationship, which seems sporting of her. "Time stopped for you about four years ago," somebody tells Robin, or maybe it is everyone who tells Robin that.

There is a subplot. When we first see Ernie the dim-witted deputy, he is drinking in a parked squad car with a local woman named Donna (Karen Sillas). He's about to make a move when he gets the call to check out the alarm at the hardware store. Throughout the entire movie, Ernie and Donna try to get horizontal, and are repeatedly interrupted. This is a running gag, or, in this movie, a walking gag. Donna grows frustrated, and wanders the deserted night streets in her nightgown—forlorn, neglected, and in heat. At one point, when Ernie arrives for yet another rendezvous, she warns him, "This is your last chance," but one senses that with Donna there are as many last chances as with Publisher's Clearing House.

All of the elements of the plot at long last fall into place, including an old tattoo that explains an earlier parable. Comes the dawn, and we are left with questions which only a policeman could answer. (Spoiler Warning—read no further if you intend to see the film.)

Attention, officers! If a perpetrator has a three-page arrest record, and during one night, angry at being dumped by an old girlfriend, he breaks a store window, breaks out of a jail cell, steals a police car, uses a police shotgun to shoot out another window, locks an officer out of the police station, locks two officers into cells, starts a fire, and tries to frame an officer for the crimes, would you, in the morning, release the kid and tell him to go home because "her old man has insurance"? Just wondering.

Renaissance Man

(Directed by Penny Marshall; starring Danny DeVito, Gregory Hines; 1993)
Renaissance Man is a labored, unconvincing comedy that seems cobbled together out of the half-understood remnants of its betters. Watching it, I felt embarrassed for the actors, who are asked to inhabit scenes so contrived and artificial that no possible skill could bring them to life. It's hard to believe that this is the work of Penny Marshall, whose films like *Big* and *A League of Their Own* seemed filled with a breezy confidence.

The movie stars Danny DeVito as a divorced and broke Detroit advertising man who is fired from his job. He applies for unemployment compensation, and his counselor eventually finds him a job—as a civilian instructor on a nearby army base. His assignment is to take a classroom of eight difficult cases and somehow increase their "basic comprehension"—of everything, I guess. This is made more difficult by DeVito's own lack of any basic comprehension of how the army works.

The class seems impossible to teach, and besides, he's no teacher. In desperation he begins to talk about Shakespeare, and the students, desperate for action, encourage him to say more. Eventually the class turns into a seminar on *Hamlet,* and we are subjected once again to the dishonest fiction that academic knowledge can somehow be gained by enthusiasm and osmosis. Why, the students' mastery of the subject is so profound that in no time they've put together a classroom rap musical based on Shakespeare's story! (It helps that one of the students is played by Marky Mark.)

My doubts about the possibility of teaching Shakespeare in this way are surpassed only by my doubts about how the exercise has anything to do with the army. Those doubts are shared by a drill sergeant (Gregory Hines), who thinks DeVito is simply wasting the time of his recruits. The formula of this story requires DeVito to eventually "prove himself" to the sergeant, and the moment I saw the base's "Victory Tower," a dangerous obstacle course involving lots of climbing and crawling, I knew with a sinking conviction that sooner or later DeVito would be climbing down walls on ropes to win the respect of the men.

Graduate students of Shakespeare are often assigned to do a "source study" on one of his plays, reading Shakespeare's own sources for one of the histories, say, and then noting what the Bard kept, and what he changed. *Renaissance Man* could also inspire a source study. It is obviously a cross between *Dead Poets Society* (unpromising students inspired by unconventional teacher) and *Private Benjamin* (desperate unemployed civilian joins the army). Advanced students might want to research the sources of *those* films—which were retreads, yes, but at least less labored than *Renaissance Man.*

One odd quality about this movie is its gloominess. It seems strangely thoughtful and morose for a comedy, especially as it develops the stories of the various class members. The screenplay also has problems with logic. Are we really supposed to believe, for example, that DeVito can pawn the award he won in an advertising competition for enough money to buy his daughter a telescope *and* a trip out of the country to view an eclipse?

The ending of the film is an exercise in phony suspense. See if you can follow this army logic. The students are not required to take a final exam in the course. *But* if they take it, and fail, they'll flunk out of basic training. Therefore, they shouldn't take it, right? But so great is their transformation that they insist on taking it, and turn up in the classroom (after the obligatory twenty seconds of suspense in which DeVito thinks they won't come, and sad music plays). But the final is verbal, not written, with all the students in the room at the same time, so apparently they will pass or fail as a class, not as individuals. I say "apparently" because the ending suggests they do pass, but the movie absentmindedly neglects to supply that information. Not that, by then, I cared.

Return to the Blue Lagoon

(Directed by William A. Graham; starring Brian Krause; 1991)

I had this great idea for a sequel to *The Poseidon Adventure.* You remember, the movie where the ocean liner was overturned by a tidal wave, and the passengers had to climb to safety through an upside-down ship. In my sequel, just as they got to their destination, another tidal wave would come along and right the ship—and they'd have to retrace their steps.

The makers of *Return to the Blue Lagoon* are working in the same great tradition. In the original 1980 movie, a boy and girl were castaways on a lost island where the adults built a house and trained them in the ways of survival and then died, leaving the boy and girl to grow up into tanned and beautiful adolescents (Brooke Shields and Christopher Atkins) who studied how the giant sea turtle made love, and drew the obvious conclusions. "All we have to look forward to," Pauline Kael wrote, "is: when are these two going to discover fornication?"

Return to the Blue Lagoon begins shortly after the young couple set sail from the island with their baby girl, but the young couple died at sea. Their drifting boat is then discovered by a passing ship, and the baby is rescued. It is immediately embraced by a widow on board (Lisa Pelikan), who has a young son of her own. Then it develops that the plague is sweeping the ship. The captain realizes that the only way to save the widow and the two children is to cast them adrift, in hopes they will find rescue or an island. Otherwise, their sure fate is death by plague.

So, the mother and the two children float away in a little boat, only to inevitably wash up on the shores of—wouldn't you know—*the very same island.* The palm-thatch cottage is still standing, all of the comforts of home are still in place, and all that is left is for the movie to repeat the earlier story. The mother raises the children until they are self-sufficient; she dies; and the kids grow into tanned and beautiful adolescents (Milla Jovovich and Brian Krause). All we have to look forward to, as Pauline Kael so presciently wrote, is: when are these two going to discover fornication?

The original *Blue Lagoon* at least had a certain purity of form. This one complicates matters by having the island discovered by a passing ship, which contains, inevitably, a young woman who makes eyes at the hero, and a bearded sailor who bodes no well for the heroine. That leads to the expected developments in which the hero and heroine decide they like each other best after all, and the evil sailor has something terrible happen to him—like, to take a random example, being eaten by a shark.

The most curious aspect of the movie is the presence of island natives on the other side of the island. They apparently visit during every full moon, beat their drums a lot, and then paddle away in the morning. There are ominous warnings about staying away from the other side of the island, staying indoors during the full moon, etc., but nothing really comes of the presence of the natives. It's as if the filmmakers felt obligated to throw in a few ominously beating drums, but didn't know where to take it from there.

The sincere idiocy of this film really has to be seen to be appreciated—not that I think there is any need for you to see, or appreciate, it. *Return to the Blue Lagoon* aspires to the soft-core porn achievements of the earlier film, but succeeds instead of creating a new genre, no-core porn.

SSSSSSS**S**SSSSSS

●●●

Salome's Last Dance

(Directed by Ken Russell; starring Glenda Jackson; 1988)
Sex is the theater of the poor.—Oscar Wilde

Whether Wilde actually said that, I cannot be sure. The line is not found in any of the standard books of quotations, but it sure sounds like Wilde, and it gets *Salome's Last Dance* off to a rousing start, from which it never recovers.

The Wilde character delivers the line as he enters a male bordello in Paris, where as a special treat the owner has planned a clandestine performance of his banned play *Salome.* The action takes place in 1892, three years before Wilde's disgrace and imprisonment, although in this freewheeling film by Ken Russell the period could be anytime in the past century. Russell's approach is to stage a play-within-a-film, so that while Wilde languishes on a sofa and drinks champagne, the hardworking bordello staff perform his play on a proscenium stage that has been set up for the occasion.

What do we learn from this approach, and indeed from this film? Not much, except that Ken Russell is addicted, as always, to excesses of everything except purpose and structure. After his previous film, *Gothic,* which recreated a weekend idyll involving Shelley and Byron, Russell demonstrates again that he is most interested in literary figures when their trousers are unbuttoned. And even then, he isn't interested in why, or how, they carry on their sex lives; like the defrockers of the scandal sheets, he wants only to breathlessly shock us with the news that his heroes possessed and employed genitals.

As Wilde (Nickolas Grace) reclines on his sofa, the performers in *Salome* perform his play with great energy. Their dialogue is more or less faithful to what Wilde wrote, but the bizarre excesses of the staging are all Russell. The plot retells Wilde's version of the biblical story of Salome's request to Herod that she be presented with the head of John the Baptist on a silver platter. But the story is complicated mightily by the use of Douglas Hodge in a dual role, playing both John the Baptist and "Bosie"—Lord Alfred Douglas, Wilde's lover. While Bosie struggles to stay in character onstage, Wilde reclines in the arms of a young page from the brothel.

Russell is known for his cheerful willingness to involve his actors in embarrassing situations, at whatever cost to their dignity, and in *Salome's Last Dance* such performers as Glenda Jackson and Stratford Johns show what good sports they are by grappling manfully with their lines while all about them disintegrates in Russellian excess. There is, for example, the matter of the three dwarfs dressed as Hassidic Jews and sent on stage to mimic their behavior. The presence of two busty British "Page Three" girls, who stand in the background of nearly every scene, with no visible purpose. The trickery by which Imogen Millais-Scott, as Salome, is replaced by a male dancer in one scene so that the character can be revealed as a transvestite.

There are, I am sometimes convinced, two Ken Russells: The disciplined and gifted director of such films as *Women in Love, Altered States,* and *Tommy,* and the orchestrator of wretched excess in films like *The Music Lovers, Gothic,* and this one. Despite the fact that *Salome's Last Dance* encompasses almost the entire text of a play by Oscar Wilde, it seems shapeless and without purpose. Russell has devised a production without inventing a goal. At the end of the film, there are some shocks and surprises, some foreshadowing of Wilde's long fall into despair, but they seemed tacked on as a favor to the history buffs. There's never the feeling that this whole film was thought out from beginning to end with any particular structure in mind.

By looking at a film like this, however, you can possibly learn something about what does and doesn't work on the screen. I would like to suggest the following postulate: When characters in a movie shock each other, it works a lot better than when they are intended to shock us. Everyone in *Salome's Last Dance*—both within and outside the play—is unshockable. Russell frames their bizarre behavior by a stage and presents it to us, presumably so that we will be shocked. But we are not. The movies are a voyeuristic medium, and to some degree we identify with the characters in a movie, so that if they aren't shocked, we aren't either. Thank God theater is not the sex of the poor.

Saturn 3

(Directed by Stanley Donen; starring Farrah Fawcett, Kirk Douglas; 1980)
Given the fact that written science fiction encourages the greatest possible free play of ideas, why is it that filmed science fiction almost always seems required to be dumb, dumb, dumb? How, this late in the game, can we still get movies like *Saturn 3*? Who paid for it? The credits name Lord Lew Grade and Elliott Kastner. They've got a tidy little partnership over in England that's well enough financed to chum out about a dozen international releases a year, some of them as good as *The Muppet Movie,* most of them as bad as *Saturn 3.*

How dumb is *Saturn 3*? I will give you an example. The movie's about Kirk Douglas and Farrah Fawcett, who are the only two crew members on *Saturn 3,* a space research station near Saturn. They have a visitor, who is supposed to be a Captain James, but is really the evil Benson (Harvey Keitel) who has killed James and replaced him for reasons of his own. Benson has brought along a robot named Hector. And, toward the end of the movie, Hector is chasing Kirk and Farrah. So what do they do? They remove the floor panels of the space station and cover the hole with a flimsy material, so that when Hector steps on it, it'll collapse, and Hector will fall through to the bitterly cold cauldron beneath. Amazing! We haven't seen this brilliant idea since Tarzan was putting stakes in the bottoms of holes to catch elephants. And Tarzan, at least, would have been bright enough to realize that if you make a hole in the floor of a space station, your atmosphere will rush out explosively. How can they still get away with disregarding all the elementary laws of physics in science fiction movies?

But this movie's dumb in other ways, too. The love triangle between Douglas, Fawcett, and Keitel is so awkwardly and unbelievably handled that we are left in stunned indifference. The purpose of Keitel's visit is left so unclear we can't believe Douglas would accept it. The hostility of the robot is unexplained.

And then there are dubious details like (a) the spaceship whizzes through the rocks in the rings of Saturn without hitting any of them; (b) the space station is rambling and spacious despite the fact that every square inch of construction would be at an incredible premium millions of miles from Earth; (c) gravity is the same as on Earth; (d) . . . but never mind.

This movie is awesomely stupid, totally implausible from a scientific viewpoint, and a shameful waste of money. If Grade and Kastner intend to continue producing films with standards this low, I think they ought instead, in simple fairness, to simply give their money to filmmakers at random. The results couldn't be worse.

The Scarlet Letter
(Directed by Roland Joffe; starring Demi Moore, Gary Oldman; 1995)
The great inconvenience of *The Scarlet Letter,* from a Hollywood point of view, is that the novel begins after the adultery has already taken place. This will not do. It is like taking up the story of Salome after she has put the veils back on. Another problem is that there is not much action in Nathaniel Hawthorne's novel, except inside the minds and souls of the characters. A third is that the Reverend Dimmesdale, who impregnates poor Hester, is the leader of the local hypocrites who persecute her. Channel surfing the other morning, I came across Demi Moore just as she was describing *The Scarlet Letter* as "a very dense, uncinematic book."

And so it is; many of the best books are. That's what rewrites are for. The film version imagines all of the events leading up to the adultery, photographed in the style of those *Playboy's Fantasies* videos. It adds action: Indians, deadly fights, burning buildings, even the old trick where the condemned on the scaffold are saved by a violent interruption. And it converts the Reverend Dimmesdale from a scoundrel into a romantic and a weakling, perhaps because the times are not right for a movie about a fundamentalist hypocrite. It also gives us a red bird, which seems to represent the devil, and a shapely slave girl, who seems to represent the filmmakers' desire to introduce voyeurism into the big sex scenes.

The story, you may recall, involves a Puritan woman named Hester Prynne (Demi Moore), who is found to be pregnant even though her husband has not arrived in the Massachusetts Bay Colony, and is feared dead. After refusing to name the father of her child, Hester is condemned to wear a scarlet letter on her bodice. Her daughter, Pearl, is born, and grows up as a willful little vixen. It is revealed that the father of the child is Arthur Dimmesdale (Gary Oldman), the leader of the local bluenoses denouncing Hester. And then her long-lost husband, Roger Prynne (Robert Duvall) turns up, assumes another identity, and tries to determine who was the thief of his wife's affections. The novel ends with poor Dimmesdale confessing his sin, crying out "His will be done! Farewell!" and dying.

It is obviously not acceptable for Dimmesdale to believe he has sinned, and so the movie cleverly transforms his big speech into a stirring cry for sexual freedom and religious tolerance. Instead of dying of a guilty seizure, he snatches the noose from Hester's neck and pulls it around his own, only to be saved when the Indians attack, driving a burning cart through the village. The roles of the puritanical local ministers are farmed out to supporting actors, and Dimmesdale is left to hang around sheepishly, keeping his guilty secret but regarding Hester with big wet eyes begging forgiveness and understanding.

Roland Joffe, who directed the film, says "the book is set in a time when the seeds were sown for the bigotry, sexism, and lack of tolerance we still battle today . . . yet it is often looked at merely as a tale of nineteenth-century moralizing, a treatise against adultery." Actually, it is more often looked upon as a tale of seventeenth-century moralizing, and a treatise against hypocrisy. But never mind. Joffe adds: "And, of course, it is also a marvelous romance."

Not so marvelous really. After insisting on living alone in a cottage outside town, which sets local tongues a-wagging, Hester is walking in the forest one day when she comes upon a man skinny-dipping in a pond. It is the reverend, although she doesn't know that. She, and we, see him in the altogether, and then she hears him preaching in church, where he sounds a good deal more like Susan Powter than a Puritan.

Hester entertains lustful thoughts about his body, and they entertain her. (Gary Oldman, marvelous actor that he is, may not be everybody's ideal of the perfect male physique—remember him as Sid Vicious?—but on the whole I think we can be relieved Brad Pitt was not cast.) Hester's comely slave girl, Mituba (Lisa Jolliff-Andoh) prepares her bath, and then Hester slowly luxuriates in it by candlelight, while dreaming of Arthur. It is hard to see for sure, but I think she may be indulging in the practice that the nuns called "interfering with yourself."

Meanwhile, through a convenient peephole, Mituba watches lustfully, for no other purpose, I believe, than to provide the additional thrill of one attractive woman observing another one naked. Will the sin that dare not speak its name make an appearance in Massachusetts Bay? Alas, no; the prospect of interracial lesbian love, appealing as it is to today's filmmakers, would not quite fit into this story, even as revised and updated.

Soon Dimmesdale visits Hester, they become powerfully attracted to one another, and commit adultery on a bed of dried beans in the shed, while Mituba again watches them, disrobing and crawling into her mistress's bath. Mituba holds a candle with its flame just above the waterline, and at the moment of their climax, she draws it under the water, extinguishing it with a hiss. This is way better than curtains blowing in the wind; it's the equal of the moment in *Ryan's Daughter* when, as the two lovers coupled, his stallion neighed and her mare whinnied.

The rest of the film is more or less as I have described it, although longer, much longer. Lurid melodrama develops after Hester's husband arrives, played by Robert Duvall as if he'd never had sex in his life and didn't want anybody else to, either. The movie's morality boils down to: Why should this old fart stand between these two nice young people? The movie has removed the character's sense of guilt, and therefore the story's drama. ("Do you believe . . . what we did was wrong?" asks Hester.) Hollywood has taken that troublesome old novel and made it cinematic at last, although I'm afraid it's still pretty dense.

S.F.W.

(Directed by Jefery Levy; starring Reese Witherspoon; 1995)
S.F.W. is the kind of movie to inspire members of Generation X to lie about their age. It qualifies Forrest Gump for a genius grant. It is a portrait of the most singularly stupid, obnoxious character I've seen on the screen in many a day—which would be promising, if he were not boring, as well.

The movie stars Stephen Dorff as Cliff Spab, who gets his fifteen minutes of fame when he is one of several hostages held inside a convenience store by mysterious terrorists. The hostage ordeal is telecast nonstop from security cameras inside the store, and Cliff soon becomes a global celebrity because of his nihilistic pronouncements and his debates with the terrorists and fellow hostages. His basic philosophy, expressed in the movie's title, is "so fucking what?" That's about as deep as it gets.

The hostage ordeal arrives at a crisis point on Day 36, when the store runs out of beer. Shortly thereafter, Cliff Spab finds himself free and back on the street, the adored hero of millions, his photo on T-shirts. Unfortunately, his parents are slow to applaud his heroism, and want him to clean up his room. He responds by trashing his private refrigerator, filled with beer, and going on a rampage before stalking out of the house.

The media hang on Cliff's every word. "Everybody wanted a piece of me," he complains in the narration. "Trouble was, there wasn't enough of me to go around." That would have been true even if they had only wanted an itsy-bitsy piece, since there is very little of Cliff to begin with. He is culturally deprived, has a low IQ, is narcissistic and alcoholic, and has one of those vocabularies in which the most popular four-letter word is used as an all-purpose substitute for thousands of other words unknown to the speaker.

Basically, Cliff's pose is, he wants to be famous for not wanting to be famous. He is a reluctant celebrity, cheered for his reluctance. This pose reaches its absurdist climax when Cliff stars at a rock concert. His act is rather simple. The orchestra plays "Thus Spake Zarathustra" while Cliff walks out onstage and stands there, projecting reluctance to be made into a celebrity, and the audience cheers wildly.

The sayings of Cliff Spab will not soon be anthologized in those books of great movie lines. "If you think about it enough, you can go nuts," he opines at one point. At another, asked "What are you rebelling against?" he rips off Marlon Brando's famous response to the same question, "What have you got?" This must I think be counted an original line of Cliff's, since the movie gives no evidence that he has ever heard of Marlon Brando, or anyone else.

In fairness to Jefery Levy, the director and cowriter, the film is intended as a satirical attack on the cult of celebrity, and it uses unconvincing looka-likes for such as Phil Donahue and Sam Donaldson in scenes where TV takes Cliff Spab seriously. One problem may be that Cliff Spab is seen at such great length that we grow very tired of him. His celebrity is no stranger, I suppose, than the attention given to such other marginal personalities as Kato Kaelin and John Wayne Bobbitt, but then again we have not been made to listen to Kato or John W. around the clock for more than a month. It only seems as if we have.

She's Out of Control

(Directed by Stan Dragoti; starring Tony Danza, Catherine Hicks; 1989)
What planet did the makers of this film come from? What assumptions do they have about the purpose and quality of life? I ask because *She's Out of Control* is simultaneously so bizarre and so banal that it's a first: The first movie fabricated entirely from sitcom clichés and plastic lifestyles, without reference to any known plane of reality.

The film stars Tony Danza as Doug, a divorced dad with an unhealthy obsession about the dating behavior of his teenage daughter, Katie (Ami Dolenz). He wants to keep her forever trapped in an asexual prepubescent hinterland, but then Doug's fiancée Janet (Catherine Hicks) takes the kid for a complete beauty makeover: hair, makeup, wardrobe, and attitude. And the next time Doug sees his daughter, she's descending the staircase looking like she stepped out of one of those soft-core perfume ads.

Doug spends a lot of time looking at his daughter. He sees her so specifically as a sexual creature, and is so obsessed by what he sees, that in another movie his attention would probably seem perverse. The character he plays in this movie is so dim-witted and lacking in psychological insight, however, that his behavior is not so much perverse as slack-jawed.

There are a couple of minute subplots in the movie, one involving the romance between Doug and Janet, and the other one involving Katie's influence on her kid sister, Bonnie (Laura Mooney). But the heart of this movie is the father's unsuccessful attempts to enforce curfews, dictate behavior, and curtail the emotional development of his daughter.

The scene that sets up this obsession is a sick one—the sicker the more you think about it. Doug takes the family to the beach, and then stares in horrified fascination as Katie comes running out of the surf in her one-piece bathing suit, her breasts bouncing in slow motion like outtakes from a TV jiggle show.

The problem with this scene is that Doug seems to regard his daughter not in parental terms but in sexual ones. The movie does not possess a shred of healthy insight into the process by which people mature; it sees adolescent girls as commodities to be protected from predatory males.

The French director Jean-Luc Godard once said that the way to criticize a movie is to make another movie. By a happy coincidence, just such a movie opened on the same day as *She's Out of Control.* It's called *Say Anything,* and it is healthy, sensitive, and true about a relationship between a father, his daughter, and her boyfriend. It is a movie about personal standards, about learning to trust, about growing up healthy and sane. The people who made *She's Out of Control* could learn a lot from it.

Sidney Sheldon's Bloodline
(Directed by Terence Young; starring Audrey Hepburn; 1979)
After six months, a week, and two days of suspense, we can now relax: The worst movie of 1979 has opened. Just avoid this one film, and anything else you see will be better. The name of the movie is *Sidney Sheldon's Bloodline,* and on second thought, I'm not recommending that you avoid it: See *Sidney Sheldon's Bloodline,* and weep for the cinema.

The movie is based on a novel by Sidney Sheldon, a fact cunningly hinted in its title. It is about a woman who gains control of her father's multi-billion-dollar pharmaceutical company after her father dies in a fishy mountain-climbing accident. The woman is played by Audrey Hepburn, making her first screen appearance in four years, and there is this much to be said: When she appears on the screen for the first time, the theater goes silent as everyone absorbs once again the fact of her extraordinary beauty. And then the theater stays silent, as everyone absorbs the astonishing extent of the artistic stupidity wreaked upon her by the screenplay.

I've jotted down a few sample lines. "When I yam feenished weev you," threatens one character, "you vell be lak ze beetle I haf killed: Almost dead!"

At another point, Hepburn learns that a chemist working for her late father's firm has made an interesting pharmaceutical discovery that may turn out to be marketable: A drug promising eternal youth.

"Normal people will be able to live 100 or 150 years," he avers.

"How soon can this drug be marketed?" she asks.

"Eighteen months."

"Make it twelve. This is urgent."

Faithful moviegoers may recall that Sidney Sheldon's *The Other Side of Midnight* was released two summers ago, and that I was unkind enough to give it a reserved review. I now apologize for that error. *The Other Side of*

Midnight was so immeasurably better than *Sidney Sheldon's Bloodline* that, in retrospect, Sheldon should have sued to have his name taken out of the title of this film and put in the other one. But why should he worry? The novel was sold for a reported $2 million, and Sheldon is laughing all the way to the remedial writing class.

The film's cast is, of course, horribly mistreated. Ben Gazzara is perhaps the worst victim. He plays Hepburn's confidant and lover. The fact that *Sidney Sheldon's Bloodline* and Gazzara's *Saint Jack* are playing at the same time in the same town offers mute evidence that a good actor in a bad movie should not necessarily be blamed for everything.

Other people we cannot blame for being in this movie include Irene Papas, arguably the most striking actress in the movies; James Mason, as civilized as ever; Romy Schneider, she of the cool elegance; and Gert Frobe, of the police department. Omar Sharif is not only blameless, he is even praiseworthy: As he plays his scenes, he finds a way to sneak past the director his obvious conviction that the dialogue he has been given is beneath contempt and may, indeed, be hilarious.

I have not yet mentioned why the movie is considered marketable. It is about the favorite fictional subject of the fast-fading seventies: the Woman in Danger. Hepburn is not only made to crawl along burning rooftops and be assaulted by industrial spies, but, such trash is this film, at one point she is almost run down by a truck that isn't even intended to hit her. In a movie built upon threats on a character's life, it is a little reprehensible to suggest that she could die in a random accident. But then, this film *is* a little reprehensible.

Silent Fall

(Directed by Bruce Beresford; starring Richard Dreyfuss, Liv Tyler; 1994)
Silent Fall is a thriller about an autistic little boy who witnesses the murder of his parents. He'd make a great witness, if only he would talk. I was reminded of a T.V. report about a parrot that witnessed a murder. The parrot talked, but was it admissible as a witness?

Psychiatrist Jack Reiner (Richard Dreyfuss) uses a deck of cards while explaining the boy to his older sister, Sylvia (Liv Tyler). Let's say the solution to the murder is the Queen. You or I might be reminded of it by a million things. But Tim can only get to the Queen from the Jack. And he can only get to the Jack from the 10. And so on, all the way back to the Ace—which is, in a sense, what the psychiatrist is searching for.

Silent Fall approaches this story in a solemn way, in one of those productions where everybody lives in big houses surrounded by autumnal woods, and spends a lot of time walking by the sides of lakes. The Dreyfuss character has retired from treating children after a child died while under his care. Now he's hauled out of retirement by the local sheriff (J. T. Walsh, playing a nice guy for a change). The parents of Sylvia and Tim have been found brutally slashed to death in their bedroom. When the cops arrive, Tim is swinging a bloody knife and Sylvia is cowering in the closet. She saw the killer, a man who escaped before she could ID him.

The cops use pretty sloppy procedure on the case. Sylvia and Tim are allowed to go back to the house to live while it is still a crime scene. Apart from the possibility they might disturb clues, nobody in the movie even *thinks* it might be dangerous for an eighteen-year-old girl to be out there unprotected, with a mad slasher on the loose and she as the only witness. Meanwhile, Reiner goes to work making friends with Tim, hoping he holds the clue to the murders.

There is more. Much more. Some of it involves Linda Hamilton *(Terminator II)*, as Jake's wife, Karen. She gets second billing but the role is just a hair this side of unnecessary. John Lithgow wanders through in a thankless role as a psychiatrist who believes in using drugs instead of therapy. Mostly the action involves Jake and the little boy, and Jake and the sexy teenage girl, who seems sorta attracted to him.

Now. There are some things about this plot I dare not reveal. Let's go carefully here. There is an attempted murder, and in terms of its planning, execution, sheer impossibility, and ultimate outcome, it is without doubt the most absurd attempted murder I have seen since Goldie Hawn got involved with that elevator in *Deceived* (1991).

There's more. There is, for example, the solution to the murders, which stars little Tim in the performance by an autistic character so remarkable that it makes Dustin Hoffman's work in *Rain Man* look like a warm-up. If you see the movie, ask yourself : Assuming (a) that Timmy could do what he does while Dreyfuss explains the mystery, and (b) that Timmy is the best impressionist since Frank Gorshin, then even so, (c) how did he get the flawless timing, so that he performs right on cue during Dreyfuss's summation?

Silent Fall has a tortuously constructed plot, but the solution to the mystery has been right there all along. I refer you to the entry on "The Law of Economy of Characters" in *Ebert's Little Movie Glossary,* which observes that since there are no unnecessary characters, the guilty person in a whodunit is inevitably the one who otherwise seems unaccounted for.

The Sixth Man

(Directed by Randall Miller; starring Kadeem Hardison, Marlon Wayans; 1997)
The Sixth Man is another paint-by-the-numbers sports movie, this one about a college basketball team that makes it to the NCAA finals with the help of the ghost of one of its dead stars. Let's not talk about how predictable it is. Let's talk about how dumb it is.

The film starts with the childhood hoop dreams of a couple of brothers, Antoine and Kenny, who are coached by their father and hope to be stars one day. The father dies before he can see them realize their dream: They're both starters for the University of Washington Huskies. Antoine (Kadeem Hardison) is the dominant brother, the play-maker who gets the ball for the crucial last-minute shots. Kenny (Marlon Wayans) is a gifted player, but in his brother's shadow.

The tragedy strikes. Antoine dunks the ball, falls to the court, and dies of heart failure on the way to the hospital. Kenny is crushed, and the Huskies embark on a losing streak until, one day at practice, Kenny throws the ball into the air and it never comes back down again.

Antoine, of course, has returned, this time as a ghost that only Kenny can see. And eventually Antoine returns to the court as an invisible sixth man on the Huskies team. He deflects the ball, tips in close shots, gives a boost to the Huskies, and trips up their opponents, and soon the team is in the NCAA playoffs.

Presumably *The Sixth Man* is intended to appeal to basketball fans. Is there a basketball fan alive who could fall for this premise? I'm not talking about the ghost—that's easy to believe. I'm talking about the details of the game.

I was out at the United Center last week for the big overtime contest between the Bulls and the Supersonics. Along with thousands of other fans, I was an instant expert, my eyes riveted on every play. If the ball had suddenly changed course in midair, do you think we would have noticed? What if a ball dropped all the way through the basket and then popped back up again? What if a player was able to hang in midair twice as long as Michael Jordan?

My guess is that any one of those moments would have inspired a frenzy of instant replay analysis, and all three of them together would have induced apoplexy in announcer Johnny (Red) Kerr. But in *The Sixth Man,* audiences and commentators don't seem to realize that the laws of physics and gravity are being violated on behalf of the Huskies. Finally a woman sportswriter (Michael Michele) for the student paper uses the stop-action button on her VCR to replay a game, and notices that Kenny never even touched a ball before it went in.

I don't want to belabor technicalities here. I know the movie's premise is that nobody notices that the ghost is affecting the game. Because nobody notices, that frees the movie to proceed with its lethargic formula, right to the bitter end. (Will the team decide it has to win on its own? Will the ghost and his brother have to accept the fact of death? Will the Huskies be way behind at half-time of the big game? Will they win? Will the sun rise tomorrow?)

You can't even begin to enjoy this game unless you put your intelligence on hold, or unless you're a little kid. A real, real, little, little kid. Why do Hollywood filmmakers hobble themselves in this way? Why be content with repeating ancient and boring formulas when a little thought could have produced an interesting movie? What if Kenny and Antoine had worked out a strategy to *secretly* affect the outcome of the game? What if they were aware that obvious tactics would be spotted? What if Kenny didn't tell his teammates about the ghost? What if Antoine, for sheer love of the game, took the other side once in a while?

The possibilities are endless. Movies like *The Sixth Man* are an example of Level One thinking, in which the filmmakers get the easy, obvious idea and are content with it. Good movies are made by taking the next step. Twisting the premise. Using lateral thinking. I imagine a lot of studio executives are sports fans. Would any of them be *personally* entertained by this movie? If this answer is "no"—and it has to be—then they shouldn't expect us to be, either.

Slaves of New York

(Directed by James Ivory; starring Bernadette Peters; 1989)

I detest *Slaves of New York* so much that I distrust my own opinion. Maybe it's not simply a bad movie. Maybe it takes some kind of special knack, some species of sly genius, to make me react so strongly. I pause. I leaf through my memories of the film. I try to analyze what I really feel.

Okay. I feel calmer now. The first thing I feel is a genuine dislike for the people in this film—the ambitious climbers on the lower rungs of the ladder in the New York art world. I dislike them because they are stupid, and have occupied my time with boring conversation. It is more than that. They are not simply stupid. They *value* stupidity. They aim their conversations below the level of their actual intelligence because they fear to appear uncool by saying anything interesting. By always being bored, they can never be passé? No wonder Andy Warhol wanted to film this material.

The second thing I feel is that their entire act is a hypocritical sham. They want to succeed so much they can not only taste it, they can choke on it. And it doesn't matter what they succeed at. They move through a world of art, fashion, photography, and design, but the actual disciplines and psychic rewards of this world are not interesting to them. They want to use art as a way of obtaining success, which is more important to them than art will ever be.

The heroine of the movie is a young woman who designs hats. They are truly hideous hats, designed to bring embarrassment and ridicule to those who wear them, but never mind what the hats look like. The important thing is, how does the designer herself feel about her hats? I have no idea. She never permits herself to react to them, to care for them, to be proud of them. She looks at them as if they were her fingernail clippings—once a part of her, but not important, and now no longer even attached.

Her boyfriend manufactures paintings he does not love. Other people in her life also play at the extrusion of art, in the hopes that their work will sell, and they will find a gallery to represent them, and that eventually they will be able to afford a really nice apartment in New York City. The title, *Slaves of New York,* is explained by its author, Tama Janowitz, to mean that life in New York is basically a matter of becoming successful enough to have a nice apartment, and that if you do not have one, you move in with someone who does, and become that person's slave. The whole idea is to eventually get your own apartment, and have slaves of your own.

I have a suspicion that, to some degree, Janowitz is right and the Slave/ Apartment syndrome does operate in New York. That would certainly explain a great deal of the bad art that's around. Watching the film, I remembered a conversation I had with the actor John Malkovich about the way that off-Broadway theater was dying in New York while thriving in the provinces. "To have off-Broadway," he said,"you have to have starving actors. And to have starving actors, you have to have a place for them to starve. New York is too expensive for that. You can't afford to starve there anymore."

There was once a time, in decades not too long ago, when life for a young artist consisted of living in a threadbare apartment while trying to create great art, instead of trying to live in a great apartment while creating threadbare art.

Sour Grapes
(Directed by Larry David; starring Steven Weber, Craig Bierko; 1998)
Sour Grapes is a comedy about things that aren't funny. It reminded me of *Crash,* an erotic thriller about things no one finds erotic. The big difference is that David Cronenberger, who made *Crash,* knew that people were not turned on by auto accidents. Larry David, who wrote and directed *Sour Grapes,* apparently thinks people are amused by cancer, accidental castration, racial stereotypes, and bitter family feuds.

Oh, I have no doubt that all of those subjects could be incorporated into a great comedy. It's all in the style and the timing. *Sour Grapes* is tone-deaf comedy; the material, the dialogue, the delivery, and even the sound track are labored and leaden. How to account for the fact that Larry David is one of the creators of *Seinfeld?* Maybe he works well with others.

I can't easily remember a film I've enjoyed less. *North,* a comedy I hated, was at least able to inflame me with dislike. *Sour Grapes* is a movie that deserves its title: It's puckered, deflated, and vinegary. It's a dead zone.

The story. Two cousins (Steven Weber and Craig Bierko) go to Atlantic City. One is a designer who wins a slot jackpot of more than $436,000. He was playing with quarters given him by the other guy. The other cousin, a surgeon, not unreasonably, thinks he should get some of the winnings. If not half, then maybe a third. The winner offers him 3 percent.

This sets off several scenes of debate about what would be right or wrong in such a situation. Even a limo driver, hearing the winner's story, throws him out of the car: "You were playing with his money!" The losing doctor nevertheless gives his cousin a blue warm-up suit for his birthday, only to discover that the louse has given the suit away to an African-American street person.

So far all we have is a comic premise that doesn't deliver laughs. Now the movie heads for cringe-inducing material. We learn about the winner's ability to perform oral sex while alone. He's alone a lot, because his wife is mad at him, but that's an opening for stereotyped Jewish Mother scenes. The feud heats up, until the enraged doctor lies to the winner: "You have terminal cancer. It's time to set your house in order." Ho, ho.

The winner wants to spare his mother the misery of watching her son die. So he gives her house key to the black bum in the warm-up suit and tells him to make himself at home. His plan: His mother will be scared to death by the sight of the black home invader. After she screams, we see the bum running down the street in Steppin' Fetchit style. Was there no one to hint to David that this was gratuitous and offensive?

Further material involves the surgeon getting so upset in the operating room that he reverses an X-ray film and removes the wrong testicle from a TV star—who then, of course, has to be told that they still had to go ahead and remove the remaining testicle. The star develops a castrato voice. Ho, ho.

This material is impossible to begin with. What makes it worse is the lack of lightness from the performers, who slog glumly through their dialogue as if they know what an aromatic turkey they're stuck in. Scene after scene clangs dead to the floor, starting with the funeral service that opens the film. The more I think of it, the more *Sour Grapes* really does resemble *Crash* (except that *Crash* was not a bad film). Both movies are like watching automobile accidents. Only one intended to be.

Species

(Directed by Roger Donaldson; starring Ben Kingsley, Michael Madsen; 1995)
Think about this. According to the movies, out there in space, untold light years from Earth, exist many alien species with the ability to travel between the stars and send messages across the universe. Their civilizations must be wonderfully advanced, and yet, when we finally encounter them, what do we

get? Disgusting, slimy morph-creatures with rows of evil teeth, whose greatest cultural achievement is jumping out at people from behind things. How do they travel through space? By jumping out from behind one star after another?

Species is the latest movie to explore this depressing vision. Like the *Alien* movies and many others, it is founded on a fear of another species, and the assumption that extraterrestrials basically want to eat us. For every rare film like *2001* or *Close Encounters of the Third Kind* with a sense of wonder about the vastness of creation, there are a dozen like this, which are basically just versions of *Friday the 13th* in which Jason is a bug-eyed monster.

There may be a reason for this. Mainstream Hollywood is so terrified of intelligent human characters that it's no wonder they don't want aliens who are even smarter than the humans: Hey, dude, you don't pay for a ticket just to hear words you don't understand. And there's a kind of smugness in the assumption that we are at the top of the evolutionary ladder; that other species, even if they do manage to travel to Earth, will look and behave like an explosion at the special-effects factory.

Species, directed by Roger Donaldson from a screenplay by Dennis Feldman, begins with an interesting premise: Radio telescopes pick up signals from space which, when decoded, include a formula for a DNA string that can be combined with our own. Thus a creature might be born that is both human and alien—able to live here, but with attributes of the other species. Scientists in a secret government lab carry out the experiment, which produces a pretty little girl. In the opening scene, they are trying to gas her to death.

One attribute of the creature is its rapid growth rate. After only a few days she looks like a ten-year-old, and by the next time we see her, she has matured into a sexy blonde (Natasha Henstridge) who could star in the *Sports Illustrated* swimsuit issue anytime. We know this because the movie spends a good deal of time having her take off her brassiere while seducing her victims in hot tubs, because she wants to mate.

Pure logic would suggest that if she can change from a ten-year-old into a twenty-one-year-old almost overnight, she should die of old age before the movie is over. But, no, she stays at the sex bomb stage for the rest of the film, except when morphing into a gruesome monster. (The ability to instantly change one's physical composition is, I believe, in violation of the laws of physics, but *Species* breaks every law but the law of diminishing returns.)

Ben Kingsley, that invaluable actor, does what he can with the lead role.

He's Fitch, the scientist in charge, and he leads a team on a chase of the escaped alien. Because the existence of the monster must remain a secret, a general alert is delayed. Instead, Kingsley gathers Press (Michael Madsen), a hired killer for the government; Dan (Forest Whitaker), an "empathist" who can sense what happened in places; Arden (Alfred Molina), an anthropologist; and Laura (Marg Helgenberger), a molecular biologist, whose primary role is to be rescued by the others.

The alien, named Sil, is a quick learner. She checks into a motel, asks the clerk, "Where can I find a man?" and picks up the first of her victims in a bar. As the search team follows her trail, the empathist picks up signals that she rejected one guy because he did not have, perhaps, the right genes. Boy, didn't he. What happens to him shouldn't happen to a bug on a windshield. And then the other guy meets her standards, and soon there is the prospect of lots of little Sils.

The movie ends with a chase through a sewer system, and into an underground oil lake. There are lots of flames and struggles and lots and *lots* of scenes where the creature jumps out from behind things. And of course there are the usual false alarms, in which you *think* it's the creature, but whew, it's only a bat/cat/rat. Eventually it develops a tongue like a frog, and can flick it out several yards to capture its enemies.

There is one line in the screenplay that suggests an interesting direction the movie could have taken. Sil, half alien, half human, is driven by instinct, not intelligence, and doesn't know why she acts the way she does. She says, "Who am I? What am I?" But the movie never tells her. I can imagine a film in which a creature like Sil struggles with her dual nature, and tries to find self-knowledge. Like Frankenstein's monster, she would be an object of pity. But that would be way too subtle for *Species,* which just adds a slick front end to the basic horror vocabulary of things jumping out from behind stuff.

Speed Zone
(Directed by Jim Drake; starring Peter Boyle, Donna Dixon; 1989)
Read my lips.

Cars are not funny. Speeding cars are not funny. It is not funny when a car spins around and speeds in the other direction. It is not funny when a car flies through the air. It is not funny when a truck crashes into a car. It is not funny when cops chase speeding cars. It is not funny when cars crash through roadblocks.

None of those things are funny.

They have never been funny.

People are not amused by them. No, not even the people unlucky or unwise enough to have paid money to see a movie like *Speed Trap*—or a movie like *Cannonball Run,* of which *Speed Trap* is a pathetic clone. Audiences sit in dead silence.

Hollywood does not seem to understand this basic principle, which is why so many movies have featured chases, crashes, and flying automobiles in recent years. Occasionally a chase will indeed be exciting—when it has something to do with the plot, as in *The French Connection* or *To Live and Die in L.A.* But when a movie is *all* chases and crashes, then the intelligent viewer will realize that what he is seeing is a big payday for a lot of stunt drivers, and he will lose interest.

Nonstop chase-and-crash comedies have provided some of the worst movies of recent years (both *Cannonball Run* movies, the *Smokey* sequels, etc.), but even in that dismal company *Speed Zone* sets some kind of record. This is a movie that lasts ninety-five minutes and contains one (1) laugh. To save you the admission price, here is the joke:

Dickie Smothers: "We've got to go to the Dulles airport."

Tommy Smothers: "What are we going to Fresno for?"

Dickie: "What makes you think we're going to Fresno?"

Tommy: "Well, you said the dullest airport, didn't you?"

None of the other jokes in *Speed Zone* measure up to that standard. The movie is still another waste of John Candy, who makes a movie like *Planes, Trains and Automobiles* that showcases his genuine talent, and then waltzes into a cynical, no-brainer ripoff like this with nothing more on his mind, apparently, than the rent check.

The movie features countless other celebrities in bit roles, but none of them make as lasting an impression as the Michelin trademark, which is displayed throughout the film in a blatant example of product promotion. Will Michelin sell more tires this way? I wonder. Would you trust your life to tires made by anyone who thought association with this film would improve their product's image?

Spice World

(Directed by Bob Spiers; starring The Spice Girls; 1998)
The Spice Girls are easier to tell apart than the Mutant Ninja Turtles, but that is small consolation: What can you say about five women whose principal distinguishing characteristic is that they have different names?

They occupy *Spice World* as if they were watching it: They're so detached they can't even successfully lip-synch their own songs. During a rehearsal scene, their director tells them, with such truth that we may be hearing a secret message from the screenwriter, "That was absolutely perfect—without being actually any good."

Spice World is obviously intended as a rip-off of *A Hard Day's Night* (1964), which gave the Beatles to the movies. They should have ripped off more—everything they could get their hands on. The movie is a day in the life of a musical group that has become an overnight success, and we see them rehearse, perform, hang out together, and deal with such desperately contrived supporting characters as a trash newspaper editor, a paparazzo, and a manipulative manager.

All of these elements are inspired in one way or another by *A Hard Day's Night*. The huge difference, of course, is that the Beatles were talented—while, let's face it, the Spice Girls could be duplicated by any five women under the age of thirty standing in line at Dunkin' Donuts.

The Beatles film played off the personalities of the Beatles. The Spice Girls have no personalities; their bodies are carriers for inane chatter. The Beatles film had such great music that every song in it is beloved all over the world. The Spice Girls music is so bad that even *Spice World* avoids using any more of it than absolutely necessary.

The film's linking device is a big double-decker bus, painted like a Union Jack, which ferries the Girls past London landmarks (so many landmarks I suspect the filmmakers were desperately trying to stretch the running time). This bus is of ordinary size on the outside but three times too wide on the inside; it is fitted with all the conveniences of Spice Girlhood, except, apparently, toilet facilities, leading to the unusual sight of the Girls jumping off for a quick pee in the woods. (They do everything together.)

So lacking in human characteristics are the Girls that when the screenplay falls back on the last resort of the bankrupt filmmaking imagination—a childbirth scene—they have to import one of their friends to have the baby.

She at least had the wit to get pregnant, something beyond the Girls since it would involve a relationship, and thus an attention span. Words fail me as I try to describe my thoughts at the prospect of the five Spice Girls bedside at a childbirth, shouting "push!"

Stanley
(Directed by William Grefe; starring Chris Robinson; 1972)

The old man climbed out of his seat in the sixth row and went shuffling up the aisle, asking people what time it was. "Do you have the time?" he kept asking. "The time? What time is it?"

A woman sitting across the aisle advised him to shut up and get lost. "I paid my money and I want to see the movie," she said. She gobbled her buttered popcorn and stared at the screen, where a stripper was biting off a snake's head.

"Ooo-eee," somebody said in the darkness.

"What time is it?" the man asked. He was back again.

"Quiet!" somebody whispered fiercely.

On the screen, a character named Tim was caressing the head of his pet rattlesnake and cooing at it: "Does that feel good, Stanley? Do you like that, Stanley?" Stanley was the rattlesnake.

Back at Tim's cabin, a cretinous game poacher had just blown off Hazel's head with a shotgun. Hazel was Stanley's wife. Then the poacher killed Hazel's three baby snakes. At about this point, a couple of other villains sunk into quicksand while screaming fearsomely.

Still to come was the big swimming pool scene, where the head villain jumps into his pool without realizing that Tim had filled it with water moccasins. This is quite a scene. The head villain's daughter comes riding up on her horse, sees her dead father, shouts "Daddy!" and then is abducted by Tim and taken back to the swamp.

The girl gets over Daddy's death pretty easily, I'd say. By the time Tim gets her back to the cabin she's making eyes at him. They kiss and caress and (so help me) the sound track bursts into a song with the lyrics "Let's play hide and seek with the world." Meanwhile, her old man has been attacked by dozens of deadly snakes. How sharper than a serpent's tooth it is, you might say, to have a thankless child.

I think it was when the stripper bit off the snake's head that I first began to ask myself what I was doing in the theater.

There's a close-up of blood running down her chin, and then a scene where she gets plowed on Jack Daniels and asks her husband if he has any idea how it feels to bite off a snake's head every day—twice on weekends. He's too happy to listen. This was opening night at the club, you see, and he explains: "It always pays to wine and dine the critics! The reviews will be terrific! They loved your act, sweetheart!"

It is my job to go to movies and write about them. If the movie is a work of art, I must try to rise to the occasion. If it's just an entertainment, then my job is to suggest how well you might be entertained. But how should I approach *Stanley*? The movie is doing business—but what kind of people are in the audience?

Are they just poor slobs who got suckered in by the ads? Or are they geeks enjoying a busman's holiday? Should I rate the movie with stars, or vomit bags? Why did the old man want to know what time it was? Had he missed the feeding at the zoo? Why wouldn't anyone tell him? Didn't they know? Didn't they care that it was late . . . very late?

Ooo-eee.

Starship Troopers
(Directed by Paul Verhoeven; starring Casper Van Dien; 1997)
Starship Troopers is the most violent kiddie movie ever made. I call it a kiddie movie not to be insulting, but to be accurate: Its action, characters, and values are pitched at eleven-year-old science fiction fans. That makes it true to its source. It's based on a novel for juveniles by Robert A. Heinlein. I read it when I was in grade school. I have improved since then, but the story has not.

The premise: Early in the next millennium, mankind is engaged in a war for survival with the Bugs, a vicious race of giant insects that colonize the galaxy by hurling their spores into space. If you seek their monument, do not look around you: Bugs have no buildings, no technology, no clothes, nothing but the ability to attack, fight, kill, and propagate. They exist not as an alien civilization but as pop-up enemies in a space war.

Human society recruits starship troopers to fight the Bug. Their method is to machine-gun them to death. This does not work very well. Three or four troopers will fire thousands of rounds into a Bug, which like the Energizer Bunny just keeps on comin'. Grenades work better, but I guess the troopers haven't twigged to that. You'd think a human race capable of interstellar travel might have developed an effective insecticide, but no.

It doesn't really matter, since the Bugs aren't important except as props for the interminable action scenes, and as an enemy to justify the film's quasi-fascist militarism. Heinlein was of course a right-wing saber-rattler, but a charming and intelligent one who wrote some of the best science fiction ever. *Starship Troopers* proposes a society in which citizenship is earned through military service, and values are learned on the battlefield.

Heinlein intended his story for young boys, but wrote it more or less seriously. The one redeeming merit for director Paul Verhoeven's film is that by remaining faithful to Heinlein's material and period, it adds an element of sly satire. This is like the squarest but most technically advanced sci-fi movie of the 1950s, a film in which the sets and costumes look like a cross between Buck Rogers and the Archie comic books, and the characters look like they stepped out of Pepsodent ads.

The film's narration is handled by a futuristic version of the TV news, crossed with the Web. After every breathless story, the cursor blinks while we're asked, "Want to know more?" Yes, I did. I was particularly intrigued by the way the Bugs had evolved organic launching pods that could spit their spores into space, and could also fire big globs of unidentified fiery matter at attacking space ships. Since they have no technology, these abilities must have evolved along Darwinian lines; to say they severely test the theory of evolution is putting it mildly.

On the human side, we follow the adventures of a group of high-school friends from Buenos Aires. Johnny (Casper Van Dien) has a crush on Carmen (Denise Richards), but she likes the way Zander (Patrick Muldoon) looks in uniform. When she signs up to become a starship trooper, so does Johnny. They go through basic training led by an officer of the take-no-prisoners school (Michael Ironside) and then they're sent to fight the Bug. Until late in the movie, when things really get grim, Carmen wears a big wide bright smile in every single scene, as if posing for the cover of the novel. (Indeed, the whole look of the production design seems inspired by covers of the pulp space opera mags like *Amazing, Imagination,* and *Thrilling Wonder Stories*).

The action sequences are heavily laden with special effects, but curiously joyless. We get the idea right away: Bugs will jump up, troopers will fire countless rounds at them, the Bugs will impale troopers with their spiny giant legs, and finally dissolve in a spray of goo. Later there are refinements, like fire-breathing beetles, flying insects, and giant Bugs that erupt from the earth. All very elaborate, but the Bugs are not *interesting* in the way, say, that the villains in the *Alien* pictures were. Even their planets are boring; Bugs live on ugly rock worlds with no other living species, raising the question of what they eat.

Discussing the science of *Starship Troopers* is beside the point. Paul Verhoeven is facing in the other direction. He wants to depict the world of the future as it might have been visualized in the mind of a kid reading Heinlein in 1956. He faithfully represents Heinlein's militarism, his Big Brother state, and a value system in which the highest good is to kill a friend before the Bugs can eat him. The underlying ideas are the most interesting aspect of the film.

What's lacking is exhilaration and sheer entertainment. Unlike the *Star Wars* movies, which embraced a joyous vision and great comic invention, *Starship Troopers* doesn't resonate. It's one-dimensional. We smile at the satirical asides, but where's the warmth of human nature? The spark of genius or rebellion? If *Star Wars* is humanist, *Starship Troopers* is totalitarian.

Watching a film that largely consists of interchangeable characters firing machine guns at computer-generated Bugs, I was reminded of the experience of my friend McHugh. After obtaining his degree from Indiana University, he spent the summer in the employ of Acme Bug Control in Bloomington, Indiana. One hot summer day, while he was spraying insecticide under a home, a trapdoor opened above his head and a housewife offered him a glass of lemonade. He crawled up, filthy and sweaty, and as he drank the lemonade, the woman told her son, "Now Jimmy—you study your books, or you'll end up just like him!" I wanted to tell the troopers the same thing.

Stealing Beauty
(Directed by Bernardo Bertolucci; starring Liv Tyler; 1996)
I wait and wait so patiently.
I'm quiet as a cup . . .
I hope you'll come and rattle me . . .
Quick! come and wake me up!

This is one of several poems written by Lucy, the heroine of *Stealing Beauty,* as she drifts through an endless house party in Tuscany. I quote Lucy's poetry because I want to set you a test question. Reading it, how old would you guess Lucy is? Nine? Fourteen? The notion of being "quiet as a cup" is not bad. "Rattle me" is better than "drink from me." Those double exclamation points, however . . .

Pencils up. Lucy is nineteen. If this poetry seems unsophisticated for a worldly nineteen-year-old, you should read some of her other poems, which are superimposed on the screen in her own handwriting, and (I am afraid) her own spelling.

Lucy is a creature without an idea in her head. She has no conversation. No interests. No wit. She exists primarily to stir lust in the loins of the men. After the death of her mother, a poet who visited these Italian hills twenty years ago, Lucy has come back to an artists' home with two things on her mind: She wants to discover the identity of her real father, and she wants to lose her virginity. Experienced moviegoers can assess the risk that she will solve these problems simultaneously.

Stealing Beauty is the new film by Bernardo Bertolucci *(Last Tango in Paris, The Last Emperor),* who like many a middle-aged man before him has been struck dumb by the beauty of a nubile young girl, and has made the mistake of trying to approach her on what he thinks is her level. The movie plays like the kind of line a rich older guy would lay on a teenage model, suppressing his own intelligence and irony in order to spread out before her the wonderful world he would like to give her as a gift. Look at these hills! These sunsets! Smell the herbed air! See how the light catches the old rose-covered villa! The problem here is that many nineteen-year-old women, especially the beautiful international model types, would rather stain their teeth with cigarettes and go to discos with cretins on motorcycles than have all Tuscany as their sandbox. (For an example of a cannier May–December seduction strategy, consider *Nelly and Monsieur Arnaud,* in which an older man fascinates a young woman by emphasizing his age and experience and pretending to be beyond her charms.)

Lucy is played by Liv Tyler, a young actress who has been profiled in all the glossies by writers who find it delightful that she thought her father was one rock star when in fact he was another. Thus there is an "autobiographical" component to her search among the artistic layabouts at the Tuscan villa for the man who seduced her mother twenty years ago. Tyler is indeed attractive, and looks enough like Lili Taylor to be her sister. But Lili Taylor usually plays smart women, and if she were in this movie her B.S. Alarm would be ringing constantly.

The villa is occupied by a sculptor (Donal McCann), who starts on a tree trunk with a chain saw and is soon sand-papering the curve of Lucy's chin. His earth-mother wife (Sinead Cusack) is tired after twenty years of cooking and keeping house for a continual house party, and no wonder. The most interesting guest is a gay playwright (Jeremy Irons) who is dying of AIDS and attracts Lucy because he is not after her. Other guests include an art dealer (Jean Marais), an advice to the lovelorn expert (Stefania Sandrelli), a designer (Miranda Fox), and an entertainment lawyer (D. W. Moffet), who sighs, "I think it would be great, you know, to just sit around all day and express yourself." Neighbors drop in, including assorted young men, one of whom may have sent Lucy a letter that she thinks was romantic and poetic—as indeed anyone who writes like Lucy would.

The movie is great to look at. Like all those other Brits-in-Italy movies (*A Month at the Lake*, *Enchanted April*, *A Room with a View*), it makes you want to find this place and go there. In this case, however, you hope the movie characters have moved out before you get there. There is a simmer of discontent beneath the surface of everyday life in the villa, a sort of sullen, selfish unhappiness that everyone has about his or her lot in life.

The purpose of the Lucy character, I guess, is to act like a catalyst or a muse, shaking up old patterns and forcing these exiles to decide where their homes really are. She is fresh and they are decadent narcissists. Only the Jeremy Irons character, absorbed in his dying, and the Donal McCann character, absorbed in his art, have lives of any meaning.

The young men who buzz about Lucy are of no substance whatever. The older men are similar, but can make better conversation, which would be useful if there were any evidence that Lucy was a conversationalist. Actually she serves for Bertolucci more as a plot device than as a person. She represents some kind of ideal of perfect virgin beauty, and the film's opening shots, in which a photographer on a plane sees her sleeping and takes close-ups of her lips and crotch, set the tone. The sad thing is that, sleeping, she embodies what she represents to this movie just as well as when she's awake.

Stealing Home
(Directed by Steven Kampmann, Will Aldis; starring Mark Harmon, Jodie Foster; 1988)

The problem is possibly with me. I detested *Stealing Home* so much, from beginning to end, that I left the screening wondering if any movie could possibly be that bad. Never mind the hoots and catcalls from others in the preview audience; they had their own problems. I resolved to sit in a quiet place and run through the movie once again in my mind, trying to see through its paralyzing sincerity to the intelligence, if any, inside.

I was not successful. *Stealing Home* is a real squirmer, a movie so earnest and sincere and pathetic and dripping with pathos that it cries out to be satirized. The only way to save this movie would be with a new sound track with savagely cynical dialogue over the sappy images. This is one of those movies where the filmmakers remember the golden days of their adolescence, and are so overcome with emotion that they fail to recognize their memories as clichés learned from other movies. There is not a second in this film that seems inspired by real life, and since the film is plugged as the hero's autobiography, that's a fairly serious flaw.

The film stars Mark Harmon as a third-rate professional baseball player who is throwing his life away, one day, when he gets a call that Katie Chandler (Jodie Foster) is dead. When he was a kid, Katie was like an older sister to him, encouraging him to do his best while simultaneously tantalizing him with her rebellious spirit. He first met her when he was ten, and they spent carefree summers together on the Jersey shore while she shone like a beacon through his teenage years. But then they sort of drifted apart, and there were reports of a couple of unhappy marriages, and now she has committed suicide.

Why has she killed herself? The movie does not dignify that sensible question with an answer, and so I will supply one. Katie Chandler killed herself so that she could be cremated and her ashes could be used as a prop in this movie. She leaves a note saying that the ashes should be given to Billy Wyatt (the Harmon character), because he will know what to do with them. And sure enough, he does. He knows that he must return to a place where he and Katie shared a very special moment, and cast her ashes into the wind. He arrives at this conclusion several scenes after the audience does, but you can't really blame him; after all, we've seen these clichés before, and he apparently has not.

The movie is told in a lot of flashbacks, to when Billy was ten, and when he was sixteen, and when he was older, and when he did this, and when he did that, and a copy of the screenplay should be provided to anyone entering the theater, since the casting of the "young" versions of various characters is so confusing, and the flashbacks so inept, that it's a guessing game most of the time as to what we're watching, and why. Things are further complicated, unnecessarily, by the addition of a Best Friend character (played by Jonathan Silverman as a youth and Harold Ramis in the present), who has his own adolescent adventures, which get confused with Billy's.

A disproportionate amount of the film is devoted to the issue of whether one of these friends did, or did not, seduce the would-be prom date of the other one. I mention this because it is symptomatic of the film's general malaise. *Stealing Home* was cowritten and codirected by Steven Kampmann and Will Aldis, who based it on some of their own memories. Much of the film suffers from the "you shoulda been there" syndrome, in which scenes feel suspiciously like family legends that should have been left around the dinner table instead of being inflicted on us.

Movies like this possibly get talked into being by the confidence of the collaborators, who are so familiar with the material that they never pause to make it accessible, comprehensible, or interesting to the rest of us. Kampmann and Aldis labored for a time in the 1970s at Second City, and have been associated with such TV shows as *WKRP in Cincinnati* and *Mork and Mindy.* Did nothing in their previous experience tip them off that this film was KRP on the Jersey shore?

Stigmata

(Directed by Rupert Wainwright; starring Patricia Arquette, Gabriel Byrne; 1999)

Stigmata is possibly the funniest movie ever made about Catholicism—from a theological point of view. Mainstream audiences will view it as a lurid horror movie, an *Exorcist* wannabe, but for students of the teachings of the church, it offers endless goofiness. It confuses the phenomenon of stigmata with satanic possession, thinks stigmata can be transmitted by relics, and portrays the Vatican as a conspiracy against miracles.

The story: In Brazil, a holy priest has come into possession of a lost gospel "told in the words of Jesus himself." In the priest's church is a bleeding statue of the Virgin Mary. The Vatican dispatches a miracle-buster, Father Andrew (Gabriel Byrne) to investigate. "The blood is warm and human," he tells his superiors. He wants to crate up the statue and ship it to the Vatican for investigation, but is prevented. (One pictures a vast Vatican storehouse of screen windows and refrigerator doors bearing miraculous images.)

The old priest has died, and in the marketplace an American tourist buys his rosary and mails it as a souvenir to her daughter, Frankie (Patricia Arquette), who is a hairdresser in Pittsburgh. Soon after receiving the rosary, Frankie begins to exhibit the signs of the stigmata—bleeding wounds on the wrists, head, and ankles, where Christ was pierced on the cross. Father Andrew is again dispatched to investigate, reminding me of Illeana Douglas's priceless advice to her haunted brother in *Stir of Echoes:* "Find one of those young priests with smoldering good looks to sort of guide you through this."

The priest decides Frankie cannot have the stigmata, because she is not a believer: "It happens only to deeply religious people." Psychiatrists quiz her, to no avail ("Is there any stress in your life?" "I cut hair."). But alarming manifestations continue; Frankie bleeds, glass shatters, there are rumbles on the sound track, she has terrifying visions, and at one point she speaks to the priest in a deeply masculine voice, reminding us of nothing so much as Linda Blair in *The Exorcist.*

Now there's the problem. Linda Blair was possessed by an evil spirit. Frankie has been entered by the Holy Spirit. Instead of freaking out in nightclubs and getting blood all over her bathroom, she should be in some sort of religious ecstasy, like Lili Taylor in *Household Saints.* It is not a dark and fearsome thing to be bathed in the blood of the lamb.

It is also not possible, according to the very best church authorities, to catch the stigmata from a rosary. It is not a germ or a virus. It comes from within. If it didn't, you could cut up Padre Pio's bath towels and start your own blood drive. *Stigmata* does not know, or care, about the theology involved, and thus becomes peculiarly heretical by confusing the effects of being possessed by Jesus and by Beelzebub.

Meanwhile, back at the Vatican, the emotionally constipated Cardinal Houseman (Jonathan Pryce) rigidly opposes any notion that either the statue or Frankie actually bleeds. It's all a conspiracy, we learn, to suppress the gospel written in the actual words of Christ. The film, a storehouse of absurd theology, has the gall to end with one of those "factual" title cards, in which we learn that the "Gospel of St. Thomas," said to be in Christ's words, was denounced by the Vatican in 1945 as a "heresy." That doesn't mean it wouldn't be out in paperback if there was a market for it. It does mean the filmmakers have a shaky understanding of the difference between a heresy and a fake.

Does the film have redeeming moments? A few. Arquette is vulnerable and touching in an impossible role. I liked the idea of placing her character within a working-class world; there's a scene where one of the customers in the beauty shop resists having her hair treated by a woman with bleeding wrists. And Nia Long has fun with the role of Frankie's best friend; when your pal starts bleeding and hallucinating, it's obviously time for her to get out of the house and hit the clubs.

Stigmata has generated outrage in some Catholic circles. I don't know why. It provides a valuable recruiting service by suggesting to the masses that the church is the place to go for real miracles and supernatural manifestations. It is difficult to imagine this story involving a Unitarian. First get them in the door. Then start them on the Catechism.

The Story of Us
(Directed by Rob Reiner; starring Bruce Willis, Michelle Pfeiffer; 1999)
Rob Reiner's *The Story of Us* is a sad-sack movie about the misery of a married couple (Bruce Willis and Michelle Pfeiffer) who fight most of the time. Watching it is like taking a three-day trip on a Greyhound bus with the Bickersons. I leave it to you to guess whether the movie has a happy ending,

but what if it does? A movie like this is about what we endure while we're watching it, not about where it finally arrives.

Meet the Jordans, Ben and Katie. He's a TV comedy writer, she composes crossword puzzles. They have two kids, Erin and Josh. Their marriage is a war zone: "Argument has become the condition for conversation," he observes. They fake happiness for the kids. How did they arrive at such pain? It is hard to say; the movie consists of flashbacks to their fights, but their problems are so generic we can't put a finger on anything.

Gene Siskel used to ask if a movie was as good as a documentary of the same actors having lunch. Watching *The Story of Us,* I imagined a documentary of the marriage of, say, Bruce Willis and Demi Moore. I do not say that to score a cheap point, but because Moore and Willis are spirited and intelligent people who no doubt had interesting fights about real issues, and not insipid fights about sitcom issues.

Example. The movie wants to illustrate Poor Communication. It shows Pfeiffer at home, where the washing machine is spewing suds all over the room and the kids are fighting. Willis calls her from outside their old apartment building, which is being torn down. He tells her the wrecking ball has just taken out their bedroom. She doesn't pay attention. His feelings are hurt.

The Marriage Counselor is in: She should shout, "The washer just exploded!" And he should say, "Catch you later!" Another marriage saved. Oh, and if I were her I'd turn off the power to the washing machine.

The movie is filled with lame and contrived "colorful" dialogue. Reiner, who plays a friend of the husband, gives him a long explanation of why appearances deceive. "We do not possess butts," he says, "but merely fleshy parts at the top of our legs." Whoa! Later there is a restaurant scene in which Willis screams angrily in a unsuccessful (indeed, melancholy) attempt to rip off Meg Ryan's famous restaurant orgasm in Reiner's *When Harry Met Sally.* At the end of his tirade, Willis jumps up and tells Reiner what he can "shove up the tops of your legs!"

Doesn't work, because (a) he's too angry to think up or stop for a punch line, (b) the line isn't funny, and (c) the setup wasn't funny either, because the concept isn't funny. Oh, and the scene ends with Reiner doing a double-take directly into the camera. How many ways can one scene be mishandled?

Who thought this movie would be entertaining? The same person who thinks we need more dialogue about why guys do the wrong thing with rolls of toilet paper. And who thinks the misery of this film can be repaired by a showboat monologue at the end that's well delivered by Pfeiffer, but reads like an audition scene?

There is a famous short story about an unhappy couple, and about what happens when it comes time to tell their children they're getting a divorce. It is called *Separating,* by John Updike. Read it to understand how much *The Story of Us* does not reach for or even guess.

Striking Distance
(Directed by Rowdy Herrington; starring Bruce Willis,
Sarah Jessica Parker; 1993)
Striking Distance is an exhausted reassembly of bits and pieces from all the other movies that are more or less exactly like this one. The credits say "written by Rowdy Herrington and Martin Kaplan," but the right word would have been "anthologized." How does it recycle its betters? Let us count the ways:

1. It is about an outspoken Pittsburgh cop (Bruce Willis), who gets in trouble by testifying against his partner in a police brutality case.

2. A serial killer is at work in the city.

3. The cop and his dad, also a cop, are on their way to the policemen's ball when they get involved in a chase to capture the serial killer suspect, and the dad is killed.

4. "The killer must be a cop," Willis says on TV, because of the way the guy drives and thinks.

5. His uncle (Dennis Farina) is on the force, and so are two of his sons, Willis's cousins.

6. There is a scene on a bridge where Willis tries to talk one of the nephews out of leaping to his death. The dialogue is amazingly familiar.

7. Willis is demoted, and assigned to the River Rescue Squad, where he remains determined to catch the serial killer (who helpfully starts dumping bodies in the river where Willis can find them).

8. Willis is assigned a new partner (Sarah Jessica Parker). She is a woman. They don't get along at first. Then they fall in love. Four durable clichés in a row. Good going.

9. Suspicion falls on Willis: Perhaps he is the serial killer?

10. One nephew goes to California, and the killings stop. Then he returns from California, and the killings resume. As veterans of this genre, we know with a certainty that this nephew is not the killer.

And so on, and on, until the ending, which cheats, indicating that all the clues in the story were simply inserted to jerk us around.

I wouldn't really mind the clichés and the tired old material so much, if the filmmakers had brought energy or a sense of style to the material. A good singer can make an old song new. But *Striking Distance* seems unconvinced of its own worth. It's a tired, defeated picture, in which no one seems to love what they're doing, unless maybe it's a few of the character actors, like Farina and John Mahoney (as the dad), who have scenes they seem to relish.

Want to write a screenplay? Why not start with these elements: A rebel cop stirs up trouble and is disciplined, but determines to stay on the trail of a serial killer, while meanwhile he is assigned a partner that first he hates and then he likes, while the killer cleverly tries to frame him. Add several chase scenes and a deadly confrontation in which all of the key characters magically congregate at the same time.

Just because it's been done before doesn't mean it can't be done again. And better. Believe me.

Stuart Little

(Directed by Rob Minkoff; starring Geena Davis, Hugh Laurie; 1999)

Any other consideration about *Stuart Little* must take second place to the fact that it is about a nice family that adopts a mouse. Yes, a mouse, in all dimensions and particulars, albeit a mouse with a cute little sports coat and an earnest way of expressing himself in piping English. Stuart is about two inches long, maybe a little longer. Early in the film Smokey, the family cat, tries to eat him, but is forced to spit him up, damp but no worse for wear.

I once read the book by E. B. White on which this story is founded. The peculiar thing about the book is that Stuart, in the imagination of the reader, swells until he occupies as much psychic space as any of the other characters. He is a mouse, but his dialogue runs from margin to margin just like the words of the humans, and his needs and fears are as great. Our intelligence tells us Stuart is a mouse, but our imagination makes him into a full-size literary character.

In the book, Stuart works just fine as a character. But movies are an unforgivably literal medium, and the fact is, no live-action movie about Stuart Little can possibly work, *because he is so much smaller than everyone else!* Stuart is definitely a mouse. He is very, very small. There is something pathetic about a scene where his new parents (Geena Davis and Hugh Laurie) tuck him in at bedtime. It doesn't matter how much they love him or how happy he is to be in this new home; all we can think about is how he hardly needs even the hem of his blanket. All through the movie I kept cringing at the terrible things that could happen to the family's miniature son. It didn't help that a few days earlier I'd seen *The Green Mile* in which an equally cute and lovable mouse was stamped on by a sadist, and squished.

The movie of course puts Stuart through many adventures and confronts him with tragic misunderstandings. He is provided with a new wardrobe and a tiny red convertible sportster to race around in, and is chased through Central Park by hungry cats. That sort of thing.

My mind reeled back to last year's grotesque family "comedy" named *Jack Frost*. That was the film in which a family's father dies and is reincarnated as a snowman. Now that is an amazing thing. If your dad came back as a snowman after being dead for a year, what would you ask him? Perhaps, is there an afterlife? Or, what is heaven like? Or—why a snowman? But no sooner does the snowman in *Jack Frost* appear than it is harnessed to a desperately banal plot about snowball fights at the high school.

Stuart Little is not anywhere near as bad as *Jack Frost* (it is twice as good—two stars instead of one). But it has the same problem: The *fact* of its hero upstages anything the plot can possibly come up with. A two-inch talking humanoid mouse upstages roadsters, cats, little brothers, everything. I tried imagining a movie that would deal seriously and curiously with an intelligent and polite child that looked like a mouse. Such a movie would have to be codirected by Tim Burton and David Lynch.

I am reminded of the old man who finds a frog in the road. "Kiss me," says the frog," and I will turn into a beautiful princess." The man puts the frog in his pocket. "Didn't you hear my offer?" asks the frog in a muffled voice. "I heard it," the old man says, "but frankly, at my age, I'd rather have a talking frog." My guess is that the makers of *Stuart Little* might not understand the point of this story.

Switchblade Sisters

(Directed by Jack Hill; starring Robbie Lee, Joanne Nail; 1975)

> *Sooner or later, every girl's got to find out—the only thing a man's got below his belt is clay feet.*—Switchblade Sisters

Insights like that were big in the exploitation movies of the 1970s. The dialogue clanked along from one dumb profundity to another, and the sentiments were as pious as political speeches. One of the characters in *Switchblade Sisters* (1975) quotes approvingly from Mao's *Little Red Book,* although enlightenment among the sisters is not universal: After the leader of a boy gang rapes a new member of a girl gang, he asks, "You all right? You were asking for it." She is inclined to agree.

Switchblade Sisters is one of the countless films viewed by Quentin Tarantino during his now-legendary employment at Video Archives in Manhattan Beach, California (the store owner should get a finder's fee based on QT's subsequent career). Now Tarantino has started a division of Miramax named Rolling Thunder Pictures to rerelease some of his discoveries. After *Switchblade Sisters* we are promised *Mighty Peking Man* (1977), the 1964 Italian horror film *Blood and Black Lace,* and the 1973 blaxploitation epic *Detroit 9000.*

Exploitation films could be a lot of fun. The director of *Switchblade Sisters,* Jack Hill, directed sixteen of them, including two of my favorites, the Pam Grier films *Coffy* and *Foxy Brown.* His other titles included *Swinging Cheerleaders, The Big Bird Cage, Snake People, Blood Bath,* and *Spider Baby.* Often they were released more than once, under various titles; *Spider Baby* became *The Liver Eaters,* and *Switchblade Sisters* was also known as *The Jezebels* and *The Playgirl Gang.*

What made the Pam Grier pictures stand out from the others was Grier's own charisma; she was an authentic movie star, and even Hill's sleazy production values and slapdash photography and editing couldn't conceal her talent. The problem with *Switchblade Sisters* is that no one on screen is any better than the talent behind the camera. The movie is badly acted, written, and directed, and while I was watching it I realized that in some unexplained but happy way, the basic level of cinematic talent has improved in the past two decades.

Few new directors today could make a film this bad. Low budgets have nothing to do with it. Consider Robert Rodriguez (whose *El Mariachi* cost $8,000), Matty Rich (*Straight Out of Brooklyn,* $24,000), and Edward Burns

(*The Brothers McMullen,* $28,000). Despite their budgets, they are born filmmakers who know where to put a camera, how to write a script, how to cast and direct actors, and how to move things along. By contrast, *Switchblade Sisters* is a series of tableaux in which stiff actors are grouped in awkwardly composed shots to say things like "Freeze, greaseball!"

The greaseball, by the way, is a sadistic bill collector trying to collect $40 in back payments on a TV set owned by a tearful welfare mother in a building that is otherwise apparently occupied only by Switchblade Sisters. As he takes the elevator to the street, another Sister gets on at every floor (are they psychic, or did they phone ahead and plan the elevator ride?). When they reach the ground floor, the greaseball gets his tie cut off. Heavy.

The plot involves a girl gang named the Jezebels, which hangs out at a burger stand. Maggie (Joanne Nail), a new girl in the neighborhood, refuses to give her seat to Lace (Robbie Lee), the Jezebels' leader, and that leads to a fight but also to mutual respect. Soon Dominic (Asher Brauner), the leader of the Silver Blades, rapes Maggie—and since he is Lace's boyfriend, this leads to a certain tension.

One thing leads to another, as the script hurries from cliché to cliché. The Jezebels are thrown into jail, where they are mistreated by a lesbian warden before getting their revenge. Later there's a hilarious rumble in a roller rink— it's a shoot-out on skates with automatic weapons—that seems to leave dozens dead, although all but one of the key characters survives.

The movie is wallpapered with the slogans of the era. The cops are "pigs," the Black Power girl gang is the repository of revolutionary wisdom, there is solidarity between the girl gangs, and at some point we are astonished to be given the information that all of these characters are still in high school, and as juveniles cannot be tried for what seems like a citywide crime wave.

The only real reason for seeing *Switchblade Sisters* would be to condescend to it, to snicker at its badness. But there are degrees of bad, and this movie falls far below Pauline Kael's notion of "great trash." There is also some amusement to be had from the costumes: The mile-wide shirt collars, leather vests, and plaid pants on the men, and the hot pants and thigh boots on the women. But such pleasures are small. Should you actually pay money to see this movie at a time when *Welcome to the Dollhouse, The Rock, Nelly and Monsieur Arnaud, The Hunchback of Notre Dame,* and *I Shot Andy Warhol* are playing? I don't think so.

TTTTTTTTTTT

· ·

Tai-Pan
(Directed by Daryl Duke; starring Bryan Brown, Kyra Sedgwick; 1986)
Tai-Pan is the embodiment of those old movie posters where the title is hewn from solid rock and tiny figures scale it with cannons strapped to their backs, while the bosoms of their women heave in the foreground. It tells the saga of men who were larger than life, except for their brains, and of the women who loved them, lost them, left them, returned to them, double-crossed them, bore their children, oppressed their servants, and still found time to rend their hearts and their underwear.

The China Coast, 1842. The Chinese object, not unreasonably, to the British practice of buying opium from the Chinese and then selling it back to them for their silver. British warships are sent to pound the Chinese mainland, and then a treaty is signed giving England the right to operate Hong Kong as a free port.

But who will control Hong Kong? Will it be Dirk Struan, the lusty buc-caneer, or Tyler Brock, the sniveling cheat? Both are extraordinary men. For one thing, they do not age visibly during the several decades of their rivalry. The movie is a little cagey about its exact time span, but try to figure this out: Struan has two grown sons near the beginning of the story, and so he must be at least forty or even forty-five when the auction is held to sell the land on which Hong Kong will be built. And yet he is still fit enough to fight a duel in the midst of a raging hurricane after principal construction has been finished on the original city. The women also hold up remarkably well—better than the buildings, which fall down around everybody's ears in the stirring climax.

Struan (Bryan Brown) is the kind of man who never apologizes and never explains. He has a British wife who came out to Hong Kong, took one look around, and went back home forever, sending him a son as a memento. He has a Chinese mistress and a Chinese son (by an earlier mistress). Brock (John Stanton) has a son, too—a vicious torturer and killer. Both fathers hope their boys will grow up to inherit Hong Kong, and soon we are on the edge of our seats with suspense over who will prevail: Will it be the two noble heirs to a hero's blood, or the snot nose sadist?

Life in early Hong Kong seems to have centered on protracted boudoir scenes, interrupted by beauty contests, formal balls, sword fights, and stormy weather, with the occasional odd bit of perfunctory diplomacy. By my estimate, twice as much time is spent on the fancy-dress contest as on the negotiations over the opium trade.

Of the women of *Tai-Pan,* it can be said that Joan Collins could have played each and every one of them at some point in her career. My favorite is Mary Sinclair (Katy Behean), who comes out to Hong Kong as a simple English lass and, through pluck and dedication, becomes a successful prostitute, inspiring the immortal line, "You're not the Mary Sinclair I knew." Then there is May-May (Joan Chen), Brown's Chinese mistress, who will-will. Their most tender moment comes when she loses face with him and wants to commit suicide, and he helps her regain face by whipping her but not really hitting her very hard. You gotta love this guy.

The conflict in the movie centers on who will be the Tai-Pan, or British ruler, of Hong Kong. Brock buys up a lot of Struan's promissory notes to force him into bankruptcy, but Struan is able to raise the money in the nick of time through a loan from the industrious Sinclair, who is the kind of girl Marlene Dietrich had in mind when she observed that you don't get to be known as Shanghai Lil in one night.

Brock remains bitter over the years and vows that he will have his revenge, and that leads to the big sword fight during the hurricane. Then all is calm, and Struan observes that we are in the "eye of the hurricane." This must be some hurricane, because the eye alone lasts longer than some of the movie's whole decades, providing Struan with time to return home for the ending, which is romantic, glorious, tempest-tossed, tragic, and way overdue.

Teaching Mrs. Tingle

(Directed by Kevin Williamson; starring Helen Mirren, Marisa Coughlan; 1999)
Helen Mirren is a very good actress. All too good for *Teaching Mrs. Tingle,* where she creates a character so hateful and venomous that the same energy,

more usefully directed, could have generated a great Lady Macbeth. She is correct to believe that comic characters are best when played straight. They depend on the situation to make them funny. There is nothing funny about the situation in *Teaching Mrs. Tingle*.

The movie resembles *Election* in its attempt to deal with the dog-eat-dog world of ambitious high-school students, where grade points can make an enormous difference. But it lacks that movie's sly observations about human nature, and bludgeons the audience with broad, crude, creepy developments. Here is a movie that leaves us without anyone to like very much, and no one to care about. It was written and directed by Kevin Williamson, whose screenplays for the *Scream* pictures depend on comic slasher situations for their appeal; here, required to create more believable characters, he finds the wrong ones for this kind of story.

Katie Holmes stars as Leigh Ann Watson, an honor student only a few percentage points shy of becoming class valedictorian. Much depends on the grade she gets in history, a class that Mrs. Tingle (Mirren) rules with an iron fist and cruel sarcasm. She seems to take an almost erotic delight in humiliating her students in public, and singles out Leigh Ann for special ridicule, maybe just because she's smart and pretty.

Also in the picture: Jo Lynn Jordan (Marisa Coughlan), Leigh Ann's best friend; their classmate and friend, Luke Churner (Barry Watson), who combines the better qualities of slobs and oafs; and Trudie Tucker (Liz Stauber), who is Leigh Ann's bitter rival for valedictorian. Oh, and there's Michael McKean as the high school principal; Mrs. Tingle knows he's in AA and threatens to blackmail him for secret drinking. And Coach Wenchell (Jeffrey Tambor), whose relationship with Mrs. Tingle is reflected in his nickname, Spanky (in this case it is best spelled Spankee).

Leigh Ann turns in a history project in the form of a journal that might have been kept by a Pilgrim woman; it's leather-bound, with meticulous calligraphy and decorations, and would make the judges of the History Book Club weep with gratitude. Mrs. Tingle scornfully mocks it after only glancing at the front page. Later, she pounces on the three friends in the gym. Luke has stolen a copy of Mrs. Tingle's final exam, and stuffs it into Leigh Ann's backpack, where Mrs. Tingle finds it. Now Leigh Ann faces expulsion.

All of this serves as setup to the heart of the movie, which is spent with Mrs. Tingle tied to her bed while the three students desperately try to figure out what to do next. If this were a serious hostage or kidnapping movie, some of the resulting material might seem appropriate. Mirren approaches Mrs. Tingle like a prisoner of war in a serious film, playing mind games with her captors. There are scenes that are intended as farce (unexpected arrivals and phone calls), but they're flat and lifeless. We have no sympathy for Mrs. Tingle, but at least she has life, while the three students are simply constructions—walking, talking containers for the plot.

Is it possible that some high school students hate their teachers so much that they'll play along with *Teaching Mrs. Tingle*? I doubt it, because Mrs. Tingle isn't hateful in an entertaining way. She belongs in one of those anguished South American movies about political prisoners and their captors facing ethical dilemmas. And the kids belong in *Scream 3*.

Teenage Mutant Ninja Turtles II: The Secret of the Ooze
(Directed by Michael Pressman; starring Paige Turco; 1991)
I bent over backward to be fair to the first movie about the Teenage Mutant Turtles. It was, I wrote, "probably the best possible Teenage Mutant Ninja Turtle movie." Now we have the sequel, subtitled *The Secret of the Ooze*. I may not get what I want, but I get what I deserve.

Once again, here are the four superhero turtles, their friends Keno and April, their enemy the Shredder, his buddies the Foot Gang, and the maddening Turtle theme music, which sounds like an berserk merry-go-round. There is also a mad scientist, necessary to explain additional details about how the turtles got that way.

Kids like the turtles. A recent national survey reported that 95 percent of grade-school teachers could trace aggressive, antisocial classroom behavior to the Ninja Turtles—high praise. As someone who was raised on Superman, Batman, Spiderman, and Wonder Woman, I think the kids are getting the short end of the stick. What kind of a superhero is an amphibian who lives in sewers, is led by a rat, eats cold pizza, and is the product of radioactive waste? Is this some kind of a cosmic joke on the kids, robbing them of their birthright, a sense of wonder? Or is it simply an emblem of our drab and dreary times?

One disturbing thing about the turtles is that they look essentially the same. All that differentiates them, in the Nintendo game that gave them birth, is their weapons. It's as if the whole sum of a character's personality is expressed by the way he does violence. The turtles are an example of the hazards of individuality. They hang out together, act together, fight together, and have a dim collective IQ that expresses itself in phrases like "Cowabunga, dude."

This is the way insecure teenage boys sometimes talk in a group, as a way of creating solidarity, masking fears of inadequacy, and forming a collective personality that is stupider than any individual member of it. The way you attain status in the group is by using violence to defend it against outsiders. People raised on these principles run a risk of starring in videotapes of police brutality.

I liked the older superheroes better. The ones that stood out from a crowd, had their own opinions, were not afraid of ridicule, and symbolized a future of truth and justice. Superman represented democratic values. Today's kids are learning from the Turtles that the world is a sinkhole of radioactive waste, that it's more reassuring to huddle together in sewers than take your chances competing at street level, and that individuality is dangerous. Cowabunga.

The Tenant
(Directed by Roman Polanski; starring Roman Polanski, Shelley Winters, Melvyn Douglas; 1976)

Roman Polanski's *The Tenant* was the official French entry at Cannes last May, and in the riot to get into the press screening one man was thrown through a glass door and two more found themselves in the potted palms. It's a wonder nobody was killed in the rush to get out. *The Tenant* is not merely bad, it's an embarrassment. If it didn't have the Polanski trademark, we'd probably have to drive miles and miles and sit in a damp basement to see it.

Like *Last Tango in Paris,* it involves the apartment shortage in Paris. An earnest and shy young man (Polanski, very earnest and shy) applies for the apartment of a young woman who attempted suicide and is in the hospital. The woman dies and Polanski gets the apartment. It's in a tall, gloomy building inhabited by hateful, spiteful people who are always spying on each other. And it has a haunted bathroom; every time Polanski looks in through the bathroom window (which he does quite frequently), there's someone standing there motionless, looking straight back at him.

Polanski throws a modest little housewarming party, and all hell breaks loose. Every other tenant in the building complains about the noise. Indeed, every time Polanski moves a chair, shifts a cabinet, plays the radio, or even coughs, the people upstairs and downstairs start banging on the walls for quiet (it's here that the movie most closely approaches a horror story).

Polanski eventually decides that the building itself is malevolent, and the people in it are out to get him. He is wrong; actually, all they want is a little quiet. But Polanski is paranoid, and that's the movie's basic problem. If he thought he were paranoid but the people really were after him, then there'd be some nice fun in the tradition of no more than perhaps six dozen movies already this year. But because he really is paranoid, and we know he is, the movie's just a study of his downward spiral.

And what a spiral. He becomes convinced that the other tenants are trying to turn him into the woman who committed suicide. He puts on her clothes and makeup, and buys shoes and a wig. He convinces himself, at times, that he *is* the dead woman. In an ending that must rank among the most ridiculous ever fashioned for an allegedly reputable movie, he dresses in drag, hurls himself from the same window the former tenant used, fails to kill himself, climbs back upstairs, and throws himself out again.

There is then an ironic ending that will come as a complete surprise to anyone who has missed every episode of *Night Gallery* or the *CBS Mystery Theater.* It turns out that—but never mind, never mind. It's been a long time since I've heard an audience talk back to the ending of a horror film. *The Tenant* might have made a decent little twenty-minute sketch for one of those British horror anthology films in which Christopher Lee, Peter Cushing, and Vincent Price pick up a little loose change. As a film by Polanski, it's unspeakably disappointing.

The Thing with Two Heads

(Directed by Lee Frost; starring Ray Milland, Roosevelt Grier; 1972)
What a heck of a thing to happen to a guy. He's a black man, convicted of murder and unable to persuade anyone of his innocence. He's sentenced to the

electric chair (apparently because the Supreme Court's jurisdiction doesn't include American International Pictures). He's willing to do anything to get another chance at life, so he volunteers for a weird medical experiment. The next thing he knows, he has Ray Milland's head parked alongside his left ear. This leads us to a philosophical point: Is it better to be alive with Ray Milland's head plugged into your neck, or to be dead?

Most of us would probably take Ray Milland, I guess. It's not often you get to meet a real movie star. But Roosevelt Grier, who plays the escaped convict, doesn't have such an easy choice.

The problem is that Ray Milland is an evil scientist who dreamed up the head transplant in order to ditch his old body because he was having a lot of trouble with arthritis. His sinister plan is to wait until his head grows on—and then cut Roosevelt Grier's head off! Not only that, but Milland is a racist with a line of lousy cracks about watermelon for dessert.

Some days you just can't win. It's bad enough to try to work with a veteran actor breathing down your back—but in your ear?

The most incredible thing in *The Thing with Two Heads* is not the head transplant, however, but what happens next. Within hours after Milland's head has been screwed on, the two-headed escapee is on a motorcycle and being chased by no less than fourteen police cars. Every one of them is destroyed during the chase, a process that takes so long that seven, or even five, squad cars might have been enough.

The publicity for the movie warns against the possibility of "apoplectic strokes, cerebral hemorrhages, cardiac seizures, or fainting spells" during the movie, but they're just trying to make themselves look good.

A Thousand Acres

(Directed by Jocelyn Moorhouse; starring Jason Robards, Michelle Pfeiffer, Jessica Lange, Jennifer Jason Leigh; 1997)

A Thousand Acres is an ungainly, undigested assembly of "women's issues" milling about within a half-baked retread of *King Lear*. The film is so unfocused that at the end of its very long 104 minutes I was unable to say who I was supposed to like and who I was supposed to hate—although I could name several characters for whom I had no feelings at all.

The movie is set on the thousand-acre Cook farm in Iowa, where the weathered and wise old patriarch Larry (Jason Robards) is the most powerful farmer for miles around. Then he announces he has decided to retire, and to divide his farm into three parts, giving shares to each of his daughters.

That's fine with Rose (Michelle Pfeiffer) and Ginny (Jessica Lange), who are married farm women—but Larry's youngest and most favored daughter, Caroline (Jennifer Jason Leigh), a lawyer, questions the wisdom of the plan. Larry instantly disowns her and later slams a door in her face, and as the other two daughters and their husbands begin running the farm, we figure it's only a matter of time until old Larry is out there in a raging storm, cursing the heavens.

We are correct, but *A Thousand Acres* wants only to borrow plot elements of *King Lear,* not to face up to its essentials. We are denied even the old man's heartbreaking deathbed scene—that goes to one of the daughters, after her second bout with breast cancer. The movie repeats the currently fashionable pattern in which men are bad and fathers are the most evil of all; there is not a single positive male character in the movie, unless you count the preacher who says grace before the church supper.

The husbands of the two older daughters, indeed, are written so thinly that when one of them (Kevin Anderson) kills himself, we're not sure why (until it's belatedly explained) and don't much care, and when the other (Keith Carradine) goes off to Texas to work on a hog farm, his wife scarcely seems to notice he's gone. Along the way, in a development so badly handled it seems to belong in another movie, Caroline gets married in Des Moines and lets her sisters find out about it only through a wedding announcement in the local weekly; as nearly as I can recall, we never meet her husband, nor is he ever referred to again.

All white male patriarchs must be guilty of something in modern women's fiction, preferably the sexual abuse of their children, and I was not surprised to find out that Larry visited the bedrooms of Rose and Ginny. Rose describes the visits in lurid detail, but Ginny cannot remember, although they took place as late as her sixteenth year; her memory lapse, I think, serves to prolong the breathless scenes of description. ("Daddy might be a drinker and a rager," Ginny says, "but he goes to church!") The youngest daughter was apparently not molested, maybe because (in the movie's laborious *Lear* parallels) she was the most favored.

Among the other subjects dutifully ticked off are a husband's rejection of his wife after she has a mastectomy; a woman who has five miscarriages because no one told her the local drinking water was poisoned with pesticides; the alcoholism of the father and one of the husbands; the inadequate sexual performance of both husbands; the betrayal of Rose and Ginny by a handsome neighbor man (Colin Firth), who is such a cad he sleeps with both of them but only tells one about the other; and a man who buys a tractor that is three times bigger than he needs—a clear case of phallic compensation. Toward the end we get the tragedy of Alzheimer's, the heartlessness of banks, the problem of unnecessary lawsuits, and the obligatory "giant agricultural conglomerate."

All of these subjects are valid and promising and could be well handled in a better movie. In *A Thousand Acres,* alas, they seem like items on a checklist. The movie is so distracted by both the issues and the *Lear* parallels that the characters bolt from one knee-jerk situation to the next.

Then there is the problem of where to place our sympathy. In *King Lear,* of course, we love Lear and his daughter Cordelia, and hate the two older sisters and their husbands. In *A Thousand Acres* it cannot be permitted for a man to be loved or a woman to be hated, and so we have the curious spectacle of the two older sisters being portrayed as somehow favorably unfavorable, while the youngest, by eventually siding with her father, becomes a study in tortured plotting: She is good because a woman, suspect because a lawyer, bad because she sues the others, forgiven because her father evolves from monstrous to merely pathetic. Many of the closing scenes are set in a courtroom, providing the curious experience of a movie legal case in which the audience neither understands the issues nor cares which side wins.

The movie is narrated by Ginny, the Lange character, apparently in an effort to impose a point of view where none exists. But why Ginny? Is she better than the others? At the end of the film she intones, in a solemn voice-over, "I've often thought that the death of a parent is the one misfortune for which there is no compensation." Say what? She doesn't remember her mother and is more than reconciled to the death of a father who (thanks to recovered memory) she now knows molested her. What compensation could she hope for, short of stealing him from his deathbed to hang him on a gallows?

A Thousand Acres is so misconceived it should almost be seen just to appreciate the winding road it travels through sexual politics. Many of the individual scenes are well acted (Michelle Pfeiffer and Jessica Lange are luminous in their three most important scenes together). But the film substitutes prejudices for ideas, formula feminism for character studies, and a signposted plot for a well-told story. The screenplay is based on a novel by Jane Smiley, unread by me, which won the Pulitzer Prize—which means that either the novel or the prize has been done a great injustice.

Three to Tango
(Directed by Damon Santostefano; starring Neve Campbell, Matthew Perry; 1999)

Neve Campbell is amazingly cute. I have admired her in other movies, but now, in *Three to Tango,* which gave me nothing else to think about, I was free to observe her intently. She has wide, intelligent eyes, kissable lips, and a face both sweet and carnal, like Doris Day's. I support her decision to never wear any garment that comes within a foot of her neck.

In *Three to Tango* she is mired in a plot of such stupidity that there is only one thing to do, and that is to look at her. In her more erotic moments she twinkles with enjoyment at her own naughtiness; consider a scene where she slithers in a bubble bath and describes a lesbian flirtation with her Brazilian roommate in college. She's having as much fun with this dialogue as we are.

She's telling the story to a character named Oscar (Matthew Perry), who she thinks is gay. It's all a misunderstanding. Oscar and his business partner Peter (Oliver Platt), who *is* gay, are architects who desperately need a $90 million commission from a rich Chicago builder (Dylan McDermott). The builder is a married man and the Neve Campbell character, named Amy, is his mistress. He assigns Oscar to "keep an eye" on Amy, assuming that Oscar is safe because gay.

Why does everyone think Oscar is gay? Because this is an Idiot Plot, in which no one ever says what obviously must be said to clear up the confusion. That's because they want that commission. We see a model for their $90 million project, which resembles the Lincoln Park Conservatory in the eighth month of its pregnancy.

Of course Oscar and Amy fall in love. And what a Meet Cute they have! On their first evening together, they go out for the evening, their taxi explodes (yes, explodes), and they run in the rain and wade in the mud and find a restaurant where they eat tuna melts that make them sick, and they run outside and hurl. This is the Meet Cute as Meet Puke. And on the same date she manages to cause Oscar incredible pain with a sharp door handle to his netherlands. No movie like this is complete without male pattern bruising.

Only about a week after first being considered gay, Oscar is named Gay Man of the Year. It's like they're waiting outside the closet with his trophy. He can't decline the honor because he wants the commission. But then, at the awards banquet, a door in the back opens and Amy walks in. (This is the old Dramatic Late-Arriving Person Who Means Everything to the Speaker Ploy.) Looking into her wide, intelligent eyes, cunningly placed eighteen inches above her wide, intelligent breasts, Oscar blurts out the truth: "I am not gay!" Then we hear the Slowly Gathering Ovation (one brave man stands up and starts to clap slowly, others follow, applause builds to crescendo).

I was wondering how easily the Gay Man of the Year could get a standing ovation for announcing at the awards banquet that he was not gay, but my question was answered in the end credits. Although skyline shots and one early scene create the impression that the movie was made in Chicago, it was actually shot in Toronto. Those Canadians are just so doggone supportive.

This review would not be complete without mention of a scene where Oscar grows distraught and runs through the streets of Chinatown. As he approaches the camera, several Peking ducks, or maybe they are only chickens, are thrown at him from offscreen. Why? Why, indeed. Why, oh why.

Tidal Wave

(Director uncredited; starring Andrew Meyer; 1975)

Bad movies are really getting awful these days. It seems like only yesterday we were savoring bombs like *The Vengeance of She* and *Godzilla vs. the Smog Monster*—movies so terrible they achieved a sort of greatness. Movies in which there were lines like "I have waited 3,000 years for this day" and newspaper reporters who let their voices trail off at the end of declarations like: "But, doctor, if your predictions are correct, this means the end of civilization on Earth. . . ."

I was hoping *Tidal Wave* would be a movie like that. When the publicity photographs arrived in the mail a few weeks ago, I was heartened by the sight of the staples holding together the cardboard skyscrapers: Here was a movie with real lack of promise! It even looked like a good bet to outflank *King Kong vs. Godzilla*. (What happened in that one, as I recall, is that King Kong lost and is currently trying to promote a bout with the Smog Monster, to establish himself as a contender once again.) But *Tidal Wave* let me down. It is purely and simply a wretched failure, a feeble attempt to paste together inept special effects (filmed in Japan) and Lorne Greene (filmed in America— to his everlasting regret, I'll bet).

The story involves ominous happenings along the Japan Trench, a vast underwater geological feature which, when it's viewed from a submarine, looks suspiciously like mud being stirred up by a garden hose. Japanese scientists regard it with horror, and no wonder: Their computers inform them all the Japanese islands will soon sink into the trench, with the possible loss of more than 100 million lives (under the circumstances, the title *Tidal Wave* becomes the understatement of the season).

This would, of course, be a great catastrophe, something the people in the movie are constantly assuring each other: "What a great catastrophe," they intone. Cut to the United Nations, where poor Lorne Greene is addressing the world's governments on plans to bail out the Japanese. There is, he observes, a certain degree of technological difficulty involved in an air and sea rescue effort involving 100 million people—but this is a catastrophe that threatens not just Japan, you understand, but all Earth's nations, since who knows what will slide into the Japan Trench next?

There's the obligatory love story, involving a scientist whose girlfriend makes a last-minute dash up Mt. Fujiyama and is trapped in a phone booth, where she calls him and makes plans, rather optimistically, I thought, to meet him in Geneva, Switzerland, when all of this is over. There are also people in boats who drift hither and yon before being swamped by tidal waves that look suspiciously like regular waves shot from a very low position with a wide-angle lens. The movie never ends, but if you wait long enough it gets to a point where it's over.

'Til There Was You

(Directed by Scott Winant; starring Sarah Jessica Parker, Jeanne Triplehorn; 1997)

Here is the most tiresome and affected movie in many a moon, a 114-minute demonstration of the Idiot Plot, in which everything could be solved with a few well-chosen words which are never spoken. The underlying story is a simple one: A man and a woman who are obviously intended for one another are kept apart for an entire movie, only to meet at the end. We're supposed to be pleased when they get together, I guess, although the movie ends with such unseemly haste that we never get to experience them as a couple.

'Til There Was You, directed by Scott Winant with a screenplay by Winnie Holzman, plays like half-digested remnants of a dozen fictional meals. We have flashbacks to the love stories of parents, college love affairs, shocking revelations about sexuality and parentage, a maladjusted former sitcom star, an architect who is a "perfectionist with low self-esteem," a ghostwriter who falls in love with a colorful old apartment building, not one but two colorful old ladies who stick to their guns, a restaurant that's an architectural nightmare, zoning hearings, bad poetry, endlessly falling rose petals, chain-smoking, gays in the closet, traffic accidents, and at the end of it all we have the frustration of knowing that 114 minutes of our lives have been wasted, never to be returned.

Oh, and we have disastrous casting decisions. I find it helpful, as a general rule, to be able to tell the characters in a movie apart. Several of the characters in this film (a gay college professor, an architect, and another guy) look so much alike I was forever getting them confused. They were all sort of would-be Pierce Brosnan clones. Since the plot depends on coincidental meetings (and close misses) involving people who should know each other but don't, and people who do know each other but shouldn't, the look-alikes grow even more confusing. The casting director no doubt thought that since several of the leads have appeared on TV sitcoms, the audience would recognize them and not be distracted by superficial physical similarities. Sorry.

The plot: A former sitcom star (Sarah Jessica Parker) owns a wonderful old apartment complex that has been earmarked for replacement by a condo. She begins to date the architect (Dylan McDermott) who will design the condo. His hero is an old lady architect (Nina Foch) who is apparently the Frank Lloyd Wright of her generation. She designed the colorful old apartment complex, but he doesn't know that. (How likely is it that an architect would be unfamiliar with one of his famous mentor's key buildings in the city where he lives? Not very.)

Meanwhile, a ghostwriter (Jeanne Tripplehorn) is hired by the sitcom star to write her autobiography. The ghostwriter and the architect met when they were children at summer camp. They are destined to meet again, but keep missing each other by inches or minutes. Some of their near-misses take place in a restaurant the architect designed.

This restaurant, of frightening ugliness, seems designed to keep personal-injury lawyers in work. When Tripplehorn enters it for the first time, she can't get the door open. Then it flies open and she staggers across the entire room and bangs into something. Later, she beans herself on a low-flying sculpture, trips over a waiter, catches her heel in the floor, falls over a chair, etc. Did she train for a Three Stooges movie?

All of the movie's heartfelt scenes are tangential. They involve major characters talking to minor ones instead of to each other. There is the heartfelt talk between the architect and his mentor. The heartfelt talk between the ghostwriter and a dotty old lady (Gwen Verdon) who lives in the colorful old building (which the writer staggered into after a coincidental car crash). There is the heartfelt talk between the writer and her old father, who tells her the childhood legends the movie began with were all fiction. There is the heartfelt love scene between the writer and her college professor, who is later revealed to be gay, and then disappears from the movie just when we thought the story would be about him.

Many details are just plain wrong. Since the Tripplehorn character is a literature student, we expect her to be a fairly sophisticated writer. Yet when we hear one of her poems read (after it accidentally sticks to the bottom of an architectural model thrown out of a window—but never mind), it turns out to be written in rhyming couplets of the sort found beneath the needlework column in women's craft magazines. All of the characters smoke unpleasantly, and want to stop, and one of the movie's near-misses, where the predestined lovers almost meet, is an "N.A." meeting, which is described as "Nicotine Anonymous." Warning: Before dropping "N.A." into your conversation, be aware that most people think it stands for something else.

And what about those rose petals? Or lilac petals, or whatever they are? The courtyard of the colorful old building, we can clearly see, has no foliage above it. Yet petals drift down in endless profusion for days and weeks during every scene—so many, I sat through the end credits in the futile hope there would be mention of the Petal Dropper.

All comes together at the end. Landmarks are saved, hearts are mended, long-deferred love is realized, coincidences are explained, the past is healed, the future is assured, the movie is over. I liked the last part the best.

The Tin Drum
(Directed by Volker Schlondorff; starring David Bennent, Mario Adorf; 1979)
Allegories have trouble standing for something else if they are too convincing as themselves. That is the difficulty with *The Tin Drum,* which is either (a) an allegory about one person's protest against the inhumanity of the world, or (b) the story of an obnoxious little boy.

The movie invites us to see the world through the eyes of little Oskar, who on his third birthday refuses to do any more growing up because the world is such a cruel place. My problem is that I kept seeing Oskar not as a symbol of courage but as an unsavory brat; the film's foreground obscured its larger meaning.

So what does that make me? An anti-intellectual philistine? I hope not. But if it does, that's better than caving in to the tumult of publicity and praise for *The Tin Drum,* which has shared the Grand Prix at Cannes (with *Apocalypse Now*) and won the Academy Award as Best Foreign Film, and is hailed on all fronts for its brave stand against war and nationalism and in favor of the innocence of childhood.

Actually, I don't think little Oskar is at all innocent in this film; a malevolence seems to burn from his eyes, and he's compromised in his rejection of the world's evil by his own behavior as the most spiteful, egocentric, cold, and calculating character in the film (all right: except for Adolf Hitler).

The film has been adapted by the West German filmmaker Volker Schlondorff from the 1959 novel by Günter Grass, who helped with the screenplay. It chronicles the career of little Oskar, who narrates his own life story starting with his mother's conception in a potato patch. Oskar is born into a world divided: In the years after World War I, both Germans and Poles live in the state of Danzig, where they get along about as well as Catholics and Protestants in Belfast.

Oskar has fathers of both nationalities (for reasons too complicated to explain here), and he is not amused by the nationalistic chauvinism he sees around him. So, on his third birthday, he reaches a conscious decision to stop growing. He provides a plausible explanation for his decision by falling down the basement stairs. And for the rest of the movie he remains arrested in growth: a solemn-faced, beady-eyed little tyke who never goes anywhere without a tin drum that he beats on incessantly. For his other trick, he can scream so loudly that he shatters glass.

There is a scene in which Oskar's drum so confuses a Nazi marching band that it switches from a Nazi hymn to "The Blue Danube." The crashing obviousness of this scene aside, I must confess that the symbolism of the drum failed to involve me.

And here we are at the central problem of the movie: Should I, as a member of the audience, decide to take the drum as, say, a child's toy protest against the marching cadences of the German armies? Or should I allow myself to be annoyed by the child's obnoxious habit of banging on it whenever something's not to his liking? Even if I buy the wretched Drum as a Moral Symbol, I'm still stuck with the kid as a pious little bastard.

But what about the other people in the movie? Oskar is right at the middle of the tug-of-war over Danzig and, by implication, over Europe. People are choosing up sides between the Poles and the Nazis. Meanwhile, all around him, adult duplicity is a way of life. Oskar's mother, for example, sneaks away on Thursday afternoons for an illicit sexual interlude. Oskar interrupts her dalliance with a scream that supplies work for half the glassmakers in Danzig. Does this make him a socialist or an Oedipus?

Soon after, he finds himself on the road with a troupe of performing midgets. He shatters glasses on cue, marches around in uniform, and listens as the troupe's leader explains that little people have to stay in the spotlight or big people will run the show. This idea is the last Oskar needs to have implanted in his mind.

The movie juxtaposes Oskar's one-man protest with the horror of World War II. But I am not sure what the juxtaposition means. Did I miss everything? I've obviously taken the story on a literal level, but I don't think that means I misread the film as it stands.

If we come in armed with the Grass novel and a sheaf of reviews, it's maybe just possible to discipline ourselves to view *The Tin Drum* as a solemn allegorical statement. But if we take the chance of just watching what's on the screen, Schlondorff never makes the connection. We're stuck with this cretinous little kid, just when Europe has enough troubles of its own.

T.N.T. Jackson

(Directed by Cirio H. Santiago; starring Jeanne Bell; 1975)
You remember the story about John Carter of Mars. He was Edgar Rice Burroughs's hero, and he galloped all over Mars on whatever passed for a horse up there. One day he was attacked and chased by a band of villains who started hacking at him with their swords.

Carter of Mars drew his own trusty blade and started hacking back at them, while trying to make it up the castle stairs. But they were too much for him. First he lost a leg. Then an arm. They were gaining on him. "The hell with this," said John Carter, throwing away his sword, drawing his atomic ray gun and zapping the bad guys into a radioactive ash heap.

I think about that story every time I see a Kung Fu movie, because Kung Fu movies depend on the same unwritten rules as John Carter novels: Nobody can have a gun. If they had a gun, they'd just shoot you, and you wouldn't get to go through the whole "aaaaaiiiiieeeee" number and leap about with your fists flashing, your foot cocked, and your elbow of death savagely bent. It's great to have a black belt, but it's better if the bad guys know the rules.

They do in *T.N.T. Jackson,* which is easily the worst movie I've seen this year (yes, worse, far worse, than *Rape Squad*). And so we get all the obligatory postures, all the menacing glares, and especially all the slow-motion leaps through the air. At the end, so great is the heroine's wrath that she propels her fingers of vengeance all the way through the villain, who looks mighty surprised at that, let me tell you.

One of the little problems with *T.N.T. Jackson,* alas, is that the Kung Fu fight scenes have been so loosely staged you can easily see the fighters aren't even touching each other. This results in some curious moments, as when the heroine thrusts her foot *at* a bad guy, who recoils violently, though he wasn't even touched. Maybe what she needs is some Dr. Scholl's deodorant powder?

The movie's about a drug-smuggling ring in Asia. T.N.T. Jackson (played by Jeanne Bell) is teamed up with one of the smugglers (Stan Shaw) and is also searching for the killer of her brother. That's not just the plot summary, it's the plot. There are innumerable badly staged fights, a confrontation with a U.S. government agent (Pat Anderson in U.S. government-issue bikinis), lots of idle threats, and the quaint notion that T.N.T. Jackson fights better when nude and in the dark.

This leads to a scene in which, after her clothes have been ripped off, she gets into a fierce battle for control of the light switch. She turns off the lights and demolishes three bad guys. The villain turns the lights back on. She turns them off. He turns them on, etc. I began mentally composing a screenplay for *Young Tom Edison Meets the Savage Sisters*.

Turbulence

(Directed by Robert Butler; starring Ray Liotta, Catherine Hicks; 1997)
Turbulence thrashes about like a formula action picture that has stepped on a live wire: It's dead, but doesn't stop moving. It looks like it cost a lot of money, but none of that money went into quality. It's schlock, hurled at the screen in expensive gobs.

The plot involves an endangered 747 flight from New York to Los Angeles. It's Christmas Eve, and there are only about a dozen passengers on board, including two prisoners and their federal marshals (anyone who has flown around Christmastime knows how empty the planes always are). One prisoner gets a gun and shoots some of the marshals, after which the other prisoner—the really dangerous one—gets a gun and kills the rest, including both pilots and one flight attendant. He locks the remaining hostages in the "crew quarters," where they are forgotten for most of the picture.

This prisoner is Ryan Weaver (Ray Liotta), a.k.a. the Lonely Hearts Killer. He claims the evidence against him was faked by an LA cop (Hector Elizondo). In a performance that seems like an anthology of possible acting choices, Liotta goes from charmer to intelligent negotiator to berserk slasher to demented madman. My favorite moment is when he's covered with blood, the plane is buckling through a Level 6 storm, bodies are littered everywhere, and he's singing "Buffalo Gals, Won't You Come Out Tonight?"

This is one of those movies where you keep asking questions. Questions like, how much money does an airline lose by flying a 747 from New York to

LA with a dozen passengers on board? Like, do passengers board 747s from the rear door? Like, can a 747 fly upsidedown? Like, have you ever seen Christmas decorations inside an airplane (lights and wreaths and bows and mistletoe)? Like, why don't the oxygen masks drop down automatically when the cabin depressurizes—and why do they drop down later, during a fire? Like, do storms reach as high as the cruising altitude of a transcontinental flight?

The big conflict involves the Lonely Hearts Killer and two flight attendants. One of them (Catherine Hicks) is strangled fairly early. The other (Lauren Holly) wages a heroic fight after both pilots are killed. It's up to her to fend off the madman and somehow land the big plane. Holly's performance is key to the movie, and it's not very good: She screams a lot and keeps shouting "Ooohhh!" but doesn't generate much charisma, and frankly I wish the killer had strangled her and left the more likable Hicks to land the plane.

The 747 spends much time weathering a big storm. ("It's a Level 6!" "Is that on a scale of 1 to 10?" "No! It's on a scale of 1 to 6!") The storm causes all of the lights inside the plane to flash on and off, including the Christmas lights. That lends to extended sequences in which the attendant and the madman crawl around the aisles in darkness illuminated by lightning bolts—and then there's the big moment when the plane flies upside down and they get to crawl on the ceiling.

On the ground, events are monitored in the Los Angeles control tower. The pilot of another 747 (Ben Cross) talks the brave attendant through the landing procedure, while a stern FBI agent argues that the plane should be shot down by the air force before it crashes in an inhabited area. Eventually he orders a fighter plane to fire—although by then the plane is already over Los Angeles and looks as if it would crash more or less into Disneyland.

There are more questions. Like, if a 747 sheers off the roof of a high-rise restaurant, wouldn't that cause it to crash? Like, if a 747 plows through an outdoor billboard, wouldn't that cause it to crash? Like, if it sweeps all the cars off the roof of a parking garage, wouldn't that cause it to crash? Like, if it gets a truck caught in its landing gear, what would happen then? ("It's a Ford!" a sharp-eyed observer says, in a line that—for once—I don't think represents product placement.)

Oh, yes, there are many moments I will long remember from *Turbulence*. But one stands out. After Lauren Holly outsmarts and outfights the berserk killer and pilots the plane through a Level 6 storm, the FBI guy still doubts she can land it. "She's only a stewardess," he says. To which the female air traffic controller standing next to him snaps, "She's a—flight attendant!"

20 Dates

(Directed by Myles Berkowitz; starring Myles Berkowitz, Elisabeth Wagner; 1999)

20 Dates tells the story of Myles Berkowitz, a man who wants to make a film and to fall in love. These areas are his "two greatest failures, professional and personal," so he decides to make a film about going out on twenty dates. By the end of the film he has won the love of the lovely Elisabeth—maybe—but his professional life is obviously still a failure.

The film has the obnoxious tone of a boring home movie narrated by a guy shouting in your ear. We learn how he gets a $60,000 investment from a man named Elie Samaha and uses it to hire a cameraman and a sound man to follow him around on his dates. Elie is never seen on film, but is taped with an (allegedly) hidden recorder while he threatens Berkowitz, complains about the quality of the footage, and insists on sex, stars—and a scene with Tia Carrere.

Elie has a point. Even though $60,000 is a low budget, you can't exactly see the money up there on the screen. I've seen features shot for half as much that were more impressive. What's worse is that Berkowitz loses our trust early in the film, and never regains it. I don't know how much of this film is real, if any of it is. Some scenes are admittedly staged, and others feel that way.

Even though Berkowitz presumably displays himself in his best light, I couldn't find a moment when he said anything of charm or interest to one of his dates. He's surprised when one woman is offended to learn she's being photographed with a hidden camera, and when another one delivers an (unseen) hand wound that requires twenty stitches. The movie's best dialogue is: "I could have sworn that Karen and I had fallen in love. And now, it's never to be, because I couldn't ever get close to her—at least not closer than ninety feet, which was specified in the restraining order."

One of his dates, Stephanie, is a Hollywood wardrobe mistress. He asks her for free costumes for his movie (if it's a doc, why does it need costumes?).

She leaves for the rest room, "and I never saw her again." Distraught, he consults Robert McKay, a writing teacher, and McKay gives him theories about screen romance that are irrelevant, of course, to an allegedly true-life documentary.

And what about Elie? He sounds unpleasant, vulgar, and tasteless (although no more so than many Hollywood producers). But why are we shown the outside of the county jail during his last conversation? Is he inside? What for? He promises to supply Tia Carrere, who indeed turns up in the film, describing Elie as a "very good friend." She may want to change her number.

There's a 1996 film available on video named *Me and My Matchmaker,* by Mark Wexler, about a filmmaker who consults a matchmaker and goes on dates that he films himself. It is incomparably more entertaining, funny, professional, absorbing, honest, revealing, surprising, and convincing than *20 Dates.* It works wonderfully to demonstrate just how incompetent and annoying *20 Dates* really is.

200 Cigarettes

(Directed by Risa Bramon Garcia; starring Christina Ricci, Courtney Love; 1999)

All those cigarettes, and nobody knows how to smoke. Everybody in *200 Cigarettes* smokes nearly all the time, but none of them show any style or flair with their cigarettes. And the cinematographer doesn't know how to light smoke so it looks great.

He should have studied *Out of the Past* (1947), the greatest cigarette-smoking movie of all time. The trick, as demonstrated by Jacques Tourneur and his cameraman, Nicholas Musuraca, is to throw a lot of light into the empty space where the characters are going to exhale. When they do, they produce great white clouds of smoke, which express their moods, their personalities, and their energy levels. There were guns in *Out of the Past,* but the real hostility came when Robert Mitchum and Kirk Douglas smoked at each other.

The cast of *200 Cigarettes* reads like a roll call of hot talent. They're the kinds of young stars who are on lots of magazine covers and have Web pages devoted to them, and so they know they will live forever and are immune to the diseases of smoking. I wish them well. But if they must smoke in the movies, can't they at least be great smokers, like my mother was? When she was smoking you always knew exactly how she felt, because of the way she used her cigarette and her hands and the smoke itself as a prop to help her express herself. She should have been good; she learned from Bette Davis movies.

The stars of *200 Cigarettes,* on the other hand, belong to the suck-and-blow school of smokeology. They inhale, not too deeply, and exhale, not too convincingly, and they squint in their close-ups while smoke curls up from below the screen. Their smoke emerges as small, pale, noxious gray clouds. When Robert Mitchum exhaled at a guy, the guy ducked out of the way.

I suppose there will be someone who counts the cigarettes in *200 Cigarettes,* to see if there are actually 200. That will at least be something to do during the movie, which is a lame and labored conceit about an assortment of would-be colorful characters on their way to a New Year's Eve party in 1981. Onto the pyre of this dreadful film are thrown the talents of such as Ben Affleck, Casey Affleck, Janeane Garofalo, Courtney Love, Gaby Hoffman, Kate Hudson, Martha Plimpton, Paul Rudd, Guillermo Diaz, Brian McCardie, Jay Mohr, Christina Ricci, Angela Featherstone, and others equally unlucky.

Ricci and Love have the kinds of self-contained personalities that hew out living space for their characters no matter where they find themselves, but the others are pretty much lost. The witless screenplay provides its characters with aimless dialogue and meaningless confrontations, and they are dressed not like people who might have been alive in 1981, but like people going to a costume party where 1981 is the theme. (There is not a single reason, by the way, why the plot requires the film to be set in 1981 or any other year.)

Seeing a film like this helps you to realize that actors are empty vessels waiting to be filled with characters and dialogue. As people, they are no doubt much smarter and funnier than the cretins in this film. I am reminded of Gene Siskel's bottom-line test for a film: "Is this movie more entertaining than a documentary of the same people having lunch?" Here they are contained by small ideas and arch dialogue, and lack the juice of life. Maybe another 200 cigarettes would have helped; coughing would be better than some of this dialogue.

U-Turn

(Directed by Oliver Stone; starring Sean Penn, Billy Bob Thornton; 1997)
Only Oliver Stone knows what he was trying to accomplish by making *U-Turn,*
and it is a secret he doesn't share with the audience. This is a repetitive, pointless exercise in genre filmmaking—the kind of movie where you distract
yourself by making a list of the sources. Much of the story comes from *Red
Rock West,* John Dahl's 1994 film about a man and a wife who both try to
convince a drifter to kill the other. And the images and milieu are out of Russ
Meyer country; his *Cherry, Harry and Raquel* and *SuperVixens* contain the
same redneck sheriffs, the same lustful wives, the same isolated shacks and
ignorant mechanics and car culture. *U-Turn* and *Cherry* both end, indeed,
with a debt to *Duel in the Sun.*

I imagine Stone made this movie as sort of a lark, after the exhausting but
remarkable accomplishments of *Nixon, Natural Born Killers, Heaven and
Earth,* and *JFK.* Well, he deserves a break—but this one? Stone is a gifted
filmmaker not afraid to take chances, to express ideas in his films and make
political statements. Here he's on holiday. Watching *U-Turn,* I was reminded
of a concert pianist playing "Chopsticks": It is done well, but one is disappointed to find it done at all.

The film stars Sean Penn, in a convincing performance all the more admirable for being pointless. He plays Bobby, a man who has had bad luck up
the road (his bandaged hand is missing two fingers), and will have a lot more
bad luck in the desert town of Superior, Arizona. He wheels into town in his
beloved Mustang convertible, which needs a new radiator hose, and encounters the loathsome Darrell (Billy Bob Thornton), a garage mechanic he will
eventually be inspired to call an "ignorant inbred turtleneck hick."

While Darrell works on the car, Bobby walks into town. Superior is one
of those backwater hells much beloved in the movies, where everyone is
malevolent, oversexed, narrow-eyed, and hateful. There are never any in-

dustries in these towns (except for garages, saloons, and law enforcement) because everyone is too preoccupied by sex, lying, scheming, embezzling, and hiring strangers to kill each other.

Bobby quickly finds a sultry young woman named Grace (Jennifer Lopez), and is invited home to help her install her drapes and whatever else comes to mind. Soon her enraged husband Jake (Nick Nolte) comes charging in, red-eyed and bewhiskered, to threaten Bobby with his life, but after the obligatory fight they meet down the road and Jake asks Bobby to kill his wife. Soon Grace will want Bobby to kill her husband (the *Red Rock West* bit), and the film leads to one of those situations where Bobby's life depends on which one he believes.

Superior, Arizona, is the original town without pity. During the course of his brief stay there, Bobby will be kicked in the ribs several dozen times, almost be bitten by a tarantula, shot at, and have his car all but destroyed—and that's all before the final scenes with the vultures circling overhead. Bobby comes across almost like a character in a computer game; you wipe him out, he falls down, stars spin around his head, and then he jumps up again, ready for action.

The film is well made on the level of craft; of course it is, with this strong cast, and Stone directing, and Robert Richardson as cinematographer. But it goes around and around until, like a merry-go-round rider, we figure out that the view is always changing but it's never going to be new. There comes a sinking feeling, half an hour into the film, when we realize the characters are not driven by their personalities and needs, but by the plot. At that point they become puppets, not people. That's the last thing we'd expect in a film by Oliver Stone.

Unforgettable
(Directed by John Dahl; starring Ray Liotta; 1996)
In the long annals of cinematic goofiness, *Unforgettable* deserves a place of honor. This is one of the most convoluted, preposterous movies I've seen—a thriller crossed with lots of Mad Scientist stuff, plus wild chases, a shoot-out in a church, a woman taped to a chair in a burning room, an exploding university building, adultery, a massacre in a drugstore, gruesome autopsy scenes,

and even a moment when a character's life flashes before her eyes, which was more or less what was happening to me by the end of the film.

What went wrong? The movie has been directed by John Dahl, a master of *noir*, whose *Red Rock West* and *The Last Seduction* were terrific movies. *Seduction* starred Linda Fiorentino, who is back this time. Her costar is Ray Liotta, from *GoodFellas*. The supporting cast includes the invaluable Peter Coyote and David Paymer. It's a package with quality written all over it. But what a mess this movie is.

The premise: Liotta is a Seattle medical examiner, working with the police. Everyone in town believes he murdered his wife, but he got off on tainted evidence. "Wear a crash helmet if you go out with him," a woman advises Fiorentino. She is a university researcher whose experiments with rats indicate that the brain stores its memories in a clear fluid which, if transferred to another rat, gives that rat the first rat's memories—but only in the presence of a strong stimulus to trigger them. A cat, for example, to chase it through a maze.

Liotta hears Fiorentino explaining her theory, and sees a way to clear his name and discover his wife's murderer. He will inject himself with his dead wife's brain fluid, mixed with Fiorentino's secret elixir, while he's in the room where his wife was murdered. The stimulus will kick in, and he'll witness her murder through her memories.

How does he obtain her brain fluid? Well, luckily, it's stored in a clear vial in the evidence room of the police department, so he can simply steal it. Good thing this stuff has a long shelf life at room temperature, eh? And so Liotta is off on his quest. Soon he's joined by Fiorentino, who warns him that 30 percent of the rats in her experiments have died of heart attacks. No problem-o: He takes a nitroglycerin pill right before injecting himself.

The plot careens through an endless series of astonishing developments. Fans of those old horror films of the 1930s will remember that all a Mad Scientist has to do is inject himself with a miraculous substance, and it works perfectly, almost every time. That's what happens here. Liotta drains brain fluids from corpses. From comatose cops. From a victim of the drugstore massacre (she was an art student, so he learns he can draw—and sketches her murderer). And the fluids kick in right on time.

It's never really explained how he deals with four or five conflicting sets of memories, all sloshing around in his brain. No matter. His mental life resembles a human channel-changer. All he needs is a stimulus, and *whoosh!*—he has a flashback. Sometimes he thinks he *is* a killer, and repeats old crimes. Meanwhile, the list of suspects grows shorter, because, as we all know, the secret killer has to be someone in the movie, and there are only so many possibilities.

Fiorentino played one of the most forcible women in recent movies in *The Last Seduction.* As her punishment, she now plays one of the least. Get this. The movie's device for keeping her in the picture is that, since Liotta may have a heart attack, she'll follow him around to be sure he's okay. That puts her on the scene for a series of amazing revelations, and gives us someone to explain the ending, which functions as without any question the single least appropriate intro in history for Nat King Cole's "Unforgettable."

The actors play this material perfectly straight, as if they thought this was a serious movie, or even a good one. That makes it all the more agonizing. At least in the old horror films, the actors knew how marginal the material was, and worked a little irony into their performances. Here everybody acts as if they're in something deep, like a Bergman film, or *Chicago Hope.*

I have nothing in principle against goofy films. Hey, I'm the guy who liked *Congo.* But *Unforgettable* is truly strange—a movie that begins with an absurd premise and follows it doggedly through a plot so labyrinthine that, at the end, I found myself thinking back to Fiorentino's experiment. The first rat couldn't find its way through the maze, and was cornered by the cat. The second rat, after an injection of brain fluid, zipped through the maze. Trying to find my way through this plot, I felt like the first rat.

Universal Soldier

(Directed by Roland Emmerich; starring Jerry Orbach, Jean-Claude Van Damme; 1992)

One of my favorite parts in science fiction movies is the explanation of the science, which is usually very heavy on the fiction. In *Universal Soldier,* for example, we are given two Vietnam-era soldiers who are killed in action (by each other) and then packed in ice so their bodies can be used in a secret government project to create "UniSols"—android fighting machines. Twenty-five years later, not having aged a day, they go into action.

How did this scientific breakthrough take place? It's up to the brilliant Dr. Gregor (Jerry Orbach) to explain. As nearly as I can recall, he "hypercharged their bodies to turn dead flesh into living tissue." So now we know. The refitted UniSols look like muscular human beings, but wear funny little monoculars that send out a TV signal (of startlingly low quality). They are strong, acrobatic, and versatile, and can be controlled by their leaders, but wouldn't you know that two of the units have combat flashbacks to Vietnam and remember that they hate one another.

The wayward units are Luc (Jean-Claude Van Damme) and Scott (Dolph Lundgren). In 'Nam, Luc wanted only to go home, and Scott wanted only to kill, and when Luc saw Scott conducting a one-man My Lai massacre, he tried to stop him and then both wound up on the recycling heap. Their minds are supposed to have been wiped clean of all memories, but when the flashbacks begin, each man's orientation has been defined by his strongest motivation at the time of his death.

Enter now the most interesting character in the movie, a TV newswoman named Veronica, played by Ally Walker with style and personality that would grace a much more ambitious movie than this one. Walker, fired by her network, goes freelance and discovers the secret of the UniSols, leading to a long series of action scenes in which Van Damme tries to protect her and Lundgren tries to kill them both.

The centerpiece of the action is a chase between a prison bus and the armored UniSols van, along narrow desert roads on the edge of deep precipices. I suppose there is a market for this sort of thing among bubblebrained adolescents of all ages, but it takes a good chase scene indeed to rouse me from the lethargy induced by dozens and dozens of essentially similar sequences. I have got to the point where the obligatory climax (vehicle hurtles over edge, bursts into fireball) is exciting only because it means the damn chase is finally over.

So back to Ally Walker. If you see this movie, watch her carefully. She is given an absurd character to play, but she has a screen personality that implies wit and intelligence even when the dialogue provides her with nothing to work with. She has some of the same qualities as Debra Winger, and brings scenes to life simply through the energy of her presence. To my astonishment I found myself interested in what she was saying, and if she can sell this dialogue, she can play anything.

As for Lundgren and Van Damme: It must be fairly thankless to play lunks who have to fight for the entire length of a movie while exchanging monosyllabic idiocies. At the Cannes Film Festival in May, the two stars found themselves on the same red carpet, going up the formal staircase to an evening screening. They exchanged words and got into a shoving match, right there in front of the world's TV cameras. Some said it was a publicity stunt. I say if you can do one thing and do it well, stick to it.

Very Bad Things
(Directed by Peter Berg; starring Cameron Diaz, Christian Slater, Daniel Stern; 1998)

Peter Berg's *Very Bad Things* isn't a bad movie, just a reprehensible one. It presents as comedy things that are not amusing. If you think this movie is funny, that tells me things about you that I don't want to know.

What bothers me most, after two viewings, is its confidence that an audience would be entertained by its sad, sick vision, tainted by racism. If this material had been presented straight, as a drama, the movie would have felt more honest and might have been more successful. Its cynicism is the most unattractive thing about it—the assumption that an audience has no moral limits and will laugh at cruelty simply to feel hip. I know moral detachment is a key strategy of the ironic pose, but there is a point, once reached, that provides a test of your underlying values.

The film involves five friends who go on a bachelor party to Las Vegas. Kyle Fisher (Jon Favreau), is on the eve of marriage to the wedding-obsessed Laura (Cameron Diaz). His pals include a Realtor named Robert Boyd (Christian Slater), the antagonistic Berkow brothers Adam (Daniel Stern) and Michael (Jeremy Piven), and a mechanic named Charles (Leland Orser) who doesn't talk much.

In Vegas, there's a montage showing them gambling, tossing back shots, and snorting cocaine. A stripper named Tina (Carla Scott) arrives, does lap dances, and is steered into the bathroom by Michael. He lurches drunkenly about the room with her until her head is accidentally impaled on a coat hook. She's dead. (When I saw the film at the Toronto festival, the audience laughed at a shot showing her feet hanging above the floor. Why?)

Some of the men want to dial 911, but Robert takes charge. How will it look that a hooker has turned up dead in their suite? "Take away the horror of the situation. Take away the tragedy of her death. Take away all the moral and ethical considerations you've had drummed into you since childhood, and what are you left with? A 105-pound problem."

His solution? Cut her up and bury her in the desert. He browbeats the others into agreement, but then a black security guard enters with a complaint about noise. The guard (Russell B. McKenzie) sees the dead body, and Robert stabs him with a corkscrew. Now there are two bodies to dispose of, and the guys stride through a hardware store like the Reservoir Dogs.

The movie makes it a point that some of the guys are Jewish, and uses that to get laughs as they bury the bodies. Jewish law, one argues, requires that the body parts be kept together—so they should dig up the dismembered pieces and sort them out. "She's Asian," says another. "Do they have Jews in Asia?" The answer is yes, although surely such a theory would apply to anyone. They start rearranging: "We'll start with black. Then we'll go to Asian."

My thoughts here are complex. The movie is not blatantly racist, and yet a note of some kind is being played when white men kill an Asian and a black. Why then make it a point that some of them are Jewish? What is the purpose, exactly? Please don't tell me it's humor. I'm not asking for political correctness, I'm simply observing the way the movie tries to show how hip it is by rubbing our noses in race.

The events described take about thirty minutes. There is not a single funny thing that happens once the men get to Vegas (Diaz has some funny early stuff about the wedding). Nor is the aftermath funny, as the men freak out with guilt and fear. Robert makes threats to hold them in line, but more deaths follow, and the last act of the film spins out a grisly, unfunny, screwball plot. By the time of the wedding, when potentially comic material crawls back in over the dead bodies, it's way too late to laugh: The movie's tone is too mean-spirited and sour.

Very Bad Things isn't bad on the technical and acting level, and Slater makes a convincing engine to drive the evil. Peter Berg shows that he can direct a good movie, even if he hasn't. If he'd dumped the irony and looked this material straight in the eye, it might have been a better experience. His screenplay has effective lines, as when Robert coldly reasons, "What we have here was not a good thing, but it was, under the circumstances, the smart play." Or when he uses self-help platitudes to rationalize murder ("Given the fact that we are alive and they are not, we chose life over death").

But the film wants it both ways. At a Jewish funeral, the sad song of the cantor is subtly mocked by upbeat jazz segueing into the next scene. Mourners fall onto the coffin, in a scene that is embarrassing, not funny. When a widow (Jeanne Tripplehorn) struggles with Robert, she bites his groin, and as he fights back we hear female ululations on the sound track. What's that about? I won't even get into the bonus material about her handicapped child and three-legged dog.

Very Bad Things filled me with dismay. The material doesn't match the genre; it's an attempt to exploit black humor without the control of tone necessary to pull it off. I left the theater feeling sad and angry. On the movie's Web site, you can download a stripper. I'm surprised you can't kill her.

Virus

(Directed by John Bruno; starring Donald Sutherland; 1999)

Ever notice how movies come in twos? It's as if the same idea descends upon several Hollywood producers at once, perhaps because someone who hates movies is sticking pins in their dolls. *Virus* is more or less the same movie as *Deep Rising,* which opened a year earlier. Both begin with small boats in the Pacific. Both boats come upon giant floating ships that are seemingly deserted. Both giant ships are inhabited by a vicious monster. Both movies send the heroes racing around the ship trying to destroy the monster. Both movies also have lots of knee-deep water, fierce storms, Spielbergian visible flashlight beams cutting through the gloom, and red digital readouts.

Deep Rising was one of the worst movies of 1998. *Virus* is easily worse. It didn't help that the print I saw was so underlit that often I could see hardly anything on the screen. Was that because the movie was filmed that way, or because the projector bulb was dimmed to extend its life span? I don't know and in a way I don't care, because to see this movie more clearly would not be to like it better.

Virus opens with berserk tugboat captain Donald Sutherland and his crew towing a barge through a typhoon. The barge is sinking and the crew, led by Jamie Lee Curtis and William Baldwin, want to cut it loose. But the barge represents the skipper's net worth, and he'd rather go to the bottom with it. This sequence is necessary to set up the skipper's avarice.

In the eye of the storm, the tug comes upon a drifting Russian satellite communications ship. In the movie's opening credits, we have already seen what happened to the ship: A drifting space cloud enveloped a *Mir* space station, and sent a bolt of energy down to the ship's satellite dish, and apparently the energy included a virus that takes over the onboard computers and represents a vast, if never clearly defined, threat to life on Earth. Sutherland wants to claim the ship for salvage. The crew board it, and soon are fighting the virus. "The ship's steering itself!" one character cries. The chilling answer: "Ships don't steer themselves." Uh, oh. The methods of the virus are strange. It creates robots, and uses them to grab crew members and turn them into strange creatures that are half man, half Radio Shack. It's up to Curtis, Baldwin, and their crewmates to outsmart the virus, which seems none too bright and spends most of its time clomping around and issuing threatening statements with a basso profundo voice synthesizer.

The movie's special effects are not exactly slick, and the creature itself is a distinct letdown. It looks like a very tall humanoid figure hammered together out of crushed auto parts, with several headlights for its eyes. It crunches through steel bulkheads and crushes all barriers to its progress, but is this an efficient way for a virus to behave? It could be cruising the Internet instead of doing a Robocop number.

The last half hour of the movie is almost unseeable. In dark dimness, various human and other figures race around in a lot of water and flashlight beams, and there is much screaming. Occasionally an eye, a limb, or a bloody face emerges from the gloom. Many instructions are shouted. If you can explain to me the exact function of that rocket tube that turns up at the end, I will be sincerely grateful. If you can explain how anyone could survive that function, I will be amazed. The last shot is an homage to *The African Queen,* a movie I earnestly recommend instead of this one.

Volcano

(Directed by Mick Jackson; starring Tommy Lee Jones, Anne Heche; 1997)
I expected to see a mountainous volcano in *Volcano,* towering high over Los Angeles. But the movie takes place at ground level; it's about how lava boils out of the La Brea Tar Pits, threatens a stretch of Wilshire Boulevard, and then

takes a shortcut through the city sewer system. The ads say "The Coast Is Toast," but maybe they should say "The Volcano Is Drano."

This is a surprisingly cheesy disaster epic. It's said that *Volcano* cost a lot more than *Dante's Peak,* a competing volcano movie, but it doesn't look it. *Dante's Peak* had better special effects, a more entertaining story, and a real mountain. *Volcano* is an absolutely standard, assembly-line undertaking; no wonder one of the extras is reading a paperback titled *Screenwriting Made Easy.*

The movie stars Tommy Lee Jones, professional as always even in this flimsy story, as the chief of the city's Office of Emergency Management. He races through the obligatory opening scenes of all disaster movies (everyday life, ominous warnings, alarm sounded by hero scientist, warnings pooh-poohed by official muckety-mucks, etc.). Soon manhole covers are being blown sky-high, subway trains are being engulfed by fireballs, and "lava bombs" are flying through the air and setting miniature sets on fire.

Jones is at ground zero when the La Brea Tar Pits erupt and lava flows down the street, melting fire trucks. Like all disaster-movie heroes, he's supplied with five obligatory companions:

1. His daughter (Gaby Hoffmann), who comes along for the ride, gets trapped by a lava flow, is rescued, is taken to a hospital, and has to be rescued from the path of a falling skyscraper that her dad has blown up to redirect the lava flow.

2. The blonde female scientist (Anne Heche), who warns that the first eruption is not the last, predicts where the lava will flow next, and at a crucial point explains to Jones that it will flow downhill, not uphill. He tells her at a critical moment: "Find my daughter!" She should have replied, "Hey, I'm the one that told you what the lava was going to do! Find her yourself! I'm needed here."

3. The African-American sidekick (Don Cheadle), whose function is to stand in the middle of the Office of Emergency Management and shout at Jones through a telephone. I don't know what he *did* at the office, but nobody else did anything either. One wall was covered by a giant screen showing hysterical anchors on the local TV news. Rows of grim technicians faced this wall, seated at computer terminals that showed the very same TV news broadcast. (All of the anchors are so thrilled to be covering a big story that they can scarcely conceal the elation in their voices.)

4. The Asian-American Female Doctor (Jacqui Kim), who arrives at the scene, gives first aid to firemen and hero's daughter, and organizes the evacuation of Cedars-Sinai Hospital as the lava flows toward it. (She doubles as the wife of the man who builds the high-rise tower that Jones blows up.)

5. The Dog. In a tiny subplot, we see a dog barking at the lava coming in the front door, and then grabbing his Doggy-Bone and escaping out the back. When that happened, not a single dog in the audience had dry eyes.

Tommy Lee Jones is a fine actor, and he does what he can. Striding into the OEM control center, he walks briskly up to a hapless technician and taps on his computer keyboard, barking: "See that, that, and that? Now watch this!" He sounds like he means business, but do you suppose someone was actually paid for writing that line?

Various subplots are rushed on and off screen at blinding speed. At one point a troublesome black man is handcuffed by police, who later release him as the lava flow approaches. He's free to go, but lingers and says, "You block this street, you save the neighborhood—right?" The cops nod. Then he pitches in and helps them lift a giant concrete barrier. The scene is over in a second, but think how insulting it is: It doesn't take a rocket scientist to figure out they're trying to save the neighborhood, so the dialogue is for our benefit, implying that the black dude cares merely for "the neighborhood," and volunteers only when his myopic concerns have been addressed.

The lava keeps flowing for much of the movie, never looking convincing. I loved it when the firemen aimed their hoses way offscreen into the middle of the lava flow, instead of maybe aiming them at the leading edge of the lava—which they couldn't do, because the lava was a visual effect, and not really there.

I also chortled at the way the scientist warns that the first eruption "is not the last," and yet after the second eruption (when it is time for the movie to end), the sun comes out, everyone smiles, and she offers Jones and his daughter a lift home. Hey, what about the possibility of a third eruption? What about that story she told about the Mexican farmer who found a mountain in his cornfield?

The movie has one perfect line: "This city is finally paying for its arrogance!" Yes, and *Volcano* is part of the price.

WWWW**W**WWW

··

⭐ The Wedding Singer

(Directed by Frank Coraci; starring Adam Sandler, Drew Barrymore; 1998)
The Wedding Singer tells the story of, yes, a wedding singer from New Jersey, who is cloyingly sweet at some times and a cruel monster at others. The film-makers are obviously unaware of his split personality; the screenplay reads like a collaboration between Jekyll and Hyde. Did anybody, at any stage, gave the story the slightest thought?

The plot is so familiar the end credits should have issued a blanket thank-you to a century of Hollywood lovecoms. Through a tortuous series of con-trived misunderstandings, the boy and girl avoid happiness for most of the movie, although not as successfully as we do. It's your basic off-the-shelf formula in which two people fall in love, but are kept apart because (a) they're engaged to creeps; (b) they say the wrong things at the wrong times; and (c) they get bad information. It's exhausting, seeing the characters work so hard at avoiding the obvious.

Of course there's the obligatory scene where the good girl goes to the good boy's house to say she loves him, but the bad girl answers the door and lies to her. I spent the weekend looking at old Astaire and Rogers movies, which basically had the same plot: She thinks he's a married man, and almost gets married to the slimy band leader before he finally figures everything out and declares his love at the eleventh hour.

The big differences between Astaire and Rogers in *Swing Time* and Adam Sandler and Drew Barrymore in *The Wedding Singer* is that (1) in 1936 they were more sophisticated than we are now, and *knew* the plot was inane, and had fun with that fact, and (2) they could dance. One of the sad by-products of the dumbing-down of America is that we're now forced to witness the goofy plots of the 1930s played sincerely, as if they were really deep.

Sandler is the wedding singer. He's engaged to a slut who stands him up at the altar because, sob, "the man I fell in love with six years ago was a rock singer who licked the microphone like David Lee Roth—and now you're only a . . . a . . . wedding singer!" Barrymore, meanwhile, is engaged to a macho monster who brags about how he's cheating on her. Sandler and Barrymore meet because she's a waitress at the weddings where he sings. We know immediately they are meant for each other. Why do we know this? Because we are conscious and sentient. It takes them a lot longer.

The basic miscalculation in Adam Sandler's career plan is to ever play the lead. He is not a lead. He is the best friend, or the creep, or the loser boyfriend. He doesn't have the voice to play a lead: Even at his most sincere, he sounds like he's doing standup—like he's mocking a character in a movie he saw last night. Barrymore, on the other hand, has the stuff to play a lead (I commend to you once again the underrated *Mad Love*). But what is she doing in this one—in a plot her grandfather would have found old-fashioned? At least when she gets a good line (she tries out the married name "Mrs. Julia Gulia") she knows how to handle it.

The best laughs in the film come right at the top, in an unbilled cameo by the invaluable Steve Buscemi, as a drunken best man who makes a shambles of a wedding toast. He has the timing, the presence, and the intelligence to go right to the edge. Sandler, on the other hand, always keeps something in reserve—his talent. It's like he's afraid of committing; he holds back so he can use the "only kidding" defense.

I could bore you with more plot details. About why he thinks she's happy and she thinks he's happy and they're both wrong and she flies to Vegas to marry the stinker, and he . . . but why bother? And why even mention that the movie is set in the mid-1980s and makes a lot of mid-1980s references that are supposed to be funny but sound exactly like lame dialogue? And what about the curious cameos by faded stars and inexplicably cast character actors? And why do they write the role of a Boy George clone for Alexis Arquette and then do nothing with the character except let him hang there on screen? And why does the tourist section of the plane have fewer seats than first class? And, and, and . . .

What Planet Are You From?

(Directed by Mike Nichols; starring Garry Shandling, Annette Bening, Greg Kinnear; 2000)

Here is the most uncomfortable movie of the new year, an exercise in feel-good smut. *What Planet Are You From?* starts out as a dirty comedy, but then abandons the comedy, followed by the dirt, and by the end is actually trying to be poignant. For that to work, we'd have to like the hero, and Garry Shandling makes that difficult. He begrudges every emotion, as if there's no more where that came from. That worked on TV's *Larry Sanders Show*—it's why his character was funny—but here he can't make the movie's U-turn into sentimentality.

He plays an alien from a distant planet, where the inhabitants have no emotions and no genitals. Possibly this goes hand in hand. He is outfitted with a penis, given the name Harold Anderson, and sent to Earth to impregnate a human woman, so that his race can conquer our planet. When Harold becomes aroused, his penis makes a loud whirling noise. Imagine Mr. Spock with a roto-rooter in his pants.

If I were a comedy writer I would deal with that humming noise. I would assume that the other characters in the movie would find it extremely disturbing. I put it to my female readers: If you were on a date with a guy and his crotch sounded like it contained an operating garbage disposal, how would you feel? I submit that a normal woman would no more want to get into his pants than stick her hand down a disposal unit.

The lame joke in *What Planet Are You From?* is that women hear the noise, find it curious, and ask about it, and Harold makes feeble attempts to explain it away, and of course the more aroused he becomes the louder it hums, and when his ardor cools the volume drops. You understand. If you find this even slightly funny, you'd better see this movie, since the device is never likely to be employed again.

On earth, Harold gets a job in a bank with the lecherous Perry (Greg Kinnear), and soon he is romancing a woman named Susan (Annette Bening) and contemplating the possibility of sex with Perry's wife Helen (Linda Fiorentino). Fiorentino of course starred in the most unforgettable movie crotch scene in history (in *The Last Seduction,* where she calls the bluff of a barroom braggart). There is a scene here with exactly the same setup: She's sitting next to Harold in a bar, his crotch is humming, etc., and I was wondering, is it too much to ask that the movie provide a hilarious homage? It was. Think of the lost possibilities.

Harold and Susan fly off to Vegas, get married, and have a honeymoon that consists of days of uninterrupted sex ("I had so many orgasms," she says, "that some are still stacked up and waiting to land"). Then she discovers Harold's only interest in her is as a breeder. She is crushed and angry, and the movie turns to cheap emotion during her pregnancy and inevitable live childbirth scene, after which Harold finds to his amazement that he may have emotions after all.

The film was directed by Mike Nichols, whose uneven career makes you wonder. Half of his films are good to great (his previous credit is *Primary Colors*) and the other half you're at a loss to account for. What went into the theory that *What Planet Are You From?* was filmable? Even if the screenplay by Garry Shandling and three other writers seemed promising on the page, why star Shandling in it? Why not an actor who projects joy of performance—why not Kinnear, for example?

Shandling's shtick is unavailability. His public persona is of a man unwilling to be in public. Words squeeze embarrassed from his lips as if he feels guilty to be talking. *Larry Sanders* used this presence brilliantly. But it depends on its limitations. If you're making a movie about a man who has a strange noise coming from his crotch, you should cast an actor who looks different when it isn't.

When Night Is Falling

(Directed by Patricia Rozema; starring Pascale Bussieres, Henry Czerny; 1995)
Patricia Rozema was raised as a Calvinist in Canada, and saw no films until she was sixteen. In this she resembles her coreligionist Paul Schrader, who saw his first film at about the same age, and went on to write *Taxi Driver* and direct *American Gigolo*. Both of the Rozema films I've seen deal with a young woman coming to terms with her unrealized sexual yearnings. One suspects an element of autobiography.

Rozema's first feature was the enchanting *I've Heard the Mermaids Singing* (1987), the story of a young Toronto woman who dreams of becoming a photographer, and goes to work for a sophisticated older woman who runs an art gallery. The young woman idealizes the older one, but discovers secrets about her: That she is a lesbian, and that she is bitter about being a dealer rather than an artist. The film is ingenious in that it seems to be about the young narrator, and ends up being at least as much about the woman she gets a crush on.

Now comes *When Night Is Falling,* again about a young woman, this one a professor in a Protestant theological college in Toronto. Her name is Camille (Pascale Bussieres), she is from Quebec, and she is engaged to marry a fellow professor named Martin (Henry Czerny). Then one day at a laundromat she encounters a woman her age named Petra (Rachel Crawford), their laundry is exchanged, not by accident, and when Camille returns Petra's clothes, Petra looks at her solemnly and says, "I'd love to see you in the moonlight with your head thrown back and your body on fire."

There is a part of me that responds to reckless romanticism like that, and I guess I understand Petra saying it, but before their first date? Slow down, girl! Camille is shocked and tells Petra she has made a mistake. But she hasn't, and Camille finds herself increasingly fascinated by Petra (whose name may or may not be inspired by the heroine of *The Bitter Tears of Petra von Kant,* Fassbinder's 1973 film about lesbianism).

The film until this point has been absorbing and sensible, but then it begins to go wrong. The emotional center is sound; we believe the growing attraction the two women felt for each other, but the details of their stories seem contrived and awkward.

Petra, for example, is a little too good to be true; she is a member of a circus troupe modeled on Cirque de Soleil, and her act (not terribly difficult although she isn't very good at it) consists of juggling balls of light in pantomime from behind a backlit screen. She lives in a trailer decorated like an ecological hippie gift shop. First seen in skin-tight leather (not strictly necessary since she is seen only as a shadow), she appears in a series of bizarre "artistic" costumes that hammer home the point: She is a wild free spirit, offering Camille the choice of remaining in the drab Calvinist environment, or running away and joining the circus. Does the symbolism feel just slightly strained when Camille seeks out Petra a second time, and Petra takes her on a surprise hang-gliding date?

Camille's relationship with Martin is strained and unconvincing (despite their sex scene together, they don't seem to know each other very well). And her scenes with Reverend DeBoer (David Fox), the president of the college, are stiffly contrived. When she and Martin are offered the job of college co-chaplains, but only if they marry, she wears one of Petra's wildly inappropriate blouses to the first interview and stumbles through a later interview designed to test her soundness on the question of homosexuality. When the reverend unexpectedly visits her apartment while Petra is there, Camille behaves so strangely that she seems to be concealing not lesbianism, but a panic attack.

The mechanics of the story are awkward. Martin discovers the affair through a convenient photograph, and by peering through a window of Petra's trailer. Petra sets an artificial deadline because the circus is leaving town. The women have ludicrous misunderstandings. Oh, and there's Bob, Camille's beloved dog, "who I realize I love more than anyone I'm supposed to love." Bob spends most of the movie dead in the refrigerator, and then Camille goes out into the wilderness on a dark and snowy night to bury him, meanwhile nipping at cherry brandy until she passes out and seems to freeze to death. . . .

The ending of the movie completely derails. Leave out such details as that Petra is able to arrive at the side of the frozen body well before the ambulance does. Put aside problems of continuity. Forget even Bob's remarkable reappearance in the end credits. Laughter is the friend of romance but the enemy of sexual passion (which seems funny only to the observer). And *When Night Is Falling* has too many unintended laughs for its passion to be convincing. We start out nodding solemnly in sympathy with Camille and Petra. We share their angst. We care about their happiness. But then we start to snicker, and all is lost. This movie needed a strict rewrite, preferably by an unsmiling Calvinist. I shouldn't have left the theater worrying about what was going to happen to Bob.

When the Whales Came
(Directed by Clive Rees; starring Paul Scofield, Helen Mirren; 1989)
When the Whales Came is the gloomy story of how the gloomy inhabitants of the gloomiest island in the world save themselves from a gloomy fate that would have forced them to leave their barren and overcast outpost in the

stormy sea, and move to the jolly mainland. Like all such movies, it features a crowd of extras who wear old clothes and materialize out of thin air on command, to portray the island's poor and weather-beaten inhabitants.

I realize I am not getting into the spirit of this movie. I know that as a responsible viewer, it is my responsibility to describe it as an urgent and important fable about the fate of Earth, and I am supposed to cheer because the islanders save some whales and thus avoid a curse that drove everyone off of a nearby island seventy years ago.

God knows I am in favor of the whales. I think we should all stop buying Japanese products until the Japanese stop their single-minded campaign to murder every last whale they can get their hands on. That should not be too great a sacrifice, since if such a boycott were really enforced, it would probably only last two days. But loving the whales and loving this movie are two different enterprises, and to the degree that *When the Whales Came* makes the fate of the whales seem like a dreary and boring subject, it is like to harm the cause.

The movie takes place on the eve of World War I, on the forbidding and rain-swept island of Bryher, off the southwest coast of England. Here the stubborn inhabitants eke out lives of poverty and hard labor. Not far away across the waters is the island of Samson, which has been deserted for years. In the opening sequence of the film, we find out what drove the people away from Samson. When a school of whales swam ashore, the inhabitants butchered them, bringing down upon their heads a series of disasters, diseases, and wells that ran dry.

Only one man remembers those events on Samson. He was a boy then, and he and his mother were the last to leave the island. Now he is an old man, deaf and reclusive, and he lives in a rude cottage on the edge of the sea. He is known as the Birdman (Paul Scofield). Two local children (Max Rennie and Helen Pearce) become friends with the Birdman, and learn to share his love of living things.

Meanwhile, life goes on. We meet the boy's parents (David Threlfall and Helen Mirren), and watch as the father goes off to fight the war and is reported missing. Later in the film, the father miraculously returns from the war, alive after all, and only a grouch would point out that the entire story of his going off to, and coming back from, the war is entirely irrelevant to the rest of the story (unless the villagers, by sparing the whales, somehow saved his life—a conclusion so banal I am reluctant to subscribe to it).

One day a rare narwhale beaches itself on the island. The inhabitants immediately plan to kill it for its rare tusk, which is long and spiraled and looks like a unicorn's. Three local juvenile delinquents meanwhile burn down the Birdman's cottage, but he disregards the tragedy, murmuring "Nothing else matters now" as he attempts to save the whale from the mob of extras who have appeared from over the nearest dune. The children help the deaf man to communicate the history of the tragic island of Samson—and the unruly crowd, once it has heard his story, immediately does an emotional about-face and pitches in to save the whale, after which they stand on the beach, waving torches to scare away other suicidal narwhales, after which there is a happy ending and a joyous kiss between the boy's reunited parents.

I have nothing but admiration for people who want to spare the lives of our fellow inhabitants on spaceship Earth, but I wish they would appear in full-witted movies. *Turtle Diary,* for example, was a wonderful and complex movie about two people who conspired to steal some giant turtles from the zoo and return them to the ocean. *When the Whales Came* is a simpleminded movie by filmmakers who have conspired to make a predictable and morose parable and bang us over the head with it until it is dead.

Wild Orchid

(Directed by Zalman King; starring Carre Otis, Mickey Rourke, Jacqueline Bisset; 1990)

We engage in a conspiacy of silence about erotic movies. We discuss their plots, their characters, the truthfulness of their worlds. We never discuss whether or not they arouse us—whether we're turned on. Critics are the worst offenders, occupying some Olympian peak above the field of battle, pretending that the film in question failed to engage their intelligence when what we want to know is whether it engaged their libido.

Wild Orchid is an erotic film, plain and simple. It cannot be read in any other way. There is no other purpose for its existence. Its story is absurd, and even its locale was chosen primarily for its travelogue value; this movie no more needs to take place in Brazil than in Kansas, which the heroine leaves in the opening scene.

And yet none of that is relevant. What is relevant is that I did not find the movie erotic. It tells the story of a virginal young woman (Carre Otis) who is hired as an international lawyer, leaves on the next flight for Rio de Janeiro, and there meets a man and woman (Mickey Rourke and Jacqueline Bisset) locked in a contest of psychological control. By the end of the film Otis will have been mentally savaged and physically ravished by Rourke and others, at first against her will, I guess, although she puts up what only her mother would consider a struggle.

Details in the opening scene almost invite us to snicker. Can we believe that Otis, who looks about eighteen, has graduated from law school, mastered three or four languages, and spent eighteen months with "a major Chicago law firm" before being hired on the spot by a top New York firm that puts her on the next plane to Brazil? Hardly, since in the few scenes where she is required to talk like a lawyer, she speaks like someone who is none too confident she has memorized the words correctly. Can we believe that Bisset is an international negotiator who wants to buy valuable beachfront property from Rourke? That Rourke is a street kid from Philadelphia who bought his first house at sixteen, fixed it up, sold it at a profit, and is now one of the world's wealthiest men?

Well, we can almost believe it about the Rourke character (what's hard to accept is that anyone so rich would still be making money by actually doing things—like buying hotels—instead of simply ripping off the less wealthy through cleverness in the financial markets). But what I couldn't believe was the chemistry between Rourke and Otis, whose passion is supposed to shake the earth but seemed more like an obligation imposed on them by their genitals.

Rourke has had chemistry before. Who can forget his relationship with Kim Basinger in *9½ Weeks*? That he doesn't have it here is largely because Carre Otis, beautiful and appealing as she is, brings little conviction to her role. It is hard for us to believe her character exists—but apparently almost impossible for her.

The screenplay by Patricia Louisianna Knop and Zalman King and the direction by King strain for a psychological complexity that simply isn't there. Rourke is a man who cannot feel, they tell us, and so he lives through others—by arranging for Otis to have an affair with a strange man, for example. His untouchability has driven Bisset mad, which is why she "sent" Otis to Rourke in the first place—to see if he is incapable of loving all women, or only Bisset. Without the sex, this could be a Henry James novel (if it had been written by Henry James, of course).

I have seen, however, movies even more unbelievable than *Wild Orchid* which nevertheless stirred me at an erotic level (the original *Emmanuelle* was one, and *9½ Weeks* was another). Apparently the lesson to be learned here is that sexuality itself is not enough, nor is nudity or passion. What is required is at least some notion that the personalities of the characters are really connecting. Unless they find each other sexy, why should we?

Wing Commander
(Directed by Chris Roberts; starring Ginny Holder; 1999)
Jurgen Prochnow, who played the submarine captain in *Das Boot,* is one of the stars of *Wing Commander,* and no wonder: This is a sub movie exported to deep space, complete with the obligatory warning about the onboard oxygen running low. "Torpedoes incoming!" a watch officer shouts. "Brace yourself!" It's 500 years in the future. If the weapons developed by the race of evil Kilrathi only inspire you to "brace yourself," we might reasonably ask what the Kilrathi have been doing with their time.

Other marine notes: "Hard to port!" is a command at one point. Reasonable at sea, but in space, where a ship is not sailing on a horizontal surface, not so useful. "Quiet! There's a destroyer!" someone shouts, and then everyone on board holds their breath, as there are subtle sonar *pings* on the sound track, and we hear the rumble of a giant vessel overhead. Or underhead. Wherever. "In space," as *Alien* reminded us, "no one can hear you scream." There is an excellent reason for that: Vacuums do not conduct sound waves, not even those caused by giant destroyers.

Such logic is of course irrelevant to *Wing Commander,* a movie based on a video game and looking like one a lot of the time, as dashing pilots fly around blowing up enemy targets. Our side kills about a zillion Kilrathi for every one of our guys that buys it, but when heroes die, of course they die in the order laid down by ancient movie clichés. The moment I saw that one of the pilots was an attractive black woman (Ginny Holder), I knew she'd go down, or up, in flames.

The plot involves war between the humans and the Kilrathi, who have refused all offers of peace and wish only to be targets in the crosshairs of video computer screens. Indeed, according to a Web page, they hope to "destroy the universe," which seems self-defeating. The Kilrathi are ugly turtleoid creatures with goatees, who talk like voice synthesizers cranked way down, heavy on the bass.

Against them stand the noble earthlings, although the film's hero, Blair (Freddie Prinze, Jr.) is suspect in some circles because he is a half-breed. Yes, his mother was a Pilgrim. Who were the Pilgrims? Humans who were the original space voyagers, and developed a gene useful for instinctively navigating in "space-time itself." (Just about all navigation is done in space-time itself, but never mind.) Pilgrims went too far and dared too much, so timid later men resented them—but if you need someone to skip across a Gravity Hole, a Pilgrim is your man.

There are actors on board capable of splendid performances. The commander of the fleet is played by David Warner, who brings utter believability to, alas, banal dialogue. Two of the other officers, played by Tcheky Karyo and Prochnow, are also fine; I'd like to see them in a real navy movie. Prinze shows again an easy grace and instant likability. Matthew Lillard, as a hotshot pilot named Maniac, gets into a daredevil competition with the Holder character, and I enjoyed their energy. And the perfectly named Saffron Burrows has a pleasing presence as the head of the pilot squadron, although having recently seen her in a real movie (Mike Figgis's *The Loss of Sexual Innocence,* at Sundance), I assume she took this role to pay the utility bills.

These actors, alas, are at the service of a submoronic script and special effects that look like a video game writ large. *Wing Commander* arrives at the end of a week that began with the death of the creator of *2001: A Space Odyssey.* Close the pod bay door, Hal. And turn off the lights.

YYYYYYYYYY

Year of the Horse

(Directed by Jim Jarmusch; starring Neil Young, Ralph Molina; 1997)

Year of the Horse plays like *This is Spinal Tap* made from antimatter. Both films are about aging rockers, but *Year of the Horse* removes the humor and energy, portraying Neil Young and Crazy Horse as the survivors of a death march. There are times, indeed, when Young, his hair plastered flat against his face with sweat, his eyes haunted beneath a glowering brow, looks like a candidate for a mad slasher role.

The film, directed by Jim Jarmusch, follows a 1996 concert tour and intercuts footage from 1986 and 1976 tours. It's all shot in muddy earth tones, on grainy Super-8 film, Hi Fi 8 video, and 16mm. If you seek the origin of the grunge look, seek no further: Young, in his floppy plaid shirts and baggy shorts, looks like a shipwrecked lumberjack. His fellow band members, Billy Talbot, Poncho Sampedro, and Ralph Molina, exude vibes that would strike terror into the heart of an unarmed convenience store clerk.

This is not a fly-on-the-wall documentary. Jarmusch's interviews take place in a laundry room, where the band members and Young's father sit on a straight chair and meditate on the band's long and lonely road. Young muses on "the trail of destruction I've left behind me," and there is solemn mention of departed band members ("Neil once said they were dropping like flies").

These séances are intercut with concert footage, during which the band typically sings the lyrics through once and then gets mired in endless loops of instrumental repetition that seem positioned somewhere between mantras and autism. The music is shapeless, graceless, and built from rhythm, not melody; it is amusing, given the undisciplined sound, to eavesdrop later as they argue in a van about whether they all were following the same arrangement.

The older footage is not illuminating. One high point, from a visit to Glasgow in 1976, is a meal in a restaurant that is interrupted when the fabric flowers in the centerpiece catch fire. The band members try smothering the flames with napkins and extinguishing them with orange juice, and eventually they join the woman who owns the place in sadly eyeing the ashes.

Later in the film, Jarmusch himself appears on camera, reading to Young from the Old Testament, a book the musician seems unfamiliar with. Jarmusch reads the parts where an angry God tells his people how he will punish them, and Young looks like God's tribulations are nothing he hasn't been through more than once.

If there is a theme to the band's musings, it is astonishment that they have been playing together for so long. They play with other groups, but when they come together, they say, there is a fusion. With touching self-effacement, Young tells Jarmusch, "The band is called 'Neil Young and Crazy Horse,' but I know it's really 'Crazy Horse.' My new jacket says 'Crazy Horse.' The others say 'Neil Young and Crazy Horse,' but mine just says 'Crazy Horse.'" Yes, but wouldn't the point come across a little better if theirs just said "Crazy Horse" too?

Index

W-Y